Shires

Sales &

Pigs

By   Clare Hastings

ELY CATTLE MARKET

GEORGE COMINS

WILL HOLD A SALE OF

HORSES

CARRIAGES, HARNESS & EFFECTS

ON

Thursday, 22nd May, 1924

ELY HORSE FAIR

Precisely at 2 o'clock.

ENTRIES ARE RESPECTFULLY SOLICITED.

GEORGE COMINS, Auctioneer, Agricultural and General Valuer, Land and Insurance Agent, Ely
Telegrams "COMINS," ELY.   Telephone 68.

W. Heffer & Sons Ltd., Hills Road, Cambridge.

Cover Design: Clare Hastings and Tim Smith

Shires

Sales &

Pigs

By   Clare Hastings

> **The Story of An Ely Family of Auctioneers**
> **George Comins 1856 - 1997**

**Dedicated to the memory
of my father**

George William Drage Comins

and grandfather

George Dobede Drage

who I never had the privilege of knowing.

Every effort has been made to ensure that the information in this book is correct at the time of going to print.

Published by John Nickalls Publications
Oak Farm Bungalow, Suton, Wymondham, Norfolk, NR18 9SH.

ISBN: 1 904136 06 0

Printed by Geo. R. Reeve Ltd.
9-11 Town Green, Wymondham, Norfolk, NR18 0BD

Contents

Foreword

When I joined the firm of George Comins and Son in 1971, Ely was a thriving market town, virtually self sufficient with the local economy dominated by agriculture. It was a different city to the one we know today which has been heavily influenced by the 'Cambridge Phenomenon.' The busiest day of the week was Thursday market day, with the stalls market which still exists on the square, and the cattle market. People poured into Ely from all points of the compass to do their weekly shop and attend to their business.

In agriculture, parents were able to bring up families on holdings of twenty to fifty acres with livestock, poultry hard and soft fruit and vegetables, a far cry from the plight of agriculture today. Thus, on Thursdays, the farmers brought their livestock to the cattle market together with their surplus produce for sale, while their wives went around the town for their weekly shopping and social interchange. They usually met up in cafes and restaurants for lunch or more likely in the White Hart or Club Hotel with their friends to catch up on the weeks gossip.

There were two firms of auctioneers in Ely then, namely George Comins and Son, whose offices were in Chequer Lane, and Cheffins Grain and Chalk, whose offices were at 14, Newnham Street with their cattle market premises adjoining. The two firms subsequently amalgamated in 1987 for form Cheffins Grain and Comins which was shortened to Cheffins in 2000.

I hope everyone connected with the market, particularly when it was in the centre of Ely with the Cathedral as a backdrop, will have fond memories. The characters, the humour, the bargains and the surprises and disappointments all gave Ely a wonderful atmosphere on a Thursday. People regularly tell me new stories and how much they enjoyed it and still miss it today.

PHILIP AMBROSE
Cheffins.

Introduction

The firm of George Comins, Auctioneers, Valuers, House and Land agents was in business in the centre of Ely and the surrounding villages from 1856, when George Comins founded the firm, until 1982 when George William Drage Comins his grandson, retired. The firm then became 'Comins' before amalgamating with Messrs. Cheffins, Grain and Chalk to become Cheffins, Grain and Comins, now Cheffins.

Clare Hastings is the, great grand daughter of the founder of the firm.

Her father, George W.D. Comins and mother went into a nursing home in Norwich in 1994 and the family home was sold. At that time it was brought to her attention that the haylofts over the stables were full of old papers. On investigation it was found that over fifty hessian sacks of papers were stored there, balanced on rotting floor boards, containing papers, bill posters, household accounts and details of furniture, house and land sales dating back to 1869. Many of these papers had been wrapped in brown paper and tied with string before putting into the sacks and in the dry loft had remained more or less in the condition they were when they were stored there, give or take a few mouse droppings and a considerable layers of dirt and dust.

These sacks were thrown down into Chantry Lane from the hay loft door and, with the help of Michael Peacock who had previously worked in the firm with her father, Clare spent many hours sifting through the papers and the dirt to reveal a fascinating insight into the history of the cattle market, and the agricultural and domestic side of Ely and district over the last one hundred and twenty odd years. Almost a complete social history of Ely emerged in addition to a detailed insight of her own family history.

Shires, Sales and Pigs gives a very brief glimpse into life in Ely during the years each of the George's were in business.

**Hay loft over the smaller garage (left)
where papers were stored, some for over 100 years.**

Acknowledgements

The majority of the material contents of this book were found in a hay loft but it could not have been compiled without the help, support and encouragement of so many people. Some people sorted papers, some moved them – many times, some gave permission for pictures to be printed, some wrote sections, took photographs and named people in photographs.

I have been surprised by the interest that has been caused and the memories of the past it has rekindled in so many people. A chance remark or memory has found its way into the pages and I would like to thank everyone very much for all their interest and encouragement.

Clare Hastings

Philip Ambrose, Bill Bradshaw, Gordon Butcher, 'Honor & Honey',
Sylvia Houghton, Mary McKittrick, Michael Peacock, Tim Smith.
Market Photographs courtesy of Brian Lane and The Ely Standard.
Cartoons reproduced courtesy of Les Garner.

****

The Author was educated at Miss Cross's school in Chapel Street, Acremont House with headmistress Mrs. Saunders and St. Felix School, Southwold. She has been living in East Sussex for thirty years and has inherited the family's interest in agriculture and auction sales.

She now divides her time between renovating properties in Ely and Agricultural Shows, The South of England and Heathfield Show, in Sussex.

Photography by Kimberly Langford – Tacoma Wa. USA

The Family Tree

GEORGE COMINS – THE ELDER
1803 –1857 A Draper from Sutton
Married FRANCES 1801 – 1858
|

RICHARD	GEORGE	JOSEPH
1831 – 1857	1838 – 1887	1841 - 1860

Married LETTICE ELIZABETH DRAGE 1863
(Father - William Drage a farmer from Sutton)

Started the Firm of
GEORGE COMINS
In Market Street in 1856
Horse Repository in Newnham Street
In 1871
Bought St. Mary's Street House
For his family home and firm's office

|

Lettice	GEORGE DOBODE DRAGE	Grace
	1866 – 1942	1873 - 1927

Married WINIFRED POWLES nee DIX

Took over family firm 1887
Becoming
GEORGE COMINS & SON
Indentured to the Firm of Ventom, Bull & Cooper, 35, Old Jewry, London. 1885
Offered the Freedom of the City of London

LETTICE WINIFRED	GEORGE WILLIAM DRAGE	JOHN DOBODE	PERCY POWLES
	1911 – 1997		Step brother —
Married EDWARD WHITE	Married RUTH ELAINE NORTON		Mayor of Ely
Veterinary Surgeon	1909 - 1996		1989 - 1990
Station Road, Ely.			
1940's – 1950's.	Took over the firm of		

GEORGE COMINS & SON
in 1942 running the business from 17, St. Mary's Street
until the1970's when the business moved to the
renovated Chequers Public House in Chequer Lane off
the High Street.
He built and opened a New Ely Cattle Market in
1955 and the last sale held there, after his
retirement, was on 25th October 1990.

|

CLARE HASTINGS (Nee COMINS)
1948 -

GEORGE COMINS – THE ELDER
1803 – 1857

George Comins The Elder was born in Spilsby, Lincolnshire on 26th August 1803. At some point the family moved to Sutton and George took up the occupation of a Grocer in the Village. He and his wife Frances had three sons, Richard, Joseph (Josh) and George.

Richard and Josh followed their father into the Grocery trade but in 1856 George, at the age of eighteen, moved to Market Street Ely to set up the auctioneering firm of George Comins.

Within four years the whole family, with the exception of George, had died. Richard died in October 1857 closely followed by his father George The Elder in November of the same year. His mother Frances died of apoplexy on 6th June 1858 only to be followed by Josh in January 1860. The cause of death of both boys was recorded as 'Phthisis pulmonaris.'

By the end of 1860 the young George was on his own to make his mark as an Auctioneer in the City of Ely.

Ely Cemetery 23rd February 1860
Rock & Co. London No. 4195
(A plate torn from a book with a hand written receipt on the back)

GEORGE COMINS
1838 – 1887

Founder of the Firm George Comins

The business of 'Auctioneer' was started in Market Street in 1856. Very little is known about the first ten years of business in Market Street but by 1863 George had met Lettice Elizabeth Drage, the daughter of local Sutton Farmer William Drage, and they were married at the Parish Church in Sutton on 3rd November 1863. George Dobede Drage was born in Market Street in 1866 followed by Grace in 1873 and Lettice.

George Comins – Auctioneer, 17, St. Mary's Street, Ely

During the ten years from the founding of the firm to the birth of his son George Dobode, all kinds of sales by auction were held in Ely but after the arrival of his only son, George and his wife Lettice, looked for a substantial family residence in the centre of the town which could accommodate, not only the family, but also the business, servants, dogs, horses and carriages. The ideal property became available in St. Mary's Street which had been built by a doctor and used as his surgery. This large property with eleven rooms, two staircases, cellar, stables, harness room, pigsty, haylofts, a yard and room for carriages with a back entrance for horses on Chantry Lane was ideal for the growing family and expanding business.

The small gatehouse to the right of the front gate was joined to the main building with a glass roof which provided space for the offices of the firm. The gardens were enclosed by a six foot wall with stone balls on the gate pillars and the trees in front of the wall facing the street were surrounded by iron railings. (The majority of these railings were demolished for use in the war.) The small circular summer house in the garden remained, with its roof covered in creepers until the 1950s. The property was later number '17'.

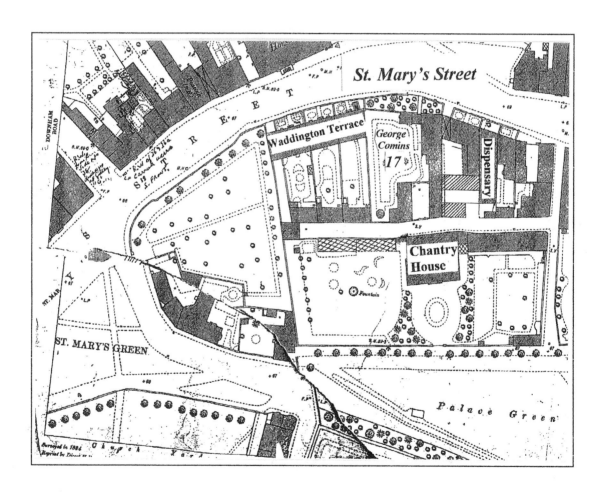

Plan of 17, St. Mary's Street in 1884

The Offices of George Comins and Son
17, St. Mary' Street

(photograph taken from St. Mary's Street in 1948 – the only remaining iron railings are on either side of the pathway to the front gate)

The brick building and wooden offices taken from the garden in the 1950s.

The stable block containing stable, harness room, pigsty taken in the late 1950s. The creeper covered summerhouse remains and the door opened onto the cobblestone yard which had been covered with tarmac.

SUTTON, ISLE OF ELY,
CAMBS.

MODERN, USEFUL, & RECENTLY NEW
HOUSEHOLD
FURNITURE
AND
EFFECTS,

Consisting of a walnut wood 6¾ octave cottage pianoforte, by *Oetzmann & Plumb* (manufacturers by appointment to the Royal Family), a handsome ditto in rosewood
case with a full fretice-work front, *by Shoebrook,* drawing room
and dining room furniture, Brussels and felt carpets, the
equipments of seven bed-rooms, consisting of feather beds,
mattresses, palliasses, 4-post, Arabian, and iron bedsteads,
kitchen requisites and effects.

GEORGE COMINS

Has been Favoured with Instructions from the Rev. L. Saywell,
who is leaving Sutton,

TO SELL BY AUCTION,

AT HIS RESIDENCE,

On WEDNESDAY, 1st day of JUNE, 1864

The whole of his Household Furniture and Effects,

Sale to commence at 12 o'clock punctually.

Catalogues may be had at the Lamb Inn, Ely, Crown Inn,
Sutton, and upon application to the Auctioneer at his Office, High
Street, Ely.

W. B. CREAK, PRINTER, HIGH STREET, ELY.

MR. GEORGE COMINS, Auctioneer, Valuer, House and Land Agent,

ST. MARY STREET, ELY, (Established in Ely, A.D. 1856),

CONDUCTS SALES OF FURNITURE AND EFFECTS
,,   VALUATIONS OF THE SAME
,,   SALES OF ALL CLASS OF STOCK-IN-TRADE
,,   VALUATIONS OF THE SAME
,,   SALES OF LIVE AND DEAD FARMING STOCK
,,   VALUATIONS OF THE SAME
,,   SALES OF GROWING CROPS OF GRASS AND OTHER CROPS
,,   VALUATIONS OF THE SAME
,,   SALES OF ALL CLASS OF GROWING AND CUT TIMBER
,,   VALUATIONS OF THE SAME
,,   SALES OF HOUSES, LANDS, REVERSIONARY INTEREST AND
               LIFE POLICIES
,,   VALUATIONS OF THE SAME
,,   VALUATIONS OF COVENANTS UPON FARMS, BETWEEN
               IN-COMING AND OUT-GOING TENANTS, FOR PROBATE
               AND SUCCESSION DUTY.

INVENTORIES PROPERLY AND STRICTLY MADE IN CASES OF LIQUIDATIONS AND IN
BANKRUPTCY. DISTRESS FOR RENTS AND BILLS OF SALE, &c.

WATERSIDE, ELY, CAMBS.

CATALOGUE OF VALUABLE

LIVE AND DEAD FARMING STOCK,

INCLUDING

5 Working Horses, 2 Ponies, 2 Cows, 3 Steers, Goat;

GREYHOUND; POULTRY;

REAPING AND MOWING MACHINE, CHAFF-CUTTER,

DRILL, PULPER,

AND OTHER FARMING IMPLEMENTS:

A LARGE ASSORTMENT OF VALUABLE

HOUSEHOLD FURNITURE

GLASS, CHINA, AND OTHER EFFECTS;

TO BE SOLD BY AUCTION, BY

GEORGE COMINS,

On the Premises of Mr. WILLIAM HAWKES, under a Distress for Rent, and a Bill of Sale,

On WEDNESDAY NEXT, the 2nd day of JUNE, 1869,

TO COMMENCE PUNCTUALLY AT ELEVEN O'CLOCK;

Granary.

LOT
1 Butter box, ladder rounds, and 14 sacks
2 Quantity of old iron, stack cloth, and sundries
3 Sacks, and sundry seeds
4 Four sieves, seed screen, cross-cut saw, and pit saw
5 Besoms, hand-barrow, and beer stall
6 Ten jugs, 2 tubs, and 18-gallon cask
7 Two waggon ropes, hay knife, and corn bin
8 Quantity of tools

Gig House.

9 Spade, and lot of tools
10 Eight sacks, pig net, and plough share

Yard.

11 Two horse cribs
12 Lot of turf, and fire-wood
13 Reed, and sundries
14 Nine sacks, and ten sacks of potatoes
15 Carpenter's bench
16 Lot of felloes, hobs, and 5 paint pots

LOT
17 Hen coop, stool, yokes, and 3 battens
18 Granary ladder, and water tub
19 Heap of manure
20 Forty-five-round ladder
21 Chaff skip, sieve, two ties, &c.
22 Riding saddle and bridle
22a A shed containing bricks, tiles, wood, &c., as erected upon the premises

Stable.

23 Set of fore-horse harness, complete
24 Ditto
25 Ditto
26 Ditto
26a Ditto
27 Set of hind-horse harness, complete
28 Ditto
29 Ditto
30 Ditto
31 Ditto
32 Plough gears
33 Ditto
34 Ditto
35 Ditto
36 Light cart harness, complete

LOT
37 Sundry lots of harness

Implements, &c.

38 Waggon
39 Mowing and reaping machine, nearly new
40 Weighing machine and weights, by *W. and R. Avery*
41 Hay drag, by *Ransome and Sims*
42 Three hand hay drags
43 Ten-coulter drill, by *Garrett and Son*
44 First-class hand and horse chaff-cutting machine
45 Cake mill
46 Mangold pulper
47 Iron pig trough, 2 wood ditto, bullock ditto, and tub
48 Vice, spouting, manure fork, and tar tub
49 Two sieves, seed blower, sacks & seeds
50 Granary ladder, and 2 tar tubs
51 Three large oak posts, and a lot of wood
52 Milk cart on springs
53 Grindstone, and frame
54 Quantity of wood

"LION" BREWERY,

SUTTON, ISLE OF ELY, CAMBS

Important to Brewers, Farmers and others.

400 Good Ale Casks

Varying in size from 4½, 6, 9, 18 and 36 Gallons,

ALSO 2-108, 2-90, AND 1-54 GALLON CASKS,

SUPERIOR MALT MILL,

A few Lots of

FARMING

IMPLEMENTS

MR. GEO. COMINS

Is favoured with instructions from Messrs. Green & Son, of Bury St. Edmunds, to SELL by AUCTION, at their "Lion" Brewery, Ale, Stout, and Spirit Stores, being a Surplus Stock not required by them there.

On WEDNESDAY, JULY 24th, 1878,

AT TWELVE O'CLOCK PROMPT.

N.B. The Auctioneer begs to call the attention of Brewers to the Casks which are in excellent condition and of A1 make.

The Train leaves Cambridge for Sutton at 10-45, arriving there at 11-45; leaves March at 10-25, and St. Ives at 10-15, arriving at Sutton Station at 10-33, which is within 5 minutes walk of the Stores.

W. B. CREAK, PRINTER, ELY.

CORN EXCHANGE,

ELY.

CATALOGUE

OF A COLLECTION OF 1100 VOLUMES

OF

VALUABLE BOOKS,

IN ALL DEPARTMENTS OF LITERATURE,

Forming part of a Clerical Library,

Which will be Sold by Auction, by

MR. GEO. COMINS

ON TUESDAY, JUNE 22nd, 1880,

AT 2 O'CLOCK PRECISELY.

The Auctioneer particularly invites the attention of the Public to the above Library, the Books are valuable and well-selected, many of them being well bound.

The Cattle market in Ely had been in existence from the 14th Century but such was the volume of livestock being offered for sale that a sale yard was opened in 1871.

THE CITY OF ELY GREAT EASTERN REPOSITORY
FOR THE SALE OF ALL KINDS OF
HORSES, BULLOCKS, SHEEP & PIGS
CARRIAGES, HARNESS, & IMPLEMENTS

MR. GEORGE COMINS

Of the City of Ely, has been wished by many of the inhabitants of Ely and the surrounding villages, to establish a Repository Sale for Horses, Fat and Store Bullocks, Sheep, Pigs, Implements, Carriages and Agricultural Produce, and trusts by perseverance, and adhering to his old system of quick and punctual settlements of Sales to obtain their patronage.

THE STABLES AND YARD IN NEWNHAM
With Office is the place appointed to hold such Sales
OPPOSITE THE 'STAR' INN AND CLOSE TO THE CATTLE MARKET
And has engaged other stables in Ely, where he can accommodate 50 Horses if required, and every accommodation for Store Stock, Fat Bullocks, Sheep and Pigs, and every attention will be paid to the care of them.   Each Sale will be conducted in a most business like form, and any reserve upon anything consigned for sale must be delivered by 10 o clock on the morning of the sale.
SALE WILL BE HELD THE FIRST AND LAST THURSDAY IN EACH MONTH
Commencing THURSDAY JANUARY 5TH 1871
THE CHARGES WILL BE AS FOLLOWS.
HORSES. For offering any Horse for Sale not sold, 5s. this includes all expenses.
Commission on every Horse Sold up to £10 10s, over £10 and upwards 2.5 per cent, this also includes all charges.
N.B.- Keep of Horse and attendance, 1s.6d. per night extra
BULLOCKS. For offering any Bullock or Cow,including penning, and attendance, 1s each if not sold.
For the Sale of any Bullock, Store or Fat Stock or Cows, 4 s. each, this also includes all expenses.
Plenty of accommodation and keep per night EXTRA according to requirement.
For offering any Sheep or Pigs, including all expenses, 3d. per head. For Selling any Sheep or Pigs, including all expenses 5d per head. For offering any Carriage, Cart or Implements of Husbandry, Harness up to £1, 1s. over £5 and up to £10.2s, over £10 and up to £20.3s.
These Terms will include all expenses, and for Warehouse Room for the Day of Sale and the day previous. If Sold, 5 per cent. Charge on such Sale.
Payments made punctually at 3 o clock in the Afternoon, at the Office of the Auctioneer, Market Street Ely, on the same day. Conditions at the time of Sale exhibited in the Yard.
The Auctioneer has engaged Messrs. William Haylock and Thomas Oakey as Managers and Assistants and Mr. Charles Topping, Clerk.
N.B.- Nothing will be spared on the part of the Auctioneer to Establish this Sale, and trusts he may be supported as he has a communication with London Dealers who will attend his Sales.
All Entries for Advertisement of the January Sale must be made and sent to the Auctioneer not later than Thursday 22nd December, 1870, or to the Managers, Messrs. Haylock and Oakey, Ely.
Ely Auction and Valuing Offices Established 1856 – Valuations of all kinds made for succession Duty: also between Landlord and Tenant upon quitting Farms, Houses &c.

Cards over printed: Notice:- Removal CATTLE MARKET Held Weekly, on Thursdays HORSES, CARRIAGES, STOCK and IMPLEMENTS. WILL BE OFFERED FREE OF CHARGE IF NOT SOLD. Ely May 17th 1871

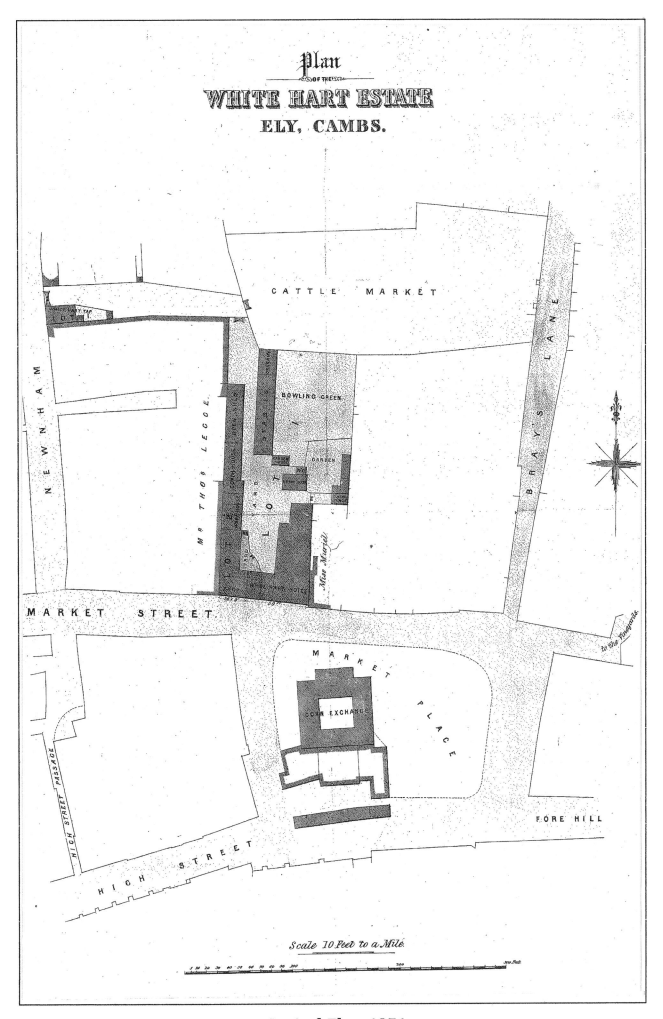

Central Ely – 1871

17

ELY, CAMBRIDGESHIRE.

DESIRABLE FREEHOLD AND COPYHOLD INVESTMENTS.

PARTICULARS AND CONDITIONS OF SALE

OF A CAPITAL

DWELLING HOUSE,

With extensive Stables, Granary, and Garden Ground, situate on the Quay, in Ely.

A COMMODIOUS

MALTING OR GRANARY,

Situate in Ship Lane, near the Quay, in Ely.

A VERY CONVENIENT

FARM HOUSE,

With the Yard, Barns, Stables, Cart Lodges, and Bullock Shed thereto belonging, situate in Ship Lane, in Ely.

A LARGE

GRANARY AND TWO COTTAGES,

With a convenient Yard, and Stables thereto adjoining, and a Frontage upon the River Ouse,
and having an entrance into Broad Street, in Ely.

BRICK AND TILED COTTAGES,

Situate on the Fore Hill, in Ely.

AND A FINE PIECE OF FREEHOLD

PASTURE LAND,

AND A LARGE FIRST CLASS FREEHOLD

TOWER
WIND MILL,

Situate in the Mill Pits Road, in St. Mary's Parish, in Ely.

TO BE SOLD BY AUCTION, BY

MR. GEORGE COMINS

At the BELL HOTEL, in ELY,

On THURSDAY, the 17th day of OCTOBER, 1872,

At FIVE O'CLOCK in the Evening punctually,

(Subject to such Conditions of Sale as will be then produced;) and in the following or such other Lots as may be determined upon
at the time of Sale.

J. H. CLEMENTS, PRINTER, ELY.

LOT 1.

All that capital MESSUAGE or DWELLING-HOUSE, situate on the Quay side, in Ely, with the entrance hall and 3 convenient reception rooms in front, together with 6 bedrooms and a back gateway or carriage entrance to a commodious office, with a large store-room over the same, abutting upon Ship Lane, and also to the kitchen, scullery, wash-house, pantry, stables, coach house, granaries, outhouses, and a large barn, (as now divided from lots 2 and 3;) and also 2 convenient pieces of garden ground, and an enclosed yard having an entrance into Ship Lane; bounded by property of Mrs. C. Cross, and R. S. J. Stevens, Esq., and lot 3 north; lots 2 and 3, west; lots 2, 3, and Ship Lane, south; and the Quay, east. Part of No. 1743 on Tithe Map.

Copyhold of the Manor of Ely Porta, with the exception of the Barn, and the smaller Piece of Garden Ground on the northern side of this Lot, which are Freehold.

LOT 2.

All that MALTHOUSE or GRANARY, with the Building at the western end thereof, formerly used as a mill-house, and the yard at the back thereof, having a frontage next Ship Lane, in Ely, of 150 feet, or thereabouts; bounded on the north and east by lot 1; on the west by lot 3; and on the south by Ship Lane. Part of No. 1743 on Tithe Map.

Copyhold of the Manor of Ely Porta.

The Walls dividing the Yard from Lot 1 are included in that Lot.

LOT 3.

All that MESSUAGE, DWELLING, or FARM-HOUSE, with two rooms in front, and a kitchen, scullery, outhouses, five bed rooms, with the yard, barn, stables, cart-lodges, bullock shed and gateway thereto belonging, (as now divided from lots 1 and 2,) conveniently situated in Ship Lane; bounded on the north by property of R. S. J. Stevens Esq.; on the west by property of the said R. S. J. Stevens, and Ship Lane; on the south by Ship Lane and lot 1, and on the east by lots 1 and 2. Part of No. 1743 on Tithe Map.

The House and the adjacent Outhouses, Barn, Bullock Sheds, and a portion of the Yard on the northern side of this Lot are Freehold, the remainder is Copyhold of the Manor of Ely Porta.

The partition walls dividing this Lot from Lot 1 are included in Lot 1, and the wall dividing this Lot from Lot 2 are included in Lot 2.

LOT 4.

All that THREE STORIED GRANARY, or WAREHOUSE, known as Taylor's Granary, containing in length 65 feet, and in width 20 feet, or thereabouts, with the stables, yard, COALWHARF, and premises thereto adjoining, situate in Ely, near to and abutting upon the river Ouse; *and also* all those TWO BRICK-BUILT COTTAGES, with the OUTBUILDINGS and PREMISES thereto belonging, situate on the west side of the said yard, and now in the several occupations of J. Bird, and — Royston, (at rents amounting to £11. 14s. 0d. per annum.) The at premises are bounded north by property of H. Hall; east by the river Ouse; south by property of the late H. W. Evans, deceased; and west partly by a roadway from this lot to Broad Street, and partly by property of H. Hall. No. 1733 on Tithe Map.

Copyhold of the Manor of Ely Porta.

There is included in this Lot a right of horse, carriage and cart way from it into Broad Street.

N.B. The lower part of the Granary and the Coalwharf are let to Messrs. Joshua Bowers and Son, at the annual Rent of £7. 0s. 0d.

LOT 5.

All those TWO Brick and Tiled COTTAGES or TENEMENTS, with the outbuildings, yards, and gardens at the back thereof, situate on the Fore Hill, in Ely; bounded on the north by property of E. Woodroffe; on the east by property of the Churchwardens of Ely Trinity; on the south by property of H. Hall; and on the west by the Public Street, called the Fore Hill; in the several occupations of — Webb, and — Green, at rents amounting to £15. 12s. 0d. per annum. No. 565 on Tithe Map.

Copyhold of the Manor of Ely Porta.

All that large Five-storied Brick-built FREEHOLD TOWER WIND MILL, with the 3 pairs of French stones, and the Smut and Flour Machines, and Going Gear thereto belonging. *And also* the convenient granaries, stable, cart lodge, piggery and yard thereto adjoining, situate upon the Mill Pits Road, in the parish of St. Mary, in Ely. Bounded on the north by the Mill Pits Road; on the west and south by land of — Hostler; and on the east by land of — Simson In the occupation, at the apportioned rent of £50. per annum, of Messrs. Wallis and Watts, whose tenancy expires on the 11th of October, 1873. No. 554 on Tithe Map.

LOT 7.

All those 3A. 0R. 12P. (more or less) of valuable FREEHOLD PASTURE LAND, with the brick and tiled lodge standing thereon, situate upon the Mill Pits Road, in the Parish of St. Mary, in Ely, (near to Lot 6.) Bounded on the north partly by the Mill Pits Road, and partly by land of — Simson; on the east by land of ———, and on the south and west by land of — Simson. In the occupation, at the apportioned rent of £10. per annum, of Messrs. Wallis and Watts, whose tenancy expires on the 11th of October, 1873. No. 553 on Tithe Map.

Possession or Receipt of Rents and Profits may be had on Completion of the Purchases.

Further Particulars may be obtained and a Plan of Lots seen on application to Messrs. ARCHER and SON, Solicitors, Ely; or to the AUCTIONEER, at his Offices, Market Street, Ely.

THE COLLEGE, ELY,
CAMBS.

Modern, Valuable and Genteel
DINING ROOM, LIBRARY,
AND BED ROOM
FURNITURE,

Comprising:

Extending dining room table, chairs, couch, easy chair, glass in gilt frame, mahogany chiffonier, sideboard, fireirons and fenders, library table with morocco top, and 4 drawers, walnut wood whatnot with plate glass back,

"Princess of Wales" Sewing Machine,

BOOKS, ENGRAVINGS, AND CHROMOS,

two very valuable oil paintings, hall chairs, two mahogany, hat stands with marble tops,

Turkey, Brussels, Kidderminster & Felt Carpets,

feather bed, spring and wool mattresses, palliasse, iron and Arabian bedsteads, dressing tables, wash stands, tray glasses, painted wardrobe, chest of drawers, cane seat and other chairs, baths, India matting,

A VERY HANDSOME MAHOGANY WARDROBE:
The Pantry and Kitchen contain

8-day English dial, butler's tray and stand, dinner and dessert services, decanters and a quantity of rich cut glass, earthenware, mangle and wringing machine,

MOWING MACHINE, MARQUEE,
Flower Stands, Garden Tools, and other effects, which

MR. GEORGE COMINS

Has the honor to announce that he is directed by J. Greenwood, Esq., (who is changing his residence), to Sell by Auction,

On TUESDAY, the 9th day of SEPTEMBER, 1873,
Commencing the sale at 12 o'clock, in consequence of the number of lots,

The Furniture may be viewed on the morning of the Sale and Catalogues may be had on application to the Auctioneer at his Offices, Market Street, Ely, or upon the premises at the time of Sale.

MEPAL RECTORY,
CAMBS.

A portion of the MODERN and VALUABLE
FURNITURE
GLASS, CHINA,
A Library of
VALUABLE BOOKS
With the Appointments of the Study,

Kitchen, cellar and scullery articles, all the stable and garden utensils, and out-door effects, a capital forcing frame, cucumber ditto, plants, wired and board chicken house, board lodge, 54 6-feet iron hurdles, lead pump, hay, manure, wood, covered carriage, basket phaeton, harness, saddle and bridle,

GREY CARRIAGE MARE,
36 Dozen of Choice Wine,
And Numerous Effects.

MR. GEORGE COMINS

Is directed to SELL by AUCTION, upon the premises of the late Rev. A. Gatenby deceased,

On TUESDAY the 5th of DECEMBER, 1876
Commencing the Sale at 11 o'clock in the Morning.

The same will be on view at 9 o'clock on the Morning of the Sale.

Catalogues may be had of the Auctioneer at his Offices, St. Mary's Street, Ely, posted free upon application to the Auctioneer, and upon the Premises at the time of Sale; or at the Cross Keys, Inn, Mepal, and at the Ship Inn, Sutton.

W. B. CREAK, PRINTER, ELY.

MANEA, ISLE OF ELY.

Catalogue of
Important & Valuable Sale of well & costly Town made

DINING & DRAWING ROOM
TOGETHER WITH
THE APPOINTMENTS OF BEDROOM
FURNITURE,

Feather Beds, Bedding, Linen, Carpets,

BOOKS, CHINA, GLASS, & SILVER,
ENGRAVINGS AND PLATE,
HANDSOME PIER GLASSES
Pianoforte,

DAIRY, KITCHEN, SCULLERY, YARD & GARDEN
UTENSILS, AND EFFECTS.

MR. GEORGE COMINS

Will Sell by Auction the Household Furniture and Effects, in the House and upon the Premises as now occupied by Mr. M. L. Sears, of Manea aforesaid,

On FRIDAY, the 17th of FEBRUARY, 1882,
At 10 o'clock punctually, (under cover).

The Auctioneer invites the attention of the Public to this Sale; the Furniture being in good condition, and many of the Articles of the best Town make, deserve the attention of all who are really seeking such. The place of Sale is within a very easy distance of the Manea GER Station, there is a Train leaves Ely at 9-14, and one from March, 9-56.

Sale will commence punctually at time named.

FIVE HUNDRED FARM,
MANEA, ISLE OF ELY.

CATALOGUE OF
13 WORKING HORSES
Seven Nag Horses, 3 Foals,
THIRTY-SIX
EXCELLENT WELL-BRED BEAST
EIGHT COWS,
40 Ewes, Shearling Tup, Poultry,
VALUABLE AGRICULTURAL
IMPLEMENTS,
Sufficient for the working of a 300-Acre Farm,
HARNESS, AND
VALUABLE EFFECTS.

MR. GEO. COMINS

Is favoured with instructions from the Administratrix of the late William Owen, Esq. deceased,

TO SELL BY AUCTION,
On WEDNESDAY, Sept. 28th, 1881,
Punctually at TEN in the Morning.

☞ Refreshments will be provided. The Farm is within 10 minutes walk of the G.E.R. Station, at Manea.

The Auctioneer particularly invites his Friends to this Sale; the Horses are all Staunch Workers, and the Beast are well bred. The Implements are in good condition.

As the Farm is Let, the whole will be Sold without Reserve.

MANEA, ISLE OF ELY.

CATALOGUE OF

12 WORKING HORSES & MARES

COB HORSE, PONY,

4 MILCH COWS,

11 Heifers and Steers, Calf,

VALUABLE AND EXCELLENT

Agricultural Implements,

CONSISTING OF

8 MANURE CARTS, 2 COLESEED DITTO,

Two Waggons, 8 Single and Double-furrow Ploughs, Potato ditto, 7 Iron and Wood Harrows, 10-Coulter Drill, 3 Iron Rolls, Dressing Machine, 2 Mangold Pulpers, Iron Water Troughs, 2 Weighing Machines, 2 Bushels, Iron and Wood Corn Bins, Sack and Heaving Barrows, Forks, Shovels, Tools, MARKET CART, all the Implements of Husbandry and effects.

HARNESS AND PLOUGH GEAR FOR 14 HORSES,

4 Sets of Light Harness,

SADDLE & BRIDLE,

HORNSBY'S PROGRESS REAPING MACHINE,

23 ACRES OF MANGOLDS,

In Graves, and lying near the G E R. Station.

MR. GEORGE COMINS

Is directed to Sell by Auction, under a Bill of Sale, upon the premises of Mr. Michael Linford Sears, of Manea aforesaid, without reserve,

On FRIDAY, the 18th DAY OF NOVEMBER, 1881,

MANEA, ISLE OF ELY.

Catalogue of

Important & Valuable Sale of well & costly Town made

DINING & DRAWING ROOM

TOGETHER WITH

THE APPOINTMENTS OF BEDROOM

FURNITURE,

Feather Beds, Bedding, Linen, Carpets,

BOOKS, CHINA, GLASS, & SILVER,

ENGRAVINGS AND PLATE,

HANDSOME PIER GLASSES

Pianoforte,

DAIRY, KITCHEN, SCULLERY, YARD & GARDEN

UTENSILS, AND EFFECTS.

MR. GEORGE COMINS

Will Sell by Auction the Household Furniture and Effects, in the House and upon the Premises as now occupied by Mr. M. L. Sears, of Manea aforesaid,

On FRIDAY, the 17th of FEBRUARY, 1882,

At 10 o'clock punctually, (under cover).

The Auctioneer invites the attention of the Public to this Sale ; the Furniture being in good condition, and many of the Articles of the best Town make, deserve the attention of all who are really seeking such. The place of Sale is within a very easy distance of the Manea GER Station, there is a Train leaves Ely at 9-14, and one from March, 9-56.

Sale will commence punctually at time named.

CORN EXCHANGE, ELY.

To Tailors, Drapers, Private 'Families, and Others.

THE

STOCK-IN-TRADE OF A TAILOR

Late the property of Mr. BENJAMIN BAILEY, of Ely, deceased,

CONSISTING OF ABOUT

452 YARDS OF WOOLLEN CLOTHS,

Grandrills, Italian Cloths, Interlinings, Velveteens, Beaverteens and others.

ANTIQUE AND MODERN

SITTING AND BED-ROOM AND KITCHEN

FURNITURE

AND OUT-DOOR EFFECTS.

QUANTITY OF THIS SEASON POPPIES,

IN BAGS,

Shop Fixtures, Wheel-barrow, Seed Potatoes,

PANTILES, AND EFFECTS.

MR. GEORGE COMINS

Is favoured with instructions from the Representatives of Mr. Benjamin Bailey deceased, to SELL by Auction,

On Wednesday, December 2nd, 1885,

PUNCTUALLY AT 11 IN THE MORNING.

Commencing with the Furniture.

☞ Catalogues may be had of the Auctioneer of the Stock-in-Trade at his Offices, St. Mary's Street, Ely, or posted free upon application to him. He also begs to state that most of the Woollen Cloths have been recently purchased and are of good quality and design.

ST. MARY'S STREET, ELY,

CAMBRIDGESHIRE.

MODERN & ANTIQUE COSTLY & TOWN-MADE
DINING & SITTING ROOM

FURNITURE,

COMPRISING A

GRAND TONED PIANOFORTE BY BROADWOOD & Co.

Dispersed throughout the house are numerous lots of Old China, articles of Virtu, Knicknacks, Worcester and other China, and Plated articles ;

ABOUT

600 VOLS. OF BOOKS, OIL PAINTINGS AND ENGRAVINGS,

A QUANTITY OF CHASTE

Silver, about 420 Ounces,

THE CONTENTS OF THE

PRINCIPAL AND SECOND BED CHAMBERS,

A VALUABLE ASSORTMENT OF

BLANKETS, FEATHER BEDS, BEDDING, TABLE AND BED LINEN,

Several Grand Spanish Mahogany Wardrobes,

THE FITTINGS OF

A Solicitor's Office, and the Contents of China and Glass Closet, Hall, Study, Pantry, Kitchen, Scullery, Landings, Laundry, Dairy and Back Kitchen ;

TWO VERY VALUABLE DOUBLE-BARREL GUNS;

ALL THE VALUABLE

Garden, Stable, and Brewing Utensils, Out-door Effects, Farming Utensils, Saddlery, Horse Clothing, valuable silver-mounted Whips, &c.;

LAWN MOWER, 30-INCH ROLL, GARDEN SEATS;

PHAETON,

Handsome 14-hands Grey Pony

VALUABLE ALDERNEY COW, POULTRY, PHEASANTS,

AND NUMEROUS EFFECTS.

MR. GEO. COMINS

Is favoured with instructions to Sell the above by Auction, upon the Premises of Henry Dench, Esq., on

Tuesday & Wednesday, the 15th & 16th June, 1886,

COMMENCING EACH DAY AT 11 O'CLOCK PROMPT, UNDER COVER.

☞ On view on Monday, the day previous to the Sale, by Ticket only, to be obtained of the Auctioneer.

Catalogues may be had of the Auctioneer, at his Offices, St. Mary's Street, Ely, or on the premises on the day of Sale.

HADDENHAM,
ALDRETH AND HILROW,
CAMBRIDGESHIRE.

DESIRABLE FREEHOLD AND COPYHOLD INVESTMENTS.

PARTICULARS WITH PLAN & CONDITIONS OF SALE

OF

63 ACRES
(MORE OR LESS) OF
ARABLE AND PASTURE
LAND,
WITH
2 Cottages and Barn,
YIELDING ANNUALLY
A NETT RENTAL OF £219.
WHICH

MR. GEORGE COMINS

Is directed by the Trustee, with the concurrence of Mrs. Comins and Miss Drage,

TO SELL BY AUCTION,

AT THE BELL HOTEL, IN HADDENHAM,

On TUESDAY, the 14th day of NOVEMBER, 1871,

At SIX O'CLOCK in the Evening,

(Subject to such Conditions as will be then produced, in Lots, or as may be determined on at the time of Sale,)

Formerly belonging to Mr. WILLIAM DRAGE, late of Sutton, Deceased.

LOT 1.

All that Piece of Old Pasture Accommodation Land, known as College Close, in Duck Lane, in the Parish of Haddenham, and numbered on the Tithe Map 177, containing 3A. 1R. 23P. (more or less ;) bounded on the south by property of Thomas Granger ; on the east by a garden in the occupation of John Stanley ; on the west by a garden of William Gothard ; and on the north by Duck Lane ; in the occupation of Mr. Drage Camps, at a rental of £17. per annum.—*Freehold.*

LOT 2.

All that Piece of Arable Land, situate in Hoghill Drove, in the Parish of Haddenham, and numbered on the Tithe Map 3182, containing 7A. (more or less ;) bounded on the south by land of Mr. Drage Camps ; on the west by the Drove ; on the north by the Commissioners' Drain, and on the east by land of O. Claude Pell, Esq. In the occupation of John Newal, at a rental of £25 per annum.—*Copyhold of the Manor of Haddenham, Fine certain.*

LOT 3.

All that Piece of Arable Land, formerly a Holt, situate in Hoghill Drove, and numbered on the Tithe Map 3181, adjoining Lot 2, containing 1A. 23P. (more or less ;) bounded on the south and east by the Commissioners' Drain ; on the west by Hoghill Drove, and on the north by land of Angier Batt. In the occupation of John Newal, at a rental of £3. 10s. per annum.—*Copyhold of the Manor of Haddenham.—Fine certain.*

LOT 4.

All that Piece of Arable Land, situate in Dairy Drove, in the Parish of Haddenham, and numbered on the Tithe Map 3233, containing 7A. (more or less ;) bounded on the south by land of William Porter's Trustees ; on the west by Dairy Drove ; on the north by land of Mr. Banham, and on the east by property of James Rose. In the occupation of Thomas Clark, at a rental of £20. per annum.—*Copyhold of the Manor of Haddenham.—Fine certain.*

LOT 5.

All that Piece of Arable Land, situate in Dam Bank, in Aldreth, in the Parish of Haddenham, and numbered on the Tithe Map 3478, containing 4A. (more or less ;) bounded on the south by the Drove ; west by land of Mr. Reed Camps ; on the east by land of Thomas Porter, and on the north by land of Mr. Wells. In the occupation of James Lucas, at a rental of £14. per annum.—*Freehold.*

LOT 6.

All that Piece of Accommodation Rich Old Pasture Land, known as Barn Close, near the village of Haddenham, and numbered on the Tithe Map 121, containing 4A. (more or less ;) and having a frontage next the highway of 229 feet, with a capital Barn thereon ; bounded on the north by lot 7 ; on the east by land of Martin Pate, Esq.; on the south by the highway leading to Aldreth, and on the west by land of Thomas Clark. In the occupation of Joseph Hosler, at a rental of £21. per annum.—*Freehold.*

The Purchaser of this Lot to keep up the Fence next to Lot 7.

LOT 7.

All that Piece of Accommodation Rich Old Pasture Land, adjoining lot 6, in the Parish of Haddenham, and numbered on the Tithe Map 121, being part of Barn Close, containing 5A. 0R. 38P. (more or less ;) bounded on the north by Berry Lane ; on the east by property of Martin Pate, Esq.; south by lot 6, and on the west by land of John Waller. In the occupation of Joseph Nightingale, at a rental of £22. per annum.—*Freehold.*

LOT 8.

All that Piece of Arable Land, abutting on to Berry Lane south, in the Parish of Haddenham, and numbered on the Tithe Map 528, containing 5A. 3R. (more or less ;) bounded on the west by land of William Cockle ; north by land of William Rowell and Elizabeth Tubbs, and east by land of Robert Porter. In the occupation of William Wright, Joseph Burton, and others, at a rental of £20. 10s. per annum.—*Copyhold of the Manor of Haddenham.—Fine certain.*

ELY, CAMBRIDGESHIRE.

Particulars and Conditions of Sale

OF THE

SUBSTANTIALLY ERECTED AND CONVENIENTLY ARRANGED

Dwelling House,

TOGETHER WITH EXTENSIVE

TIMBER YARD, GRANARIES, AND OUT-OFFICES.

ALSO,

3 COTTAGES,
WITH GARDENS AND OUT-HOUSES,
WHICH,

MR. GEORGE COMINS

Is favoured with instructions from the Mortgagees to Offer for Sale by Auction,

At the Lamb Hotel, Ely,

On THURSDAY, the 21st of JULY, 1887,

At 5 o'clock in the Afternoon precisely.

IN TWO LOTS.

MESSRS. FOSTERS & LAWRENCE,
SOLICITORS,
10, TRINITY STREET,
CAMBRIDGE.

LOT 1

Comprises all that substantially brick-built and slated

DWELLING HOUSE

situated in Silver Street, Ely; and containing, in the basement excellent Cellarage, on the ground floor Entrance Hall, 2 Sitting-rooms, Kitchen, Scullery, and Pantry, on the first floor 5 Bed-rooms, Box-room, Bath-room, and W.C.

The Outbuildings comprise: 3 brick-built and slated Store-rooms, with Granaries over, (which could easily be converted into 6 excellent cottages), 4 stalled brick-built and tiled Stables, with Chaise House, 3 open Sheds, Engine Shed, W.C., and enclosed Yard.

Bounded on the north by lot 2, and property of Major Baldwin ; south by Smock Mill Alley ; east by Silver Street ; and west by property of Major Baldwin. Having a frontage of 26 feet to Silver Street, also a frontage of 190 feet to Smock Mill Alley, or thereabouts. Containing in the whole 2 roods 4 poles (more or less).

COPYHOLD OF THE MANOR OF ELY BARTON.

LOT 2

Comprises all those

3 BRICK-BUILT AND SLATED COTTAGES

situated in Silver Street, Ely; each containing 2 upper and 2 lower-rooms. 3 boarded and tiled Lodges, Bake-house, W.C., and Garden.

Bounded on the north by property of Henry Hall, Esq.; south and west by lot 1 ; and east by Silver Street. Having a frontage of 37 feet, and a depth of 63 feet 5 inches, or thereabouts. All let to good tenants at an aggregate rental of £21 per annum.

The Purchaser of this lot to block up the door-way and entrance at the side of lot 1; and keep in repair the fence at the back of this lot.

COPYHOLD OF THE MANOR OF ELY BARTON.

THE BOARD OF HEALTH WATER SERVICE IS LAID ON.

QUIT RENT: 2s. TO BE APPORTIONED.

Furniture Sale – St. Mary's Street
Tuesday 26th April & Wednesday 27th April 1887
In conjunction with Messrs. Catling & Mann

ST. MARY'S STREET, ELY,
CAMBRIDGESHIRE.

MODERN AND VALUABLE

FURNITURE,
CONSISTING OF

Several mahogany glazed and open Bookcases, dining-room, loo, Pembroke, gipsy, card, occasional and other Tables; ladies' occasional Chairs in needle-work, mahogany inlaid Writing Desks, Whatnots, Pier Glasses, Engravings, tapestry, Kidderminster and other Carpets; Music Stools, mahogany Side-boards, easy and American Chairs, Counters, &c., &c.;

7-Octave **PIANETTE** in Mahogany Case, by Chappell;

6½-Octave *Pianette in Mahogany Case, by Broadwood;*

A GRAND CHAMBER PIPE ORGAN IN MAHOGANY CASE,
By Hill & Co.;

PLATED ARTICLES, QUANTITY OF LINEN.
THE WHOLE OF THE
Contents of the Bedrooms,
INCLUDING

Massive mahogany and birch Arabian Bedsteads; feather Beds, Palliasses, hair Mattresses, Toilet Glasses, double and single marble-top Washstands, dressing Tables, Ottomans, double chest of oak and other Drawers, Wardrobes, &c.;

THE CONTENTS OF THE HALL, LANDING, AND OUT-OFFICES;
ALL THE
STOCK-IN-TRADE OF A MUSIC SELLER,
COMPRISING

A large quantity of Music, also numerous volumes of Books, and a grand Stock of Brass and String Instruments, which might be expected to be found, and selected by the late Mr. Meacham;

To be Sold by Auction, by

Mr. GEO. COMINS & Messrs. CATLING & MANN,

Who are favoured with instructions from the Executor of the late Mr. JOHN MEACHAM, (and are jointly concerned on this occasion,)

On Tuesday & Wednesday, 26th & 27th April, 1887,
AT 10 FOR 11 O'CLOCK PUNCTUALLY EACH DAY.

Full descriptive Catalogues may be had of the Auctioneers, St. Mary's Street, Ely, and Corn Exchange Street, Cambridge.

The above will be removed to the Corn Exchange for convenience of Sale, and can be viewed on Monday preceding the Sale, between the hours of 12 noon and 5 p.m., by Ticket only.

Suddenly on the 27th April 1887 at 11.40 p.m. George Comins died at his home in St. Mary's Street.

> ### *Death of Mr.George Comins*
> *We regret to record the death of this gentleman, which took place on Wednesday night last. Mr. Comins, who was 49 years of age, was a well known auctioneer of this city, in which place he had been a resident for a quarter of a century. He was a native of Sutton, and was of indefatigable business habits. He was ever genial, and held in high esteem by all who had the pleasure of his acquaintance. A few months ago he was apparently of robust health and of a strong constitution. About Christmas time he broke a blood vessel, from the effects of which he never recovered. This calamity was followed by rapid consumption and diabetes, and he has passed away in the very meridian of life, respected and regretted by numerous friends and acquaintances.*

GEORGE DOBODE DRAGE COMINS
1866 – 1942

The young George Dobode Drage, the only son with two sisters Grace and Lettice, was educated at The King's School an became an Old Elean, possibly one of the oldest members of the Club. From the papers found, although hardworking i business, he was probably the most flamboyant of all the Georges, he lived life to the full taking advantage of the privilege society in which he found himself, and was given the best possible opportunities to be educated to take over the business After leaving school he was apprenticed to the firm of Ventom, Bull & Cooper, 35, Old Jewry, London for a period of seve years from 16th February, 1885. This apprenticeship was cut short by the sudden death of his father and he returned to El to run the business.

> Ely, May 9th, 1887.
>
> Sir.
>
> I beg respectfully to inform you that the business of an Auctioneer and Valuer lately carried on by my deceased Father at Ely, will for the future be continued by me; and I shall be grateful for any business that you may be good enough to favour me with, which I will endeavour to conduct to the best of my ability and your satisfaction; and you may depend upon prompt completion and settlement. I may mention that I have been articled with the well-known and old-established firm of Messrs. Ventom, Bull, & Cooper, 35, Old Jewry, London.
>
> I am, Sir,
> Your obedient servant.
> G. D. D. COMINS.

The first sale the young George D.D. conducted was in Littleport in 1886. The first two sales held after his father's death were on the New Barnes Estate and in Stretham.

"Who says another guinea"?   6934 E

George D.D.Comins selling at a 'Cock' Sale held at the side of the Corn Exchange on the Market Square (opposite what is now the fish and chip shop) at 5.30 p.m. The cockerel being sold is perched on top of the basket.

NEW BARNES ESTATE,

ELY, CAMBS.

A Heavy Fall of

TIMBER TREES

CONSISTING OF

OAK, ASH, ELM, AND POPLAR.

TOGETHER WITH THE

Bark, Brush and Lop

WOOD.

MR. GEORGE COMINS

Is favoured with instructions from the Ecclesiastical Commissioners to SELL by Auction,

On *WEDNESDAY, JUNE the 1st, 1887,*

At 11 for 12 o'clock, prompt.

Credit will be given for Two Months on a joint promissory note.

The above timber is lying on Clayway Drove, between Thistle Corner and the G.E.R. Gates, (where the sale will commence), and on lands in the occupation of Mr. Coy; the same are within an easy distance of the River and the G.E.R. Station, and the roads are now in good condition for removal.

Catalogues may be had of the Auctioneer, at his offices, St. Mary's Street, Ely.

W. B. Creak, Printer and Stationer, Ely.

STRETHAM, ISLE OF ELY.

MODERN AND VALUABLE

FURNITURE

CONSISTING OF

Mahogany chiffonnier, walnut ditto with plate-glass back and panels, mahogany loo, dining, papier mache, claw, and other tables, mahogany hall, Windsor, and cane-seated chairs, ottomans, pier glasses, tapestry, Kidderminster, and other carpets, engravings, oil paintings, musical box, mahogany sofas, cases of stuffed birds, &c., &c.

IRON DEED SAFE, DOUBLE-BARREL GUN,

The whole of the contents of the Bed-rooms,

INCLUDING,

Mahogany Arabian and French bedsteads, feather beds, palliasses, mattresses, toilet glasses, marble-top wash-stands, dressing tables, mahogany chests of drawers, ottomans, linen, &c.

THE CONTENTS OF

The Hall, Landing, Pantry, Kitchen, and Scullery.

IRON-GREY PONY.

Norfolk Car. Set of Plated Harness.

THE OUT-DOOR EFFECTS:

Core of hay, 6 coombs of oats, straw, weighing machine and weights, churn, stand, butter scales, ladder, sacks, stack cloth, quantity of tools, and numerous effects.

MR. GEORGE COMINS

Is favoured with instructions from the Executrixes of the late Mr. Wm. Charles, (deceased); to SELL by Auction,

UPON THE PREMISES, AFORESAID,

On TUESDAY, JUNE the 14th, 1887,

At 11 for 12 o'clock, prompt.

Catalogues may be had of the Auctioneer, at his offices, St. Mary's Street, Ely.

William B. Creak, Printer, High Street, Ely.

As the successful, young batchelor was enjoying his various pursuits in Ely, London and the country the family were becoming concerned about his moral welfare.

In 1896 his sisters Grace and Lettice went to stay with 'Fred Palmer'. A letter to George thanking him for some game birds he had sent 'Fred' included a few word of advice.

11th October 1896   *37, Liverpool Lawn*

Dear George,   Thank you very much for the Birds you so kindly sent we enjoyed them immensely, our larder does not

often contain game as you can imagine. I only hope you had good sport shooting them

Grace is getting on very fairly with her 'bike' lessons I think she has changed her first instructor because he was too ugly.

You have not been up yet as you promised, am quite longing for a real good <u>bust</u>, it seems ages since I had one. I wish

you could manage to run down if only for a few days, I will do my best to treat you <u>real proud.</u>

Well old man, keep straight.   I can't be always looking after you but do come and try our British four and a clay pipe.

We all send love to your Mother and yourself and again thanking you for your kindness. I am, Yours sincerely, Fred

---

Despite the family concerns George worked hard both at work and play and in 1909 was offered the Freedom of the City of London.

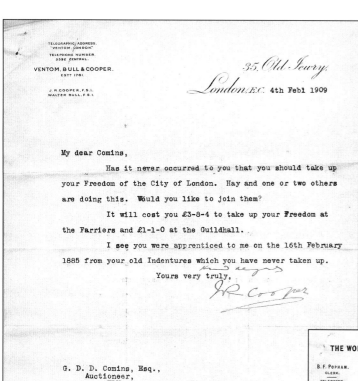

TELEGRAPHIC ADDRESS.
"VENTOM. LONDON."
TELEPHONE NUMBER.
3392 CENTRAL.

VENTOM, BULL & COOPER.
EST? 1761.

J.R.COOPER, F.S.I.
WALTER BULL, F.S.I.

35, Old Jewry,
London, E.C. 4th Febl 1909

My dear Comins,

      Has it never occurred to you that you should take up
your Freedom of the City of London. Hay and one or two others
are doing this. Would you like to join them?

      It will cost you £3-8-4 to take up your Freedom at
the Farriers and £1-1-0 at the Guildhall.

      I see you were apprenticed to me on the 16th February
1885 from your old Indentures which you have never taken up.

      Yours very truly,

      J R Cooper

G. D. D. Comins, Esq.,
    Auctioneer,
      ELY.

THE WORSHIPFUL COMPANY OF FARRIERS

B. F. POPHAM.
CLERK.

TELEPHONE—
AVENUE 2883.

A.

140, LEADENHALL STREET,
LONDON, E.C.

16th February 1919 09

Dear Sir,

      I beg to acknowledge receipt
of your letter of the 10th instant, inti-
mating your desire to take up the Freedom
of the Farriers Company, which will then
entitle you to the freedom of the City of
London. It will be necessary for you to
attend here, and I would suggest that you
arrange an appointment with me when you are
next in Town, when I shall be pleased to
admit you to the Freedom of the Company.

      The fee payable to the
Company on the taking up of the Freedom
by servitude is £3. 8. 4, and on your
taking up the Freedom of the City, a fee

of £1. 1. 0 is charged by the Corporation
towards the Funds of the City Orphans'
Schools. —

      Yours faithfully,

G. D. D. Commins Esq.,
    Auctioneer,
      Ely.

The 'Urban District Councillors' Handicap 1901 Posters were displayed all over the town, written by an anonymous person signing himself AM-PAR-TIC-U-AR .

The Urban District Councillors' Handicap, 1901.

BAPTIE BOB is on the job, and so is BARBER JOE ;

THE CAMPBELLS are coming, so mind how far you go ;

STEAM-ENGINE-JIMMY is the man, be sure you put him in ;

PAINT-POT-GEORGE— The Soldier's Friend—Back him for a win ;

BARTLE is a fine made horse, on him you'll surely bet ;

CHARLIE up the other end is not trained properly yet ;

ST. CLEMENT knows the course too well, on him you'll put some cash ;

And some on BASKET-BILLY, Who's got a lot of dash ;

The old horse called the TAILOR, don't leave him in the mud

For the new horse called the DOLBY. the horse of SHELTON BLOOD ;

HANSLIP is a good old horse, he's got a bit of pace ;

LOTS-FARM is in splendid form, back him for a place ;

TIMBER-DEAL is fairly fit, on him keep your eye ;

ARCHER's up, and means to have a finger in the pie ;

LACEBY'S Mare is scratched you know, and BIDDY's done a bunk.

There are 3 horses trained on BEER, let's hope they will not funk ;

PUNCHARD is all fit again and ready for the fray,

And so is CALICO-THE-FIRST, if only he can stay ;

WOOD-HOUSE is a steady horse and very good at startin',

But some are laying 2 to 1 upon St. Mary's MARTIN ;

CRUSOE is in the swim, but hardly knows the track ;

GOLF is a heavy-weight upon his poor old back.

All you Ely Voters just keep yourselves alive

And dot down all the best of them on March the Twenty-five.

AM-PAR-TIC-U-AR.

Printed and Published by GEORGE H. TYNDALL, Minster Place, Ely

Horses, Carriages and Harness
In Ely in the early 1900s

The horse was still used as the main means of transport with hackneys being in demand for carriages and shire horses to work the land. .

Ely had its own carriage builders, saddlers, horse physicians and machinery agents.

 *From* **VINCE & SONS,**
Coach Builders,
MARKET STREET & EGREMONT STREET,

ESTAB. 1868.

F. G. A. FENNINGS,
Lynn Road Carriage Works,
ELY, CAMBS.

Carriages of every description made to order.

SPECIALITIES IN DOG CARTS, GIGS, &c.
Estimates given on application.

Vehicles entrusted to me are carefully protected, and covered by Insurance.

TELEGRAMS: "FENNINGS, ELY."

Nov 25 1905

M

To H. RAYNER, & Son
Builder, Wheelwright & General Smith,
WAGGON AND CART BUILDER.
House Painter and Glazier,
LITTLE DOWNHAM, near ELY.
ESTABLISHED 1790.

Wheels New Tyred and all kinds of Smiths' Work done
ON THE PREMISES.
Estimates given for Repairing and Painting Waggons, Carts and Traps.

Memorandum.

From
C. E. LONGSTAFF,
SADDLER AND HARNESS MAKER,
HIGH STREET, SUTTON,
(Isle of Ely).

April 22 1905

To

Horse Clothing, Rugs &c., to Order.
ALL STABLE NECESSARIES KEPT IN STOCK.

28

HIGH STREET
ELY, *Mich* 190*8*.

Mr G Comins

Dr. to **W. CRAWLEY,**

Horse Clothing and all Stable Requisites.
—◦○◦—
RUGS, ROPES, BRUSHES, & CART GREASE.
—◦○◦—
Gears Contracted for. Work done on the Farms.

. Saddler .
AND
Harness Maker.

FARM AND NAG HORSE HARNESS,
ALL HOME MADE,
CAN BE SUPPLIED AT ONCE.

REPAIRS PROMPTLY EXECUTED.

⊣ MEMORANDUM. ⊱

From

H. PALMER,

HORSE BREAKER,

SOHAM.

To *Mr Comins*   190*8*

Telegrams: "MOTT, Littleport."

Fol. *356C*

LITTLEPORT,   *Mich* 190*4*
Cambs.

Mr S Wayman

TO **T. MOTT,**

Sole Proprietor and Manufacturer of the

Celebrated HORSE POWDER LOTION.

ALL HORSE & CATTLE MEDICINES.

ALL ACCOUNTS MUST BE PAID TO THE HEAD OFFICE, LITTLEPORT.

Granby St., Littleport,

March 190*5*

Mr Comins

Bought of E. Luddington & Sons,

Blacksmiths & Coal Merchants.

. . HORSES AND TRAPS FOR HIRE. . .

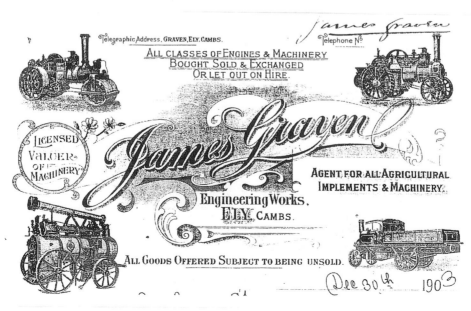

Telegraphic Address. GRAVEN, ELY, CAMBS.   Telephone N°

ALL CLASSES OF ENGINES & MACHINERY
BOUGHT SOLD & EXCHANGED
OR LET OUT ON HIRE.

LICENSED VALUER OF MACHINERY

James Graven

AGENT FOR ALL AGRICULTURAL
IMPLEMENTS & MACHINERY.

Engineering Works,
ELY, CAMBS.

ALL GOODS OFFERED SUBJECT TO BEING UNSOLD.

Dec 30th 190*3*

FRIDAY NEXT.
THETFORD,
ISLE OF ELY.

SALE OF SITTING ROOM
FURNITURE
BED ROOM & KITCHEN APPOINTMENTS,
CART HORSE,
MANURE CART
Set of Hind Harness,
AND
AGRICULTURAL IMPLEMENTS,
WHICH

MR. GEORGE COMINS

Is favoured with instructions to SELL by AUCTION (under a Bill of Sale), upon the Premises in the occupation of Mr. John Thomas Hinkin,

On FRIDAY next, 7th Dec., 1900,

Precisely at TWELVE o'clock.

For further particulars apply to Mr. GEORGE COMINS, Auctioneer, Valuer, and Land Agent, and Agent to the "Alliance" Life & Fire Assurance Company.

J. H. Clements & Son, Printers, Ely.

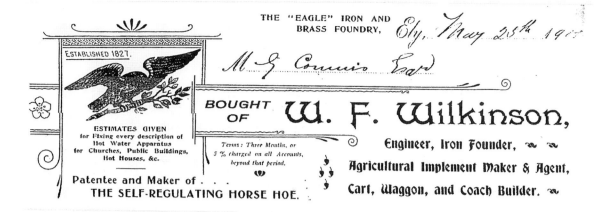

THE "EAGLE" IRON AND BRASS FOUNDRY, *Ely, May 25th 190...*

M. G. Comins Esqr

ESTABLISHED 1827.

ESTIMATES GIVEN
for Fixing every description of
Hot Water Apparatus
for Churches, Public Buildings,
Hot Houses, &c.

Terms: Three Months, or
5 % charged on all Accounts,
beyond that period.

Patentee and Maker of . . .
THE SELF-REGULATING HORSE HOE.

BOUGHT OF **W. F. Wilkinson,**

Engineer, Iron Founder,

Agricultural Implement Maker & Agent,

Cart, Waggon, and Coach Builder.

Re. W. F. WILKINSON.

CITY OF ELY.

THE STOCK=IN=TRADE

OF AN

AGRICULTURAL ENGINEER

AND

COACH BUILDER,

COMPRISING

An eight H.P. Portable Engine, 5 new Manure Carts on iron arms with copes and ladders, 9 new square spring Carts on patent axles, new Dog Cart, 2 Gigs and Pony Cart in good condition, baker's covered Hand Barrow, new flat wrought iron Roll with scrapers, 3 new "Cambridge" crease Rolls with shafts and 2 ditto with swing frames, A and square iron Harrows, rear discharge "Adrience" Binder and *Hornsby's* ditto, (nearly new,) 2 Reaping Machines by *Hornsby & Wood*, 5-tine Cultivator, set of Horse Works for driving elevator, patent Mangold Roll, cast iron Cattle Troughs, circular and long Pig Troughs, about 2,000 dry ash and elm felloes, 50 pairs of turned and unturned dry Naves, 380 dressed Spokes (various sizes,) new pair of 6in. Cart Wheels, pair of 3in. tired ditto, lance wood and elm cart Shafts, quantity of rain water Guttering and Fittings, Furnace Grates, Doors and Frames, and False Bottoms, double and single dog cart Steps, 20 Carriage Lamps, 3ft. Circular Saw, cast iron Plough, Sack Barrow and Scuffle Wheels, 3¼in. copper lined Force Pump and 3in. galvanized ditto, mahogany Wardrobe, cart Back Bands, new and second hand axles, and various other effects.

A Black Nag Gelding (7 years old, quiet,) set of Silver Plated Driving Harness, set of Hind Harness, Riding Saddle and Bridle.

WHICH

MR. GEO. COMINS

Will Sell by Auction, under a Deed of Assignment

UPON THE PREMISES, EAGLE FOUNDRY, ELY,

AND IN A PADDOCK NEAR,

On Wednesday, 22nd MAY, 1901,

AT 11 O'CLOCK PRECISELY.

Catalogues may be had of Mr. GEORGE COMINS, Auctioneer, Valuer and Land Agent, Ely, and Agent to the "Alliance" Life and Fire Assurance Company.

G. H. TYNDALL, PRINTER, MINSTER PLACE, ELY.

COLVILLE HOUSE, LITTLEPORT, ISLE OF ELY.

Sale of HOUSEHOLD FURNITURE, GARDEN, OUTDOOR & MISCELLANEOUS EFFECTS, CART, HARNESS, SWINE & POULTRY; which Mr. GEORGE COMINS is favoured with instructions from Mr. J. H. C. Allen, (who is leaving Littleport), to sell by Auction, upon the premises, (close to the G.E. Railway Station), on Monday, 12th October, 1903, precisely at 12.30 o'clock.

CATALOGUE.

Kitchen, Pantry and Scullery.

LOT
1 Four framed pictures
2 Weighing machine and weights
3 Dinner service 53 pieces
4 Six meat dishes
5 Six ditto
6 Twenty plates
7 Cheese stand and 6 waiters
8 Two tureens with lids and soup tureen
9 A well dish, cheese dish and cover, and 2 earthen drainers
10 Two metal teapots, breakfast cruet, glass fly catcher and sundry earthen ware
11 Two earthen pork pots and milk pan
12 Filter by *Lipscombe* and meat safe
13 Wooden box, 2 fold linen horse and paraffine hanging lamp
14 Bottle roasting jack and screen
15 Large iron boiler
16 New tin fish kettle
17 2 earthen milk pans and ditto ham pan
18 The "Knoll" washer by *Schultz Bros.* in good order
19 Two ft. patent mangle
20 Three iron saucepans
21 Two ditto
22 Two wooden wash keelers and washing board
23 Coal scoop, iron fender and deal table
24 Pair of 9 tread folding steps
25 Three wicker linen baskets, &c.
26 Three windsor chairs and pair of arm ditto
27 Copper kettle
28 Deal table with drawer, 5 ft. by 3 ft.
29 Sundry tinware
30 Ditto
31 Five flat irons, box iron and charcoal ditto
32 Enamelled saucepan, ditto cullender and sundries
33 Painted round table and pair of striped tapestry curtains
34 Three ft. 2 in. pierced iron fender and set of steel fireirons

Hall.

35 Five bordered fibre mats
36 Large fibre mat and one bordered ditto
37 Three framed pictures
38 A pair of oil paintings "Hunting Scenes" in massive carved gilt frames, each 3 ft. 6 in. by 2 ft. 6 in.
40 A carved oak hat and umbrella stand with plate glass and tiled back, coloured marble top and a drawer, 4 ft. wide by 7 ft. high

LOT
41 A stuffed bird in glass case
42 Ditto
43 Ditto

Dining Room.

A Carved Mahogany Suite upholstered in leather, comprising:—
51 Six chairs
52 Gentleman's easy chair on castors
53 Lady's ditto
54 Couch
55 Pair of engravings in Maple frames "Departure of the Highland Bride" and "Highland Ferry Boat"
56 Pair of engravings in Maple frames, Scriptural subjects
57 A ditto in ditto
58 Musical box with 3 cylinders, each playing 6 tunes (in good order) in inlaid rosewood case.
59 American walnut brass bound coal vase with liner and server
60 Quantity of Cassell's History of England illustrated
61 Four ft. 6 in. iron curb fender and ash pan
62 Polished extending dining table with extra leaf, 5 ft. 9 in. by 4 ft.
63 Ditto
64 A sewing machine

Drawing Room

A Carved Walnut Suite upholstered in green plush, comprising:—
74 Six chairs
75 Gentleman's circular easy chair
76 Lady's ditto
77 Double end couch

LOT
78 A carved walnut cheffoneer with shaped marble top and plate glass back; lower part fitted with 3 cupboards enclosed by 3 carved folding doors 4 ft. wide by 4 ft. 10 in. high
79 A 6¾ octave cottage pianoforte by *Oetzmann and Plumb*, 56, Great Russell Street, London, in rosewood case
80 Wooden flower stand decorated with cork, on castors, 3 ft. 7 in. by 1 ft. 8 in.
81 A handsome carved ebonized and gilt overmantel with 3 bevel plate glass panels and 4 maroon plush ditto, 6 brackets and 2 china cabinets with glazed panels, 5 ft. 4 in. wide by 4 ft. 4 in. high
82 A burr walnut oval loo table on carved pillar, and 4 chairs
83 A velvet pile table cloth with art tapestry border and fringe
84 Walnut brass bound coal scoop with liner and server
85 Handsome 4 ft. 8 in. pierced brass fender and ditto ash pan
86 A burr walnut 4 tier whatnot
87
88
89
90
91
92
93
94
95

Bedroom Furniture.

96 Japanned hip bath and ditto foot bath
97 Two pictures in Maple frames
98 Three ft. 6 in. shaped pierced iron fender with steel top
99 Ditto ash pan and set of steel fireirons
100 Three imitation rosewood caneseated chairs
101 3 ft. painted deal dressing table and valance
102 Three ft. mahogany wash stand
103 Mahogany towel airer and toilet service
104 Three ft. 4 in. mahogany chest of 5 drawers
105 Shaped mahogany toilet glass with spiral supports
106 Shaped birch toilet glass
107 Mahogany commode
108 Carved mahogany Arabian bedstead with spiral supports, 6 ft. 6 in. by 4 ft. 8 in. and crimson damask furniture
109 Mattress and pair of palliasses
110 Feather bed, bolster and 2 pillows
111 Picture in gilt frame

LOT
112 Two ft. 8 in. pierced iron fender, ditto ash pan and set of steel fireirons
113 Four chairs with cane seats
114 Three ft. mahogany dressing table with 3 drawers
115 Two ft. 4 in. mahogany washstand with drawer
116 Toilet set
117 Three ft. 2 in. mahogany chest of 5 drawers
118 Mahogany toilet glass with spiral supports
119 Brass bound pierced fender with 3 brass foot and ash pan
120 Chimney glass in rosewood and gilt frame, plate 24 in. by 14 in.
121 Timepiece and sundry ornaments
122 Painted wood bedstead with valance, mattress and pair of palliasses
123 Feather bed bolster and 2 pillows
124 Grained wash stand with drawer and toilet ware
125 Two ft. 10 in. grained chest of 4 drawers
126 Mahogany toilet glass with drawer
127 Linen chest, chair and timepiece
128 Iron French bedstead 6 ft. 6 in. by 3 ft. 6 in. and valance
129 Two-light forcing frame, 8 ft. 2 in. by 4ft. 8 in.
130 Woven wire spring mattress
131 Wool mattress
132 Wool mattress, feather pillow and bolster
133 Iron French bedstead
134 Painted deal linen chest with drawer 3 ft. 6 in. by 1 ft. 6 in.
135
136
137
138
139
140

Cart, Harness, &c.

141 Square spring cart
142 Mangel pulper
143 Two knife chaff cutter
144 Riding saddle and bridle
145 Set of breechen, 2 saddle girths, &c.
146 Set of strong brass mounted driving harness
147
148
149
150
151

Swine and Poultry.

152 Fat pig
153 Ditto
164 fowls
155 fowls

Outdoor Effects.

LOT
156 Quantity of old iron
157 Ditto
158 Ditto
159 Three wooden hen coops
160 Three ditto and 2 wooden fowl troughs
161 Long iron pig trough
162 Two white canvas boat sails and pair of oars
163 Two wooden tressels and 7 wooden boxes
164 Iron shovel, rake and ladle
165 Two iron garden rakes and wooden drag rake
166 Wooden corn bin
167 Set of 3 potato riddles and stand
168 Thirteen iron augers
169 Iron crow bar, tar brush and 4 draw hoes
170 Riveted galvanised iron water trough 5 ft. 3 in. long
171 Six ft. iron frame wooden garden seat
172 Twenty-three in. iron garden roll
173 Fourteen in. lawn mower by *Barnard & Co.*
174 Fourteen in. lawn mower
175 Two-light forcing frame, 8 ft. 2 in. by 4ft. 8 in.
176 Ditto 8 ft. 2 in. by 6 ft. 2 in.
177 Ditto 6 ft. 6 in. by 5 ft. 8 in.
178 Ditto 6 ft. 6 in. by 5 ft. 6 in.
179 Quantity of plants
180 Ditto
181 Ditto
182 One dozen tomato plants in pots
183 Ditto
184 Ditto
185 One-and-a-half dozen ditto
186 Four draw hoes and 2½ gallon water can
187 Three 2-gallon water cans
188 Carpenter's bench with screw 7 ft. 2 in. by 2 ft. 6 in.
189 Large painted wooden flower box
190 Mangel pulper
191 Ditto
192 Ditto
193 Quantity of dahlia stakes
194 Quantity of flower canes
195 Garden syringe and small wooden forcing frame
196 Quantity of flower pods
197 Ditto
198 Ditto
199 Quantity of wooden seed boxes
200
201
202
203
204

Catalogues may be had of MR. GEORGE COMINS, Auctioneer, Valuer and Land Agent, Ely, and Agent for the "Alliance" and the "Law" Accident Assurance Companies.

G. H. TYNDALL, PRINTER, ELY.

CATALOGUE.

LOT 1.

Seven lbs.

of

Findlay's

"Northern Star"

(White Round)

New (1902) Disease-Resisting Potato.

A heavy cropper, of fine shape and quality, and the
most disease-resisting and weather defying Potato
which Mr. Findlay has ever known. In 1902 he was
selling them at 20s. per lb., which is equivalent to
£2,240 per ton.

---

10   MR. GEORGE COMINS, AUCTIONEER,

LOT 328.

Half a Ton

of

Findlay's

"Royal Kidney"

(White Kidney)

New (1901) Disease-Resisting Potato.

This is an excellent Potato, most hardy. Disease-
Resisting, a heavy cropper and a grand keeper. It
has a fine appearance and its table qualities are of the
highest order, firm, dry and of fine flavour. The crop
ripens off the third week in September.

LOT.
329   A similar lot
330   Ditto

---

16   MR. GEORGE COMINS, AUCTIONEER,

LOT 475.

Half a Ton

of

"Sutton's Ninety=fold"

(Earliest on Record.)

A Wonderful Cropper and has won The Royal
Horticultural Society's Award of Merit.

Experienced growers have expressed their astonish-
ment at the enormous yield and to the knowledge of
Mr. Ambrose, customers have sold entire crops on the
ground for marketing at high figures. For two years
in succession it has been impossible to supply the
demand for this Potato.

LOT.
476   A similar lot

---

14   MR. GEORGE COMINS, AUCTIONEER,

LOT 429.

Half a Ton
of
Findlay's

"Evergood"

New Mid-Season Disease-Resisting Potato.

This Potato will in every way bear out that it has got
an appropriate name, being at all times of first class
cooking quality, admitting of it taking its place as mid-
season early and keeping so well as to rank with any
late or maincrop Potato; is of nice plump oval shape,
with fine white clear skin; a heavy cropper of equal
sized tubers. In the years it has been under the obser-
vation of Mr. Findlay he has not seen a diseased tuber.

LOT.
430   A similar lot
431   Ditto

ST. MARY'S STREET, ELY.   17

LOT 487.

Three lbs.
of

"Sutton's Discovery"

(New late Potato.)

Handsome Tubers and the heaviest cropping variety
Mr. Ambrose has ever grown, far better than "Up-to-
Date. A very strong grower. Not a single diseased
tuber could be found. A splendid late variety, and at
the present time Messrs. Sutton & Sons are charging
20/- per pound.

LOT.
488   A similar lot
489   Ditto
490   Ditto
491   Ditto
492   Ditto
493   Ditto
494
495
496

LOT 497.

One cwt.
of

"King Edward VII."

(Second Early)

A Marvellous Cropper.

It was introduced by a Lincolnshire Farmer and sold
for £40 per ton. Twenty-one Tons per acre were grown
last year. A great future is predicted for this Potato.

LOT.
498   A similar lot
499   Ditto
500   Ditto

An etching of Stuntley Hall

Twenty Pence Ferry,
WILBURTON,
ISLE OF ELY.

SALE of a High-Class GROWING

CROP OF OZIERS

Comprising an area (more or less) of

TWO ACRES,

Situate abutting upon the Bank of the Old West River, within a few yards of Twenty Pence Ferry,

WHICH

MR. GEORGE COMINS

Is favoured with instructions from MARTIN PATE, Esq., to Sell by Auction,

In about Half-Acre Lots, as now staked out,

Upon the Land, Twenty Pence Ferry,

On FRIDAY, 18th MARCH, 1904,

At 3.30 o'clock precisely.

The Oziers have been carefully selected, consisting of Nottingham Long Skins, Spaniards, Black Holland, Black Maul, New Kind, &c.; and are suitable for the manufacture of high-class Goods.

They are well situated for removal, adjoining the Old West River, which runs into the Ouse and 100-Foot Rivers, and a few yards from the Twenty Pence Hard Road.

For further particulars apply to Mr. GEORGE COMINS, Auctioneer, Valuer, and Land Agent, Ely, and Agent for the "Alliance" Life and Fire, and the "Law" Accident Insurance Companies.

J. H. Clements & Son, Printers, Ely.

CITY OF ELY.

SALE OF THE

Plant of a Miller

WHICH

MR. GEORGE COMINS

Will sell by Auction,

UPON THE PREMISES, ANNESDALE, ELY,

(Close to the G.E. Railway Station), in the occupation of Mr. Alfred Hone.

On Friday, 25th November, 1904,

PRECISELY AT 2.30 O'CLOCK.

Catalogues may be had of Mr. George Comins,
Auctioneer, Valuer and Land Agent, Ely.

G. H. TYNDALL, THE MINSTER PRESS, ELY.

CATALOGUE.

1 Quantity of cinders and a bag of lime
2 Two iron cart arms, quantity of wire and iron
3 Iron crow bar, besom and sundry tools
4 Stone staff and tin scoop
5 Five step ladder and wooden water butt
6 Waterproof cart cover
7 Tool box fitted with lock and key 3 ft. long by 1 ft. wide
8 Deal plank 9 ft. 6 in. long by 7 in. by 2¼ in.
9 A length of ditto 4 ft. 6 in. long by 9 in. by 3 in. and various pieces of wood
10 Sixteen chaff bags
11 Ten two bushel bags
12 Ten flour ditto
13 Ten ditto
14 Twelve sacks
15 One dozen mill bills and 2 bill holders
16 Loading board 8 ft. 10 in. long by 1 ft. 8 in. wide
17 Weighing machine and weights up to 21 stone by *Day & Millward* in good condition
18 Sack barrow
19 Pair of 4 ft. peak stones recently fitted with all new brasses and box with oak hurst silent feed and crane fitted to take up stones
20 Seven H.P. Portable Engine in first class condition by *Barrows & Stewart, No. 386*, 30 ft. run of iron chimney and accessories. The engine has been recently fitted with new box and tubes
21 A leather belt 56 ft. long by 5 in. wide
22 Wooden corn hopper 4 ft. 4 in. long by 2 ft. 5 in. wide by 3 ft. 7 in. deep
23 Wooden sack hoist complete
24 Fifty ft. of ⅝ steel chain and pulley
25 Forty ft. of 4 in. Ply webbing strap
26 Strong Miller's cart on springs and patent axle to carry 25 cwt.
27 A set of heavy harness
28 Leather horse collar and tie
29
30
31

CITY OF ELY.

Sale of COWS, MANURE, and Miscellaneous Effects, which Mr. GEORGE COMINS is favoured with instructions from Mr. Matthew Hitch (who is giving up his Dairy Business), to Sell by Auction, upon the Premises, Potters Lane, Back Hill, Ely, on WEDNESDAY, 12th OCTOBER, 1910, at TWO o'clock precisely.

CATALOGUE.

Miscellaneous.

LOT
1 Tin milk pail
2 Ditto
3 Ditto
4 Two 1 pint tin measures and 1 small ditto
5 Tin funnel, 2 butter boards and butter marker
6 Two butter patties, milk rack and cream pot
7 Cream pot and 2 earthen milk pans
8 Two earthen milk pans
9 Two ditto
10 Two ditto

LOT
11 Two earthen milk pans
12 Three ditto
13 A barrel churn and stand in good order
14 Iron boiler and 2 meat tins
15 Ditto and 1 ditto
16 Calving rope
17 Wooden half-tub
18 Ditto
19 Ditto
20 Two sides for shed, an inch thick
21 Three ditto
22 Three ditto

LOT
23 Two sides for shed, an inch thick
24 One pair of barn doors
25 Three Wood doors
26 Three ditto
27 Two iron and wood doors
28 Two ditto
29 Two ditto
30 Three pieces of fencing
31 Two poultry wire doors
32 Two ditto
33 Two ditto
34 Four wooden benches
35 Wooden corn bin

LOT
36 Fourteen 4-ft. corrugated sheets
37 Eight 6 ft. 6 in. ditto
38 Nine 8 ft. ditto
39 Twelve 5 ft. ditto
40 Ten odd ditto
41 Ten odd ditto
42 Square spring market cart
43 A large heap of well-made manure

MILCH COWS.

LOT
1 Red Cow in full profit, due to calve in March
2 Red Roan Cow in full profit
3 Red and White Cow in full profit, due to calve early in January
4 Red Cow in full profit, due to calve in June
5 Red Heifer, about 18 months old

CATALOGUES may be had of Mr. GEORGE COMINS, Auctioneer, Valuer, and Land Agent, Ely.

J. H. CLEMENTS AND SON, PRINTERS, ELY.

MANOR FARM, WITCHAM, ISLE OF ELY

SALE OF

4 STACKS OF EXCELLENT HAY

COMPRISING

Well got Highland Meadow, First Cut Clover & Wash Hay

WHICH

GEORGE COMINS

Is favoured with instructions from Mr. WILLIAM VYE (who is leaving the Farm) to Sell by Auction,

On WEDNESDAY, 29th NOVEMBER, 1922

AT 12 O'CLOCK PRECISELY.

Catalogues may be obtained of GEORGE COMINS, Auctioneer, Agricultural and General Valuer, Land and Insurance Agent, Ely.

Winifred Comins
Winifred Powles (Nee Dix)
1881 - 1955

By 1910 George had met and married a widow, Winifred Powles (nee Dix) from Lowestoft who, with her son Percy by her previous marriage moved into the family home. Winifred, born in 1881 joined the British Red Cross from 1914 –1918, became Nursing Commandant from 1935 – 1938 and continued running a mobile unit from 1939 – 1945. She joined the Women's Institute at its formation in 1921 and was President of the Ely Centre from 1937 – 1947. She was also a member of the Operatic Society, the Women's Conservative Club and joined the British Legion Women's Section at its formation in 1948.

George and Winifred had three children, George William Drage, John Dobede Drage and Lettice Winifred. All the children lived in the three rooms, including a nursery, on the top floor of 17, St. Mary's Street.

Winifred Comins seated to the left of Nurse Clarke (third row from the top) between 1935- 1938 during her time as Nursing Commandant.

George D.D.Comins was a great animal lover keeping Hackneys for his driving carriages and cocker spaniels.
In 1905 after a visit to the Morgan & Co. Showrooms in London he bought a Morgan car for £60 which he had sent to El
on the train.   Although this car seemed to have a repaint quite regularly he kept it until 1914.

He was a member of the Ely Constitutional Club and the Isle of Ely Coursing Club.   He was also often asked to sell good
for charities and held sales for the Red Cross Fund.

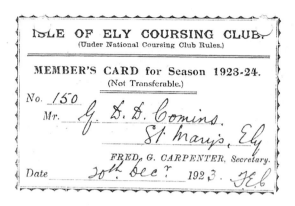

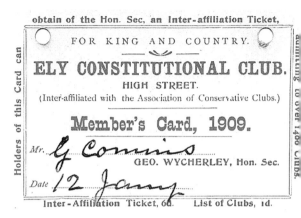

George did, when not working, appear to be a little careless and on two occasions lost his diamond ring and had to hav
posters printed to try and secure its return.   The ring was returned and the diamond still remains intact although now ha.
been reset as a ladies ring.

CITY OF ELY.

REWARD
£2 : 2 : 0

A Gold Ring may have been lost between the Co-operative Stores, St. Mary's Street, High Street, Butter Market, Market Place to Post Office and High Street Passage.

Any person taking the ring to the Police Station will receive the above reward.

40

The hackney horse was in great demand for riding and carriage driving and great importance was placed on breeding top quality animals. Stallions, travelling on the railway, were able to visit mares in the towns and villages. Adbolton St. George, the property of the Hunston Stud, Hunstanton had, at the age of five, travelled to shows all over the country was at stud in 1915 visiting towns and villages by train.

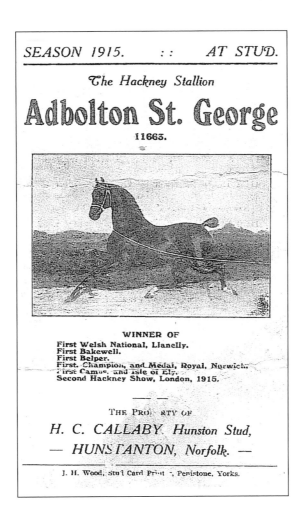

SEASON 1915. :: AT STUD.

The Hackney Stallion

Adbolton St. George
11663.

WINNER OF

First Welsh National, Llanelly.
First Bakewell.
First Belper.
First Champion, and Medal, Royal, Norwich.
First Cambs. and Isle of Ely.
Second Hackney Show, London, 1915.

THE PROPERTY OF

H. C. CALLABY, Hunston Stud,
— HUNSTANTON, Norfolk. —

J. H. Wood, Stud Card Printer, Penistone, Yorks.

Adbolton St. George
11663
will travel Norfolk and Cambridgeshire,
standing:

MONDAY - Wisbech, Swan Hotel, 9.30 a.m. to 3 p.m.,
March, White Hart Hotel from 4 p.m. to 12.30 p.m. Tuesday

TUESDAY Ely 2 p.m. and stay the night "Duke of Wellington"

WEDNESDAY Cambridge, Mr. Saint's.

THURSDAY Aylsham, Mr. Boddy's Marsham.

FRIDAY The Greyhound, East Dereham

SATURDAY At home, Hunston Stud.

TERMS - - £5 5s. each.

Groom's Fee 5s.

All Nominations booked to him must be paid for and will be charged full fee, due at end of season.

Every reasonable care will be taken of mares sent, but they will be at their Owner's own risk absolutely, and Mr. Callaby will not take any responsibility.

Keep of Mares at Grass - - 7/6 per week.

Keep of Mares and Foals at Grass - 10/6 per week.

Corn at Market prices.

N.B. All Mares should be booked to Hunstanton, Norfolk (G.E.R.), and can be met by appointment. The Stud is 5 minutes from the Station.

STALLIONS AND MARES ON SALE.

Telegrams--"CALLABY, HUNSTANTON."
Telephone—3 HUNSTANTON.

The auctioneer was always very happy to sell anything in any place for a commission but when the vendor was not always willing to pay the commission he was quick to make his point. A series of letters over payment of commission on the sale of a drill became somewhat heated when the purchaser informed George that he was unable to pay because he was being called up to fight in the war.

From the vendor:
In answer to your letter I am expecting to be called away very shortly for my country if you care to accept five shillings for what trouble you consider I have been to you in ref to drill I will send it by return before I go as for sending you a guinea I have not one by me to send awaiting your reply

George's Reply to the vendor:
I am in receipt of your letter of yesterdays date and note that you are using the War to shirk your liability. If you are joining <u>Lord Kitcheners Army</u> I will accept five shillings in discharge of my claim, if you are not doing so I shall require the Guinea sending at once or I shall put the matter in Court without further delay. I must say that I am surprised at your treatment. My Sale was the means of finding you a purchaser and I took the purchaser to my Repository Yard and showed him the Drill and through me you made a very good price of it. This offer is without prejudice.
Yours faithfully, GDDC

Reply:
Dear Sir, In answer to yr letter I am sorry that you should think ill of me after I have done my best, also that you should doubt my word about offering my services to my country I have not fallen so low as that yet to send you word I was expecting if I had not offered myself. But at the same time I thank you for accepting five shillings in settlement to save me any further trouble I am enclosing 5s. postal order as requested trusting you will acknowledge the same. Yrs. Faithfully.

George was not giving up on this commission
Dear Sir,
I am in receipt of P.O.value 5/- which I accept on the conditions named in my last letter of the 25th ultimo but on no other conditions whatsoever, so you will hear from me again later on.Yours faithfully, GDDC

Manufacturers of goods from as far away as Birmingham, Derby and Liverpool were sending surplus stock to auction in sales in Ely by train. Roses, plants and shrubs even came from Holland.

TELEPHONE 803.   Telegrams: "CARPETS, DERBY."

J. HOPLEY DODD,   *160, London Road,*
ENGLISH & ORIENTAL CARPET   *Derby.*
FACTOR AND IMPORTER.
ESTABLISHED OVER A QUARTER OF A CENTURY.   June 8th 1914.

Mr. George Comins,

    E L Y .

Dear Sir,

      Can you include about a dozen lots of Carpets and Rugs (say three Carpets and nine Rugs) in a good Furniture Sale during this month.?

      Providing my lots are offered about the middle of your Furniture Sale, I will pay you a commission of Fifteen per cent (15%) on the amount sold (no charge for unsolds). The commission to include EVERY EXPENSE – I pay carriage only.

      I could select you a dozen lots from enclosed catalogue.

      Please say if you find the cheaper qualities or the better qualities sell best.?

                  Yours truly, *J Howell*

Nat. Telephone 30Y4.   Telegrams: "CARPETS, DERBY."

J. HOPLEY DODD,   *160, London Road,*
CARPET FACTOR.   *Derby*

Particulars of Consignment.

		RESERVE		
LOT.		£	S.	D.
100.	Best Quality Tapestry Brussels Bordered Carpet, handsome pattern 9ft. × 6ft.9	0	16	3
101.	Floral Designed Sofa Rug	0	8	0
102.	Best Quality Tapestry Brussels Bordered Carpet, handsome pattern 9ft. × 9ft. ...	1	2	6
103.	,, ,, ,, ,, ,, ,, ,, ,, 10ft.6 × 9ft.	1	6	0
104.	,, ,, ,, ,, ,, ,, ,, ,, 12ft. × 9ft.	1	10	0
105.	Oriental Designed Hearth Rug, fringed ends	0	8	9
106.	Roll of superior Tapestry Brussels Stair Carpet, 10 yards	0	14	9
107.	Best Quality Tapestry Brussels Bordered Carpet, rich design 12ft. × 10ft.6 ...	1	16	3
108.	,, ,, ,, ,, ,, ,, ,, ,, 13ft.6 × 10ft.6 ...	2	0	0
109.	Oriental Designed Hearth Rug, fringed ends	0	10	6
110.	Best Quality Tapestry Brussels Bordered Carpet, rich design, 9ft. × 7ft.6 ...	0	18	0
111.	**Best Quality Brussels Pile Bordered Carpet, rich design, 10ft.6 × 9ft.** ...	1	17	6
112.	Grey Goat Skin Hearth Rug, lined and mounted on cloth	0	8	9
113.	**Best Quality Brussels Pile Bordered Carpet, rich design, 12ft. × 9ft.** ...	2	4	0
114.	,, ,, ,, ,, ,, ,, ,, ,, 12ft. × 10ft.6 ...	2	12	6

Terms—Twelve-and-Half per cent. inclusive commission on the amount sold, (no charge for unsolds), the commission to include **every expense except carriage.**

1/10/04.

TELEPHONE 803.

Telegrams: "CARPETS, DERBY."

Exors. of the Late

J. HOPLEY DODD,

ENGLISH & ORIENTAL CARPET
FACTOR AND IMPORTER.

ESTABLISHED OVER A QUARTER OF A CENTURY.

160, London Road,

Derby

September 2nd 1919.

Cheques to be made payable to
"Exors. late J.H.Dodd".

Mr. George D. Comins,
Ely.

Dear Sir,

We are desirous of having a Carpet Sale in Ely this
autumn. Will you kindly let us know per return of post on what
terms you can undertake this for us. We would pay you a Commission
of Five per cent. on the amount sold and pay your expenses, providing
same were reasonable. Will you please let us know what these would
be ?

Yours faithfully,

per pro. Exors. late J.H.Dodd.

A Knight

CORN EXCHANGE,

ELY.

Tuesday, November 16th, 1920,

At 2 o'clock p.m. precisely.

Mr. GEORGE COMINS

Has received instructions from a well-known Firm of Carpet Factors and Importers
to SELL BY AUCTION, as above, a

FIRST-CLASS STOCK OF BRITISH AND ORIENTAL

CARPETS
AND RUGS.

Superfine Velvet Pile,
English Seamless Axminster,
Real Mirzapore, Best
Quality Brussels, and
Superior Oriental Carpets.

English Axminster and other Stair Carpetings in various lengths.
Hearth Rugs, Corridor Carpets, Hall Rugs, Door Mats, etc., etc.

GOODS ON VIEW DAY PRIOR AND MORNING OF SALE.

Auctioneer's Offices : Ely, Cambridgeshire.

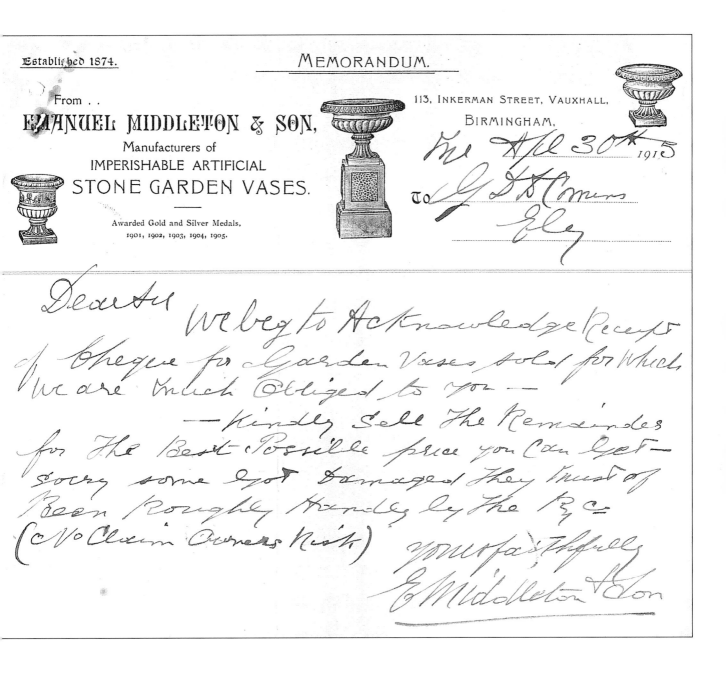

Established 1874.

MEMORANDUM.

From . .

EMANUEL MIDDLETON & SON,

Manufacturers of
IMPERISHABLE ARTIFICIAL
STONE GARDEN VASES.

———

Awarded Gold and Silver Medals,
1901, 1902, 1903, 1904, 1905.

113, INKERMAN STREET, VAUXHALL,
BIRMINGHAM,

The H/e 30th 1915

To G. D. Corners Ely

Dear Sir We beg to Acknowledge Receipt of Cheque for Garden Vases sold for which we are much Obliged to you —

— Kindly Sell The Remainder for The Best Possible price you can get — sorry some got Damaged they must of Been Roughly Handled by the Rc (No Claim Owners Risk)

yours faithfully

E M Middleton & Son

Sales of these Stone Garden Vases carried on in Ely for over 30 years

Telephone:
CENTRAL 1564, BIRMINGHAM.

MPF/TH.

Telegrams:
"QUICKLY, BIRMINGHAM."

JAMES & KEITH, Ltd.,

ELECTRO-PLATE MANUFACTURERS,

55, Newhall Street, BIRMINGHAM.

22nd., Feb. 1922,

Mr. G. Comins,
    Auctioneer,
    ELY.

Dear Sir,

    To keep our people employed and to turn some of our stock into cash, we are prepared to send out a quantity for auction and shall be glad to know whether you think they will realise fair prices, say not less than half the regular prices marked on illustration enclosed.

    We may say that these goods are all new and good medium quality made for Jewellers, etc.,— not common stuff made for auction purposes — and we are only offering to sell in this way to tide over the slack period between Christmas and Easter..

    No doubt you have frequent sales of household furniture etc., at private houses, where these could easily inc included and to advantage— an assortment similar to illustration would carry in two boxes by parcels post, and double this quantity would only cost a little more by post than by rail, and you would get the goods next day.

    Please let us know per return of post when your next sale will be held in which some could be included and your charge for selling these goods, also whether you have regular sales on your own premises and if so, the latest day for sending particulars for next sale.

    We are also winding up our Tool Department and have for disposal a quantity of various Tools, Motor Horns, etc., — are there any sales of Motor Accessories in Ely — if so we should appreciate any particulars you can give us regarding these and thank you in anticipation.

             Yours faithfully,

          FOR J

1 Egg Spoon not included in Assortment, and will be sent in place of 1 Jam Spoon.

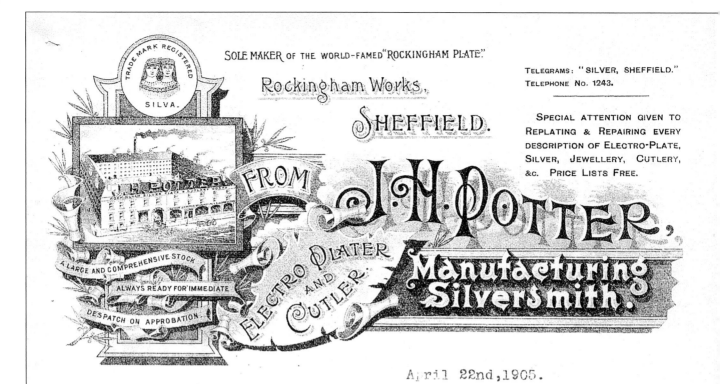

SOLE MAKER OF THE WORLD-FAMED "ROCKINGHAM PLATE."

Rockingham Works,
SHEFFIELD.

TRADE MARK REGISTERED
SILVA.

A LARGE AND COMPREHENSIVE STOCK
ALWAYS READY FOR IMMEDIATE
DESPATCH ON APPROBATION

FROM

J.H. POTTER,
ELECTRO PLATER AND CUTLER.
Manufacturing Silversmith.

TELEGRAMS: "SILVER, SHEFFIELD."
TELEPHONE No. 1243.

SPECIAL ATTENTION GIVEN TO
REPLATING & REPAIRING EVERY
DESCRIPTION OF ELECTRO-PLATE,
SILVER, JEWELLERY, CUTLERY,
&c. PRICE LISTS FREE.

April 22nd,1905.

Dear Sirs,

We purpose holding an Exhibition of highclass Plate & Cutlery
for 14 days, finishing up with an Auction Sale of the unsold portion.
If this is in your line, kindly say terms of selling, and give us infor
ation of rooms available for the purpose, andyour opinion as to the
best time of year. If you can conveniently communicate with owners
of rooms, asking them to forward particulars and terms for 14 days, to
us,we shall esteem it a favor.

Yours truly,

J.H.POTTER.

A. MOONEN - NURSERYMAN
EXPORTER OF PLANTS
BOSKOOP - HOLLAND

Prices of RHODODENDRONS — CONIFERS
DWARF-, CLIMBING– and STANDARD ROSES
free on demand

Boskoop, 17th Jan: 192 9.

G. D. D. Comins, Esq.
       Ely.

Dear Sir,

    I will be glad to know, or You can keep a sale of Roses, Plants and Shrubs for me, in Febr or March next.

    Please, say also Your terms.

Your early reply will very much oblige.

        Yours faithfully,

        A. Moonen -

Horse Sales

Horse Sales took place regularly at 'The Horse Repository' Cambridge Road, on farms in Ely and the surrounding villages and on the Market Hill. Horse Fairs and Prize Horse Sales added to the volume of weekly sales. Shire horses, hackneys, vanners, ponies and 'nags' all came under the hammer along with carriages, carts and harness.

Telegrams: COMINS, ELY.

GEORGE COMINS,
Auctioneer, Agricultural and
General Valuer, Land Agent and
—— Surveyor, ——
ELY, Cambridgeshire.

AGENT FOR THE
"ALLIANCE" ASSURANCE COMPANY, FIRE
LIFE, EMPLOYERS' LIABILITY, ACCIDENT, LIVE
AND DEAD FARMING STOCK, FARM PRODUCE,
CROPS DAMAGED BY HAIL, AND OTHER
INSURANCE.

ELY PRIZE HORSE SALE.

ON THURSDAY, 29th MAY NEXT.

Ely, May, 1913.

DEAR SIR,

I beg to advise you that the next Sale will be held on Thursday, 29th May next (Ely Horse Fair). The Great Eastern Railway Company have been good enough to announce this Sale on their handbills relating to express service of trains from London to Ely on the Horse Fair day, 29th May next, so that this forthcoming Sale will be specially advertised amongst London buyers, and catalogues will be sent to all the best buyers in London and elsewhere.

At the first Sale held on the 2nd April last, there was a large company present, including many good buyers, nearly all the horses being sold. Cart Horses, Vanners and Shire Colts realised 37, 36, 33 and 21½ guineas, Harness Horses and Ponies 26 and 19 guineas. There was a large entry of Carriages, Harness, Agricultural Implements, Farm Produce and miscellaneous effects which realized satisfactory prices.

I enclose entry form and you will observe that I am offering £10 in prizes. I should esteem it a favour if you would be good enough to send me some entries which should, if convenient to you, be made as soon as possible, but *not later* than Thursday, 22nd May next, so that the same may appear in the catalogue.

Horses will be stood in separate standings under cover, and loose boxes are provided for unbroken horses.

Thanking you in anticipation.

Yours faithfully,

GEORGE COMINS.

50

MARKET HILL, ELY.

GEORGE COMINS

WILL SELL BY AUCTION,

THIS DAY THURSDAY,

PRECISELY AT 2.30 O'CLOCK,

A

GREY HORSE

For further particulars apply to the Auctioneer, Ely.

G. H. TYNDALL, PRINTER, ELY.

1905

Telegrams: COMINS, ELY.

ELY, CAMBS.

Conveniently situated on the Main Line of the Great Eastern Railway. There is a good service of trains from London, Bishop's Stortford, Cambridge, the North of England, Norwich, King's Lynn, Peterborough, Ipswich and other Towns.

HORSE REPOSITORY

GEORGE COMINS

begs to announce that he will hold in his REPOSITORY YARD, CAMBRIDGE ROAD, ELY,

Periodical Sales of

CART HORSES,

Van & Harness Horses,

COBS & PONIES,

SHIRE & NAG COLTS & FOALS

ALSO

CARRIAGES, HARNESS, AGRICULTURAL IMPLEMENTS,

Hay, Straw, Roots and other Farm Produce, and Miscellaneous Property.

A SALE WILL BE HELD

On Wednesday, 2nd April, 1913.

AT 11.30 O'CLOCK PRECISELY.

PRIZES WILL BE OFFERED:

£3 3s. for the best CART MARE or GELDING, quiet and a good worker.

£2 2s. for the best VANNER, quiet and a good worker.

£1 1s. for the best HARNESS MARE or GELDING, quiet in harness, 14.2 h.h. or over.

Judging will be at 10.30 o'clock punctually. All horses must be in the Sale Yard not later than 10 o'clock.

ENTRIES ARE RESPECTFULLY SOLICITED,

which should be made on or before 26th MARCH.

Entry Forms and detailed Particulars may be had of

GEORGE COMINS,

Auctioneer, Agricultural and General Valuer and Land Agent, Ely.   Established in Ely 1856.

G. H. TYNDALL, THE MINSTER PRESS, ELY. [15794]

George Comins' Horse Repository
CAMBRIDGE ROAD.

THE NEXT SALE WILL BE HELD

On Tuesday next, 10th February, 1914

At **11-30** o'clock precisely;

WHEN

All the Prize Sires of the

TOWER FARM SHIRE STUD,

The property of Mr. W. E. STOCKDALE, will be offered for Sale by Auction at this sale (subject to conditions exhibited in the Sale Yard), viz., the following Lots—10, 11, 12, 13 and 14.

Lot 10. A Brown Shire Stallion,

"JAMESON BOY"

35 Vol. (31543), rising 2 years old.
Sire—"CLIFFORD JAMESON" (26053).
Dam—"HALSTEAD GUELDER ROSE" (42122).
Third at Downham Show, 1912.

Lot 11. A Brown Shire Stallion,

"CLIFFORD JAMESON"

(26053), rising 7 years old. 17.1 h.h.
Winner of 17 Prizes.
Sire—"DUNSMORE JAMESON" (17972).
Dam—"RANSOM GIFT" (46070) by "CALWICH BLEND" (17226) by "HAROLD" (3703).

Lot 12. A Brown Shire Stallion,

"ROYAL LAD"

34 Vol. (30856), rising 3 years old.
Sire—"LUDBORO' ROYAL" (23465).
Dam—"FLOWER," Vol. 33 (67027) by "GABEL'S ALMA" (18027).
First at Downham Foal Show, 1911.

Lot 13. A Bay Shire Mare,

"FLOWER"

Vol. 33 (67027), 9 years old. 16.1 h.h.
Quiet, and a good worker. Sound: Veterinary Surgeon's Certificate.
Sire—"GABEL'S ALMA" (18027).
Dam—"BEAUTY" by "WILLENHALL PRINCE" (14435).
g Dam—by "STUNTNEY DUKE" (3341).
Won Prizes—Second, Ely Show, 1910. Reserve for Medal, Littleport Show, 1911.
Bred 5 consecutive foals which have won several prizes.

Lot 14. Brown Hackney Mare,

"TOWER PARK QUEEN"

(22264), 8 years old. 15.2 h.h.
Quiet to ride and drive, and pass all road traffic. Sound: Veterinary Surgeon's Certificate.
Sire—"PRICKWILLOW CONNAUGHT" (7573).
Dam—"TOWER QUEEN" by "LORD DONOGHUE" (2743).
g Dam—"PEPPERMINT" (771).
Won Prizes at Ely and Littleport Foal Shows.
This mare's stock has taken prizes: a two-year-old took Second King's Lynn, 1911, and other prizes have been won by her foals.

Catalogues of other entries can be had of the Auctioneer, Ely.

JOHN P. TIBBITTS, ELY.

Clifford Jameson

26053.

BROWN.   FOALED 1907.

CLIFFORD JAMESON is a horse having the best of sound limbs, with the best quality bone, hair, and feet.

His substance with quality is very remarkable; he has won a number of prizes, and stood well in his class at London Shire Horse Shows, 1909 and 1910.

CLIFFORD JAMESON was bred by the late King, and sold at the Sandringham sale.

CLIFFORD JAMESON'S Foals won the following Prizes: 1912.

First and Champion Silver Cup (value £5) at Cottenham Foal Show.

First and two Seconds at Cambs. and Isle of Ely Agricultural Show, held at Chatteris.

Three Firsts, two Seconds, and Reserve for Champion, Littleport.

Three Firsts, two Seconds, and two Thirds, being 7 prizes out of 8 awards, at Downham.

THESE FOALS WON OVER £40 IN PRIZES.

PEDIGREE.

Sire—DUNSMORE JAMESON 17972.
Dam—22191 MOORS BONNY by REGENT II 6316.
g Sire—MOORS ZEALOT 15731 by POTENTATE 12086.

Dam—46070 RANSOM GIFT by CALWICH BLEND 17226 by HAROLD 3703.
g Dam—24568 RANSOM BOUNTY by LINCOLNSHIRE BOY 3188.

Service Fee = £5/5/=.

Bona-fide Tenant Farmers, £2/12/6.

PRIZES
won by
CLIFFORD JAMESON 26053.

1908.

Herefordshire and Worcestershire, Kidderminster	Third
Ludlow Agricultural Society, Ludlow	First
Welsh National Society, Aberystwyth	Third
Hereford Horse Show, Hereford ...	First
Cardiff Horse Show, Cardiff	Third
Kington Horse Show, Kington ...	Second

1909.

Shire Horse Show, London	Commended
Bath and West Society, Exeter ...	Reserve
Shropshire and West Midland, Shrewsbury	First
Do. do.	Second
Welsh National Society, Aberystwyth	Second
Cardiff Horse Show, Cardiff	Third

1910.

Shire Horse Show, London	Commended
Somerset Agricultural Society, Bridgewater	Second
Gloucestershire Agricultural Society, Cheltenham	First
Shropshire and West Midland, Shrewsbury	Third
Welsh National Society, Llanelly ...	First

Clifford Jameson was sold for 60 guineas and went to Whittlsea, Peterborough.

54

15 Bay Shire Stallion, rising 2 years old, eligible for the Stud Book.
  Sire, "Childwick Harold" (19494), bred by the late Sir Blundell Maple. *Dam*, No. 36324
  Shire Horse Stud Book.

16 Bay Shire Filly, rising 2 years old, eligible for the Stud Book.
  Sire, "Stretham Marvel" (28819), Vol. 32. *Dam,* "Daisy," by "Ely Oak" (17337).
  G. Dam by "Ely Castern Admiral" (9085).

17 Brown Shire Filly, rising 2 years old. Eligible for the Stud Book.
  Sire, "Stretham Marvel" (28819) Vol. 32. *Dam* by "Hendre Duke" (16178). *G. Dam* by
  "Castern Admiral" (9085).

18

19

20

21

22

23

Mr. George Clarke, Grange Road, Littleport.

24 Red Roan Hackney Mare, 5 years old, 14.2 h.h., quiet to ride and drive, sound.

Mr. G. Clarke, Brandon.

25 Grey Harness Mare, 11 years old, 15.3 h.h., pass all road traffic, and has been driven
  by owner for past seven years.

The Property of a Farmer.

26 Bay Van Mare, 6 years old, 15.2 h.h., quiet in all gears.

Mr. Arthur Wood, Witchford.

27 Bay Nag Mare, 15 h.h., quiet to ride and drive, and pass all road traffic.

Mr. F. Baxter, Waterbeach.

28 Bay Strong Nag Mare, 8 years old, 16 h.h., quiet to drive and in all gears, and pass
  all road traffic.

29 Roan Cob, 5 years old, 14 h.h., quiet to ride and drive, and pass all road traffic;
  sound.

 The following three lots will first be offered as a Turn-Out in one lot.

30 Bay Cob, 13 h.h., quiet to ride and drive, and pass all road traffic.

31 Governess Car on rubber tyres.

32 Set of Brass-mounted Driving Harness.

Other horses entered in the sale made high prices – almost double the prices of the previous year

ESTABLISHED IN ELY 1856.
Telegrams: COMINS, ELY.

GEORGE COMINS,
Auctioneer, Agricultural and
General Valuer, Land Agent and
—— Surveyor, ——
ELY, Cambridgeshire.

AGENT FOR THE
"ALLIANCE" ASSURANCE COMPANY, FIRE
LIFE, EMPLOYERS' LIABILITY, ACCIDENT, LIVE
AND DEAD FARMING STOCK, FARM PRODUCE,
CROPS DAMAGED BY HAIL, AND OTHER
INSURANCE.

DEAR SIR,   *Ely, March, 1914.*

ELY HORSE SALE.

ON WEDNESDAY, 8th APRIL, 1914.

  I beg to inform you that I am holding a Sale of Cart, Van and Harness
Horses, Ponies, Colts and Fillies, Carriages, Harness, Implements, etc., in my Sale
Yard, Cambridge Road, Ely, on Wednesday, 8th April, 1914. I enclose Entry Form,
and would esteem it a favour if you could send me some Entries, which should, if
convenient to you, be made as soon as possible, but not later than Thursday,
2nd April next, so that the same may appear in the catalogue.

  Good prices were realized at my Sale on the 10th February last. Shire
Horses fetched 74, 60, 48, 41½, and 20 guineas, Shire Colts, and Fillies 49½, 30 and 28
guineas, and the Carriages, Harness and Implements realised satisfactory prices.

  Horses will be stood in separate standings under cover, and Loose Boxes are
provided for unbroken Horses.

  Thanking you in anticipation,

      Yours faithfully,

      GEORGE COMINS.

Horse Repository Requisitioned by the Military
1st January 1915

The successful horse sales of 1914 were potentially threatened by the receipt of a letter from the Garrison Office, Ely requisitioning the stables for War Horses.

Garrison Office, Ely   *1st January 1915*

Dear Sir,

> *Please note that your repository stables in the Cambridge Road will be required for the use of the Military from tomorrow the 2nd instant.*
> *Sixteen horses will be put in them tomorrow and probably a further number later on.*
> *Payment will be made at the rate of 9d (ninepence) per horse nightly.*

I have the honor to be
Sir,
Your obedient servant,
A.J. Handley - Lieut.
Garrison Quartermaster

After some initial disagreement about who would be paying for the oil to light the stables George D.D. Comins managed to negotiate a lease whereby he still had the use of the stables for sales one day a month.   Exactly where the horses, equipment and manure would be removed to on this sale day is unknown.

Item 5 of the lease states
The Landlord shall have the right to use the Yard one day in every month for the purpose of holding a Repository Sale of Horses, Carriages and other Effects, between the hours of   7.30 a.m. and 5 p.m. and the Tenant shall remove from off the ground floor of the Yard all Horses, Guns, Saddlery, Manure, fodder and all other Effects whatsoever, except mangers and water trough and give vacant possession to the Landlord of the whole of the said ground floor, of the premises hereby let including Stables, Yard and Office etc. between the hours aforesaid for the purpose of holding such a sale.

By the following month, February, the inconvenience of this military takeover was working to George's benefit as he was requested to sell the military horses as and when required.
Over the next few years this became a very profitable addition to the regular, local horse sales.

THURSDAY NEXT.

MARKET HILL, ELY.

SALE OF

3 HORSES

VIZ.:—

Brown Mare, 9 years old,
2 Brown Mares, aged.

The above are certified free from disease,

WHICH

GEORGE COMINS

Is favoured with instructions from Lieutenant-Colonel
Spragge, D.S.O., Commanding Troops, Ely (being the
property of His Majesty's Government),

TO SELL BY AUCTION,

On the Market Hill, Ely,

ON

Thursday next, 25th Feb. 1915,

At 2.30 o'clock precisely.

*For further particulars apply to GEORGE COMINS, Auctioneer,
Agricultural and General Valuer and Land Agent, Ely.*

J. H. CLEMENTS AND SON, PRINTERS, ELY.

By 1917 all horses sold were subject to a 'SALE OF HORSES ORDER 1917' issued by the Agricultural Executive Committee at County Hall, March.

The licence issued stated that horses changing owners may only be sold or transferred to an occupier of an Agricultural Holding, or to a person authorised by the Board of Agriculture, Fisheries or the Army Council . This licence may have resulted in a fall of horses being put up for sale and possibly had a bearing on the prices raised.

In 1919, George D.D.Comins felt that insufficient horses were being auctioned so he wrote to the Secretary of State for War asking if he might sell some Surplus Army Horses.

12th March 1919

Sir,   Sale of Army Horses

I trust that you will permit me writing to you hereon, but should you require any more Surplus Army Horses, disposing of by Auction, in this City, I shall be pleased to conduct the sales for you.

I may say that I hold periodical Horse Sales, in this City. I can refer you to my Bankers Messrs. Barclay & Co., of this City and any other references that you may require.

I may add that I have acted for members of Lord Fulham of Downham Family (Hayes Fisher Esqre) and his Lordship might probably be kind enough to give you some information about my firm.

Trusting to be favoured with your instructions, which would receive every personal attention.

                              Yours obediently,
                              George D.D.Comins

To: The Right Honorable His Majesty's Secretery of State for War,
*   War Office, Whitehall. S.W.*

Horses which were entered in the Horse Repository Sales were required to be brought to the sales yard and tied up 'to the halter'. Stables were provided for unbroken horses.

'To the halter' became unsatisfactory so George purchased ten leather and brass bridles to be used for the sales. They were bought to be used at the sales but the good condition in which they were found in the hay lofts indicates that they were in fact never used.

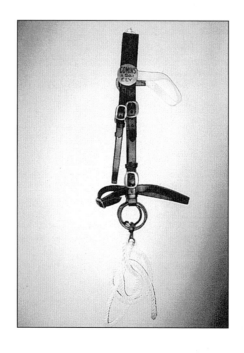

The Corn Exchange
Market Place

...uction sales of any kind were conducted in the Corn Exchange. When goods were to be sold from premises which were ...ot suitable for the public to be able to view and bid the items were '**Removed thereto for convenience of the Sale.**'

...ccasionally, if the Corn Exchange sale date did not fit in with the vendor the goods were just brought to the Market Hill ...d sold in the open. A letter, written in pencil, from J.W.How of Broad Street to George Comins in the early 1900s gives ... illustration of the sales held in the open.

To Mr. Comins Dear Sir,

I am moving a good cottage of furniture to the Market Hill today as early as I can. I expected the people had made arrangements but I find they have not and they have left it with me and I would prefer you to sell them. Kindly let bearer know and have the Town Cryed.

They are nice clean goods 2 couch easy chairs, 6 or 8 arm chairs, about 18 small chairs, 3 bedsteads, 2 feather beds, boulsters and pillars, tables, good chest draws and every thing usual in a 6 roomed cottage. I shall be glad if you can sell them.

Yours faithfully, J.W.How Broad Street

ASK FOR
HIGH CASTE TEA.

Oct ___ 1910

Mr Comins
Bought of
J. W. HOW,
Painter, Glazier, Paperhanger & General Dealer

THURSDAY NEXT, 14th APRIL, 1921.

MARKET HILL, ELY

AT 2.30 P.M. PRECISELY,

GEORGE COMINS

Will Sell by Auction, Without Reserve, about

200 GOOD OAK POSTS

QUANTITY OF HARDWOOD RAILS, SCANTLINGS AND BOARDS

AND SOME

SEASONED ASH PLANKS

AUCTIONEER'S OFFICES: ST. MARY'S STREET, ELY.

THE COLLEGE, ELY,
KING'S SCHOOL HOUSE & HEREWARD HALL.

CATALOGUE OF

Valuable Dining Room, Library and Reception Room

FURNITURE

A QUANTITY OF LINEN, BLANKETS, ELECTRO PLATED ARTICLES AND CUTLERY,

The Contents of the Principal Bedrooms

AND DORMITORIES,

THE EFFECTS IN THE HALLS, CORRIDORS, KITCHENS AND PANTRIES,

WHICH

MR. GEORGE COMINS

Is favoured with instructions from the REV. F. W. HAWES, Head Master of the King's School, who has resigned and is leaving Ely, to sell by Auction,

IN THE CORN EXCHANGE, ELY,

(Removed thereto for convenience of Sale).

On TUESDAY, 4th OCTOBER, 1904,

PRECISELY AT 10.30 O'CLOCK,

(Owing to the number of Lots).

Catalogues may be had of MR. GEORGE COMINS, Auctioneer, Valuer and Land Agent, Ely, and Agent to the "Alliance" Life and Fire and the "Law" Accident Assurance Companies.

re Joseph Tindall.

ST. MARY'S STREET, ELY

SALE OF

STOCK-IN-TRADE

OF A

GROCER AND PROVISION MERCHANT
FIXTURES AND FITTINGS,

WHICH

MR. GEORGE COMINS

Will sell by Auction, under a Deed of Assignment, in Convenient Lots,

IN THE CORN EXCHANGE, ELY,

(Removed thereto for convenience of Sale),

On TUESDAY, 24th MAY, 1910,

AT 12 O'CLOCK PRECISELY,

COMPRISING:

A Patent Cash Till by *T. O'Brien* in Mahogany Case, Mahogany Top Counter fitted with drawers, several Nests of Mahogany Drawers, Mahogany Show Case with Glazed Front, 3-tier Mahogany Biscuit Cabinet with Marble Slab, Marble and Slate Butter Slab, Mahogany Glazed Chocolate Case, Wire Fruit Stand, Japanned Tea Cannisters, Shelving, Deal Table and Form, Beer Stalder, Hand Cart on Springs, Deal Bench, Coffee Mill, Currant Sieves, 3-division Coffee Box, Quantity of Tea, Coffee, Cocoa, Sugar, Rice, Tapioca, Currants, Raisins, Sultanas, Cornflour, Starch, Essences, Pepper, Mustard, Salt, Vinegar, Matches, Candles, Plain and Fancy Soaps, Jellies, Ginger, Spices, Borax, Blue, Chutney, Custard Powder, Bovril, Ju-Vis, and Oxo, Biscuits, Tinned Pears, Peaches, Apricots, Pineapple, and other Fruits, Bottles of Apricots and Various Fruits, Jars of Strawberry, Gooseberry, Plum, Raspberry, Marmalade and other Jams, Bottles of Pickles, Relishes and Sauces, Quaker Oats, Grape Nuts, Force, Walnuts, Brazil and Barcelona Nuts, Figs, Treacle, Chocolates and Sweets, Lemon and Orange Peel, Macaronie, Prunes, an Assortment of Hand, Hair, Scrub, Saucepan, Whitewash and Stable Brushes, Carpet and Yard Brooms, Mops, Emery Paper, Blacklead, Brass and Boot Polishes, Firelighters, Quantity of Brown and other Papers and Paper Bags, Bacon Wrappers and Sacks, Empty Sweet and Biscuit Tins, Vinegar Casks and Miscellaneous Effects.

The above will be sold from a written Catalogue.

AUCTIONEER'S OFFICES: ST. MARY'S STREET, ELY.

G. H. TYNDALL, THE MINSTER PRESS, ELY. [13239]

CORN EXCHANGE, ELY.

Sale of SURPLUS WAR STORES, which GEORGE COMINS is instructed to Sell by Auction, in the CORN EXCHANGE, ELY, on WEDNESDAY, 14th June, 1922, at 11 o'clock precisely.

CATALOGUE.

The Sale will commence in the Cattle Market, Ely, with Lots 1 to 50.

LOT	
1	Two shed sections about 6 ft. by 4 ft. suitable for fowl houses and piggeries
2—50	A similar lot
51	Ten tent pegs; iron spiked and ringed
52—55	A similar lot
56	Ten baking tins
57	Ditto
58	Ditto
59	Five nearly new galvanized and painted fire buckets
60—68	A similar lot
69	Five new pick handles
70—88	A similar lot
89	Two moul heads with handles
90—98	A similar lot
99	Twelve new broom handles
100—123	A similar lot
124	Two new picks with handles
125	Ditto
126	One ditto
127	Three new large builder's pails
128—150	A similar lot
151	Four folding candle lanterns in cases
152—155	A similar lot

The following 4 Lots will all join up in one length.

156	A 12 ft. length of wired (inside and out) suction hose with brass unions
157	Ditto
158	Ditto
159	Ditto
160	Large new galvanized bath
161—165	A similar lot
166	Five round galvanized wash tubs
167—169	A similar lot

LOT	
170	Iron boiler (equal to new)
171—174	A similar lot
175	Three 3-gallon tin pails with lips
176—179	A similar lot
180	Four new 3-gallon oval camp boilers with lids
181—184	A similar lot
185	Three ditto
186	Two ditto
187	Two new very heavy white enamelled pails
188—198	A similar lot
199	Set of 5 new enamelled saucepans with lids
200—222	A similar lot
223	Two tin saucepans and steamer; and heavy enamelled kettle
224—228	A similar lot
229	Pair of canvas shoes
230—233	A similar lot
234	A new length of linoleum
235	Ditto
236	Well-made cocoa mat
237—241	A similar lot
242	Two new army stools
243	Ditto
244	One ditto
245	Door (as new)
246—254	A similar lot
255	Two new shovels
256	Ditto
257	Ditto
258	Two 4-prong forks
259	Ditto
260	Ditto

LOT	
261	Two hay forks
262	Ditto
263	New manilla waggon rope, 20 yards long
264	Ditto
265	Two felling axes
266	Ditto
267	One ditto
268	Two hedging hooks
269	Ditto
270	One ditto
271	Two bushel skeps with handles
272	Three ditto
273	Two galvanized sanitary buckets
274	Three ditto
275	Roll of new sanded felt roofing, 15 yards long
276—299	A similar lot
300	Portable marquee table, 12 ft. by 3 ft.
301	Two portable forms, 6 ft. by 9 in., 2 in. tops
302—325	A similar lot
326	Three new kitchen chairs
327—332	A similar lot
333	New stick back arm chair
334	Ditto
335	New upholstered wicker arm chair
336—338	A similar lot
339	New 12-gallon portable copper with all fittings
340	Ditto
341	Ditto
342	New 10-gallon ditto
343	Ditto
344	New portable water sterilizer complete in case

LOT	
345	Corn bin
346	Ditto
347	New round ditto
348—350	A similar lot
351	Water tank
352	Ditto
353	Pair of all wool white blankets
354—357	A similar lot
358	New waterproof waggon cover
359—362	A similar lot
363	Waterproof waggon cover
364—372	A similar lot
373	Waterproof stack cover
374—382	A similar lot
383—397	
398	Two heavy horse rugs
399	Ditto
400	One ditto
401	Five trestles
402	Ditto
403	Two bedside lockers
404	Ditto
405	One ditto
406	Six scrubbing brushes
407—412	A similar lot
413	Twelve odd brushes
414	One dozen branding irons
415	Ditto
416	Two leather headstalls
417—425	A similar lot
426	One dozen odd straps
427	Ditto
428	Sundry harness
429	Ditto

Catalogues may be obtained of GEORGE COMINS, Auctioneer, Valuer, Land and Insurance Agent, Ely.

G. H. TYNDALL, THE MINSTER PRESS, ELY. 21444

By order of Miss E. Davison and Dr. Louis Warner.

CORN EXCHANGE, ELY

Catalogue of the

VALUABLE REMAINING FURNISHINGS

(Removed from 47, Cambridge Road and 30, Egremont Street, Ely)

For Sale by Auction by

GEORGE COMINS & SON

TUESDAY, 24th AUGUST, 1948, AT 11 a.m.

OUTDOOR

LOT	
1	Sundry boxes
2	2 door scrapers
3	Garden spade, fork and shears
4	Lawn mower
5	Pair of 3-tread steps
6	7 wood framed shutters
7	7 ditto
8	10 wood fruit trays
9	10 ditto
10	10 ditto
11	10 ditto
12	Quantity of glazed tiles
13	Quantity of fairy lights
14	2 galvanised baths
15	Deal table
16	Mangle
17—22	

KITCHEN

LOT	
23	Sundries
24	Tinware
25	Sausage machine and icing set
26	Pastry board, trencher, cannister, etc.
27	Various pie dishes
28	Quantity of Well dishes
29	Earthen tea and coffee pots
30	2 stone jars and various moulds
31	Ham pan and 2 stone jars
32	2 pork pots
33	Various plant vases
34	Ditto
35	6 various jardinieres
36	6 various flower vases
37	5 ditto
38	2 glass pedestal dishes
39	Sundry glassware
40	2 copper kettles
41	3 iron saucepans and 3 steamers
42	Brass preserve pan, 13-in. diameter
43	Enamelled kettle, frying pan, etc.
44	Large egg preserving pail
45	Folding airer and small chair
46	Iron umbrella stand
47	Carpet chair and 2 stools
48	4'6" deal table with drawer
49	4' ditto with 2 drawers
50	3 sets of brass stair rods
51	1'10" 3-tier oak bookshelf
52	3'3" mahogany folding side leaf
53	Tea board and hanging bracket
54	Gas fire
55	Carpet sweeper
56	Ditto
57	Electric iron
58	Green curtain
59—64	

CHINA AND GLASS

LOT	
65	Sundry china
66	Sundry pottery
67	Ditto
68	*Limoges* china cake stand, etc.
69	China coffee service, complete
70	Green *Wedgewood* fruit stand and dish
71	Hand painted china dessert service, 16 pieces
72	Glass jugs and cake stand
73	3 glass powder bowls
74	Engraved glass water jug, 3 pickle and 3 various jars
75	Set of 3 cut glass decanters
76	Pair of decanters and single ditto
77	½ dozen engraved tumblers
78	½ ,, ruby custard glasses
79	½ ,, engraved ditto
80	½ ,, cut champagne glasses
81	½ ,, plain ditto
82	½ ,, engraved sherry glasses
83	Various glasses
84	Ditto
85	Sundry glassware
86—91	

HALL, OFFICE AND SPORTS GOODS

LOT	
92	Hall brush set
93	*Admiral Fitzroy* barometer and thermometer
94	3' walnut hat and umbrella stand
95	Oak smokers cabinet
96	Sewing machine
97	Indoor crocquet set
98	Golf clubs and bag
99	Set of Clock Golf numerals and 2 putters
100	3'9" mahogany sideboard with cellarette
101	8-day mantel clock in black marble case
102	3'3" mahogany overmantel
103	Upholstered easy armchair
104	Ditto
105	Letter press
106	2 small book shelves
107	Pair of oak book ends and wooden bowl
108	Mahogany table with drawer
109	Model schooner
110	**20" mahogany Canterbury**
111	**Ditto**
112	Draught screen
113	Coal box and server
114	Wire fireguard
115	*Vactric* electric cleaner
116	Square oak framed mirror
117	**Large mahogany table desk with drawer**
118	Set of 4 mahogany office elbow chairs
119	Electric reading lamp
120	Metal music stand in case
121	Oval oak gateleg table
122	Mains radio
123	Electric clock
124	*Pedigree* perambulator
125	Child's push chair
126	Folding ditto
127	Gent's bicycle
128	Lady's ditto
129	Carpet, 9' × 9'
130	Hair cord stair carpet
131	Cord stair carpet, in 2 lengths
132	Adjustable copper desk lamp
133—138	

BOOKS

139 "The Works of H. G. Wells," 12 vols.
140 "The International Library of Famous Literature," 20 vols.
141 "The Popular Encyclopaedia," 14 vols.
142 Various novels
143 Ditto
144 Ditto
145 Ditto
146 Ditto
147 Various books
148 Ditto
149—154

RECEPTION ROOMS

155 Pair of gilt framed water colours and pair of oak framed engravings
156 Pair of 15" mantel vases
157 3' oval oak gateleg table
158 2 iron fenders and large framed picture
159 Set of painted shelves
160 *Courtier* stove
161 **2'3" modern oak bureau bookcase**
162 Oak pedestal desk with drawers
163 Walnut extending dining table with 2 insertions
164 Set of 6 walnut dining chairs with loose leather seats
165 **3'10" mahogany bookcase** with 2 pairs of glazed doors, adjustable shelves and dome top
166 4 mahogany dining chairs in red plush
167 5' mahogany sideboard with mirror back
168 Various slip mats
169 **Bordered Axminster carpet,** 16'6" × 12'
170 Mahogany reading stand
171 1'10" shaped mahogany coal compendium with plate glass panelled back
172 3-fold firescreen and brass fire companion
173 3'3" mahogany writing table with leather inlay
174 Pair of gilt framed water colours
175 4'6" shaped oval walnut occasional table with under-shelf
176 3-tier brass cake stand, Indian brass jardiniere and copper ditto
177 4'6" mahogany china cabinet with plate glass panelled back
178 2'10" mahogany fall-leaf table
179 **3'9" walnut bureau–bookcase**
180 4'2" mahogany overmantel with 3 plate glass panels
181 Set of 3 decorated mantel vases and 1 other
182 365 day timepiece under glass dome
183 Set of open bookshelves
184 Indian carpet, 13' × 11'
185 Hair stuffed settee
186 Various cushions
187 Red plush curtain
188 *Berkeley* lounge chair
189 **2 Louis XVI chairs,** in petit point
190 **5' drop end settee,** in uncut moquette
191 **Fully sprung lounge armchair,** en suite
192 2 hassocks
193 Black skin rug
194 Pegged rug
195 **Excellent Axminster strip carpet,** 18' × 14', with underfelt
196 **New Axminster carpet,** 9' × 9', in 2 shades of rust
197 **New rug,** 6' × 4', in rust-green
198—201

SILVER AND PLATE

202 Silver specimen vase, plated tea strainer and pair of carver rests
203 Silver butter knife, sugar dredger and various plated forks
204 Plated steriliser with lamp
205 6-bottle cruet in plated stand
206 Plated tea pot
207 7-bar toast rack and 3-bottle breakfast cruet
208 Preserve dish on plated stand and stand with prong
209 Pair of gravy spoons
210 Bread knife, carving knife and fork
211 Carving knife, fork and steel

212 ½ dozen stainless table knives
213 ½ dozen dessert knives
214 ½ dozen table forks
215 5 ditto and 2 table spoons
216 ½ dozen dessert forks
217 5 ditto
218 ½ dozen dessert spoons
219 5 ditto
220 1 dozen tea spoons
221 3 pairs of sugar bows (1 silver)
222 Set of 6 plated serviette rings in case
223—225

BEDROOMS

226 Stained nursery shelving
227 Collapsible play pen with floor
228 Painted chest of 5 drawers
229 Ebonised wardrobe with interior mirror
230 Various clothes and hair brushes
231 Dressmaker's dummy
232 *Lloyd Loom* linen basket
     Satin Walnut Bedroom Suite, i.e.
233   3'9" Wardrobe
234   3'6" Dressing chest with triple mirrors and 3'6" Washstand
235 2 cane seat chairs and airer
236 2'6" oak occasional table with undershelf
237 4'6" satin walnut bedstead and box spring
238 4'6" feather bed and feather bolster
239 Wicker armchair
240 Modern gas fire
241 **Gent's 4' antique mahogany wardrobe** with 4 drawers and 4 sliding trays
242 Stained linen chest
243 3'6" antique mahogany chest of 5 drawers
244 Mahogany step commode
245 3' combination bedstead
246 3' wool overlay
247 Double toilet service
248 Ditto
     Satin Walnut Bedroom Suite, i.e.
249   3'8" semi-fitted wardrobe
250   3'6" Dressing chest with swing mirror and 3'6" washstand with marble top and back
251   2 cane seat chairs
252 3'6" oak bedstead with woven wire spring mattress
253 3'6" wool overlay
254 4' hair mattress
255 3'3" grained chest of 5 drawers
256 3 leather bags
257 Portable oil heater
258 Stained chest of 5 drawers
259 Grained linen chest
260—274

LINEN

(In new condition)

275 Double eiderdown
276 Ditto
277 Coloured quilt
278 Ditto
279 Ditto
280 White cotton bedspread
281 **New double Whitney blanket**
282 **Ditto**
283 Pair of double blankets
284 Ditto
285 Large *Marcella* counterpane
286 Ditto
287 Ditto
288 ½ dozen frill pillow cases
289 4 toilet covers
290 Various Duchess sets, etc.
291 **New table cloth** and 4 serviettes
292 White linen table cloth
293 Ditto
294 Ditto
295 Ditto
296 Ditto
297 Afternoon tea cloth
298

House, Farm and Land Sales

Auction sales were held for all property sales which took place mostly in the evenings in public rooms such as the Be[ll] Hotel, the Public Rooms or Public Houses in Ely and surrounding villages. Almost every house in Ely and many of th[e] farms in the villages came under the hammer, several being offered for sale more than once over the years.

On SATURDAY, 1st October, 1921, at 11.30 o'clock precisely.

Fourth Drove, Fodder Fen, Downham, Isle of Ely.

About 1¼ miles from the Black Bank Station, on the Ely and March Branch of the G. E. Railway.

Sale of Live and Dead Farming Stock, Household Furniture and Effects, which GEORGE COMINS is favoured with instructions from the Executor of the late Mr. JOHN PARSON, to Sell by Auction, upon the Premises, on SATURDAY, 1st October, 1921, precisely at 11.30 o'clock.

CATALOGUE.

Miscellaneous.

LOT
1 Quantity of old iron
2 Ditto
3 Quantity of wood
4 Ditto
5 2 nesting boxes
6 2 ditto
7 2 wooden half tubs
8 2 ditto
9 Quantity of round fencing wire
10 Iron twitch fork and 2 iron shovels
11 Hand saw and hammer
12 Scythe and roding hook
13 Iron twitch rake, Tommy-hawk and lantern
14 3—2-tine steel hand forks
15 Iron potato fork and potato ladle
16 Iron potato fork and iron potato stand
17 4-tine steel manure fork and 3 draw hoes
18 A similar lot
19 2 tray gates
20 2 good hen coops
21 Ditto
22 Ditto
23 10 corn sacks
24 10 bags
25 Stack cover 10 yds. by 10 yds.
26 Wheelbarrow
27 Iron plough and ditto skeif
28 Double iron pig trough, with divisions; 3 ft. 2 in. long by 1 ft. wide
29 Circular iron ditto
30 Square boarded crib
31 Ditto
32 Wooden manger, 12 ft. 6 in. long by 2 ft. 2 in. wide, and wooden drag rake
33 18-round ladder
34 21-round ditto
35 Zinc server and pail
36 Wooden corn bin with division
37 Potato masher
38 2 wire potato riddles
39 2 ditto
40 3 ditto
41 Wooden fowl house fitted with nesting boxes, perches and slatted floor, on 2 pairs of iron wheels, 7 ft. 10 in. long by 6 ft. 2 in. wide by 8 ft. 3 in. high
42 200 gallon circular galvanized iron water cistern
43 Ditto
44 Hay knife and cart rope
45 Cart rope (as good as new)
46 Ditto
47—56
57 3—9-ft. sheets of corrugated iron
58 3 ditto
59 3 ditto
60 3 ditto
61 2 ditto
62 4—8 ft. ditto
63 4 ditto
64 4 ditto
65 4 ditto
66 4 ditto
67 4 ditto
68 4 ditto
69 4 ditto
70 4 ditto
71 2 ditto
72 4—7 ft. ditto
73 4 ditto
74 4 ditto
75 4 ditto
76 4 ditto
77 4 ditto
78 3 ditto
78a 4—5 ft. ditto
79 4 ditto
80 3 ditto
Quantity of posts, boards, doors, sleepers, rafters, &c., arising from the pulling down of buildings, in convenient lots
81—99

Implements.

100 Sack barrow

LOT
101 Root Cutter, "The Perfect," P. P. 2, by *Bamford*
102 2-knife chaff cutter, by *Hunt & Co.*
103 Weighing machine and weights up to 20 stone, by *Burchfield & Son*
104 Ditto up to 1 cwt. and weights, class 3, by *Avery*
105 Single iron horse hoe, with 6 shares
106 2-horse [A] iron harrow
107 2-horse iron square harrow
108 Set of 3—2-horse iron barrows and iron whippletree
109 Single furrow iron plough, H. 2., by *Howard*
110 Single furrow iron plough, by *Ransome & Co.*
111 Iron ridging plough, by *Howard*
112 Double furrow iron plough, X. L. R. N., by *Cooke*
113 New ditto X. L. R. H., by *Cooke*
114 9-coulter corn and seed drill
115—120

Carts.

121 3½-in. wheel iron arm manure cart, with copes and ladders (in good condition)
122 Ditto
123 Ralli car on rubber tyres, by *H. J. Clark*
124 Pair of carriage lamps
125 Gig umbrella
126 Full size ralli car painted dark green, lined yellow
127—130

Harness.

131 Set of hind harness
132 Ditto
133 Set of fore harness
134 Ditto
135 Pair of plough gears
136 Ditto
137 Ditto
138 Leather cart horse bridle
139 Ditto, and collar with hames
140 2 pairs of hames
141 Hemp wanty and 2 horse ties
142 2 hemp wanties
143 Leather nag horse collar, pair of hames, traces and crupper
144 Set of 3 horse-trees
145 2—3 horse horse-trees
146 Riding saddle, leathers and stirrups and leather cart horse collar
147 2 fly nets
148 Set of plated cob harness
149 Set of pony ditto
150

Horses.

1 Captain, Black Shire Gelding, 5 years old, a quiet worker in all gears
2 Cheerley, Brown Shire Mare, 5 years old, a quiet worker in all gears, seasoned by Mr. Jackson's Horse
3 Brown mare pony, 13.2 h.h., 10 years old, quiet to ride and drive, and pass all road traffic
4 Chestnut Shire Colt Foal
5 Bay Shire Filly Foal, Sire Mr. Jabez Martin's Horse
6—10

Straw and Manure.

Lots 11 and 12 are on land adjoining Fourth Drove; lots 13 and 14 are at place of sale, and these lots will be sold there.
11 Stack of wheat straw, the produce of 7½ acres
12 Stack of rye straw off 6 acres and 1½ acres of wheat straw (in one stack)
13 Stack of wheat straw
14 A large heap of well-made manure
15—18

Poultry.

19 10 fowls
20 Ditto
21 Ditto
22 Ditto
23 Ditto
24—30

Household Furniture.

LOT
Wash-House.
1 2 iron saucepans
2 2 ditto, frying pan and oil tin
3 2 ditto saucepans and coal scoop
4 Iron kettle, zinc pail and linen basket
5 2 hand-brushes, toilet glass and 2 bowls
6 Earthen milk pan, washing board and kneeling mat
7 Large zinc keeler
8 Wooden ditto
9 20-in. patent iron mangle
10 Deal table

Pantry.
11 Tea ware and tea pot
12 China tea pot and 2 large tea plates
13 Glass cake dish, sugar basin and cruet
14 4 jugs
15 Cheese dish and cover and cucumber dish
16 8 meat plates
17 6 white china plates and 3 basins
18 2 tureens and 5 dishes
19 3 glass cake dishes
20 3 ditto
21 Pie dish and sundry earthenware
22 Bread trencher, waiter and 2 pastry boards
23 Earthen bread pot and jars
24 Sundry tin ware
25 Meat safe with perforated zinc sides
26 Deal table
27 Carving knife and fork with white handles
28 9 small table knives with ditto
29 9 ditto forks
30 4 ditto knives and 4 ditto forks
31 3 plated table spoons
32 7 dessert ditto
33 6 tea ditto and 4 ditto forks
34 Knife box, wicker basket and chip ditto
35 Enamelled cullender, paste board, 2 cooking spoons, pastry cutters, bread grater, &c.
36 China fruit dish and glass cake stand
37 Gold and white china tea service, floral pattern, 11 cups, 11 saucers, basin, cream jug, 14 plates and 2 large ditto
38 Dinner service, floral pattern, 39 pieces
39 3 plates, tea pot and sugar basin
40 4 engraved tumblers
41 7 ditto
42 4 pony tumblers, water jug, and ale glass
42a 3 plain and 3 engraved wine glasses
43 Sugar basin, butter dish and pickle jar
44 Sugar sifter, and engraved wine decanter
45 Plated dinner cruet with 4 glass bottles

Kitchen.
46 5 Windsor chairs
47 Arm ditto
48 Ditto with high lath back
49 2 feather cushions, antimacassar and 2 pictures
50 2 pictures, pair of ornaments and tin boxes
51 Duplex table lamp, knitted hearth-rug and mat
52 Table lamp and iron pot-top fender
53 Deal table
54 3 pieces of cocoa matting
55—69

Sitting Room.
Walnut Suite in leather, viz :—
70 6 chairs
71 Gentleman's easy chair on casters
72 Couch on ditto
73 Walnut rocking arm chair in tapestry
74 2 cushions and fire screen
75 3 ft. 4 in. iron fender, set of steel fire irons and ash pan
76 2 pairs of vases
77 Pair of ditto and 3 coloured glass vases

LOT
78 Tapestry hearth rug
79 Walnut overmantel with 5 plate glass panels and 2 china shelves
80 Walnut sideboard, upper part fitted with 3 bevelled plate glass panels and 2 china shelves, lower part with cupboard enclosed by 2 doors; and a drawer; 5 ft. 10 in. high by 3 ft. 6 in. wide
81 2 pairs of vases and 2 glass flower ditto
82 An antique solid mahogany table with 2 folding leaves, on round tapered legs and club feet; 4 ft. 3 in. long by 3 ft. 4 in. wide
83 Mahogany circular stand, length of carpet and various pieces of ditto
84 Bordered tapestry carpet
85 5 ft. mahogany cornice pole with 2 ends, 10 rings and 2 brackets
86 2 down cushions in needlework covers
87 Glass duplex lamp on brass reeded support
88 Brass hanging lamp with fittings
89—94

Bed Room, No. 1.
95 Polished washstand with drawer
96 Toilet service, water bottle and glass
97 Cornice pole and 3 pictures
98 3 ft. polished dressing table, fitted with toilet glass, 2 jewel drawers and long drawer
99 Pair of large Staffordshire china dogs, 13 inches high
100 Set of 3 green painted flower vases and stuffed birds, in 2 glass cases
101 3 pairs of vases
102 Pair of tall painted vases
103 Ditto
104 2 vases and 2 figures
105 3 polished Windsor chairs
106 3 ditto
107 Pair of engravings in Maple frames
108 2 ditto
109 1 ditto and 2 coloured prints
110 Bordered tapestry carpet
111 2 hearth rugs
112 1 ditto and piece of carpet
113 China trinket set, hand glass, comb and brush

Bed Room, No. 2.
114 3 cane seated chairs
115 3 ditto
116 Polished washstand with drawer and toilet ware
117 Double mahogany towel airer
118 Cornice pole, bamboo occasional table, iron fender and ornaments
119 Deal dressing table and valance
120 Mahogany toilet glass
121 Satin walnut commode chair
122 3 ft. 4 in. mahogany chest of 5 drawers
123 3 ft. 6 in. iron French bedstead
124 3 ft. 6 in. pair of palliasses
125 3 feather pillows
126 Piece of linoleum, 11 ft. by 6 ft.
127 Ditto 11 ft. by 5 ft.
128 Pair of coloured prints in gilt frames
129 Pair of prints in oak frames and time-piece
130 7 pictures

Bed Room, No. 3.
131 5 cane seated chairs
132 Painted washstand and toilet ware
133 Polished dressing table with drawer
134 Mahogany toilet glass
135 Cornice pole and 4 scripture texts
136 Pair of prints in oak frames and 3 pictures
137 4 ft. 6 in. brass and iron French bedstead
138 4 ft. 6 in. pair of palliasses
139 4 ft. 6 in. wool mattress
140 Ditto
141 Feather bed
142 3 toilet covers
143 5 pieces of carpet
144 Piece of floor cloth, stair carpeting and 9 brass stair rods

---

CATALOGUES may be obtained of GEORGE COMINS, Auctioneer, Agricultural and General Valuer, Land and Insurance Agent, Ely.

DOWNHAM, ISLE OF ELY

WITH VACANT POSSESSION.

SALE OF A FREEHOLD

DWELLING HOUSE

OUTBUILDINGS, YARD AND GARDEN

Situate Town's End, in the Village of Downham.

WHICH

GEORGE COMINS

Is favoured with instructions from Mrs. ELIZABETH COOKE, to Sell by Auction,

AT THE BELL HOTEL, ELY

On THURSDAY, 28th AUGUST, 1924

AT 4.30 P.M. PRECISELY.

Subject to such Conditions of Sale as will then be produced.

PARTICULARS.

A Freehold **brick built, thatched and tiled DWELLING HOUSE**, with cement stucco front, situate Town's End, in the Village of Downham, with Garden in the front enclosed by iron and wood palisades, having a frontage to the Main Street of about 41 ft. 4 in. and a frontage to the Road of 154 ft. 4 in. or thereabouts.

In the occupation of Mrs. ELIZABETH COOKE, the Owner.

Vacant Possession will be given on completion of the Purchase.

The **HOUSE** contains on the Ground Floor:—2 SITTING ROOMS each with Modern Stove with tiled sides and hearth, and one with Cupboard; DAIRY with Shelves and Counter; KITCHEN with Range and Dresser; timber built and boarded SCULLERY with tiled roof; and a brick built and tiled CELLAR. On the First Floor:—LANDING with Clothes Cupboard; 2 BEDROOMS (one with Fireplace and Cupboard) and BOX ROOM opening on to Landing.

The **OUTBUILDINGS** comprise:—Brick built WASH HOUSE with corrugated iron roof and concrete floor, fitted with 2 Coppers and Furnaces and Cooking Stove; timber built and boarded CLOSET with tiled span roof; timber built and boarded enclosed COAL PLACE; boarded and wire FOWL HOUSE; timber built enclosed CART SHED; 3 timber built PIGGERIES, 2 with brick floors; and a brick built BARN with brick floor, all with corrugated iron roofs; brick built and boarded STABLES for 3 Horses with tiled and corrugated iron roof; open CART SHED with tiled roof and brick REFUSE BIN.

YARD (partly concreted) with Carriage Entrance from the Road, and PUMP with a good supply of Water.

Bounded North by the Main Street, South by property of Mrs. Holmes, East by property of Mr. John Stevens, and West by a Road.

Present Outgoings—

Apportioned Tithe Rent Charge, 1s. 0d.   Land Tax, 3s. 6d.

The Purchaser will be required to pay £3 6s. 0d. for Fixtures and Fittings, whether mentioned in the Particulars of Sale or not, an Inventory of which can be seen at the Offices of the Auctioneer, in Ely.

Particulars of Sale may be obtained of
Messrs. HALL & CAMPBELL,   or of   GEORGE COMINS,
Solicitors, Ely;   Auctioneer, Valuer and Land Agent, Ely.

G. H. TYNDALL, THE MINSTER PRESS, ELY   2278.

WITH VACANT POSSESSION.

LITTLEPORT, ISLE OF ELY

SALE OF A VALUABLE
FREEHOLD DETACHED
BUNGALOW

With SOUTH ASPECT, and

AN ENCLOSED GARDEN

Known as **"NASUS BUNGALOW,"**

CONTAINING AN AREA OF

340 SQUARE YARDS

(MORE OR LESS).

Situate at the junction of Hithe Road and Ponts Hill, in the Town of Littleport, as recently
in the occupation of the late Mr. CORNELIUS CAWTHORNE.

**Vacant Possession will be given on Completion of the Purchase, or earlier by
arrangement.**

WHICH

GEORGE COMINS

Is favoured with instructions from the Personal Representatives of Mr. CORNELIUS CAWTHORNE,
deceased, to Sell by Auction,

AT THE CROWN INN, LITTLEPORT

On FRIDAY, 8th APRIL, 1927

At **7** p.m. Precisely.

SUBJECT TO SUCH CONDITIONS OF SALE AS WILL BE THEN PRODUCED.

PARTICULARS.

A FREEHOLD DETACHED BUNGALOW with South aspect; built in Brick covered
with Cement Stucco and roofed with Tiles. There is a **GARDEN** with ornamental Shrubs in the
front of the Bungalow, enclosed by white enamelled palisades, also an enclosed **GARDEN** with Side
Entrance from Ponts Hill, Lawn, Shrubs and Rose Trees.

Situate at the junction of Hithe Road and Ponts Hill, in the Town of Littleport, with a frontage to Hithe
Road of about 80 ft. 4 in., a return frontage to Ponts Hill of 32 ft. 6 in., an average width of 36 ft , and
covering an area of 340 Square Yards (more or less), until recently in the occupation of the late Mr.
CORNELIUS CAWTHORNE.

The Bungalow contains :—Sitting Room with Bay Window, Register Stove with tiled hearth and 2-light
brass Gas Chandelier. Bed Room with bronzed Gas Bracket. Kitchen with portable Cooking Stove and
bronzed Gas Bracket.

Timber built and boarded Tool House with corrugated iron roof; and a Closet.

Bounded North by property of Mrs. George Hall; South by Hithe Road and property of the Representatives of the late Mrs. Grubb; East by properties of Miss Pond and the Representatives of the late Mrs.
Grubb, and West by Ponts Hill.

Present Outgoings—Land Tax 10d.

Gas is laid on and Water from the Council's Main.

The Purchaser shall pay in addition to the Purchase Money the sum of £3 0s. 6d. for Fixtures
and Fittings (whether mentioned in the Particulars of Sale or not), an Inventory of which may be seen at
the Offices of the Auctioneer, in Ely.

Particulars of Sale may be obtained of

Messrs. BENDALL & SONS,	or of	GEORGE COMINS,
Solicitors,		Auctioneer, Valuer and Land Agent, Ely,
Newmarket, Soham, Ely, & Mildenhall;		of whom Orders to view can be obtained.

G. H TYNDALL, THE MINSTER PRESS, ELY 24494

29, NEWNHAM STREET, ELY

SALE OF A BRICK BUILT AND TILED

COTTAGE

DOMESTIC OFFICES & GARDEN

In the occupation of **Mr. ROBERT GREAVES**, a Weekly Tenant at 5s. per week, which produces a gross **Rent of £13 per annum.**

LANDLORD PAYING OUTGOINGS.

WHICH

GEORGE COMINS

Is favoured with instructions from the Owner, to Sell by Auction,

IN THE PUBLIC ROOM, ELY

On THURSDAY, 2nd MAY, 1929

AT 4.30 P.M. PRECISELY,

SUBJECT TO SUCH CONDITIONS OF SALE AS WILL BE THEN PRODUCED.

The Property has a frontage to Newham Street of about 27 feet 3 inches, a depth of 105 feet 9 inches and a width at the back of 14 feet and covers an area of 268 square yards (more or less).

The COTTAGE contains on the Ground Floor:—Entrance Passage, Sitting Room, Living Room, brick built Pantry and Wash House with corrugated iron and tiled span roof. On the First Floor:—2 Good Bedrooms. Gas is laid on.

The OUTBUILDINGS consist of a brick built and boarded Lodge with tiled span roof, brick built and tiled W.C., and Garden.

Bounded North by properties of Mrs. Weatherhead and Mr. Basham, South by property of Mr. J. Stubbings, East by Newnham Street and West by Property of Mr. Davison.

Enfranchised Copyhold subject to the Incidents of the Manor of Ely Porta, including compensation under the Law of Property Act 1922, as amended to the Lord and Steward of the Manor. Quit Rent 1s. 0d. Land Tax 2s. 9d.

Fixtures and Fittings belonging to the Tenant are not included in the Sale.

Further Particulars may be obtained of

Messrs. UNDERWOOD, PIPER & HEYS-JONES,

Solicitors, 13, Hollis Street, Cavendish Square, London, W.1;

or of the AUCTIONEER, Ely. Telephone 65.

G. H. TYNDALL, THE MINSTER PRESS, ELY. 25763

Farm, House and Furniture Sales
Michaelmas 1938

Farm sales were an always an important part of the business and over the years sales were held in a large percentage of farms in Ely and surrounding villages. House and furniture sales made up a fully diary for the autumn of 1938

2nd September	Hill House, Coveney	Live and dead stock Threshing tackle
9th September	Watson's Farm Littleport	Live and dead stock
20th September	Bridge Farm, Ely	Live and dead stock
22nd September	At Central Hall, Ely City of Ely & Chettisham	Auction of Property Cottages, lock up shop and buildings
	Witchford	Dwelling /orchard
	Padnal, Ely	4 acres Arable fen land
30th September	Miller's Farm, Hilgay	Live and dead stock
1st October	Soham	Furniture & effects
5th October	First Westmoor, Littleport	Live and dead stock
7th October	Burwell	Furniture, butchers equipment & effects
8th October	Wolvey Holes Farm, Coveney	Live and dead stock
11th October	40, Lynn Road, Ely	Furnishings
21st October	Bell's Farm, Littleport	Live and dead stock
28th October	Mare Fen, Littleport	Live and dead stock
1st November	4th Road, Little Downham	Live and dead stock
4th November	Bedwell Hey Farm	Live and dead stock
8th November	Blockmoor Farm, Sutton	Live and dead stock
11th November	Primrose Hill Farm, Pymoor	Live and dead stock
2nd December	California, Little Downham	Live and dead stock
7th December	Mildenhall Road, Littleport	Live/dead stock/tractor
10th December	Bull Lane Farm, Coveney	Live and dead stock
13th December	'Covent Garden' Haddenham	Live/dead stock/poultry

No. 3, PALACE GREEN
ELY

SALE OF THE REMAINING SUPERIOR

ANTIQUE AND MODERN

FURNISHINGS

comprising 6 Mahogany and 6 Oak Dining Chairs, Oak Carver Chair, Mahogany Writing Desk, Upholstered Easy Chairs, Settee, Mahogany Arm Chairs in leather, Mahogany Sideboard and Cabinets, Hall and Oval Mirrors, Occasional Tables, Oak Coal Cabinet, Walton Carpets, Turkey Rugs, Pictures, 2 Rosewood Card Tables, Books, Brass Gong, Ornaments, Overmantels, Antique Circular Carved Oak Table, Hall Lantern.

7-OCTAVE PIANOFORTE by Pleyel

3-valve 'Pye' Receiver, Sewing Machine, Pianola in mahogany case

CHOICE TABLE GLASS and PLATED GOODS

'Velour,' Chenille, Plush, Serge and Brocade Window Curtains

BEDROOM APPOINTMENTS

Oak Bedsteads, Hair Mattresses, Chests of Drawers, Toilet Ware, Commode, Bidet, Bedroom Carpets, Linoleum, Toilet Cupboards and Glasses, Oak Wardrobes.

MAHOGANY AND OAK BEDROOM SUITES

Antique Tall-Boy Chest and Toilet Glass, Blankets, Bed and Table Linen

KITCHEN AND PANTRY REQUISITES

Dinner and Tea Services, Soap-Stone, Dessert Service, Copper Kettle and Stew Pans

SMALL QUANTITY OF WINES AND CHAMPAGNE

GARDEN AND OUTDOOR EFFECTS

PATENT MANGLE, GARDEN HOSE, ROLL, FLOWER POTS, TOOLS, ETC.

GEORGE COMINS & SON

Are favoured with instructions from The Misses HARVEY, to Sell by Auction

UPON THE PROPERTY

On Tuesday, 13th September, 1938
AT 11.30 A.M. PRECISELY.

Further particulars may be obtained of the AUCTIONEERS—Head Office, ELY (Tel. 65), and at Soham and Burwell.

MASON & DORMAN LTD., THE MINSTER PRESS, ELY. 3677

ACREMONT HOUSE,

EGREMONT STREET, ELY.

Catalogue of

VALUABLE ANTIQUE & MODERN DINING & DRAWING ROOM

FURNITURE

Persian, Axminster and Brussels Carpets and Rugs, Art Tapestry, Silk, Fine Lace, Indian, Moorish and Persian Curtains, Dados and Table Covers worked in Silk and Wax

THE CONTENTS OF

SIX BED AND DRESSING ROOMS

THE EFFECTS IN THE HALL, STAIRCASES AND LANDINGS

Handsome Walnut Hall Table with Marble Top, Pair of China Seats, Table Glass, Large Handsome Dinner Services, China Breakfast and Tea Services

Quantity of Table and Bed Linen, Whitney Blankets, Lace and Art Bedspreads, Marcella Counterpanes and Down Cushions in Silk and Old Gold.

WHICH

GEORGE COMINS

Is favoured with instructions from the Executors of the late Mrs. M. LUDDINGTON, to sell by Auction,

IN THE CORN EXCHANGE, ELY

Removed thereto for convenience of Sale.

On TUESDAY, 20th JUNE, 1916

AT 10. 0 O'CLOCK PRECISELY.

Owing to the number of Lots.

Catalogues may be had of GEORGE COMINS, Auctioneer, Agricultural and General Valuer, Land and Insurance Agent, Ely.

G. H. TYNDALL, THE MINSTER PRESS, ELY. 18337

**Houses/Property
For Sale by Auction
1916 – 1953**

By order of R. J. Wallace King, Esq.

CITY OF ELY

16 Miles Cambridge, 13 Newmarket, 28 King's Lynn and 68 London.

WITH VACANT POSSESSION

PARTICULARS AND CONDITIONS OF SALE OF

A DESIRABLE FREEHOLD

CHARACTER RESIDENCE

"ACREMONT HOUSE"

30, EGREMONT STREET

With

ATTRACTIVE ENCLOSED GARDEN

For Sale by Auction

THE WHITE HART HOTEL, ELY

THURSDAY, 30th JUNE, 1949

4 p.m. precisely

Solicitors—	Auctioneers—
Messrs.	**GEORGE COMINS & SON**
COZENS–HARDY & JEWSON	Head Office—ELY. (Tel. 65)
Castle Chambers	And at Churchgate St., SOHAM
NORWICH. (Tel. 25231).	Ely Cattle Market and Burwell.

W. Jefferson & Son Ltd., Printers, Ely.   56135

VINE COTTAGE
WICKEN, CAMBS.

SALE OF
HOUSEHOLD
FURNITURE

3-piece Suite, Settee and 2 Chairs, Dining Table, Chairs in leather, Time Piece, Pictures, Cocoa Matting, Oil Paintings in gilt frames, Fire Screen, Ornaments, Books, Sideboard, Medicine Chest, Lamps, Rugs, Book Rest, Plants, 4 Mahogany Chairs, 6 ft. fitted Gentleman's Wardrobe.

Dressing Table, Washstand, Bedside Cabinet, 4 Chairs, Towel Airer (en suite)

Mirror, Oak Linen Chest, Mahogany Chests of Drawers, Bed Linen, Trunk, Mattresses, Toilet Ware, Bed Pan, Baths, Pails, Iron Bedstead.

DINNER, GLASS AND TEA WARE

Oil Stoves, Washing Machine and Mangle complete

Hand Tools and Miscellaneous Effects

WHICH

GEORGE COMINS & SON

Are instructed by the Personal Representatives of the late Mrs. M. A. TURNER to Sell by Auction

UPON THE PREMISES

SATURDAY, 13th DECEMBER, 1941

ONE O'CLOCK PRECISELY.

NO CATALOGUES.   Auctioneers' Offices—ELY (Tel. 65).   And at Soham and Burwell.

MASON & DORMAN LTD., THE MINSTER PRESS.   6121

12.5. 1941

Mem Geo Comins & Son

In Account with

The Bell Hotel, Ely

Cambridgeshire.

Proprietor: WILLIAM INGHAM

CAR meets all trains.

April 1941	Hire of Room for Sale		1	1	0
	Received with thanks				
	Ingham				
	13/5/4				

33236

By order of Mrs. S. E. BLAKE.

CITY OF ELY

FREEHOLD
PAIR of COTTAGES

Nos. 1 & 3, BERNARD STREET

PRODUCING

£28 12s. 0d. per annum

For Sale by Auction

THE BELL HOTEL, ELY

THURSDAY, 9th SEPTEMBER, 1943

4 P.M.

(Subject to Conditions of Sale to be then produced)

Solicitors—
MESSRS. HALL, HARRISS & ENNION

ELY. (Tel. 50)
And at Littleport

Auctioneers—
GEORGE COMINS & SON

Head Office—ELY. (Tel. 65)
Ely Cattle Market
Soham & Burwell

PRICE 1d.

By order of Mrs. S. CHILDS.

CITY OF ELY

A

FREEHOLD RESIDENCE
"Henley House"

19, STATION ROAD

For Sale by Auction

THE BELL HOTEL, ELY

THURSDAY, 9th SEPTEMBER, 1943

4 P.M.

(Subject to Conditions of Sale to be then produced)

Solicitors—
MESSRS. BENDALL & SONS
ELY. (Tel. 199)
And at Soham
Newmarket & Mildenhall

Auctioneers—
GEORGE COMINS & SON
Head Office—ELY. (Tel. 65)
Ely Cattle Market
Soham & Burwell

PRICE 1d.

Price 1d.

By order of Mrs. G. A. MARKWELL.

HOP ROW, HADDENHAM

A VALUABLE FREEHOLD

DWELLING HOUSE

with

OUTBUILDINGS & GARDEN

Producing

£15 12s. 0d. per Annum

FOR SALE BY AUCTION BY

GEORGE COMINS & SON

THE CHURCH HALL, HADDENHAM

THURSDAY, 24th AUGUST, 1944

7 p.m. precisely

(Subject to Conditions of Sale to be then produced)

PARTICULARS

A DETACHED DWELLING HOUSE of substantial brick and slate construction together with OUTBUILDINGS & GARDEN situate abutting Hop Row, Haddenham, as let to Mr. J. W. Rutterford under a weekly tenancy at 6/- per week (5/6 plus 6d. water). Landlord paying all outgoings.

The ACCOMMODATION comprises ENTRANCE LOBBY; SITTING ROOM with modern tiled fireplace; PANTRY with fitted shelving; KITCHEN with boarded floor, cooking range and built-in cupboard.

FIRST FLOOR—3 GOOD BEDROOMS (one with fireplace).

OUTSIDE—Brick and iron roofed WASH HOUSE, Corrugated iron built E.C. Similar built STORE PLACE, 2 galvanized tanks and GARDEN fronting Hop Row.

E.R.D.C. Water is laid on.

The Property has a frontage to Hop Row of 89 Ft. 10 ins., and is bounded North-East by Hop Row, North-West and South-East by properties of Mr. Dick Burkitt and South-West by the Recreation Ground.

OUTGOINGS—None traced.

Vendor's Solicitors—Messrs. H. COPLEY & SON, St. Ives and Ely.

MASON & DORMAN LTD. 7250

By order of Mr. G. H. SPARKS.

HIGHTOWN, BURWELL

Particulars of a Freehold Detached

RANGE of 3 COTTAGES

with

the whole forming a

OUTBUILDINGS & SPACIOUS WALLED-IN GARDEN

VALUABLE SITE IN HIGH ST. WITH 98 FT. FRONTAGE

(opposite Brooks' Stores)

VACANT POSSESSION of one Cottage will be given on completion of the purchase, two are subject to the Weekly Tenancies of Messrs. G. A. King and A. Barton at 4s. and 2s. 6d. per week respectively totalling £16 18s. 0d. per annum, Landlord paying all Outgoings.

ACCOMMODATIONS:

THE VACANT COTTAGE is of new brick construction with tiled roof and contains Sitting Room with modern fireplace and cupboard, Scullery with sink and cupboard. 1ST FLOOR—2 Bedrooms. Electric lighting throughout. (Key for view obtainable of Vendor at Will-en-Dene, Burwell).

THE TWO COTTAGES are of clunch and tiled construction and contain 2 lower and 2—3 upper Rooms.

OUTSIDE—A timber and iron roofed Store Place and Closet are attached to the vacant Cottage. The remaining Outhouses consist of a Lean-to Scullery, Lodge and 2 Closets. The Garden has a double entrance from High Street subjected to a right-of-way to property of Mr. A. Granger.

Bounded North by property of A. Granger, South and West by property of Col. C. J. O'Callaghan and East by High Street.

N.R.D.C. Water Standard adjoins.

FOR SALE BY AUCTION BY

GEORGE COMINS & SON

THE FOX INN, BURWELL

MONDAY, 23rd DECEMBER, 1946

7 p.m. precisely

(Subject to Conditions of Sale to be then produced)

Vendor's Solicitors—

MESSRS. ENNIONS

NEWMARKET. (Tel. 80).

And at Soham, Ely, Burwell and Littleport.

AUCTIONEERS' HEAD OFFICE—ELY. (Tel. 65). And at Ely Cattle Market, Burwell, and Churchgate Street, SOHAM.

THE QUAY, ELY

IMPORTANT 3-DAYS' SALE OF THE VALUABLE ANTIQUE & MODERN

CONTENTS OF THE RESIDENCE

COMPRISING

HANDSOME GEORGIAN BUREAU

Georgian Sideboards, 11 Georgian Dining Chairs, Sheraton-style Music Cabinets, Jacobean, Card & Console Tables, Stuart Pattern Chairs, Antique Wine Tables, Musical Box, Lounge Chairs, Settee, Mahogany Dining Tables, Wellington Secretaire, Globe Wernicke Bookcases, Mahogany Hall Chairs, Writing Desks & Tables in Walnut, Mahogany & Oak, Pier Glasses, Floor Lamps, Bracket & Mantel Clocks, Carriage & Skeleton Timepieces, Barometer, 3 Deed Safes, Photographic Equipment

STEINWAY PIANOLA PIANO & H.M.V. ELECTRIC GRAMOPHONE

QUEEN ANNE & 2 MAHOGANY GRANDFATHER CLOCKS

WILTON, TURKEY & AXMINSTER CARPETS
SOFT FURNISHINGS & HOUSEHOLD LINEN

400 ozs. OLD ENGLISH SILVER

PLATE, PEWTER & TABLE GLASS

ANTIQUE CHINA, IVORIES & SPECULATIVE OIL PAINTINGS

APPOINTMENTS OF 7 BEDROOMS

KITCHEN & PANTRY REQUISITES

AND

GARDEN & GREENHOUSE EFFECTS

WILL BE HELD BY

GEORGE COMINS & SON

GARDEN EFFECTS : THE QUAY (Broad Street Entrance)
MONDAY, 3rd FEBRUARY, 1947 at 1.30 p.m.

FURNISHINGS : CORN EXCHANGE, ELY
TUESDAY & WEDNESDAY, 4th & 5th FEB., 1947
AT 10 A.M. PRECISELY EACH DAY

VIEW—(Corn Exchange, ELY) on Monday 3rd Feb. from 10.30 to 4 p.m. by CATALOGUE (1/- each) obtainable of the Auctioneers, Head Office— ELY (Tel. 65), Churchgate Street, SOHAM, Ely Cattle Market & Burwell

PARTICULARS

A SUPERIOR FULLY–APPOINTED FREEHOLD

PERIOD RESIDENCE

EXCEPTIONALLY WELL PRESERVED AND MAINTAINED

with

GARAGE, CONSERVATORY AND SUMMER–HOUSE

All within Most Attractive

ENCLOSED GROUNDS

Comprising

LAWNS, TENNIS COURT, KITCHEN GARDEN AND CHOICE ORCHARD

The whole superbly situate and being

No. 31, EGREMONT STREET

with long frontage thereto and a long and valuable return frontage to Downham Road, as now occupied by Mrs. S. Daniels who will give

VACANT POSSESSION

on completion of the purchase or earlier by arrangement.

THE RESIDENCE

is detached and has considerable character afforded by its substantial brick construction, plain tiled roof, front door with pediment, front windows with folding shutters and stucco overlay to the upper front wall. Complete external decoration was carried out last year and the following accommodation is in good decorative state, mainly light colours in harmony with a generous exposure of the original oak beams throughout.

On the Ground Floor:

HALL, 16′ 3″ x 12′ 6″, with coloured tiled floor, lincrusta dado, exposed beam and fitted with " Cozy " stove in red brick recess and a 13-section radiator.

CHINA PANTRY AND CUPBOARD (off).

DRAWING ROOM, 16′ 9″ x 16′, with bay french window, tiled fireplace with overmantel fitted for china display, boarded floor, china ledge, exposed beam and 3 independent electric bracket lights.

DINING ROOM, 17′ 8″ x 13′, with boarded floor, modern tiled fireplace in mahogany mantelpiece with fitted gas fire, built-in double cupboard, 2 exposed beams, china ledge and 19-section radiator, communicating Hall and Corridor.

CONSERVATORY (off Corridor) with staging.

FOR SALE BY AUCTION BY

GEORGE COMINS & SON

By direction of the Owner

THE WHITE HART HOTEL, ELY

THURSDAY, 30th OCTOBER, 1952. At 4 p.m.

(Subject to Conditions of Sale to be then produced).

By order of the Executrix of A. C. Leeding, deceased.

WITCHAM, Cambridgeshire

(On A.142, 6 miles from the City of Ely, 14 from March and 20 from the City of Cambridge).

WITH VACANT POSSESSION

PARTICULARS AND CONDITIONS OF SALE OF

A VALUABLE SMALL FREEHOLD

GENTLEMAN'S RESIDENCE

'THE OLD VICARAGE'

(FULLY MODERNISED)

HALL,   LOUNGE,   DINING ROOM

4 BEDROOMS,   BATHROOM,   USUAL OFFICES

GARAGE   MODERN DOMESTIC BLOCK

WELL KEPT GROUNDS

LAWN   PRODUCE ORCHARD.

3 ROODS   6 POLES   IN ALL

FOR SALE BY AUCTION BY

GEORGE COMINS & SON

THE WHITE HART HOTEL, ELY

THURSDAY, 16th APRIL, 1953

At 4 p.m. precisely.

Vendor's Solicitors:

MESSRS. ROSE, JOHNSON & HICKS,

9, Suffolk Street, Pall Mall, LONDON, S.W.1.

(Tel.: Whitehall 2933 & 9129).

AUCTIONEERS' HEAD OFFICES: ELY (Tel. 2665). Branch Office: 30, Churchgate Street, SOHAM (Tel. 264). And at Ely Cattle Market and Burwell.

W. JEFFERSON & SON, LTD., PRINTERS, ELY.   67904

ISLE OF ELY COURSING CLUB.

(Under National Coursing Club Rules.)

President :   Vice-President :
SIR FREDERICK HIAM, K.B.E.   OWEN S. AMBROSE, Esq.
Hon. Treasurer : F. W. GREEN, Esq.

A COURSING MEETING

WILL TAKE PLACE

On Wednesday, November 25th, 1931,

ON THE

SHIPPEA HILL FARM, PRICKWILLOW,

By kind permission of the President of the Club
(Sir Frederick Hiam, K.B.E.)

JUDGE: Mr. ERNEST LEDGER.   SLIPPER: A. E. Newman.

RIVERS CUP STAKES

For 8 (all-ages).

Entrance Fee—Members, £3 10s. ; Non-Members, £4 10s.
Winner, £14 and Cup value £5, kindly presented by Capt.
W. G. Rivers and W. V. Rivers, Esq. ; Runner-up, £10.
(Provided the Stakes are run out.)

LARK STAKES

For 8 Mixed Puppies.

Entrance Fee—Members, £3 10s. ; Non-Members, £4 10s.
Winner, £13 and Cup value £5, or cash at option of winner
(presented by the Club) ; Runner-up, £9.
(Provided the Stakes are run out.)

MILE END STAKES

For 8 (all-ages).

Entrance Fee—Members, £3 ; Non-Members, £4.
Winner, £10 and Cup value £5, or cash at option of winner
(presented by the Club) ; Runner-up, £8.
(Provided the Stakes are run out.)

STUNTNEY STAKES

For 8 (all-ages).   To be nominated by Ladies.   Open.
Entrance Fee—£2 10s.

Winner, £8 and a Cup value £5 (presented by the Vice-
President of the Club, O. S. Ambrose, Esq., providing the
Stakes are run out) ; Runner-up, £8.   P.T.O.

Meet at the Hemp Factory at 9.45 a.m.
20 minutes walk from Shippea Hill Station L.N.E.R.- Main Line
First brace of Greyhounds to be in the Slips at 10 a.m. sharp

—

Refreshments will be provided.
P.G.BRIDGEMAN   Secretary   11, Ely Road, Stretham. ELY

Death of George D.D.Comins
11th October 1942

A handsome dapple-grey horse, the pride of the late Mr. G.D.D.Comins and his faithful companion on many of his travels, accompanied its master on his last journey on Friday afternoon when the funeral took place at Ely Cemetery.

It was selected to draw the hearse which carried its master's remains and this reversion to the old method in these days of mechanisation, was a fitting tribute to the memory of a man in whose life the love of animals played such a great part.

The horse was in charge of two of Mr.Comins' employees - Messrs. John Carter and W.Dennis.

Mr. Comins' two sons walked behind the hearse and the beautiful floral tributes were carried on two biers.

In addition to the family mourners present were the firms' employees Miss V. Vincent, Messrs. A.L.Taylor, L.E.Seward, J.Beezley, A.J.Pearson and H.Woodbine.

'With his attention devoted to his home and his business, Mr. Comins took no part in public affairs, the only offices which he held having a direct bearing on his lifes work. He had been President of the Wisbech and district Tenant-right Valuers' Association, the Cambridgeshire and Isle of Ely Agricultural Valuers' Association and a member for many years of the Norfolk Association of Agricultural Valuers.

Mr. Comins will be remembered too, for his love of animals. While he was fond of animals of every kind, his chief weakness was where horses were concerned. He had horses of his own, and he was the proud possessor of one of the finest turnouts in the district. It was his delight to go driving behind these fine animals, and although he did own a car, as it were under provocation, he returned to his beloved horses at every opportunity.

It is interesting to note that he conducted a Red Cross sale at Ely during the last war – on 11th April 1916 – and his son Mr. G.W.D.Comins, was one of the auctioneers at the Agricultural Red Cross Sale held on August 1st this year.'

Excerpts from the Ely Standard and Soham Advertiser October 1942 courtesy of 'The Ely Standard'

NOTICE

CHILDREN

1. <u>ONLY</u> admitted if accompanied

2. <u>MUST BE</u> quiet and behave

3. <u>WILL BE</u> ejected for noise or nuisance

GEORGE COMINS & SON
Auctioneers, ELY.

GEORGE WILLIAM DRAGE COMINS
1911 – 1997

George W.D. Comins, the last in the line of the auctioneering firm, was born at 17, St. Mary's Street on 3rd September 1911 and was brought up with his brother John, stepbrother Percy and sister Letty in the family home. As the eldest son he was educated at the Kings School, along with John, and then qualified as a surveyor before taking over George Comins and Son on the death of his father in 1942 although he had been working in the firm prior to that time.

He was a sickly child who suffered from meningitis and polio, the legacy of which left him with a withered leg so he always carried a walking stick, this stick becoming a useful prop when auctioneering. During his illness St. Mary's Street was covered with straw round the area of the house to deaden the noise of the cart wheels on the road. When at home George kept this stick behind a heavy velvet curtain in the sitting room 'ready to use on badly behaved children'. This threat was aired almost daily but very seldom did the stick ever get taken from behind the curtain. Even when it did, fortunately, it was never used .

As an auctioneer he was described by Philip Ambrose:
'I have seen dozens of auctioneers at work in my career and they all have their own individual styles and patter. However,anyone who had witnessed George auctioneering is unlikely to forget him. As an auctioneer, he was undoubtedly a legend and had a style all of his own. He always had a walking stick when he was selling, mainly to point at the lot offered, but without warning used to thrust the walking stick like a sword horizontally and pirouette through 360 degrees which certainly kept the assembled company of buyers very much on their toes. He had a powerful selling voice and the cry of 'I shall not dwell' will be long remembered.'.

Another local comment heard about his auctioneering abilities indicating that he would sell anything and everything and would get the last penny out of a buyer before bringing down the hammer:

'If he could sell the squeak of a pig he would do so'

Young George Comins Aged 23 at a Presentation in the Corn Exchange in 1935

George, unlike his father, was not an animal lover and after the death of George D.D. the stables and pig sty at 7, St. Mary's Street were never used again.

The pig float was kept in the yard and the horse was allowed to be tied up there during the hours of the Thursday market before being walked back to the field in West Fen Road.

While sitting in his offices in St. Mary's Street, supposedly working but looking out of the window, he often noticed a young lady walking her dog down St. Mary's Street. George organised a meeting with this lady, Ruth Norton, who was visiting her aunt Suzanna Daniels at Orchard Cottage in Lynn Road and eventually married her in 1942. Ruth Comins, a shy person, did not really become involved in the community but she did participate in, enjoy and become Chairman of the Blue Birds Club at the Tower Hospital on Friday afternoons for adults with learning difficulties.

From left to right:
Dr. Brian Bamford   —-   Mrs. Vinith Williams Ruth Comins   Ruth Whetstone

The birth of a still born son in 1945 was a tragic event for George and Ruth, so much so that it was never spoken about and was a fact that only came to light from some papers found in 2000. This was followed by the birth of their only daughter Clare which meant there was no son to follow on into the family business. George was often asked if his daughter would go into the business and his answer, always the same, silenced his audience at the time.

Do you think……..I would allow……any daughter of mine to stand in the Corn Exchange beside a double bed and say…… Any Offers ?

The love of the motor car was inherited down the family line after the purchase of the Morgan Car by George.D.D. in 1905.

For driving round farms George used a succession of cars including a Morris Traveller, a Ford Consul and Ford Anglia until he came across the cream, seven seater, four wheel drive Landrover with windows. This model then remained the vehicle for the business.

The 'other' car was kept in a centrally heated garage and was washed every Saturday morning regardless of whether it had been out of the garage during the week or not. Mileage was kept to a minimum and the car was serviced more often than required. When these vehicles came to be sold they always fetched a premium, although being several years old they were always in perfect condition with less than ten thousand miles on the clock.

In the early 1950's a grey Humber Super Snipe took pride of place followed by a grey Rover Saloon. This was replaced by a large maroon three litre Rover and subsequent cars were always made by Rover.

Ely Cattle Market

Pig Sales

The first sale of pigs to be held in the Cattle Market by George Comins was held on the 14th September 1922. The area of the market used by the firm was accessed from Brays Lane and the adjacent area accessed from Newnham Street and the White Hart Yard was used by Messrs. A.T.Grain and Sons. Both firms held weekly pig auctions, A.T.Grain and Son dealt in more cattle although George Comins began selling calves in 1924.

ELY CATTLE MARKET.

(Bray's-lane Entrance).

George Comins

BEGS to announce that he will hold a Weekly Sale EVERY THURSDAY, Precisely at 11.30 o'clock, of

Fat and Store Pigs.

The First Sale will be held on THURSDAY. 14th SEPTEMBER, 1922, when the Auctioneer will give the following Prizes, subject to the Pigs being Sold:

£1 10s. for the Best Pen of Store Pigs, not less than five.

£1 for the Second Best Pen of ditto.

10s. for the Third Best Pen of ditto.

£1 10s. for the Best Pen of Fat Pigs, not less than three.

£1 for the Second Best Pen of ditto.

10s. for the Third Best Pen of ditto.

£1 10s. for the Best Fat Sow.

£1 for the next best ditto.

£1 for the Best Cottagers' Pig.

10s. for the next best ditto.

Judging at 11 o'clock. Owners of Pigs sold will be paid on the Day of Sale.

Entries are respectfully solicited.

George Comins, Auctioneer, Agricultural and General Valuer, Land and Insurance Agent, Ely.

ELY FAIR, THURSDAY NEXT.

ELY CATTLE MARKET.

George Comins

Begs to announce that he will hold a Sale of

Fat and Weaning Calves,

EVERY THURSDAY, at 12 o'clock precisely.

At the FIRST SALE on THURSDAY NEXT, 30th OCTOBER, 1924, the following Prizes will be given :—

For the Best FAT CALF: First Prize, £2 2s.; Second Prize, £1 1s.; Third Prize, 10s. 6d.

For the Best WEANING CALF: First Prize, £1 1s.; Second Prize, 15s.; Third Prize, 10s. 6d.

Entries are Respectfully Solicited. No Entrance Fees.

Calves are required to be in the Sale Yard not later than a quarter to Twelve o'clock, when Judging will commence.

GEORGE COMINS, Auctioneer, Agricultural and General Valuer, Land and Insurance Agent, Ely.

Entries for the pig auctions in the weeks up to and including the Christmas sale were becoming so large that George D.D. Comins was finding it difficult to sell all the fat pigs and sows.

He heard of a dealer in Birmingham and in December wrote him the following letter.

Dear Sir   *7th December 1923*

    I may have occasion at times to dispose of some Fat Pigs and Fat Sows, and I have been advised to send them to you.

    I hold a weekly sale of pigs and sometimes some do not get sold.   The Sale is held on Thursdays, and I could probably send them off after the Sale or the next day Friday. Is this suitable to you ?

    Shall I send them alive or slaughtered ?   In the case of small fat pig porkers I think the carriage would be less, if sent slaughtered.

    Is there any particular Station to send them to in Birmingham ?

                                     Yours faithfully,

                                          G.D.D.C.

Mr. George Samworth,
Pig Salesman, 15, Heath Mill Lane, Birmingham.

OFFICE.
15, HEATH MILL LANE,   **BIRMINGHAM,** Dec. 8th. 1923.
OFFICE TELEPHONE, CENTRAL, 1625
MARKET TELEPHONE, CENTRAL, 6679
    PRIVATE RESIDENCE,
    RYLSTONE, SCHOOL Rᵈ. MOSELEY,   TELEGRAPHIC ADDRESS,
    TELEPHONE, SOUTH 23   "SAMWORTH, BIRMINGHAM"

MEMO FROM **GEORGE SAMWORTH** LIMᵈ.

CATTLE, SHEEP & FAT HOG

SALESMAN &ᶜ.

ESTABLISHED 1870.

Mr. G. D. D. Comins.

Dear Sir,

      Thank you for your letter to hand this morning. I shall be very pleased to do my best with any pigs that you send, and I can assure you that any business contracted will be strictly private. I know that Mr. Bryan and Mr. Borebank attend the Sales.

If convenient to you Friday would be the better day to load. There is no particular station, and if you book them to "Samworth, Birmingham" they will be quite all right. I only sell pigs alive, as the butchers here will not buy them when they come slaughtered.

      Trusting we shall do business together.

          Yours faithfully,

             p.p. George Samworth.

regular consignment of pigs, was taken from the market by pig float (horse and cart) to Ely Station each week and put on the train to Birmingham.

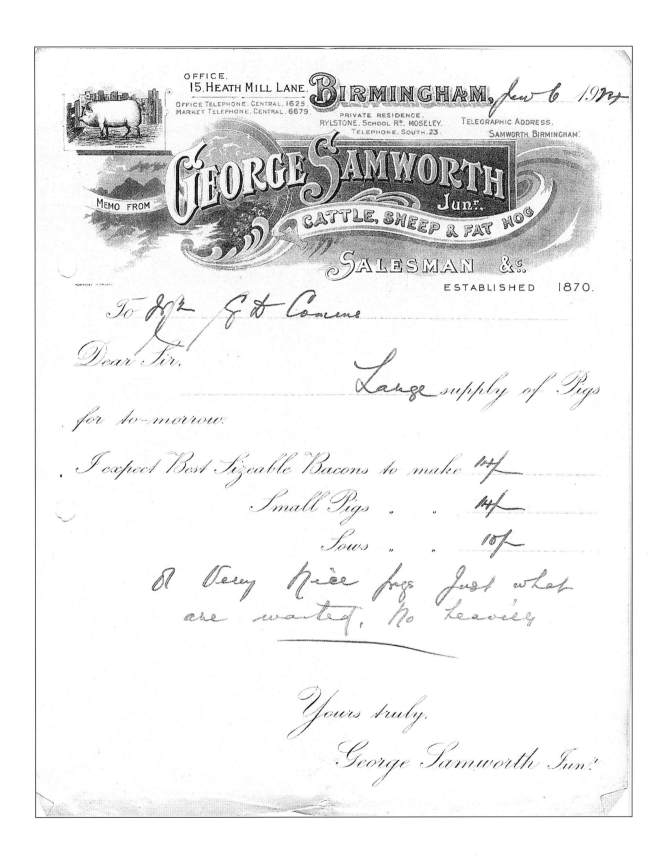

OFFICE.
15. HEATH MILL LANE.
BIRMINGHAM, *Jan 6 1904*

OFFICE TELEPHONE. CENTRAL. 1625.
MARKET TELEPHONE. CENTRAL. 6679.

PRIVATE RESIDENCE.
RYLSTONE. School Rᵈ. MOSELEY.
Telephone. SOUTH. 23.

TELEGRAPHIC ADDRESS.
"SAMWORTH. BIRMINGHAM."

MEMO FROM

GEORGE SAMWORTH
Junʳ.

CATTLE, SHEEP & FAT HOG

SALESMAN &ᶜ.

ESTABLISHED 1870.

To *Dʳ. G H Coates*

Dear Sir,

Large supply of Pigs for to-morrow.

I expect Best Sizeable Bacons to make 14/

Small Pigs " " 14/

Sows " " 10/

A very nice lot just what are wanted, No heavies

Yours truly,

George Samworth Junʳ

ELY CATTLE MARKET.

Messrs. A. T. GRAIN & SONS

will hold their Annual

SHOW AND SALE OF

XMAS FAT STOCK

On Thursday, December 14, 1922,

when the following Prizes will be offered :

CATTLE:

By Messrs. Lloyds Bank, Limited, Ely.

	1st prize	2nd prize	3rd prize
	£ s. d.	£ s. d.	£ s. d.
For the Best Pen of 3 Fat Bullocks or Heifers, fed and owned by a Farmer residing in the Isle of Ely or within 8 miles of Ely Cattle Market	2 2 0	1 1 0	

By Messrs. A. T. Grain & Sons.

For the Best Fat Bullock	2 0 0	
For the Best Fat Heifer	2 0 0	
For the Best Fat Calf	1 0 0	

PIGS:

For the Best Pen of 3 Bacon Hogs	2 0 0	1 0 0	
For the Best Fat Hog	1 10 0	15 0	
For the Best Pen of 3 Fat Pigs not weighing more than a total of 40 stone live weight	1 10 0	15 0	
For the Best Fat Sow	2 0 0	1 0 0	10 0
For the Best Fat Pig fed by a Cottager or Smallholder ...	1 0 0	10 0	
For the Best Pen of Store Pigs under 3 months old	1 0 0		
For the Best Pen of Store Pigs under 6 months old	1 0 0		

Also on the same day will be held the

4th Special Autumn Sale of

Store and Dairy Cattle

at 1.30 o'clock.

EARLY ENTRIES ARE REQUESTED.

Order of Sale : Pigs, Judging 10.30, Sale commences 11.30 ; Cattle, Judging 11.30, Sale commences 1 o'clock.

Pigs for Competition to be in the Sale Yard by 10.30 a.m. ; Cattle by 11.30 a.m. Cattle sent previous to the Sale will be carefully boxed, fed and attended to.

Auctioneers' Offices : 8, Rose Crescent, Cambridge.

ELY CATTLE MARKET.

George Comins

Begs to Announce that he will hold his

Christmas Sale of Fat and Store Pigs,

ON THURSDAY, 13th DECEMBER, 1923, at One o'clock precisely, commencing with Fat Pigs.

£18 3s. IN PRIZES

Will be given, viz. :—

	1st Prize.	2nd Prize.
	£ s. d.	£ s. d.
For the Best Pen of 3 Fat Pigs	2 12 6	1 11 6
For the Best Fat Pig	2 12 6	1 11 6
For the Best Fat Sow (1st Prize given by Messrs. Barclay's Bank, Ltd., Ely)	2 12 6	1 15 0
For the Best Fat Pig belonging to a Cottager or Small Holder	1 15 0	1 0 0
For the Best Pen of not less than 6 Store Pigs	1 11 6	
For the Best Pen of not less than 6 Store Pigs under 12 weeks old	1 1 0	

Pigs entered for Prizes are required to be in the Sale Yard not later than 12 o'clock. Judging at 12.15 a.m.

Entries are Respectfully Solicited.

No Entrance Fees.

GEORGE COMINS, Auctioneer, Valuer, Land and Insurance Agent. Offices: 17, St. Mary's Street, and Cattle Market, Ely.

Telephone 90.   17, FORE HILL,

ELY, *Jan 3* 192 3

M *r Comins*

Bought of **H. HOLROYD,**

High Class BEEF & PORK Butcher.

Families waited upon. — Prime Pickled Ox-Tongues. — Fresh Pork & Beef Sausages daily.

Telephone : SOHAM, 21.
Telegrams :
"LEONARD, Butcher, SOHAM."

SOUTHDOWN HOUSE, SOHAM, *Xmas* 192 3

M *r Comins*

BOT. OF **EDW. LEONARD & SON,**

FAMILY BUTCHERS.

Families waited on Daily for Orders.

Your Recommendations Respectfully Solicited.

Lamb and Veal in Season. Sausages Daily.

Home-cured Bacon and Hams.

Maker of Melton Mowbray Pork Pies.

Dec: 21	Ham 13 11	£ 1 4 4½

REFERENCE TO SIRES.

DOWNHAM KINGMAKER 41073 (Vol 40). Farrowed June 16th, 1923 : bred by W. E. Stockdale & Son.

Sire—†Spalding Kingmaker 30449 by *Kingmaker 24151.

Dam—Histon Queen 6th 106110 by Snowman of Wall 34089.

g Dam—Queen of Histon 2nd 80398.

†Spalding Kingmaker won first prize at the R.A.S.E. Show at Cambridge and first at Peterborough, 1922. He was bred by Mr. A. W. White.

*Kingmaker, bred by Mr. E. Wherry, was the sire of the first prize pair of Boars and the second prize pair of gilts at the Peterborough Show, 1921.

DUSTON DIPLOMAT 2nd (Ear No. 856), and entered for Vol. 42. Farrowed August 19th, 1924 ; bred by Messrs. C. W. King & Co., Ltd.

Sire—Duston Diplomat 4119 by ‡Bourne Baron 3rd 33059.

Dam—*Culthorpe Lady Dorothy 3rd 77958 by Turk of Culthorpe 30709.

g Dam—Culthorpe Lady Beatrice 58812.

‡Bourne Baron 3rd won second prize at the R.A.S.E. Show, 1922.

*A Boar out of Culthorpe Lady Dorothy 3rd was recently sold for £65.

CATALOGUE.

LOT

1. **SOW** DOWNHAM BEAUTY 89964 (Vol. 39).
   Farrowed Dec. 28th, 1921.
   Sire—†Cantab M.M. 29121 by Bourne Cantab 26069.
   Dam—Histon Bess 6th 67372 by *Histon Lion Heart 22481.
   g Dam—Histon Bess 2nd 41406.

   DOWNHAM BEAUTY reared 8 pigs in her last litter.
   Served Nov. 9th, 1925, by Downham Kingmaker 41073. (See reference to Sires.)
   †Cantab M.M. was bred on the Cambridge University Farm.
   *Histon Lion Heart won first prize, Champion and N.P.B.A. Silver Medal at the Royal Norfolk Show and third at the R.A.S.E. Show, 1919. At the Histon Sale, 1920, seven gilts by Histon Lion Heart were sold at an average of nearly £65.

2. **GILT** (Ear No. 34) Farrowed Jan. 3rd, 1925.
   Sire—Downham Kingmaker 41073.
   Dam—Downham Bess 89960, litter sister to Lot 1.
   Served Nov. 3rd, 1925, by Duston Diplomat 2nd. (See reference to Sires.)

3. **GILT** (Ear No. 136) Litter sister to Lot 2.
   Served Jan. 15th, 1926, by Duston Diplomat 2nd.

4. **GILT** (Ear No. 144) Farrowed March 10th, 1925.
   Sire—Downham Kingmaker 41073.
   Dam—Lot 1.
   Served Nov. 12th, 1925, by Duston Diplomat 2nd.

5. **GILT** (Ear No. 148) Farrowed August 1st, 1925.
   Sire—Downham Kingmaker 41073.
   Dam—Downham Bess 89960, litter sister to Lot 1.

6. **GILT** (Ear No. 150) Litter sister to Lot 5.

7. **GILT** (Ear No. 152) Litter Sister to Lot 5.

8. **GILT** (Ear No. 174) Farrowed July 30th, 1925.
   Sire—Downham Kingmaker 41073.
   Dam—Downham Bliss 89966, litter sister to Lot 1.

9. **BOAR** (Ear No. 41) Litter Brother to Lot 5.

10. **BOAR** (Ear No. 43) Farrowed Sept. 24th, 1925.
    Sire—Downham Kingmaker 41073.
    Dam—Histon Damsel 9th 106016 by *Histon Snowmans' 33655.
    g Dam—Damsel of Histon 78092.

    *Histon Snowman 5th is litter brother to Histon Amy 14th that was sold for 115 guineas at the Histon Sale, 1921.

11. **SOW** Large White and Lincolnshire Cross. Last Litter (the third), Oct. 21st, 1925 ; reared 9 pigs.
    Served Dec. 24th, 1925, by Duston Diplomat 2nd.

Rebuilding the Pig Market
1954
Brays Lane

The Opening of the New Ely Pig Market

Councillor Vernon Cross open the New Market
Left to right on the Rostrum Councillor Vernon Cross, George Comins
Walter Dennis standing below on the left

George Comins selling the first pen of pigs

Councillor Vernon Cross makes his speech as George Comins reads his notes.

Vernon Cross was the proprietor of the tea rooms and museum on Fore Hill.

Ye Olde Tea Rooms
FORE HILL, ELY

Still the resort for Luncheons and Teas, as it has been throughout all our National joys and troubles for many generations.

F, VERNON CROSS, Proprietor

An advertisement taken from the top of the front page of the Ely Standard and Soham Advertiser October 1942

Pigs being unloaded into the Market

By the 1960s the number of pigs being sold by auction had increased so much that a new extension was built onto the Pig Market.

Opening the New Extension
February 1963

Standing in the Pig ring from left to right
Tommy Housden - Mr. Palmer (Haddenham) - Albert Plumb -
George Dawson - Bill Sutton.
George Comins on the Rostrum - Michael Taylor (Clerk) by the weighbridge.

Stephen Legge
Partner in the firm from 1957 – 1987

Stephen Legge selling a pen of store pigs in the New Pig Market

The Pig Float
Transport of Pigs to Ely Cattle market from the Villages on Market Day

F. Carter – with 'Queenie'

The two wheeled pig float, painted dark green and yellow, was seen in Ely and surrounding villages every Thursday morning bringing pigs to market. Pigs were driven up the ramp and a heavy rope net fastened over the top of the float to prevent escape. The driver would sit on the plank at the front of the float to control the horse.

'Queenie', a part bred Suffolk Punch was walked up from her field belonging to the Hameys in West Fen Road early on Thursday morning, brushed until she gleamed and harnessed to the float in the yard at St. Mary's Street. The angle of her ears portrayed her usually unpleasant disposition. A nip or kick from Queenie was suffered by most people who handled her. It was brought to George's attention by a farmer in the market that she had a problem with her hoof. Mr. Runciman, the vet, was summonsed and the mare was swiftly replaced with the altogether different 'Prince.'

'Prince' a 17 hand, dapple grey Percheron was a gentle giant without a bad thought in his head. He would wander up to St. Mary's Street with his then groom Walter Dennis early Thursday morning, eagerly dispose of the handfuls of carrots waiting for him at the house, undergo the same grooming and harnessing procedure, collect the pigs and then be brought back to the yard, unharnessed and tied to the float until after market had finished. Although of gentle temperament he became bored easily and on several occasions managed to untie his halter and wander off round the town.

When Walter Dennis retired in the 1950's it was not possible to find another man to work with the horse so the float and harness along with 'Prince' were sold and pigs were transported to market by lorry.

The George Comins Silver Pig Championship Cup

An antique, solid silver cup on a black plinth was purchased in 1959 to be presented to the winner of the Champion Pig at the Christmas Show and Sale each December.

Winners from 1959 - 1975

1959	W.H.Cutworth	Stowbridge
1960	W.H.Cutworth	Stowbridge
1961	D.H.Sulman	Witcham
1962	G.J. Johnson	Wicken
1963	Carter Bros	Welney
1964	S. Rogers & Sons	Littleport
1965	Carter Bros	Welney
1966	D.H.Sulman	Witcham
1967	(No Show and sale due to Foot and Mouth Disease)	
1968	Mrs. J.M.Few	Forty Foot Bank
1969	Carter Bros.	Welney
1970	Carter Bros.	Welney
1971	Carter Bros.	Welney
1972	Carter Bros.	Welney
1973	Carter Bros.	Welney
1974	P.Barker	Walton Highway
1975	P. Barker	Walton Highway.

(Winners names taken from the silver band surrounding the plinth on the cup.)

The Clare Hastings Perpetual Challenge Cup

In 1986 George Comins gave the pig cup to his daughter Clare to be re-engraved and presented as the Championship Sheep Cup for the new sheep breed classes which she had helped to set up at Heathfield Agricultural Show in Sussex.

The Pure Bred Sheep Classes that first year consisted of: Jacob Sheep classes and four other classes for any other breed of pure bred sheep.   The classes consisted of :

Shearling Ram, ram lamb, pair of shearling ewes and pair of ewe lambs.   The classes attracted 75 entries from over 30 exhibitors.   The judge was Frank Grantham and steward Henry Noakes.   The Cup was won by V.J.R.Wadey with a Suffolk Ram.

Over the next 13 years the show became of the largest one day shows for sheep in the country with breed classes for Suffolks, Texels, Southdowns, Any other breed British Longwool, Shortwool, any other breed foreign and fleece classes with as many as 500 sheep exhibited.   Clare became Sheep Chairman and eventually Show Chairman for three years from 1997 – 2000.   The show was cancelled because of bad weather in 2001 and livestock classes were cancelled in 2001 and 2002 because of the Foot and Mouth Outbreak

Winners of the Clare Hastings Perpetual Challenge Trophy

1986	V.J.R.Wadey	Suffolk Sheep
1987	Mrs.P.Exwood	Suffolk Sheep
1988	Mrs V.Price & Sons	Suffolk Sheep
1989	Mr & Mrs. R. Walton	Wensleydale
1990	Mr & Mrs. J.H.Marshall	Texel
1991	Highfields Farm	Texel
1992	D.M. & S. Roberts	Suffolk Sheep
1993	Marshall Farms	Texel
1994	G.L.& M.J.Reynolds	Hampshire Down
1995	D.M.& S. Roberts	Suffolk Sheep
1996	Marshall Farms	Texel
1997	D.M. & S.Roberts	Suffolk Sheep
1998	Mrs Lampshire	Border Leicester
1999	R.J. Jupp & K.T.Manning	Suffolk Sheep

**Mrs. Penny Exwood receiving the Challenge Cup in 1987
At Heathfield Agricultural Show
From Show Vice President - Mrs. Ruby Browning.
Steward: Mr. Jim Gower**

George Comins & Son
&
Ely Cattle Market.

1940's – 1990's and beyond

During the 1940's/50s the firm of George Comins and Son had offices in Ely, Soham and Burwell. The villag[e] offices were eventually closed but the Old Chequers Public House in Chequer Lane, Ely was purchased an[d] renovated so that the business could move to a more central part of the town.

Stephen Legge joined the firm as a partner in 1957 and remained with the firm until 1987 when he retired. I[n] addition to the Ely Market and business he and George between them sold at the Monday Cambridge Pig Marke[t] on Mondays which was run under the name of Parker and Comins.

Stephen Legge selling at a 'junk' sale in the old pig ring.

Philip Ambrose joined the firm in 1971 and writes his memories of the firm from that time until the present day:

'*When I joined the firm in 1971 there were two firms of auctioneers in Ely, namely George Comins and Son, whose offices were in Chequer Lane, and Cheffins Grain and Chalk, whose offices were at 14, Newnham Street with their cattle market premises adjoining.*

Cheffins Grain and Chalk sold cattle, sheep and pigs with their sale starting at 12 noon. George Comins and Son sold the live poultry, rabbits and goats at 10.30 a.m., followed by dressed poultry, game, eggs and produce at 11 a.m. I had the task of dealing with these two sales and in the height of the summer season, when there was an abundance of fruit and vegetables, the sale would often continue well into the afternoon. Meanwhile at 12 noon, (the same time as Cheffins Grain and Chalk) George Comins would sell the fat pigs in competition with Cheffins Grain and Chalk and at 1.30 p.m. Stephen Legge would sell the breeding sows and litters and store pigs. At 2 p.m. George Comins started selling the 'deadstock', which at the time mainly comprised of building materials and workshop equipment.

The two auction markets adjoined linking Brays Lane and Newnham Street, the site broadly taken up now by the Brays Lane Car Park. In the early/mid seventies there were gates at each end, but they were eventually removed to allow car parking on the site during the week.

The Pig Market continued until 1976, when the country was hit by Swine Vesicular Disease and the market had to close to stop the spread of the disease and become a licensed collection centre. Unfortunately, when the regulations were eventually removed, a lot of farmers had given up pig farming and the pig market closed as it was uneconomical.

George Comins, Stephen Legge and I then converted the buildings to what can only be described as one of the most basic salerooms in the country. Nevertheless, it seemed to catch the public imagination and George then started selling the deadstock at 11 a.m. and would often have a three hour sale. Stephen Legge sold the furniture and household effects at 1.30 in the new saleroom and regularly had over 300 lots to sell on a weekly basis. Meanwhile, I was still dealing with the poultry and produce. Although we had stopped selling livestock there was a great interest in all the sales and we dealt with hundreds of house clearances. People came to Ely every week from London and towns and cities up to a fifty mile radius for a good fun day out.

The highlight of the year was the special fatstock and poultry sale held in the week prior to Christmas. The atmosphere at the sale encapsulated the start of the Christmas Festivities, and following the sale the hoarse auctioneers usually repaired to the local hostelries to imbibe freely of the Christmas spirit.

George retired in 1982 and Edwin Lee had joined us and taken over most of George's sales. Stephen Legge retired in 1987, the same year as the two firms' amalgamation. Unfortunately the firm did not own the market but leased it from the Council. In the late 1980's the Council decided that they required a new shopping centre and after a few false starts the Cloisters has been built with the adjoining car park on the former market site.

I am sure similar stories are true in market towns throughout the country.
We tried to transfer the site to the Council premises at Littleport but with a combination
of their requirement for the premises for their own use together with the increasing
burden of consumer legislation, the weekly market finally closed at the end of 1997.'

The last sale held in Ely Cattle Market was on 25th October 1990 before the site was taken over for redevelopment and is now Waitrose Car Park. Philip Ambrose sold the last lot of furniture, which was an armchair, in the miscellaneous sale. George Comins took the rostrum at the end of the sale and thanked customers and recalled some high points of the history of the market over the past 100 years.

Regulars who had attended the Thursday market all their lives were heard to make comments about the closure. One said it would be the end of an era. Another announced, as he wiped fish and chips from his fingers, that they may as well drop a bomb on Ely now. A third, leaning on his walking stick, said it would be the end of shopping in Ely.

Farmers traditionally came into Ely on Market Day and while their wives did the shopping they met up in the Market. The weekly sales were held at Portley Hill, Littleport for a time before eventually closing down but the central meeting point of the Cattle Market was never quite the same again.

Philip Ambrose selling the last lot on the Cattle Market Site.

ACCA

PERFORMANCE MANAGEMENT (PM)

P
R
A
C
T
I
C
E
&
R
E
V
I
S
I
O
N
K
I
T

BPP Learning Media is an **ACCA Approved Content Provider** for the ACCA qualification. This means we work closely with ACCA to ensure our products fully prepare you for your ACCA exams.

In this Practice & Revision Kit, which has been reviewed by the **ACCA examining team,** we:

- Discuss the **best strategies** for revising and taking your ACCA exams

- Ensure you are well **prepared** for your exam

- Provide you with **lots of great guidance** on tackling questions

- Provide you with **three** mock exams

- Provide **ACCA exam answers** as well as our own for selected questions

Our **Passcards** also support the Performance Management syllabus.

FOR EXAMS IN SEPTEMBER 2018, DECEMBER 2018, MARCH 2019 AND JUNE 2019

First edition 2008

Twelfth edition February 2018

ISBN 9781 5097 1667 8
(previous ISBN 9781 5097 0857 4)
e-ISBN 9781 5097 1697 5

Cataloguing-in-Publication Data
A catalogue record for this book
is available from the British Library

Published by
BPP Learning Media Ltd
BPP House, Aldine Place
London W12 8AA

www.bpp.com/learningmedia

Printed and bound by CPI Group (UK) Ltd
Croydon
CR0 4YY

Your learning materials, published by BPP Learning Media Ltd, are
printed on paper obtained from traceable sustainable sources.

We are grateful to the Association of Chartered Certified
Accountants for permission to reproduce past examination
questions. The suggested solutions in the Practice & Revision Kit
have been prepared by BPP Learning Media Ltd, except where
otherwise stated.

BPP
LEARNING MEDIA

About this Practice & Revision Kit

ACCA have commenced the transition of this paper to computer-based examination (CBE), beginning with a pilot in limited markets in September 2016. Students will initially have the choice of CBE or paper exams and as a result, changes will be made to BPP's learning materials to ensure that we fully support students through this transition.

This Practice & Revision Kit is valid for exams from the September 2018 sitting through to the June 2019 sitting and in this Practice & Revision Kit you will find questions in both multiple choice question (MCQ) and objective testing question (OTQ) format. OTQs include a wider variety of questions types including MCQ as well as number entry, multiple response and drag and drop. More information on these question types will be available on the ACCA website.

OTQ's will only appear in computer-based exams but these questions will still provide valuable practice for all students whichever version of the exam is taken. These are clearly marked on the contents page as either CBE style OTQ bank or CBE style OTQ case.

More information on the exam formats can be found on page xi.

All timings given throughout this Practice & Revision Kit are based on the computer-based exam which is 3 hours and 20 minutes long. Within session CBEs there will be additional questions used for quality assurance purposes, to ensure that all students now and in the future receive fair and equal exams. These extra questions are referred to by the technical term 'seeded questions' and do not contribute to a student's results. As a result, session CBEs will contain 110 marks of exam content, 100 marks contributing to the student result. Exam timings are allocated on the basis of 110 marks across the 3 hours and 20 minutes. Time management is a key skill for success in this exam and so we recommend you use these indicative timings when attempting questions to time on paper.

ACCA are recommending that all students consult the ACCA website on a regular basis for updates on the launch of the new CBEs.

These materials are reviewed by the ACCA examining team. The objective of the review is to ensure that the material properly covers the syllabus and study guide outcomes, used by the examining team in setting the exams, in the appropriate breadth and depth. The review does not ensure that every eventuality, combination or application of examinable topics is addressed by the ACCA Approved Content. Nor does the review comprise a detailed technical check of the content as the Approved Content Provider has its own quality assurance processes in place in this respect.

Contents

Review Form

Question index

The headings in this checklist/index indicate the main topics of questions, but questions often cover several different topics.

Questions set under the old syllabus *Financial Management and Control* and *Performance Management* papers are included because their style and content are similar to those which appear in the PM exam. The questions have been amended to reflect the current exam format.

Mock exam 1 (September 2016 CBE)

Mock exam 2 (Specimen exam CBE)

Mock exam 3 (December 2016 PBE)

Topic index

Listed below are the key Performance Management syllabus topics and the numbers of the questions in this Kit covering those topics.

If you need to concentrate your practice and revision on certain topics or if you want to attempt all available questions that refer to a particular subject, you will find this index useful.

Syllabus topic	Question numbers
Activity based costing	31–35, 36–40, 41–45, 46–50
Balanced scorecard	270–274, 280–284, 320
Budgetary systems and types	218, 219, 222, 225
Cost volume profit (CVP) analysis	141
Decision rules	116–120, 131–135, 140
Learning curve	172–176, 177–181, 182–186, 212–216, 217
Limiting factors	121–125
Linear programming	137
Make-or-buy decisions	111–115, 139
Management information systems	306
Mix and yield variances	192–196, 220, 224, 227
Performance measurement	308, 309, 310, 311, 312, 313, 314, 315, 319
Planning and operational variances	187–191, 197–201, 202–206, 207–211, 220, 221, 223, 224, 226, 228, 229
Pricing decisions	131–135, 136, 138
Relevant costs	106–110, 129–130
Return on investment and residual income	275–279, 285–289, 290–294, 295–299, 300–304, 305, 316, 318
Target costing	61–65
Throughput accounting	56–60, 66–70
Transfer pricing	265–269, 307, 317, 318

Helping you with your revision

BPP Learning Media – Approved Content Provider

As an ACCA **Approved Content Provider**, BPP Learning Media gives you the **opportunity** to use revision materials reviewed by the ACCA examining team. By incorporating the ACCA examining team's comments and suggestions regarding the depth and breadth of syllabus coverage, the BPP Learning Media Practice & Revision Kit provides excellent, **ACCA-approved** support for your revision.

Tackling revision and the exam

Using feedback obtained from the ACCA examining team review:

- We look at the dos and don'ts of revising for, and taking, ACCA exams
- We focus on Performance Management (PM); we discuss revising the syllabus, what to do (and what not to do) in the exam, how to approach different types of question and ways of obtaining easy marks

Selecting questions

We provide signposts to help you plan your revision.

- A full **question index**
- A **topic index** listing all the questions that cover key topics, so that you can locate the questions that provide practice on these topics, and see the different ways in which they might be examined

Making the most of question practice

At BPP Learning Media we realise that you need more than just questions and model answers to get the most from your question practice.

- Our **top tips** included for certain questions provide essential advice on tackling questions, presenting answers and the key points that answers need to include.
- We show you how you can pick up **easy marks** on some questions, as we know that picking up all readily available marks often can make the difference between passing and failing.
- We include **marking guides** to show you what the examining team rewards.
- We include **comments from the examining team** to show you where students struggled or performed well in the actual exam.
- We refer to the **BPP Study Text for exams in September 2018, December 2018, March 2019 and June 2019** for detailed coverage of the topics covered in questions.

Attempting mock exams

There are three mock exams that provide practice at coping with the pressures of the exam day. We strongly recommend that you attempt them under exam conditions. **Mock exam 1** is the September 2016 CBE. **Mock exam 2** is the Specimen CBE. **Mock exam 3** is the December 2016 PBE.

Revising Performance Management

All questions are compulsory so you must revise the **whole** syllabus. Since the exam includes 15 multiple choice questions, you should expect questions to cover a large part of the syllabus. Selective revision **will limit** the number of questions you can answer and hence reduce your chances of passing. It is better to go into the exam knowing a reasonable amount about most of the syllabus rather than concentrating on a few topics to the exclusion of the rest.

Practising as many exam-style questions as possible will be the key to passing this exam. You must do questions under **timed conditions** and ensure you write full answers to the discussion parts as well as doing the calculations.

Make sure you practise written sections as well as the calculations.

Avoid looking at the answer until you have finished a question. Your biggest problem with PM questions may be knowing how to start, and this needs practice.

Also ensure that you attempt all three mock exams under exam conditions.

Passing the PM exam

Displaying the right qualities

- You are expected to have a core of management accounting knowledge from your previous studies of MA.

- You will be required to identify the requirements of multiple choice questions quickly, so that you can make your answers confidently within the available time.

- You will be required to carry out calculations, with clear workings and a logical structure.

- You will be required to interpret data.

- You will be required to explain management accounting techniques and discuss whether they are appropriate for a particular organisation.

- You must be able to apply your skills in a practical context.

- You must understand what numbers tell you about the performance of a business.

Avoiding weaknesses

- There is no choice in this exam, all questions have to be answered. You must therefore study the entire syllabus, there are no short-cuts.

- Ability to answer multiple choice questions and cases improves with practice. Try to get as much practice with these questions as you can.

- The longer questions will be based on simple scenarios and answers must be focused and specific to the organisation.

- Answer plans for the longer questions will help you to focus on the requirements of the question and enable you to manage your time effectively – but there will not be much time.

- Answer all parts of the longer questions. Even if you cannot do all the calculation elements, you will still be able to gain marks in the discussion parts.

Gaining the easy marks

Easy marks in this exam tend to fall into three categories.

Objective test questions (OTQs)

Some OTQs are easier than others. Answer those that you feel fairly confident about as quickly as you can. Come back later to those you find more difficult. This could be a way of making use of the time in the examination most efficiently and effectively. Some OTQs will not involve calculations. Make sure that you understand the wording of 'written' OTQs before selecting your answer.

Calculations in Section C questions

There will be some relatively straightforward calculations at the start of the question and they will then probably get progressively more difficult. If you get stuck, make an assumption, state it and move on.

A Section C question may separate discussion requirements from calculations, so that you do not need to do the calculations first in order to answer the discussion part. This means that you should be able to gain marks from making sensible, practical comments without having to complete the calculations.

Discussions that are focused on the specific organisation in the question will gain more marks than regurgitation of knowledge. Read the question carefully and more than once, to ensure you are actually answering the specific requirements.

Pick out key words such as 'describe', 'evaluate' and 'discuss'. These all mean something specific.

- 'Describe' means to communicate the key features of
- 'Evaluate' means to assess the value of
- 'Discuss' means to examine in detail by argument

Clearly label the points you make in discussions so that the marker can identify them all rather than getting lost in the detail.

Provide answers in the form requested. Use a report format if asked for and give recommendations if required.

Tackling Objective Test Case Questions

First, read the whole case scenario. Make a note of any specific instructions or assumptions such as ignore inflation.

Then skim through the requirements of the five questions. The questions are independent of each other and can be answered in any order.

Some of the OTs will be easier than others. For example, you may be asked to identify the advantages of ABC costing compared with traditional absorption costing. Answer these OTs quickly.

Other OTs will be more difficult and/or complex. There are two types of OT that may take you longer to answer.

The first more time-consuming OT will involve doing a computation. For example, you may be asked to calculate the throughput accounting ratio of a product. You will probably need to jot down a quick proforma to answer a computational question like this. If the OT is a multiple choice question, remember that the wrong answers will usually involve common errors so don't assume that because you have the same answer as one of the options that your answer is necessarily correct! Double check to make sure you haven't made any silly mistakes. If you haven't got the same answer as any of the options, rework your computation, thinking carefully about what errors you could have made. If you still haven't got one of the options, choose the one which is nearest to your answer.

The second more time-consuming OT is one where you are asked to consider a number of statements and identify which one (or more) of them is correct. Make sure that you read each statement at least twice before making your selection. Be careful to follow the requirements of the OT exactly, for example if you are asked to identify **TWO** correct statements.

Exam formulae

Set out below are the formulae **which you will be given in the exam** in a formulae sheet. You should learn to use them. If you are not sure what the symbols mean, or how the formulae are used, you should refer to the appropriate chapter in the Study Text.

Exam formulae	*Chapter in Study Text*

Demand curve 5

$P = a - bQ$

$b = \dfrac{\text{Change in price}}{\text{Change in quantity}}$

a = price when $Q = 0$

$MR = a - 2bQ$

Learning curve 9

$Y = ax^b$

Where Y = the cumulative average time per unit to produce X units

a = the time taken for the first unit of output

x = the cumulative number of units

b = the index of learning (log LR/log 2)

LR = the learning rate as a decimal

Exam information

Computer-based exams

ACCA have commenced the launch of computer-based exams (CBEs) for this exam. They have been piloting computer-based exams in limited markets since September 2016 with the aim of rolling out into all markets internationally over a five-year period. Paper-based examinations will be run in parallel while the CBE's are phased in and BPP materials have been designed to support you, whichever exam option you choose.

Format of the exam

The exam format is the same irrespective of the mode of delivery and will comprise three exam sections:

Section	Style of question type	Description	Proportion of exam, %
A	Objective test (OT)	15 questions × 2 marks	30
B	Objective test (OT) case	3 questions × 10 marks Each question will contain 5 subparts each worth 2 marks	30
C	Constructed Response (Long questions)	2 questions × 20 marks	40
Total			100

Section A and B questions will be selected from the entire syllabus. The paper versions of these objective test questions contain multiple choice only and the computer based versions will contain a variety. The responses to each question or subpart in the case of OT cases are marked automatically as either correct or incorrect by computer.

Section C questions will mainly focus on the following syllabus areas but a minority of marks can be drawn from any other area of the syllabus:

- Decision-making techniques (syllabus area B)
- Budgeting and control (syllabus area C)
- Performance measurement and control (syllabus area D)

The responses to these questions are human marked.

Additional information

The study guide provides more detailed guidance on the syllabus and can be found by visiting the exam resource finder on the ACCA website: www.accaglobal.com/uk/en/student/exam-support-resources.html

Useful websites

The websites below provide additional sources of information of relevance to your studies for *Performance Management*.

- www.accaglobal.com

  ACCA's website. The students' section of the website is invaluable for detailed information about the qualification, past issues of Student Accountant (including technical articles) and a free downloadable Student Planner App.

- www.bpp.com

  Our website provides information about BPP products and services, with a link to the ACCA website.

Questions

PART A: SPECIALIST COST AND MANAGEMENT ACCOUNTING TECHNIQUES

Questions 1 to 70 cover Specialist cost and management accounting techniques, the subject of Part A of the BPP Study Text for PM.

Section A questions

MCQ bank – Specialist cost and management accounting techniques

54 mins

1   The following costs have arisen in relation to the production of a product:

    (i)   Planning and concept design costs
    (ii)   Testing costs
    (iii)   Production costs
    (iv)   Distribution and customer service costs

In calculating the life cycle costs of a product, which of the above items would be included?

    O   (iii) only
    O   (i), (ii) and (iii)
    O   (i), (ii) and (iv)
    O   All of the above   **(2 marks)**

2   In which of the following ways might financial returns be improved over the life cycle of a product?

    (1)   Maximising the breakeven time
    (2)   Minimising the time to market
    (3)   Minimising the length of the life cycle

    O   1 and 2
    O   1 and 3
    O   2 only
    O   2 and 3   **(2 marks)**

3   One of the products manufactured by a company is Product X, which sells for $40 per unit and has a material cost of $10 per unit and a direct labour cost of $7 per unit. The total direct labour budget for the year is 50,000 hours of labour time at a cost of $12 per hour. Factory overheads are $2,920,000 per year.

The company is considering the introduction of a system of throughput accounting. It has identified that machine time is the bottleneck in production. Product X needs 0.01 hours of machine time per unit produced. The maximum capacity for machine time is 4,000 hours per year.

What is the throughput accounting ratio for Product X?

    O $3.41
    O $2.80
    O $2.10
    O $1.90   **(2 marks)**

4   The following statements have been made about material flow cost accounting (MFCA).

(1)   In material flow cost accounting, waste is treated as a negative product and given a cost.

(2)   Material flow cost accounting should encourage management to focus on ways of achieving the same amount of finished output with less material input.

Which of the above statements is/are true?

○   1 only
○   2 only
○   Neither 1 nor 2
○   Both 1 and 2   **(2 marks)**

5   Which of the following statements about activity based costing is true?

○   The cost driver for quality inspection is likely to be batch size.

○   The cost driver for materials handling and despatch costs is likely to be the number of orders handled.

○   In the short run, all the overhead costs for an activity vary with the amount of the cost driver for the activity.

○   A cost driver is an activity based cost.   **(2 marks)**

6   The following information relates to the expected cost of a new product over its expected three-year life.

	Year 0	Year 1	Year 2	Year 3
Units made and sold		25,000	100,000	75,000
R&D costs	$850,000	$90,000		
Production costs				
Variable per unit		$30	$25	$20
Fixed costs		$500,000	$500,000	$500,000
Selling and distribution costs				
Variable per unit		$6	$5	$4
Fixed costs		$700,000	$500,000	$300,000
Customer service costs				
Variable per unit		$4	$3	$2

What is the expected average life cycle cost per unit?

○ $35.95
○ $46.25
○ $48.00
○ $50.95   **(2 marks)**

7   The following statements have been made about throughput accounting.

(1)   Inventory has no value and should be valued at $0.
(2)   Efficiency is maximised by utilising direct labour time and machine time to full capacity.

Which of the above statements is/are true?

○   1 only
○   2 only
○   Neither 1 nor 2
○   Both 1 and 2   **(2 marks)**

8   In environmental costing, the future cost of cleaning up operations for a product or activity may be classified as which of the following?

○   Carbon footprint
○   Contingent cost
○   Hidden cost
○   Relationship cost   **(2 marks)**

9   The following statements have been made about throughput accounting.

        (1)   Direct labour should always be treated as a factory cost when measuring throughput.

        (2)   If machine time is the bottleneck resource, there is no value in taking measures to improve direct labour efficiency.

        Which of the above statements is/are true?

        ○   1 only
        ○   2 only
        ○   Neither 1 nor 2
        ○   Both 1 and 2   **(2 marks)**

10   The following statements have been made about traditional absorption costing and activity based costing (ABC).

        (1)   Traditional absorption costing may be used to set prices for products, but activity based costing cannot.

        (2)   Traditional absorption costing tends to allocate too many overhead costs to low-volume products and not enough overheads to high-volume products.

        (3)   Implementing ABC is expensive and time consuming

        Which of the above statements is/are true?

        ○   1 only
        ○   2 only
        ○   3 only
        ○   1 and 2   **(2 marks)**

11   Which of the following statements about target costing is **NOT** true?

        ○   Target costing is better suited to assembly orientated industries than service industries that have a large fixed cost base.

        ○   Costs may be reduced in target costing by removing product features that do not add value.

        ○   A target cost gap is the difference between the target cost for a product and its projected cost.

        ○   Products should be discontinued if there is a target cost gap.   **(2 marks)**

12   Which of the following should be categorised as environmental failure costs by an airline company?

        (1)   Compensation payments to residents living close to airports for noise pollution caused by their aircraft

        (2)   Air pollution due to the airline's carbon emissions from their aircraft engines

        (3)   Penalties paid by the airline to the government for breaching environmental regulations

        ○   2 only
        ○   1, 2 and 3
        ○   1 and 3
        ○   2 and 3   **(2 marks)**

13   In material flow cost accounting (MFCA), which of the following is **NOT** a category used?

        ○   Output flows
        ○   Material flows
        ○   Delivery and disposal flows
        ○   System flows   **(2 marks)**

14   In the theory of constraints and throughput accounting, which of the following methods may be used to elevate the performance of a binding constraint?

Method 1: Acquire more of the resource that is the binding constraint

Method 2: Improve the efficiency of usage of the resource that is the binding constraint

- O   Method 1 only
- O   Method 2 only
- O   Method 1 and Method 2
- O   Neither method would be effective   (2 marks)

15   ABC Company uses throughput accounting. Machine time is the current binding constraint on production output, and management are looking for ways to increase the throughput accounting (TA) ratio for a product that the machine is used to manufacture.

Which of the following will have **NO** effect on the TA ratio?

- O   Increasing the selling price of the product
- O   Obtaining a lower purchase price for materials for the product
- O   Reducing factory costs
- O   Reducing the machine time per unit to make the product   (2 marks)

                                                                          (Total = 30 marks)

CBE style OTQ bank – Specialist cost and management accounting techniques   54 mins

16   Are the following statements about environmental management accounting true or false?

A system of environmental management accounting provides environmental information for internal use by management, but not for external reporting.	TRUE	FALSE
Environmental management accounting systems typically make use of life cycle costing.	TRUE	FALSE

                                                                                        (2 marks)

17   Which **TWO** of the following statements about throughput accounting and the theory of constraints are true?

☐   A principle of throughput accounting is that a buffer inventory should be built up for output from the bottleneck resource.

☐   Unless output capacity is greater than sales demand, there will always be a binding constraint.

☐   The production capacity of a bottleneck resource should determine the production schedule for the organisation as a whole.

☐   Idle time should be avoided in areas of production that are not a bottleneck resource.   (2 marks)

18   The following data refers to a soft drinks manufacturing company that passes its product through four processes and is currently operating at optimal capacity.

Process	Washing	Filling	Capping	Labelling
Time per dozen units	6 mins	3 mins	1.5 mins	2 mins
Machine hours available	1,200	700	250	450

Product data	$ per unit
Selling price	0.60
Direct material	0.18
Direct labour	0.02
Factory fixed cost	$4,120

Which process is the bottleneck?

Select...   ▼
Washing
Filling
Capping
Labelling

(2 marks)

19   Which **TWO** of the following statements about activity based costing (ABC) are true?

☐ Implementation of ABC is unlikely to be cost effective when variable production costs are a low proportion of total production costs.

☐ In a system of ABC, for costs that vary with production levels, the most suitable cost driver is likely to be direct labour hours or machine hours.

☐ Activity based costs are the same as relevant costs for the purpose of short-run decision making.

☐ Activity based costing is a form of absorption costing.   (2 marks)

20   Are the following statements about target costing true or false?

A risk with target costing is that cost reductions may affect the perceived value of the product.	TRUE	FALSE
An effective way of reducing the projected cost of a new product is to simplify the design.	TRUE	FALSE
The value of target costing depends on having reliable estimates of sales demand.	TRUE	FALSE
Target costing may be applied to services that are provided free of charge to customers, such as costs of call centre handling.	TRUE	FALSE

(2 marks)

21   Which **TWO** of the following statements about life cycle costing are true?

☐ A product is usually most profitable during the growth phase of its life cycle.

☐ Life cycle costing is useful for deciding the selling price for a product.

☐ An important use of life cycle costing is to decide whether to go ahead with the development of a new product.

☐ Life cycle costing encourages management to find a suitable balance between investment costs and operating expenses.   (2 marks)

22 The selling price of Product X is set at $550 for each unit and sales for the coming year are expected to be 800 units.

A return of 30% on the investment of $500,000 in Product X will be required in the coming year.

What is the target cost for each unit of Product X?

$ [ ]   (2 marks)

23 Are the following statements about environmental cost accounting true or false?

The majority of environmental costs are already captured within a typical organisation's accounting system. The difficulty lies in identifying them.	TRUE	FALSE
Input/output analysis divides material flows within an organisation into three categories: material flows; system flows; and delivery and disposal flows.	TRUE	FALSE

(2 marks)

24 Budget information relating to a company that manufactures four products is as follows.

Product	Maximum sales demand	Machine hours per unit	Maximum machine hours required	Sales price per unit	Material cost per unit
	Units			$	$
A	1,000	0.1	100	15	6
B	500	0.2	100	21	10
C	2,000	0.3	600	18	9
D	1,000	0.2	200	25	16
			1,000		

Only 750 machine hours are available during the period. Applying the principles of throughput accounting, how many units of Product B should be made if the company produces output to maximise throughput and profit?

[ ] units   (2 marks)

25 The following estimates have been produced for a new product with an expected life of four years.

	Year 1	Year 2	Year 3	Year 4
Units made and sold	5,000	10,000	25,000	10,000
	$	$	$	$
R&D costs	0.9 million	0.3 million		
Marketing costs	0.3 million	0.3 million	0.1 million	0.1 million
Production cost per unit	80	40	30	30
Customer service cost per unit	20	15	10	5
Disposal costs				0.2 million

What is the expected life cycle cost per unit?

$ [ ]   (2 marks)

26 Product YZ2 is made in a production process where machine time is a bottleneck resource. Production of one unit of Product YZ2 takes 0.25 machine hours. The costs and selling price of Product YZ2 are as follows:

	$
Materials	10
Labour (0.5 hours)	7
Other factory costs	7
	24
Sales price	30
Profit	6

In a system of throughput accounting, what is the return per factory hour?

$ [ ]   (2 marks)

27 A company manufactures Product Q, which sells for $50 per unit and has a material cost of $14 per unit and a direct labour cost of $10 per unit. The total direct labour budget for the year is 18,000 hours of labour time at a cost of $10 per hour. Factory overheads are $1,620,000 per year. The company has identified machine time as the bottleneck in production. Product Q needs 0.05 hours of machine time per unit produced. The maximum capacity for machine time is 6,000 hours per year.

What is the throughput accounting ratio for Product Q (to 1 dp)?

| | |

(2 marks)

28 Which **TWO** of the following statements about activity based costing (ABC) are true?

☐ ABC recognises the complexity of modern manufacturing by the use of multiple cost drivers

☐ ABC establishes separate cost pools for support activities

☐ ABC reapportions support activity costs

☐ ABC is an appropriate costing system when overheads vary with time spent on production **(2 marks)**

29 ABC is felt to give a more useful product cost than classic absorption costing (with overheads absorbed on labour hours) if which of the following **TWO** apply?

☐ Labour costs are a relatively minor proportion of total costs

☐ Overheads vary with many different measures of activity

☐ Overheads are difficult to predict

☐ Cost drivers are difficult to identify **(2 marks)**

30 Which **TWO** of the following costs are likely to rise when just-in-time (JIT) manufacturing is introduced?

☐ Set-up costs

☐ Raw material handling costs

☐ Raw material storage costs

☐ Customer order costs **(2 marks)**

(Total = 30 marks)

Section B MCQ case questions

Linacre Co

The following scenario relates to questions 31 – 35.

Linacre Co operates an activity based costing system and has forecast the following information for next year.

Cost pool	Cost	Cost driver	Number of drivers
Production set-ups	$105,000	Set-ups	300
Product testing	$300,000	Tests	1,500
Component supply and storage	$25,000	Component orders	500
Customer orders and delivery	$112,500	Customer orders	1,000

General fixed overheads, such as lighting and heating, which cannot be linked to any specific activity, are expected to be $900,000 and these overheads are absorbed on a direct labour hour basis. Total direct labour hours for next year are expected to be 300,000 hours.

Linacre Co expects orders for Product ZT3 next year to be 100 orders of 60 units per order and 60 orders of 50 units per order. The company holds no inventories of Product ZT3 and will need to produce the order requirement in production runs of 900 units. One order for components is placed prior to each production run. Four tests are made during each production run to ensure that quality standards are maintained. The following additional cost and profit information relates to product ZT3:

Component cost:	$1.00 per unit
Direct labour:	10 minutes per unit at $7.80 per hour
Profit mark up:	40% of total unit cost

Required

31 What are the activity based recovery rates for production set ups and product testing?

  ○ Production set up $350 per set up, product testing $600 per test.
  ○ Production set up $350 per set up, product testing $200 per test.
  ○ Production set up $210 per set up, product testing $200 per test.
  ○ Production set up $210 per set up, product testing $1,000 per test. **(2 marks)**

32 What are the activity based recovery rates for component supply and storage, and customer orders and delivery?

  ○ Component supply and storage $50 per order, customer orders and delivery $112.50 per order.
  ○ Component supply and storage $50 per order, customer orders and delivery $225 per order.
  ○ Component supply and storage $25 per order, customer orders and delivery $225 per order.
  ○ Component supply and storage $25 per order, customer orders and delivery $112.50 per order. **(2 marks)**

33 What are the general overhead per unit and the direct labour cost per unit of Product ZT3?

  ○ General overhead $0.50 per unit, Direct labour cost $7.80 per unit.
  ○ General overhead $3 per unit, Direct labour cost $1.30 per unit.
  ○ General overhead $3 per unit, Direct labour cost $7.80 per unit.
  ○ General overhead $0.50 per unit, Direct labour cost $1.30 per unit. **(2 marks)**

34   The following statements have been made about Linacre.

(1)   The use of a mark up to determine the price and profit per unit of ZT3 may lead to the incorporation of components which are not valued by the customer.

(2)   A target costing approach would place an emphasis on the planning and design stage of products in Linacre.

Which of the above statements is/are true?

○   1 only
○   2 only
○   Neither 1 nor 2
○   Both 1 and 2   **(2 marks)**

35   The following statements have been made about Linacre.

(1)   Unlike traditional absorption costing, ABC identifies variable overhead costs in the production of ZT3, for allocation to product costs.

(2)   ABC can be used as an information source for budget planning based on activity rather than incremental budgeting.

Which of the above statements is/are true?

○   1 only
○   2 only
○   Neither 1 nor 2
○   Both 1 and 2   **(2 marks)**

                                                                                    (Total = 10 marks)

Section B CBE OT case questions

Triple

18 mins

The following scenario relates to questions 36 – 40.

Triple Co makes three types of gold watch: the Diva (D), the Classic (C) and the Poser (P). A traditional product costing system is used at present, although an activity based costing (ABC) system is being considered. Details of the product lines for a typical period are:

	Hours per unit		Materials	Production
	Labour hours	Machine hours	Cost per unit $	Units
Product D	½	1½	20	750
Product C	1½	1	15	1,250
Product P	1	3	10	7,000

Direct labour costs $6 per hour and production overheads are absorbed on a machine hour basis. The overhead absorption rate for the period is $28 per machine hour.

Total production overheads are $654,500 and further analysis shows that the total production overheads can be divided as follows:

	%
Costs relating to machinery	20
Costs relating to materials handling	15

The following total activity volumes are associated with each product line for the period as a whole:

	Number of movements of materials
Product D	12
Product C	21
Product P	87
	120

Required

36 What is the cost per unit for product D using traditional methods, absorbing overheads on the basis of machine hours?

$ [   ] per unit   (2 marks)

37 What is the total amount of machining overhead that would be allocated to Product C for the period using ABC?

$ [   ]   (2 marks)

38 What is the overhead assigned to Product D in respect of materials handling using ABC?

$ [   ]   (2 marks)

39   Triple Co is attempting to identify the correct cost driver for a cost pool called quality control.

        Using the drop down list below, which would be the correct cost driver to use?

Select...   ▼
Number of units produced
Number of inspections
Labour hours
Number of machine set ups

                                                                                                (2 marks)

40   If Triple Co decides to adopt ABC, which of the following is a disadvantage that Triple Co may encounter as a
        result of this decision?

        O   ABC can only be applied to production overheads.
        O   The cost per unit may not be as accurate as it was under traditional absorption costing.
        O   The benefits obtained from ABC might not justify the costs.
        O   It will not provide much insight into what drives overhead costs.   (2 marks)

                                                                                            (Total = 10 marks)

Brick by Brick   18 mins

The following scenario relates to questions 41 – 45.

Brick by Brick (BBB) is a building business that provides a range of building services to the public. Recently it has
been asked to quote for garage conversions (GC) and extensions to properties (EX) and has found that it is winning
fewer GC contracts than expected. In addition, BBB also produces and sells different types of brick to the
construction industry. The three types of brick produced are clay, concrete and reclaimed bricks.

BBB has a policy to price all jobs at budgeted total cost plus 50%. Overheads are currently absorbed on a labour
hour basis. BBB thinks that a switch to activity based costing (ABC) to absorb overheads would reduce the costs
associated with GC and hence make them more competitive.

You are provided with the following data:

Overhead category	Annual overheads $	Activity driver	Total number of activities per year
Supervisors	90,000	Site visits	500
Planners	70,000	Planning documents	250
Property related	240,000	Labour hours	40,000
Total	400,000		

A typical GC takes 300 labour hours to complete. A GC requires only one site visit by a supervisor and needs only
one planning document to be raised. An EX requires six site visits and five planning documents.

41   What are the total overheads assigned to a GC using labour hours to absorb the overheads?

        GC $ [   ]   (2 marks)

42   What are the total overheads assigned to a GC using ABC principles in respect of supervisor costs?

        GC $ [   ]   (2 marks)

43   What are the total overheads assigned to an EX using ABC principles in respect of planning costs?

        EX $ [   ]   (2 marks)

44   The absorption cost and ABC cost per service have now been correctly calculated as follows:

	GC	EX
Absorption cost	$11,000	$20,500
ABC cost	$10,260	$20,980

Are the following statements true or false?

Changing to a system of ABC costing should lead to a more competitive price being charged for the GC.	TRUE	FALSE
Using ABC would cause total overhead costs to increase.	TRUE	FALSE

(2 marks)

45   Which of the following statements about Brick by Brick and the use of ABC is true?

○   The traditional absorption approach gives a better indication of where cost savings can be made.
○   ABC is a cheaper system for BBB than absorption costing.
○   ABC eliminates the need for cost apportionment.
○   ABC improves pricing decisions.

(2 marks)

(Total = 10 marks)

Jola Publishing Co   18 mins

The following scenario relates to questions 46 – 50.

Jola Publishing Co publishes two forms of book.

The company publishes a children's book (CB), which is sold in large quantities to government-controlled schools. The book is produced in four large production runs. The second book is a comprehensive technical journal (TJ). It is produced in monthly production runs, 12 times a year.

The directors are concerned about the performance of the two books and are wondering what the impact would be of a switch to an activity based costing (ABC) approach to accounting for overheads. They currently use absorption costing, based on number of books produced for all overhead calculations. Overheads amount to $2,880,000.

The CB will be inspected on 180 occasions next year, whereas the TJ will be inspected just 20 times.

Machine time per unit is 6 minutes for the CB and 10 minutes for the TJ.

Jola Publishing will produce its annual output of 1,000,000 CBs in four production runs and approximately 10,000 TJs per month in each of 12 production runs.

Required

46   What is the overhead cost per unit of the CB using the current system of absorption costing?

$ [   ] per unit   (2 marks)

47   Jola Publishing Co has decided to adopt ABC. Management has put together a list of steps. Match each of the steps in ABC to the correct order in which they should be carried out.

List of steps	Correct order	
Calculate the overhead cost per unit of CB and TJ.	Step 1	
Calculate the absorption rate for each 'cost driver'.	Step 2	
Determine what causes the cost of each activity – the 'cost driver'.	Step 3	
Identify major activities within each department which creates cost.	Step 4	
Create a cost centre/cost pool for each activity – 'the activity cost pool'.	Step 5	

(2 marks)

48 The overheads involved have been analysed as follows:

Overhead	$	Activity driver
Production costs	2,160,000	Machine hours
Quality control	668,000	Number of inspections
Production set up costs	52,000	Number of set ups
	2,880,000	

What is the total activity based allocation of production overheads for production of the CB?

$ [   ]   **(2 marks)**

49 What is the total activity based allocation of quality control overheads for production of the TJ?

$ [   ]   **(2 marks)**

50 If Jola Publishing Co decides to introduce an ABC costing system, which of the following is an advantage of ABC that they can expect to benefit from?

○ A reduction in overhead costs
○ Cost savings compared to absorption costing
○ Simplification of the costing process
○ More accurate costs per unit   **(2 marks)**

(Total = 10 marks)

Corrie   18 mins

The following scenario relates to questions 51 – 55.

Corrie produces three products, X, Y and Z. The capacity of Corrie's plant is restricted by process alpha. Process alpha is expected to be operational for eight hours per day and can produce 1,200 units of X per hour, 1,500 units of Y per hour and 600 units of Z per hour.

Selling prices and material costs for each product are as follows.

Product	Selling price $ per unit	Material cost $ per unit	Throughput contribution $ per unit
X	150	70	80
Y	120	40	80
Z	300	100	200

Conversion costs are $720,000 per day.

Required

51 What is the profit per day if daily output achieved is 6,000 units of X, 4,500 units of Y and 1,200 units of Z?

$ [   ]   **(2 marks)**

52 What is the efficiency of the bottleneck process given the output achieved is 6,000 units of X, 4,500 units of Y and 1,200 units of Z?

[   ] %   **(2 marks)**

53 What are the conversion costs per factory hour?

$ [   ]   **(2 marks)**

54   A change in factory cost arose, giving a new figure for conversion costs per factory hour of $80,000. What is the revised throughput accounting (TPAR) ratio for each product?

X [   ]

Y [   ]

Z [   ]   **(2 marks)**

55   Which **TWO** of the following statements about using TA are true?

☐   Corrie Co's priority, using TA, should be given to products with the highest throughput contribution per unit.

☐   TA assumes that labour costs are largely fixed.

☐   The TA ratio for each product should be less than 1.

☐   TA assumes that material costs can be controlled in the short term.   **(2 marks)**

(Total = 10 marks)

A Co   **18 mins**

The following scenario relates to questions 56 – 60.

A Co makes two products, B1 and B2. Its machines can only work on one product at a time. The two products are worked on in two departments by differing grades of labour. The labour requirements for the two products are as follows:

	Minutes per unit of product	
	B1	B2
Department 1	12	16
Department 2	20	15

There is currently a shortage of labour and the maximum times available each day in Departments 1 and 2 are 480 minutes and 840 minutes, respectively. The bottleneck or limiting factor is labour in Department 1. The current selling prices and costs for the two products are shown below:

	B1	B2
	$ per unit	$ per unit
Selling price	50.00	65.00
Direct materials	10.00	15.00
Direct labour	10.40	6.20
Variable overheads	6.40	9.20
Fixed overheads	12.80	18.40
Profit per unit	10.40	16.20

As part of the budget-setting process, A Co needs to know the optimum output levels. All output is sold.

Required

56   What is the maximum number of each product that could be produced each day?

B1 Department 1 [   ] units

B1 Department 2 [   ] units

B2 Department 1 [   ] units

B2 Department 2 [   ] units   **(2 marks)**

57   Using traditional contribution analysis, what is the contribution per unit of limiting factor of B1 (to two decimal places)?

$ [   ]   **(2 marks)**

58   What is the throughput per minute of bottleneck resource of B2 (to two decimal places)?

$ [   ]   **(2 marks)**

59   A Co needs to decide whether to base its decisions about optimum levels of production using a throughput accounting approach, or a limiting factor approach.

Which of the following is an example of an advantage of choosing a throughput accounting approach?

○   The throughput accounting approach eliminates employee idle time.

○   The throughput accounting approach eliminates bottlenecks in manufacturing.

○   The throughput accounting approach eliminates the cost of holding inventory.

○   The throughput accounting approach is more suitable for short-term decision making than limiting factor analysis.   **(2 marks)**

60   If A Co decides to apply the theory of constraints, match each of the steps to the correct order in which they should be carried out.

List of steps	Correct order	
Subordinate everything else to the decisions made about exploiting the bottlenecks.	Step 1	
Elevate the system's bottlenecks.	Step 2	
Identify A Co's bottlenecks.	Step 3	
Decide how to exploit the system's bottlenecks.	Step 4	

(2 marks)

(Total = 10 marks)

Cam Co   **18 mins**

The following scenario relates to questions 61 – 65.

Cam Co manufactures webcams, devices which can provide live video and audio streams via personal computers. It has recently been suffering from liquidity problems and hopes that these will be eased by the launch of its new webcam, which has revolutionary audio and video quality.

The webcam is expected to have a product life cycle of two years. Market research has already been carried out to establish a target selling price and projected lifetime sales volumes for the product. Cost estimates have also been prepared, based on the current proposed product specification. Cam Co uses life cycle costing to work out the target costs for its products. You are provided with the following relevant information for the webcam:

Projected lifetime sales volume   50,000 units
Target selling price per unit $200
Target profit margin   35%

Note. Estimated lifetime cost per unit:

	$	$
Manufacturing costs		
Direct material (bought in parts)	40	
Direct labour	26	
Machine costs	24	
Quality control costs	10	
	100	
Non-manufacturing costs	60	
Estimated lifetime cost per unit	160	

The following information has been identified as relevant:

(1)   Direct material cost: all of the parts currently proposed for the webcam are bespoke parts. However, most of these can actually be replaced with standard parts costing 55% less. However, three of the bespoke parts, which currently account for 20% of the estimated direct material cost, cannot be replaced, although an alternative supplier charging 10% less has been sourced for these parts.

(2)   Direct labour cost: the webcam uses 45 minutes of direct labour, which costs $34.67 per hour. The use of more standard parts, however, will mean that while the first unit would still be expected to take 45 minutes, there will now be an expected rate of learning of 90% (where 'b' = – 0.152). This will end after the first 100 units have been completed.

Required

61   What is the target cost of the new webcam?

$ [   ]   **(2 marks)**

62   What is the direct material cost per unit in light of the new information in point (1)?

$ [   ]   **(2 marks)**

63   What is the average direct labour cost per unit in light of the new information in point (2)?

$ [   ]   **(2 marks)**

64   Are the following statements about Cam Co's target costing system true or false?

Target costing ensures that new product development costs are recovered in the target price for the webcam.	TRUE	FALSE
A cost gap is the difference between the target price and the target cost of the webcam.	TRUE	FALSE

(2 marks)

65   Which of the following in the drop down list represents a possible method for closing the target cost gap for the webcam?

Select... ▼
Increase its selling price
Employ more specialist staff in its production
Redesign the webcam
Increase the number of bespoke components

(2 marks)

(Total = 10 marks)

Yam Co

The following scenario relates to questions 66 – 70.

Yam Co is involved in the processing of sheet metal into products A, B and C using three processes: pressing, stretching and rolling. The factory has many production lines, each of which contains the three processes. Raw material for the sheet metal is first pressed, then stretched and finally rolled. The processing capacity varies for each process and the factory manager has provided the following data:

Processing time per metre in hours

	Product A	Product B	Product C
Pressing	0.50	0.50	0.40

The total annual processing hours for the factory is 225,000. On average, one hour of labour is needed for each of the 225,000 hours of factory time. Labour is paid $10 per hour.

The raw materials cost per metre is $2.50 for product B. Other factory costs (excluding labour and raw materials) are $18,000,000 per year. Selling prices per metre are $60 for product B. The return per factory hour of product A is $134.

Yam carries very little inventory. Pressing has been identified as the bottleneck.

Required

66   What is the maximum output capacity per year for the bottleneck 'pressing' for each product?

Product A

metres

Product B

metres

Product C

metres

(2 marks)

67   What is the conversion cost per factory hour?

$ [   ]

(2 marks)

68   What is the return per factory hour of product B?

$ [   ]

(2 marks)

69   Yam Co is considering increasing the labour rate per hour. This would result in a conversion cost per factory hour of $95.

What is the throughput accounting ratio (TPAR) for product A assuming that this change occurs and the bottleneck process is fully utilised? (to 2 dp)

[   ]

(2 marks)

70   Are the following statements about throughput accounting in Yam Co true or false?

When the bottleneck 'pressing' is overcome ('elevated'), a new bottleneck will appear.	TRUE	FALSE
It should be expected that the throughput accounting ratio for any product in Yam Co will exceed 1.	TRUE	FALSE

(2 marks)

(Total = 10 marks)

PART B: DECISION-MAKING TECHNIQUES

Questions 71 to 141 cover Decision-making techniques, the subject of Part B of the BPP Study Text for PM.

Section A questions

MCQ bank – Decision-making techniques   54 mins

71   A decision tree is a way of representing decision choices in the form of a diagram. It is usual for decision trees to include probabilities of different outcomes.

The following statements have been made about decision trees.

(1)   Each possible outcome from a decision is given an expected value.
(2)   Each possible outcome is shown as a branch on a decision tree.

Which of the above statements is/are true?

○   1 only
○   2 only
○   Neither 1 nor 2
○   Both 1 and 2   **(2 marks)**

72   The following statements have been made about price elasticity of demand.

(1)   When sales demand is inelastic, a company can increase profits by raising the selling price of its product.

(2)   Price elasticity of demand is measured as the amount of change in sales price (measured as a percentage of the current sales price) divided by the amount of change in quantity demanded (measured as a percentage of the current sales volume).

Which of the above statements is/are true?

○   1 only
○   2 only
○   Neither 1 nor 2
○   Both 1 and 2   **(2 marks)**

73   The following statements have been made about cost plus pricing.

(1)   A price in excess of full cost per unit will ensure that a company will cover all its costs and make a profit.

(2)   Cost plus pricing is an appropriate pricing strategy when jobs are carried out to customer specifications.

Which of the above statements is/are true?

○   1 only
○   2 only
○   Neither 1 nor 2
○   Both 1 and 2   **(2 marks)**

74 The following statements have been made about decision making under conditions of uncertainty.

   (1)   Expected value is a more reliable basis for decision making where the situation and outcome will occur many times than for a one-off decision.

   (2)   A risk-averse decision maker avoids all risks in decision making.

   Which of the above statements is/are true?

   ○   1 only
   ○   2 only
   ○   Neither 1 nor 2
   ○   Both 1 and 2   **(2 marks)**

75 Which method of pricing is most easily applied when two or more markets for the product or service can be kept entirely separate from each other?

   ○   Price discrimination
   ○   Product line pricing
   ○   Skimming
   ○   Volume discounting   **(2 marks)**

76 A company has fixed costs of $1.3 million. Variable costs are 55% of sales up to a sales level of $1.5 million, but at higher volumes of production and sales, the variable cost for incremental production units falls to 52% of sales.

   What is the breakeven point in sales revenue, to the nearest $1,000?

   ○ $1,977,000
   ○ $2,027,000
   ○ $2,708,000
   ○ $2,802,000   **(2 marks)**

77 A company wishes to go ahead with one of three mutually exclusive projects, but the profit outcome from each project will depend on the strength of sales demand, as follows.

	Strong demand Profit $	Moderate demand Profit $	Weak demand Profit/(Loss) $
Project 1	70,000	10,000	(7,000)
Project 2	25,000	12,000	5,000
Project 3	50,000	20,000	(6,000)
Probability of demand	0.1	0.4	0.5

   What is the value to the company of obtaining this perfect market research information, ignoring the cost of obtaining the information?

   ○ $3,000
   ○ $5,500
   ○ $6,000
   ○ $7,500   **(2 marks)**

78   A manufacturing company makes two joint products, CP1 and CP2, in a common process. These products can be sold at the split-off point in an external market, or processed further in separate processes to produce products FP1 and FP2. Details of these processes are shown in the diagram.

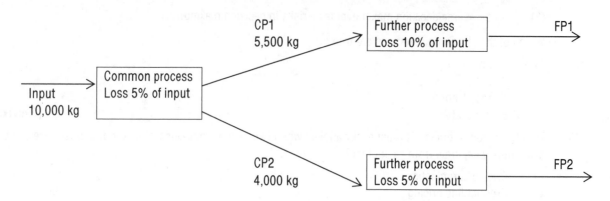

CP1 has a market price of $6 per kg and CP2 has a market price of $5 per kg. Relevant further processing costs are $2 per input kg in the process to make FP1 and $3 per input kg in the process to make FP2. Both FP1 and FP2 sell for $9 per kg.

For each 10,000 kg input to the common process, how much additional profit is obtained by further processing each of the joint products instead of selling them at the split-off point?

O $2,750
O $4,450
O $8,750
O $9,500   (2 marks)

79   A company makes and sells a single product. When sales per month are $6.8 million, total costs are $6.56 million. When sales per month are $5.2 million, total costs are $5.44 million. There is a step cost increase of $400,000 in fixed costs when sales are $6.0 million, but variable unit costs are constant at all levels of output and sales.

What is the breakeven point for sales revenue per month?

O $6.0 million
O   There are two breakeven points: $5.64 million and $6.36 million
O $5.64 million only
O $6.36 million only   (2 marks)

80   Analysing the range of different possible outcomes from a particular situation, with a computer model that uses random numbers, is known as which of the following?

O   Probability analysis
O   Sensitivity analysis
O   Simulation modelling
O   Stress testing   (2 marks)

81   A company produces and sells a single product. Budgeted sales are $2.4 million, budgeted fixed costs are $360,000 and the margin of safety is $400,000. What are budgeted variable costs?

O $1.640 million
O $1.728 million
O $1.968 million
O $2.040 million   (2 marks)

82   A company uses linear programming to decide on the production and sales budget that will maximise total contribution and profit for a financial period. The optimal solution involves using all available direct labour hours, for which the shadow price is $4.50 per hour, and machine hours, for which the shadow price is $3 per machine hour. Direct labour is paid $8 per hour.

If the objective of the company is to maximise total contribution and profit in each period, how much should the company be willing to pay per hour to obtain additional direct labour hours of production capacity?

   ○   Up to but not including $4.50
   ○   Up to but not including $9.50
   ○   Up to but not including $12.50
   ○   Up to but not including $15.50   (2 marks)

83   The demand for a product at its current price has a price elasticity greater than 1.0 (ignoring the minus sign). Which of the following statements must be correct?

   (1)   A reduction in the sales price will increase total revenue.

   (2)   A reduction in the sales price by x% will result in a percentage increase in sales demand which is greater than x%.

   (3)   An increase in the selling price will increase total profit.

   ○   Statements 1 and 2
   ○   Statements 1 and 3
   ○   Statements 2 and 3
   ○   Statements 1, 2 and 3   (2 marks)

84   A company makes two products, X and Y, using the same type of direct labour. Production capacity per period is restricted to 60,000 direct labour hours. The contribution per unit is $8 for Product X and $6 for Product Y. The following constraints apply to production and sales:

   x $\leq 10,000$ (Sales demand for Product X)
   y $\leq 12,000$ (Sales demand for Product Y)
   5x + 4y $\leq 60,000$ (Direct labour hours)

The contribution-maximising output is to produce and sell 10,000 units of Product X and 2,500 units of Product Y.

What is the shadow price per direct labour hour and for how many additional hours of labour does this shadow price per hour apply?

   ○ $1.50 per hour for the next 38,000 direct labour hours
   ○ $1.50 per hour for the next 47,500 direct labour hours
   ○ $1.60 per hour for the next 38,000 direct labour hours
   ○ $1.60 per hour for the next 47,500 direct labour hours   (2 marks)

85   In a linear programming problem to determine the contribution-maximising production and sales volumes for two products, X and Y, the following information is available.

	Product X per unit	Product Y per unit	Total available per period
Direct labour hours	2 hours	4 hours	10,000 hours
Material X	4 kg	2 kg	14,000 kg
Contribution per unit	$12	$18	

The profit-maximising level of output and sales is 3,000 units of Product X and 1,000 units of Product Y.

What is the shadow price of a direct labour hour?

   ○ $1.00
   ○ $2.40
   ○ $4.00
   ○ $4.50   (2 marks)

                                                                            (Total = 30 marks)

86   A business produces three products, Z1, Z2 and Z3. Each of these products requires different amounts of material (material X), which is a scarce resource. The following budgeted data relates to the three products:

Per unit:	Z1	Z2	Z3
	$	$	$
Selling price	200	150	100
Materials ($5 per kg)	(35)	(20)	(10)
Labour ($20 per hour)	(50)	(25)	(10)
Variable overheads	(45)	(45)	(30)
Fixed overheads	(30)	(25)	(20)
Profit per unit	40	35	30

Match the products to the order in which they should be manufactured to ensure profit is maximised.

Product
Z1
Z2
Z3

Ranking	
1st	
2nd	
3rd	

(2 marks)

87   The price elasticity of demand for a product at its current price level is inelastic. What will happen to the total revenue and the profit if the price of the product is reduced?

	Increase	Fall
Total revenue	O	O
Profit	O	O

(2 marks)

88   A company makes and sells four products. Direct labour hours are a scarce resource, but the company is able to sub-contract production of any products to external suppliers. The following information is relevant.

Product	W	X	Y	Z
	$ per unit	$ per unit	$ per unit	$ per unit
Sales price	10	8	12	14
Variable cost	8	5	8	12
Cost of external purchase	9	7.1	10	13
Direct labour hours per unit	0.1	0.3	0.25	0.2

Match the products to the order of priority in which the company should make them in-house, rather than purchase them externally.

Product
W
X
Y
Z

Ranking	
1st	
2nd	
3rd	
4th	

(2 marks)

89   H Co uses a marginal cost plus pricing system to determine the selling price for one of its products, Product X.

Product X has the following costs:

	$
Direct materials	12
Direct labour	5
Variable overheads	3
Fixed overheads	40

Fixed overheads are $20,000 for the year. Budgeted output and sales for the year are 500 units and this should be sufficient for Product X to break even.

What profit mark-up would H Co need to add to the marginal cost to allow H Co to break even?

⬚ %

(2 marks)

90   What method of uncertainty or risk analysis is also called 'What if?' analysis?

Select...   ▼
Decision tree analysis
Sensitivity analysis
Simulation modelling
Stress testing

(2 marks)

91   To calculate and use expected values in decision making, we must be able to do which **TWO** of the following?

☐ Identify all possible outcomes and their probabilities

☐ Assume the investor is risk neutral

☐ Assume the decision will often be repeated

☐ Assume the decision is a 'one-off'

(2 marks)

92   A benefit sacrificed by taking one course of action instead of the most profitable alternative course of action is known as which of the following?

Select...   ▼
Opportunity cost
Incremental cost
Relevant cost
Sunk cost

(2 marks)

93   A special job for a customer will require 8 tonnes of a Material M. The company no longer uses this material regularly although it holds 3 tonnes in inventory. These originally cost $44 per tonne, and could be resold to a supplier for $35 per tonne. Alternatively these materials could be used to complete another job instead of using other materials that would cost $126 to purchase. The current market price of Material M is $50 per tonne.

The company must decide whether to agree to the customer's request for the work, and to set a price. What would be the relevant cost of Material M for this job?

$ ⬚

(2 marks)

BPP
LEARNING MEDIA

94 A company wishes to decide on a selling price for a new product. Weekly sales of each product will depend on the price charged and also on customers' response to the new product. The following pay-off table has been prepared.

	Probability	Price P1 $	Price P2 $	Price P3 $	Price P4 $
Price		5.00	5.50	6.00	6.50
Unit contribution		3.00	3.50	4.00	4.50
Weekly demand		Units	Units	Units	Units
Best possible	0.3	10,000	9,000	8,000	7,000
Most likely	0.5	8,000	7,500	7,000	6,000
Worst possible	0.2	6,000	5,000	4,000	3,000

If the choice of selling price is based on a maximin decision rule, which price would be selected?

P [   ]

(2 marks)

95 The following decision tree shows four decision options: 1, 2, 3 and 4

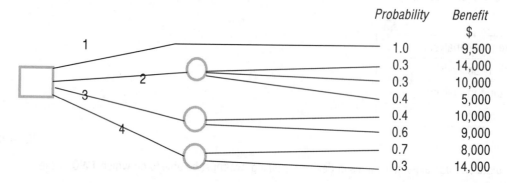

	Probability	Benefit $
1	1.0	9,500
	0.3	14,000
2	0.3	10,000
	0.4	5,000
	0.4	10,000
3	0.6	9,000
	0.7	8,000
4	0.3	14,000

Using the expected value rule, which choice should be made so as to optimise the expected benefit?

Choice [   ]

(2 marks)

96 A company wants to decide whether to make its materials in-house or to sub-contract production to an external supplier. In the past it has made four materials in-house, but demand in the next year will exceed in-house production capacity of 8,000 units. All four materials are made on the same machines and require the same machine time per unit: machine time is the limiting production factor.
The following information is available.

Material	W	X	Y	Z
Units required	4,000	2,000	3,000	4,000
Variable cost of in-house manufacture	$8 per unit	$12 per unit	$9 per unit	$10 per unit
Directly attributable fixed cost expenditure	$5,000	$8,000	$6,000	$7,000
Cost of external purchase	$9 per unit	$18 per unit	$12 per unit	$12 per unit

Directly attributable fixed costs are fixed cash expenditures that would be saved if production of the material in-house is stopped entirely.

If a decision is made solely on the basis of short-term cost considerations, what materials should the company purchase externally?

Select... ▼
4,000 units of W and 1,000 units of Z
4,000 units of W and 4,000 units of Z
3,000 units of Y and 2,000 units of Z
1,000 units of Y and 4,000 units of Z

(2 marks)

97   If the price elasticity of demand is zero, which **TWO** of the following are true?

☐ Demand is 'perfectly inelastic'.

☐ There is no change in price regardless of the quantity demanded.

☐ The demand curve is a horizontal straight line.

☐ There is no change in the quantity demanded, regardless of any change in price.   **(2 marks)**

98   A company wishes to decide on a selling price for a new product. Weekly sales of each product will depend on the price charged and also on customers' response to the new product. The following pay-off table has been prepared.

	Probability	Price P1 $	Price P2 $	Price P3 $	Price P4 $
Price		5.00	5.50	6.00	6.50
Unit contribution		3.00	3.50	4.00	4.50
Weekly demand		Units	Units	Units	Units
Best possible	0.3	10,000	9,000	8,000	7,000
Most likely	0.5	8,000	7,500	7,000	6,000
Worst possible	0.2	6,000	5,000	4,000	3,000

If the choice of selling price is based on a minimax regret decision rule, which price would be selected?

P [   ]   **(2 marks)**

99   A company wishes to go ahead with one of two mutually exclusive projects, but the profit outcome from each project will depend on the strength of sales demand, as follows.

	Strong demand Profit $	Moderate demand Profit $	Weak demand Profit/(Loss) $
Project 1	80,000	50,000	(5,000)
Project 2	60,000	25,000	10,000
Probability of demand	0.2	0.4	0.4

The company could purchase market research information, at a cost of $4,500. This would predict demand conditions with perfect accuracy.

What is the value to the company of obtaining this perfect market research information?

$ [   ]   **(2 marks)**

100   A company budgets to sells its three products A, B and C in the ratio 2:3:5 respectively, measured in units of sales. Unit sales prices and variable costs are as follows.

Product	A $ per unit	B $ per unit	C $ per unit
Sales price	20	18	24
Variable cost	11	12	18

Budgeted fixed costs are $1.2 million. What sales will be needed to achieve a target profit of $400,000 for the period? Give your answer in millions, to 3 dp.

$ [   ]   **(2 marks)**

101   What is the main purpose of sensitivity analysis?

○ To calculate the expected value of an outcome that is uncertain

○ To predict the future outcome from an uncertain situation

○ To gain insight into which assumptions or variables in a situation are critical

○ To determine the outcome from a situation in the event of the worst possible outcome   **(2 marks)**

102   Market research into demand for a product indicates that when the selling price per unit is $145, demand in each period will be 5,000 units; if the price is $120, demand will be 11,250 units. It is assumed that the demand function for this product is linear. The variable cost per unit is $27.

What selling price should be charged in order to maximise the monthly profit?

$ [   ]

(2 marks)

103   A company makes and sells three products. The budget for the next period is as follows:

Product	A	B	C
	$ per unit	$ per unit	$ per unit
Sales price	12	18	20
Variable cost	3	6	11
	9	12	9
Fixed cost	6	9	6
Profit	3	3	3
Number of units	30,000	40,000	10,000

What is the breakeven point in sales, to the nearest $1,000?

$ [   ]

(2 marks)

104   Which **TWO** pieces of information are required when deciding, purely on financial grounds, whether or not to process a joint product further?

☐ The final sales value of the joint product

☐ The further processing cost of the joint product

☐ The value of the common process costs

☐ The method of apportioning the common costs between the joint products

(2 marks)

105   Which **TWO** statements are true when using linear programming to solve production problems?

☐ If the aim is to minimise costs, the solution is where the total cost line touching the feasible area at a tangent is as far away from the origin as possible.

☐ If the aim is to minimise costs, the solution is where the total cost line touching the feasible area at a tangent is as close to the origin as possible.

☐ If the aim is to maximise profit, the solution is where the total cost line touching the feasible area at a tangent is as far away from the origin as possible.

☐ If the aim is to maximise profit, the solution is where the total contribution line touching the feasible area at a tangent is as close to the origin as possible.

☐ If the aim is to maximise profit, the solution is where the total contribution line touching the feasible area at a tangent is as far away from the origin as possible.

(2 marks)

(Total = 40 marks)

Section B questions

MCQ case questions

Ennerdale

The following scenario relates to questions 106 – 110.

Ennerdale has been asked to quote a price for a one-off contract. The company's management accountant has asked for your advice on the relevant costs for the contract. The following information is available:

Materials

The contract requires 3,000 kg of material K, which is a material used regularly by the company in other production. The company has 2,000 kg of material K currently in inventory which had been purchased last month for a total cost of $19,600. Since then the price per kilogram for material K has increased by 5%.

The contract also requires 200 kg of material L. There are 250 kg of material L in inventory which are not required for normal production. This material originally cost a total of $3,125. If not used on this contract, the inventory of material L would be sold for $11 per kg.

Labour

The contract requires 800 hours of skilled labour. Skilled labour is paid $9.50 per hour. There is a shortage of skilled labour and all the available skilled labour is fully employed in the company in the manufacture of product P. The following information relates to product P:

	$ per unit	$ per unit
Selling price		100
Less:		
Skilled labour	38	
Other variable costs	22	
		(60)
		40

Finance costs

In order to complete the contract, a member of the finance team will be required to work 8 hours overtime. The individual's annual salary is $25,000, and they work a 37.5 hour week. Overtime is paid at a rate of $15 per hour. Alternatively, an experienced contract accountant can be hired to administer the project in 75% of the time it would take the internal finance department member to complete. The contractor's rate is $25 per hour. It took the member of the finance team three hours to put together the information for this quote and no overtime was required.

Required

106 What is the relevant cost of material K which should be included in the contract?

    ○ $29,400
    ○ $29,890
    ○ $30,870
    ○ $30,380   **(2 marks)**

107 What is the relevant cost of material L which should be included in the contract?

    ○ $2,200
    ○ $2,500
    ○ $3,125
    ○   NIL   **(2 marks)**

108　What is the relevant cost of skilled labour which should be included in the contract?

- ○ $8,000
- ○ $15,600
- ○ $7,600
- ○ $12,400

(2 marks)

109　What is the relevant cost of finance which should be included in the contract?

- ○ Nil
- ○ $120
- ○ $150
- ○ $158.46

(2 marks)

110　The following statements have been made about Ennerdale's relevant costing system.

(1)　Sunk costs can never be a relevant cost for the purpose of decision making.

(2)　If Ennerdale charges the minimum price for a product or service, based on relevant costs, it will not improve its overall profitability.

Which of the above statements is/are true?

- ○ 1 only
- ○ 2 only
- ○ Neither 1 nor 2
- ○ Both 1 and 2

(2 marks)

(Total = 10 marks)

Pixie Pharmaceuticals

18 mins

The following scenario relates to questions 111 – 115.

Pixie Pharmaceuticals is a research-based company which manufactures a wide variety of drugs for use in hospitals. The purchasing manager has recently been approached by a new manufacturer based in a newly industrialised country who has offered to produce three of the drugs at their factory. The following cost and price information has been provided.

Drug	Fairyoxide	Spriteolite	Goblinex
Production (units)	20,000	40,000	80,000
	$	$	$
Direct material cost, per unit	0.80	1.00	0.40
Direct labour cost, per unit	1.60	1.80	0.80
Direct expense cost, per unit	0.40	0.60	0.20
Fixed cost per unit	0.80	1.00	0.40
Selling price each	4.00	5.00	2.00
Imported price	2.75	4.20	2.00

Required

111　What profit will the company make by producing all the drugs itself?

- ○ $96,000
- ○ $136,000
- ○ $48,000
- ○ $216,000

(2 marks)

112   What saving/(increased cost) per unit would be made/(incurred) if Fairyoxide was purchased from the overseas producer?

○ $0.85
○ $0.05
○ $0.45
○ $(0.05)   **(2 marks)**

113   What saving/(increased cost) would be made/(incurred) per unit if Spriteolite was purchased from the overseas producer?

○ $(0.80)
○ $0.20
○ $0.80
○ $(0.20)   **(2 marks)**

114   What saving/(increased cost) would be made/(incurred) if Goblinex was purchased from the overseas producer?

○ $0.60
○ $(0.20)
○ $0.20
○ $(0.60)   **(2 marks)**

115   The following two statements have been made about the decision Pixie Pharmaceuticals has to make about producing the products in house or purchasing from the overseas producer:

(1)   In a make-or-buy decision with no limiting factors, the relevant costs are the differential costs between the make and buy options.

(2)   Cost is the only relevant factor in Pixie Pharmaceutical's make-or-buy decision.

Which of the above statements is/are true?

○   1 only
○   2 only
○   Both 1 and 2
○   Neither 1 nor 2   **(2 marks)**

(Total = 10 marks)

CBE OT case questions

BDU Co

The following scenario relates to questions 116 – 120.

BDU Co is a manufacturer of baby equipment and is planning to launch a revolutionary new style of sporty pushchair. The company has commissioned market research to establish possible demand for the pushchair and the following information has been obtained.

If the price is set at $425, demand is expected to be 1,000 pushchairs; at $500 it will be 730 pushchairs and at $600 it will be 420 pushchairs. Variable costs are estimated at $170, $210 or $260.

A decision needs to be made on what price to charge.

The following contribution table has been produced showing the possible outcomes.

Price		$425	$500	$600
Variable cost	$170	255,000	240,900	180,600
	$210	215,000	211,700	163,800
	$260	165,000	175,200	142,800

116 What price would be set if BDU were to use a maximin decision criterion?

$ _____ **(2 marks)**

117 What price would be set if BDU were to use a minimax regret decision criterion?

$ _____ **(2 marks)**

118 If the probabilities of the variable costs are $170: 0.4; $210: 0.25; and $260: 0.35, which price would the risk-neutral decision maker choose?

$ _____ **(2 marks)**

119 Which **TWO** of the following, used by BDU Co, reduce uncertainty in decision making?

☐ Expected value analysis
☐ Market research
☐ Focus groups
☐ Relevant costing

(2 marks)

120 Indicate, by selecting the relevant boxes in the table below, whether each of the following statements regarding BDU Co's use of expected values is correct or incorrect.

Expected-value analysis is suitable for risk-averse decision makers, as all likely outcomes are presented.	CORRECT	INCORRECT
The average profit calculated will correspond to one of the possible outcomes.	CORRECT	INCORRECT

(2 marks)

(Total = 10 marks)

Questions

BPP
LEARNING MEDIA

Metallica Co

The following scenario relates to questions 121 – 125.

Metallica Co is an engineering company that manufactures a number of products, using a team of highly skilled workers and a variety of different metals. A supplier has informed Metallica Co that the amount of M1, one of the materials used in production, will be limited for the next three-month period.

The only items manufactured using M1 and their production costs and selling prices (where applicable) are shown below.

	Product P4 $/unit	Product P6 $/unit
Selling price	125	175
Direct materials:		
M1*	15	10
M2	10	20
Direct labour	20	30
Variable overhead	10	15
Fixed overhead	20	30
Total cost	75	105

* Material M1 is expected to be limited in supply during the next three months. These costs are based on M1 continuing to be available at a price of $20 per square metre. The price of M2 is $10 per square metre.

Required

121 What is the contribution per unit for each product?

P4 $	
P6 $	

(2 marks)

122 Metallica Co carried out some market research which suggested that a change should be made to the selling price of both Product P4 and P6. As a result, the new contribution per unit for P4 is $85 and for P6 it is $95. Which of the following answers is correct?

○ The contribution per limiting factor of P4 and P6 is $85 and $47.50 respectively, therefore P4 should be produced first.

○ The contribution per limiting factor of P4 and P6 is $113.33 and $190 respectively, therefore P6 should be produced first.

○ The contribution per limiting factor of P4 and P6 is $85 and $47.50 respectively, therefore P6 should be produced first.

○ The contribution per limiting factor of P4 and P6 is $113.33 and $190 respectively, therefore P4 should be produced first.

(2 marks)

123 Indicate, by selecting the relevant boxes in the table below, whether each of the following costs would be included in the calculation of throughput contribution if Metallica Co operated in a throughput accounting environment.

Selling price	YES	NO
Direct materials	YES	NO
Direct labour	YES	NO

(2 marks)

124 Indicate, by selecting the relevant boxes in the table below, which of the following constraints would necessitate the performance of limiting factor analysis by Metallica Co?

Limited demand for P4 or P6	YES	NO
Limited M1 or M2	YES	NO
Limited labour	YES	NO

(2 marks)

125 Once a scarce resource is identified, Metallica Co carries out a limiting factor analysis using four steps. Match each of the steps to the correct order in which they should be carried out.

List of steps	Correct order	
Rank the products in order of the contribution per unit of the scarce resource.	Step 1	
Allocate resources using the ranking.	Step 2	
Calculate the contribution per unit of the scarce resource for each product.	Step 3	
Calculate the contribution per unit for each product.	Step 4	

(2 marks)

(Total = 10 marks)

T Co

18 mins

The following scenario relates to questions 126 – 130.

The Telephone Co (T Co) is a company specialising in the provision of telephone systems for commercial clients.

T Co has been approached by a potential customer, Push Co, which wants to install a telephone system in new offices it is opening. While the job is not a particularly large one, T Co is hopeful of future business in the form of replacement systems and support contracts for Push Co. T Co is therefore keen to quote a competitive price for the job. The following information should be considered:

(i) One of the company's salesmen has already been to visit Push Co, to give them a demonstration of the new system, together with a complimentary lunch, the costs of which totalled $400.

(ii) The installation is expected to take one week to complete and would require three engineers, each of whom is paid a monthly salary of $4,000. The engineers have just had their annually renewable contract renewed with T Co. One of the three engineers has spare capacity to complete the work, but the other two would have to be moved from Contract X in order to complete this one. Contract X generates a contribution of $200 per engineer per week. There are no other engineers available to continue with Contract X if these two engineers are taken off the job. It would mean that T Co would miss its contractual completion deadline on Contract X by one week. As a result, T Co would have to pay a one-off penalty of $500. Since there is no other work scheduled for their engineers in one week's time, it will not be a problem for them to complete Contract X at this point.

(iii) 120 telephone handsets would need to be supplied to Push Co. The current cost of these is $18.20 each, although T Co already has 80 handsets in inventory. These were bought at a price of $16.80 each. The handsets are the most popular model on the market and are frequently requested by T Co's customers.

(iv) Push Co would also need a computerised control system called 'Swipe 2'. The current market price of Swipe 2 is $10,800, although T Co has an older version of the system, 'Swipe 1', in inventory, which could be modified at a cost of $4,600. T Co paid $5,400 for Swipe 1 when it ordered it in error two months ago and has no other use for it. The current market price of Swipe 1 is $5,450, although if T Co tried to sell the one it has, it would be deemed to be 'used' and therefore only worth $3,000.

126 What figure should be included in the relevant cost statement for engineers' costs?

| $ | |

(2 marks)

127 What figure should be included in the relevant cost statement for telephone handsets?

| $ | |

(2 marks)

128 What figure should be included in the relevant cost statement for the computerised control system?

- ○ $7,600
- ○ $10,800
- ○ $10,050
- ○ $10,000

(2 marks)

129 Indicate, by selecting the relevant boxes in the table below, whether each of the following statements about T Co's decision to quote for the contract are true or false?

	TRUE	FALSE
The opportunity cost is defined as the relevant cost of taking a business opportunity to install the telephone system for Push Co.	TRUE	FALSE
The decision to install the telephone system should be taken purely on the basis of whether it improves profit or reduces costs for T Co.	TRUE	FALSE

(2 marks)

130 Use the drop down list to select the type of cost that is detailed in point (i).

Select... ▼
Sunk cost
Opportunity cost
Relevant cost
Committed cost

(2 marks)

(Total = 10 marks)

Rotanola Co   18 mins

The following scenario relates to questions 131 – 135.

Rotanola Co manufactures mobile phones. It has been extremely successful in the past but the market has become extremely competitive. The company is considering a number of different strategies to improve its profitability.

The most successful product is the RTN99 which is sold for $110. Weekly demand is currently 20,000 phones. Market research has revealed that if Rotanola Co reduced the price of the RTN99 by $10, demand would increase by 2,000 phones.

Each time the phone is produced, Rotanola Co incurs extra costs of $30 for materials, $18 for labour, $14 for variable overheads and $23 for fixed costs, based on expected weekly output of 20,000 phones. The most expensive component in the phone is the battery which costs $15. Rotanola has been offered a discounted price of $12 by the supplier if it buys 22,000 batteries per week.

The company needs to come up with innovative new products as the technology moves very fast and what is useful today becomes obsolete tomorrow. The latest idea is to produce a phone incorporating virtual touch technology which makes the phone vibrate in a number of ways.

The following estimates for this phone (the RTNBZ) have been produced.

		$	$
Sales	(25,000 units @ $150)		3,750,000
Materials	(@ $50)	1,250,000	
Labour	(@ $18)	450,000	
Variable overheads	(@ $16)	400,000	
			2,100,000
Attributable fixed overheads			575,000
Profit			1,075,000

There is some doubt as to the likely cost of materials. The probability of it being $50 as expected is 0.6, the probability of it rising it to $60 is 0.3 and the probability of it falling to $40 is 0.1.

Forecast sales units are also subject to economic conditions. There is a 50% chance that sales will be as expected, a 40% chance that sales will be 10% lower than expected and a 10% chance that sales will be 5% higher than expected.

Required

131 What is the straight line demand equation for the RTN99?

P = [   ] – [   ] Q   (2 marks)

132 What is the total cost function for the RTN99 before the volume discount?

TC = [   ] + [   ] Q   (2 marks)

133 What is the total cost function for the RTN99 after the volume discount?

TC = [   ] + [   ] Q   (2 marks)

134 What is the expected profit on the RTNBZ?

$ [   ]   (2 marks)

135 The following statements have been made about Rotanola Co.

Indicate, by selecting the relevant boxes in the table below, whether each of the following statements are true or false.

	TRUE	FALSE
Rotanola Co can use market research to reduce uncertainty and monitor performance.	TRUE	FALSE
Rotanola Co could use market research to estimate by how much costs and revenues would need to differ from their estimated values before the decision would change.	TRUE	FALSE

(2 marks)

(Total = 10 marks)

Section C questions

136 RB Co

36 mins

Just over two years ago, RB Co was the first company to produce a specific 'off-the-shelf' accounting software package. The pricing strategy for the packages, decided on by the managing director, was to add a 50% mark-up to the budgeted full cost of the packages. The company achieved and maintained a significant market share and high profits for the first two years.

Budgeted information for the current year (Year 3) was as follows.

Production and sales	15,000 packages
Full cost	$400 per package

At a recent board meeting, the finance director reported that although costs were in line with the budget for the current year, profits were declining. They explained that the full cost included $80 for fixed overheads. This figure had been calculated by using an overhead absorption rate based on labour hours and the budgeted level of production of 15,000 packages. They pointed out that this was much lower than the current capacity of 25,000 packages.

The marketing director stated that competitors were beginning to increase their market share. They also reported the results of a recent competitor analysis which showed that when RB Co announced its prices for the current year, the competitors responded by undercutting them by 15%. Consequently, they commissioned an investigation of the market. They informed the board that the market research showed that at a price of $750 there would be no demand for the packages but for every $10 reduction in price the demand would increase by 1,000 packages.

The managing director appeared to be unconcerned about the loss of market share and argued that profits could be restored to their former level by increasing the mark-up.

Required

(a) Discuss the managing director's pricing strategy in the circumstances described above. **(5 marks)**

(b) Suggest and explain two alternative strategies that could have been implemented at the launch of the packages. **(4 marks)**

(c) Based on the data supplied by the market research, derive a straight line demand equation for the packages. **(3 marks)**

(d) RB's total costs (TC) can be modelled by the equation TC = 1,200,000 + 320Q. Explain the meaning of this equation. **(3 marks)**

(e) Explain what is meant by price elasticity of demand and explain the implications of elasticity for RB's pricing strategy. **(5 marks)**

(Total = 20 marks)

137 The Cosmetic Co (12/10)

36 mins

The Cosmetic Co is a company producing a variety of cosmetic creams and lotions. The creams and lotions are sold to a variety of retailers at a price of $23.20 for each jar of face cream and $16.80 for each bottle of body lotion. Each of the products has a variety of ingredients, with the key ones being silk powder, silk amino acids and aloe vera. Six months ago, silk worms were attacked by disease causing a huge reduction in the availability of silk powder and silk amino acids. The Cosmetic Co had to dramatically reduce production and make part of its workforce, which it had trained over a number of years, redundant.

The company now wants to increase production again by ensuring that it uses the limited ingredients available to maximise profits by selling the optimum mix of creams and lotions. Due to the redundancies made earlier in the year, supply of skilled labour is now limited in the short term to 160 hours (9,600 minutes) per week, although unskilled labour is unlimited. The purchasing manager is confident that they can obtain 5,000 grams of silk powder and 1,600 grams of silk amino acids per week. All other ingredients are unlimited. The following information is available for the two products:

	Cream	Lotion
Materials required: silk powder (at $2.20 per gram)	3 grams	2 grams
– Silk amino acids (at $0.80 per gram)	1 gram	0.5 grams
– Aloe vera (at $1.40 per gram)	4 grams	2 grams
Labour required: skilled ($12 per hour)	4 minutes	5 minutes
– Unskilled (at $8 per hour)	3 minutes	1.5 minutes

Each jar of cream sold generates a contribution of $9 per unit, while each bottle of lotion generates a contribution of $8 per unit. The maximum demand for lotions is 2,000 bottles per week, although demand for creams is unlimited. Fixed costs total $1,800 per week. The company does not keep inventory although if a product is partially complete at the end of one week, its production will be completed in the following week.

Required

(a) On the graph paper provided, use linear programming to calculate the optimum number of each product that the Cosmetic Co should make per week, assuming that it wishes to maximise contribution. Calculate the total contribution per week for the new production plan. All workings **MUST** be rounded to 2 decimal places.

(14 marks)

(b) Calculate the shadow price for silk powder and the slack for silk amino acids. All workings **MUST** be rounded to 2 decimal places.

(6 marks)

(Total = 20 marks)

138 Bits and Pieces (6/09)   36 mins

Bits and Pieces (B&P) operates a retail store selling spares and accessories for the car market. The store has previously only opened for 6 days per week for the 50 working weeks in the year, but B&P is now considering also opening on Sundays.

The sales of the business on Monday through to Saturday averages at $10,000 per day with average gross profit of 70% earned.

B&P expects that the gross profit % earned on a Sunday will be 20 percentage points lower than the average earned on the other days in the week. This is because they plan to offer substantial discounts and promotions on a Sunday to attract customers. Given the price reduction, Sunday sales revenues are expected to be 60% **more than** the average daily sales revenues for the other days. These Sunday sales estimates are for new customers only, with no allowance being made for those customers that may transfer from other days.

B&P buys all its goods from one supplier. This supplier gives a 5% discount on **all** purchases if annual spend exceeds $1,000,000.

It has been agreed to pay time and a half to sales assistants who work on Sundays. The normal hourly rate is $20 per hour. In total, five sales assistants will be needed for the six hours that the store will be open on a Sunday. They will also be able to take a half-day off (four hours) during the week. Staffing levels will be allowed to reduce slightly during the week to avoid extra costs being incurred.

The staff will have to be supervised by a manager, currently employed by the company and paid an annual salary of $80,000. If they work on a Sunday they will take the equivalent time off during the week when the assistant manager is available to cover for them at no extra cost to B&P. They will also be paid a bonus of 1% of the extra sales generated on the Sunday project.

The store will have to be lit at a cost of $30 per hour and heated at a cost of $45 per hour. The heating will come on two hours before the store opens in the 25 'winter' weeks to make sure it is warm enough for customers to come in at opening time. The store is not heated in the other weeks.

The rent of the store amounts to $420,000 per annum.

Required

(a) Calculate whether the Sunday opening incremental revenue exceeds the incremental costs over a year (ignore inventory movements) and on this basis reach a conclusion as to whether Sunday opening is financially justifiable. **(12 marks)**

(b) Discuss whether the manager's pay deal (time off and bonus) is likely to motivate them. **(4 marks)**

(c) Briefly discuss whether offering substantial price discounts and promotions on Sunday is a good suggestion. **(4 marks)**

(Total = 20 marks)

139 Robber (6/12)   36 mins

Robber Co manufactures control panels for burglar alarms, a very profitable product. Every product comes with a one-year warranty offering free repairs if any faults arise in this period.

It currently produces and sells 80,000 units per annum, with production of them being restricted by the short supply of labour. Each control panel includes two main components – one key pad and one display screen. At present, Robber Co manufactures both of these components in-house. However, the company is currently considering outsourcing the production of keypads and/or display screens. A newly established company based in Burgistan is keen to secure a place in the market, and has offered to supply the keypads for the equivalent of $4.10 per unit and the display screens for the equivalent of $4.30 per unit. This price has been guaranteed for two years.

The current total annual costs of producing the keypads and the display screens are:

	Keypads	Display screens
Production	80,000 units	80,000 units
	$'000	$'000
Direct materials	160	116
Direct labour	40	60
Heat and power costs	64	88
Machine costs	26	30
Depreciation and insurance costs	84	96
Total annual production costs	374	390

Notes

(1) Materials costs for keypads are expected to increase by 5% in six months' time; materials costs for display screens are only expected to increase by 2%, but with immediate effect.

(2) Direct labour costs are purely variable and not expected to change over the next year.

(3) Heat and power costs include an apportionment of the general factory overhead for heat and power as well as the costs of heat and power directly used for the production of keypads and display screens. The general apportionment included is calculated using 50% of the direct labour cost for each component and would be incurred irrespective of whether the components are manufactured in-house or not.

(4) Machine costs are semi-variable; the variable element relates to set-up costs, which are based upon the number of batches made. The keypads' machine has fixed costs of $4,000 per annum and the display screens' machine has fixed costs of $6,000 per annum. Whilst both components are currently made in batches of 500, this would need to change, with immediate effect, to batches of 400.

(5) 60% of depreciation and insurance costs relate to an apportionment of the general factory depreciation and insurance costs; the remaining 40% is specific to the manufacture of keypads and display screens.

Required

(a) Advise Robber Co whether it should continue to manufacture the keypads and display screens in-house or whether it should outsource their manufacture to the supplier in Burgistan, assuming it continues to adopt a policy to limit manufacture and sales to 80,000 control panels in the coming year. **(8 marks)**

(b) Robber Co takes 0.5 labour hours to produce a keypad and 0.75 labour hours to produce a display screen. Labour hours are restricted to 100,000 hours and labour is paid at $1 per hour. Robber Co wishes to increase its supply to 100,000 control panels (ie 100,000 each of keypads and display screens).

Advise Robber Co as to how many units of keypads and display panels they should either manufacture and/or outsource in order to minimise their costs. **(7 marks)**

(c) Discuss the non-financial factors that Robber Co should consider when making a decision about outsourcing the manufacture of keypads and display screens. **(5 marks)**

(Total = 20 marks)

140 Gam Co (6/14)   36 mins

Gam Co sells electronic equipment and is about to launch a new product onto the market. It needs to prepare its budget for the coming year and is trying to decide whether to launch the product at a price of $30 or $35 per unit. The following information has been obtained from market research:

Price per unit $30		Price per unit $35	
Probability	Sales volume	Probability	Sales volume
0.4	120,000	0.3	108,000
0.5	110,000	0.3	100,000
0.1	140,000	0.4	94,000

Notes

1 Variable production costs would be $12 per unit for production volumes up to and including 100,000 units each year. However, if production exceeds 100,000 units each year, the variable production cost per unit would fall to $11 for all units produced.

2 Advertising costs would be $900,000 per annum at a selling price of $30 and $970,000 per annum at a price of $35.

3 Fixed production costs would be $450,000 per annum.

Required

(a) Calculate each of the six possible profit outcomes which could arise for Gam Co in the coming year.

(8 marks)

(b) Calculate the expected value of profit for each of the two price options and recommend, on this basis, which option Gam Co would choose. **(3 marks)**

(c) Briefly explain the maximin decision rule and identify which price should be chosen by management if they use this rule to decide which price should be charged. **(3 marks)**

(d) Discuss the factors which may give rise to uncertainty when setting budgets. **(6 marks)**

(Total = 20 marks)

141 Cardio Co (Sep/Dec 15 amended)   36 mins

Cardio Co manufactures three types of fitness equipment: treadmills (T), cross trainers (C) and rowing machines (R). The budgeted sales prices and volumes for the next year are as follows:

	T	C	R
Selling price	$1,600	$1,800	$1,400
Units	420	400	380

The standard cost card for each product is shown below.

	T	C	R
	$	$	$
Material	430	500	360
Labour	220	240	190
Variable overheads	110	120	95

Labour costs are 60% fixed and 40% variable. General fixed overheads excluding any fixed labour costs are expected to be $55,000 for the next year.

Required

(a) Calculate the weighted average contribution to sales ratio for Cardio Co. **(4 marks)**

(b) Calculate the margin of safety in $ revenue for Cardio Co. **(3 marks)**

Chart

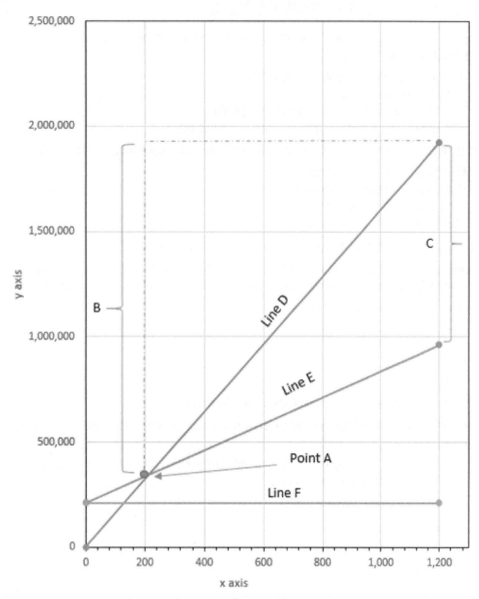

(c) A chart has been drawn assuming that the products are sold in a constant mix. State the type of chart shown, the axis labels and point A, length B, length C, line D, line E and line F. **(6 marks)**

(d) Explain what would happen to the breakeven point if the products were sold in order of the most profitable products first. **(2 marks)**

(e) Explain the limitations of cost volume profit (CVP) analysis. **(5 marks)**

(Total = 20 marks)

PART C: BUDGETING AND CONTROL

Questions 142 to 229 cover Budgeting and control, the subject of Part C of the BPP Study Text for PM.

Section A questions

MCQ bank – Budgeting and control   54 mins

142   Which of the following is the **LEAST** likely reason why standard costs might not easily be applied to road haulage and distribution services?

   ○   It is difficult to measure labour times reliably
   ○   Variable costs are negligible
   ○   It is difficult to identify a standard item for costing
   ○   Standard costing applies to manufacturing industries only   **(2 marks)**

143   For which of the following variances should a production manager usually be held responsible?

   ○   Material price planning variance
   ○   Material price operational variance
   ○   Material usage planning variance
   ○   Material usage operational variance   **(2 marks)**

144   The following statements have been made about standard mix and yield variances.

   (1)   Mix variances should be calculated whenever a standard product contains two or more direct materials.
   (2)   When a favourable mix variance is achieved, there may be a counterbalancing adverse yield variance.

   Which of the above statements is/are true?

   ○   1 only
   ○   2 only
   ○   Neither 1 nor 2
   ○   Both 1 and 2   **(2 marks)**

145   The following statements have been made about flexible budgets.

   (1)   Flexible budgets enable proper comparisons to be made between actual and expected revenues and costs.

   (2)   In every variance reporting system with flexible budgets that compares budgeted and actual profit, there must be a sales volume variance.

   Which of the above statements is/are true?

   ○   1 only
   ○   2 only
   ○   Neither 1 nor 2
   ○   Both 1 and 2   **(2 marks)**

146   A company sells two products X and Y. Product X sells for $30 per unit and achieves a standard contribution of $12 per unit, which is 40% of the selling price. Product Y, a new product, sells for $80 per unit and achieves a standard contribution of just $10 per unit, which is 12.5% of the selling price. Budgeted sales are 5,000 units of X and 3,000 units of Y.

   However, the sudden cancellation of an advertising campaign for Product Y has meant that sales for the product will be well below budget, and there has been some price discounting in an attempt to obtain sales for the product. Sales of X were in line with the budget.

   Which of the following sales variances, if calculated, would you expect to show a favourable variance for the period?

   ○   Sales mix variance
   ○   Sales price variance
   ○   Sales quantity variance
   ○   Sales volume variance   **(2 marks)**

147   Which of the following provides the most suitable definition of the controllability principle in business?

     ○   A fundamental principle of management is the responsibility to control the organisation

     ○   Managers should be held accountable only for costs and revenues over which they have some influence or control

     ○   Organisations should be divided into budget centres for the purpose of operational control

     ○   Performance measures should be reported to managers to enable them to control operations

                                                                                                   (2 marks)

148   The following statements have been made about standard mix and yield variances.

    (1)   Mix and yield variances enable management to resolve problems with the quality of production output.

    (2)   Persistent adverse mix variances may have an adverse effect on sales volume variances and direct labour efficiency variances.

Which of the above statements is/are true?

     ○   1 only
     ○   2 only
     ○   Neither 1 nor 2
     ○   Both 1 and 2   **(2 marks)**

149   The following statements have been made about the application of standard costing systems.

    (1)   Standard costing systems are compatible with a Total Quality Management approach to operations.

    (2)   Standard costing systems are less commonly used in an industry that operates in a rapidly changing environment.

Which of the above statements is/are true?

     ○   1 only
     ○   2 only
     ○   Neither 1 nor 2
     ○   Both 1 and 2   **(2 marks)**

150   The following statements have been made about learning curves.

    (1)   Learning curves are easier to apply in companies with a high labour turnover than those with a lower rate of staff turnover.

    (2)   Learning rates are not affected by time gaps between the production of additional units of a product.

Which of the above statements is/are true?

     ○   1 only
     ○   2 only
     ○   Neither 1 nor 2
     ○   Both 1 and 2   **(2 marks)**

151   The following statements have been made about the use of expected values in budgeting.

    (1)   Expected values may not be expected to occur, which means that probabilistic budgets are of limited value for budgetary control.

    (2)   The use of expected values and probabilities in budgeting is most useful when there is a high level of uncertainty about the future.

Which of the above statements is/are true?

     ○   1 only
     ○   2 only
     ○   Neither 1 nor 2
     ○   Both 1 and 2   **(2 marks)**

152 What are the three building blocks in Fitzgerald and Moon's performance model for a service business?

    ○   Objectives, standards and rewards
    ○   Dimensions, standards and rewards
    ○   Objectives, standards and measures
    ○   Dimensions, rewards and measures   **(2 marks)**

153 For which of the following reasons is zero-based budgeting (ZBB) often considered more suitable for public sector service organisations than for private sector companies?

    ○   ZBB is more suited to costs where there is little discretionary spending, as in the public sector services

    ○   The public sector is better able to afford the high cost of ZBB

    ○   ZBB is used in a top-down approach to budgeting, which is more common in the public sector than the private sector

    ○   It is easier to put public sector activities into decision packages because they are more easily definable than in the private sector   **(2 marks)**

154 The following statements have been made about the use of spreadsheets for budgeting.

    (1)   Spreadsheets greatly assist sensitivity analysis during the planning process.

    (2)   Spreadsheets greatly assist the budgeting process by facilitating the preparation of alternative draft budgets.

    Which of the above statements is/are true?

    ○   1 only
    ○   2 only
    ○   Neither 1 nor 2
    ○   Both 1 and 2   **(2 marks)**

155 A company operates in export and import markets, and its operational cash flows are affected by movements in exchange rates, which are highly volatile. As a result, the company has great difficulty in establishing a budgeting system that is reliable for more than three months ahead.

    Which of the following approaches to budgeting would be most appropriate for this company's situation?

    ○   Flexible budget
    ○   Incremental budget
    ○   Rolling budget
    ○   Zero-based budget   **(2 marks)**

156 Tech World is a company which manufactures mobile phone handsets. From its past experiences, Tech World has realised that whenever a new design engineer is employed, there is a learning curve with a 75% learning rate which exists for the first 15 jobs.

    A new design engineer has just completed their first job in five hours.

    Note. At the learning rate of 75%, the learning factor (b) is equal to −0·415.

    How long would it take the design engineer to complete the sixth job?

    ○   2.377 hours
    ○   1.442 hours
    ○   2.564 hours
    ○   5 hours   **(2 marks)**

                             (Total = 30 marks)

157 The following cost information relates to product XY, which is produced in a continuous process from several different materials.

	$
Actual quantity of materials at standard price	19,960
Actual quantity of materials at actual price	23,120
Actual yield at standard materials cost	20,800
Standard yield from actual input of materials at standard cost	19,552

What is the materials yield variance for the period?

Note. Use minus sign to denote adverse variance.

$ [   ]   **(2 marks)**

158 Which **TWO** of the following statements correctly describe an attainable standard?

☐ This standard is the least useful and most rarely used type of standard.

☐ This standard makes allowances for expected wastage and inefficiencies.

☐ This standard is based on perfect operating conditions.

☐ This standard should give employees a realistic, but challenging target of efficiency   **(2 marks)**

159 The first item of a new product took 2,000 hours to manufacture (at a labour cost of $15 per hour). A 90% learning curve was expected to apply, and it was decided to establish a standard time as the time required to manufacture the 50th item of the product, rounded to the nearest hour. The 50th item actually took 980 hours.

Select two boxes to indicate the labour efficiency variance for the 50th unit produced and whether it is favourable or adverse.

Value ($)	Sign
645	Favourable
43	Adverse
1,860	
1,905	

(2 marks)

160 The following information is given about standard and actual material costs during one month for a production process.

Material	Standard cost per kg	Actual cost per kg	Standard mix	Actual mix kg
P	3.00	3.50	10%	820
Q	2.50	2.75	20%	1,740
R	4.00	3.50	30%	2,300
S	5.25	5.00	40%	2,640
				7,500

What was the materials mix variance?

Note. Use minus sign to denote adverse variance.

$ [   ]   **(2 marks)**

161 A company makes and sells three products. Budgeted and actual results for the period just ended were as follows.

Product	Budgeted sales	Budgeted profit per unit	Actual sales	Actual profit per unit
	Units	$	Units	$
X	800	10	700	8
Y	1,000	6	1,200	6
Z	600	12	350	16
	2,400		2,250	

What was the sales mix variance?

Note. Use minus sign to denote adverse variance.

$ [   ]   **(2 marks)**

162 Which **TWO** of the following are arguments that variance analysis from a standard costing system is redundant in a total quality management environment?

☐ For standard costing to be useful for control purposes, it requires a reasonably stable environment.

☐ The ethos behind a system of standard costing is that performance is satisfactory if it meets predetermined standards.

☐ The control aspect of standard costing systems is achieved by making individual managers responsible for the variances relating to their part of the organisation's activities.

☐ Standard costs are set based on ideal standards rather than attainable ones. **(2 marks)**

163 A standard product uses 3 kg of direct material costing $4 per kg. During the most recent month, 120 units of the product were manufactured. These required 410 kg of material costing $4.50 per kg. It is decided in retrospect that the standard usage quantity of the material should have been 3.5 kg, not 3 kg.

What is the materials operational usage variance, if it is chosen to use planning and operational variances for reporting performance?

Note. Use minus sign to denote adverse variance.

$ [   ]   **(2 marks)**

164 A company makes and sells three products. Budgeted and actual results for the period just ended were as follows.

Product	Budgeted sales	Budgeted profit per unit	Actual sales	Actual profit per unit
	Units	$	Units	$
X	800	10	700	8
Y	1,000	6	1,200	6
Z	600	12	350	16
	2,400		2,250	

What was the sales quantity variance?

Note. Use minus sign to denote adverse variance.

$ [   ]   **(2 marks)**

165   In which **TWO** of the following ways might a budgetary control be a disincentive to management to achieve targeted performance?

☐   Control reports are provided too late

☐   Targets are too easy

☐   Targets are not communicated

☐   Budgets are prepared on a bottom-up basis   **(2 marks)**

166   Which **TWO** of the following statements are true in the context of a just in time (JIT) inventory system?

☐   It can result in much reduced inventory holding costs

☐   It inevitably increases the need for safety inventories

☐   It requires suppliers to operate sound quality control procedures

☐   It works best if supplies are obtained from a number of different suppliers   **(2 marks)**

167   Which **TWO** of the following points state why it is generally regarded to be more difficult to set standards for service function costs than for manufacturing costs?

☐   There is often no measurable output from service functions

☐   The activities of many service functions are of a non-standard nature

☐   The costs of many service functions are predominantly variable

☐   Tasks in many service industries are usually quick and simple   **(2 marks)**

168   Which of the following correctly describes a standard hour?

○   An hour during which only standard units are made
○   An hour during which no machine breakdowns occur
○   The quantity of work achievable at standard performance in an hour
○   An hour for which standard labour rates are paid   **(2 marks)**

169   A company operates in the energy market, and its operational cash flows are affected by movements in the price of oil, which is highly volatile. As a result, the company has great difficulty in establishing a budgeting system that is reliable for more than two or three months ahead.

Which of the following approaches to budgeting would be most appropriate for this company's situation?

○   Flexible budget
○   Incremental budget
○   Rolling budget
○   Zero-based budget   **(2 marks)**

170   What is an attainable standard?

○   A standard which is based on currently attainable working conditions.

○   A standard which is established for use over a long period, which is used to show trends.

○   A standard which can be attained under perfect operating conditions, and which includes no allowance for wastage, spoilage, machine breakdowns and other inefficiencies.

○   A standard which can be attained if production is carried out efficiently, machines are operated properly and/or materials are used properly. Some allowance is made for waste and inefficiencies.

                                                                                         (2 marks)

171   Capacity levels used in setting standard absorption rates for production overheads are often related to performance standards.

To which performance standard is budgeted capacity often associated?

○   Basic standard
○   Attainable standard
○   Ideal standard
○   Current standard   **(2 marks)**

(Total = 30 marks)

Section B questions

MCQ case questions

Crush Co   18 mins

The following scenario relates to questions 172 – 176

Crush Co has developed a new product. The first batch of 100 units will take 1,500 labour hours to produce. Crush Co has estimated that there will be an 85% learning curve that will continue until 6,400 units have been produced. Batches after this level will each take the same amount of time as the 64th batch. The batch size will always be 100 units.

Note. The learning index for an 85% learning curve is –0.2345

Ignore the time value of money.

172   What is the cumulative average time per batch for the first 64 batches?

     ○   567.7 hours
     ○   565.6 hours
     ○   433.3 hours
     ○   570 hours   **(2 marks)**

173   The total time for the first 16 batches of 100 units was 9,000 hours.

     What was the actual learning rate closest to (to the nearest %)?

     ○   80%
     ○   75%
     ○   78%
     ○   73%   **(2 marks)**

174   The following statements have been made about Crush Co and the learning curve:

     (1)   Decisions about allocating resources and costing the new product should be based on the time taken to produce the 64th batch.

     (2)   The learning process does not start until the second batch comes off the production line.

     Which of the above statements is/are true?

     ○   1 only
     ○   2 only
     ○   Neither 1 nor 2
     ○   Both 1 and 2   **(2 marks)**

175   The following statements have been made about the learning curve:

     (1)   The learning curve must assume a certain degree of motivation among employees of Crush Co
     (2)   The learning curve phenomenon is not always present

     Which of the above statements is/are true?

     ○   1 only
     ○   2 only
     ○   Neither 1 nor 2
     ○   Both 1 and 2   **(2 marks)**

176   Which of the following conditions, if present in Crush Co, would allow the learning curve to flourish?

    O   The process is a repetitive one
    O   There is a continuity of workers
    O   There are no prolonged breaks during the production process
    O   All of the above   **(2 marks)**

(Total = 10 marks)

BBB Co   18 mins

The following scenario relates to questions 177 – 181.

BBB Co has developed a new product. The first batch of 50 units will take 750 labour hours to produce. There will be an 90% learning curve that will continue until 3,550 units have been produced. Batches after this level will each take the same amount of time as the 71st batch. The batch size will always be 50 units.

Note. The learning index for a 90% learning curve is –0.152

Ignore the time value of money.

177   What is the time taken for the 71st batch?

    O   392.35 hours
    O   330.75 hours
    O   393.23 hours
    O   345.65 hours   **(2 marks)**

178   The total time for the first 16 batches of units was 8,500 hours.

What was the actual learning rate closest to (to the nearest %)?

    O   92%
    O   89%
    O   78%
    O   85%   **(2 marks)**

179   The following statements have been made about BBB Co and the learning curve:

(1)   The learning effect comes to an end in BBB Co after the 71st unit; however, some learning effects can continue indefinitely.

(2)   The learning curve is restricted to the manufacturing industry.

Which of the above statements is/are true?

    O   1 only
    O   2 only
    O   Neither 1 nor 2
    O   Both 1 and 2   **(2 marks)**

180   The costs of producing more units in BBB Co has been reduced due to the following factors. Which factor from those below is due to the learning curve effect?

    O   Bulk quantity discounts received from the supplier
    O   Lower labour costs
    O   A reduction in materials price
    O   Economies of scale achieved in energy costs   **(2 marks)**

181   The learning curve effect in BBB Co could be extended by which of the following?

    O   Increasing staff turnover
    O   Increasing the level of staff training
    O   Allowing extended breaks in production
    O   Introducing a new mechanised process   **(2 marks)**

(Total = 10 marks)

Spinster Co

18 mins

The following scenario relates to questions 182 – 186.

Spinster Co has developed a new product. The first batch of 10 units will take 300 labour hours to produce. There will be an 80% learning curve that will continue until 540 units have been produced. Batches after this level will each take the same amount of time as the 54th batch. The batch size will always be 10 units.

Note. The learning index for an 80% learning curve is –0.3219

Ignore the time value of money.

182   What is the cumulative average time per batch for the first 54 batches?

    O   4485.78 hours
    O   83.57 hours
    O   83.07 hours
    O   82.58 hours   **(2 marks)**

183   The total time for the first 16 batches of units was 3,300 hours.

    What was the actual learning rate, to the nearest %?

    O   85%
    O   91%
    O   90%
    O   87%   **(2 marks)**

184   Once a 'steady state' was reached in production, Spinster Co set the standard costs for the new product. Which of the following best describes an attainable standard?

    O   A standard which can be attained under perfect operating conditions

    O   A standard based on current working conditions

    O   A long-term standard which remains unchanged over the years and is used to show trends.

    O   A standard which can be achieved if production is carried out efficiently, machines are properly operated and/or materials are properly used.   **(2 marks)**

185   The staff at Spinster Co received incentives based on monthly variance analysis. Six months after setting the standards for the new product, the operating manager reported back to the board to say that despite unfavourable variances being reported each month, staff seemed less motivated to improve the situation in month six, than they were after the first couple of months.

    Based on this information, which of the following standards do you think was applied to the new product?

    O   Ideal
    O   Attainable
    O   Current
    O   Basic   **(2 marks)**

186   Spinster Co wishes to improve its standard costing system by holding managers accountable for the costs over which they have some influence.

    Which of the following costs are not controllable by a production department manager?

    O   Variable production overheads

    O   Direct labour rate

    O   Increases in overall material costs due to high levels of wastage caused by poor supervision of production workers

    O   An increase in the level of idle time because of poorly maintained machines by the production department   **(2 marks)**

                                                                          (Total = 10 marks)

CBE OT case questions

Birch Co

The following scenario relates to questions 187 – 191.

Birch Co budgeted to make and sell 20,000 units of Product X in a four-week period, as follows:

	$
Budgeted sales ($4 per unit per week)	80,000
Variable costs ($2.50 per unit)	50,000
Contribution	30,000
Fixed costs	3,000
Profit	27,000

The actual results for the period were as follows.

	$
Budgeted sales ($4 per unit)	64,000
Variable costs ($2.50 per unit)	40,000
Contribution	24,000
Fixed costs	3,000
Profit	21,000

In retrospect, it is decided that the optimum budget would have been to sell only 17,500 units in the period.

187   Select two boxes to indicate the sales volume planning variance and whether it is favourable or adverse.

Value ($)	Sign
2,250	Favourable
3,750	Adverse

(2 marks)

188   Select two boxes to indicate the sales volume operational variance and whether it is favourable or adverse.

Value ($)	Sign
2,250	Favourable
3,750	Adverse

(2 marks)

189   In a subsequent 4-week period, Birch Co's actual fixed costs were $3,500. There were 18,000 units produced. The budgeted fixed costs was $3,000 based on budgeted production of 17,500 units.

Select two boxes to indicate the fixed production overhead total variance and whether it is favourable or adverse.

Value ($)	Sign
440	Favourable
500	Adverse
525	

(2 marks)

190   Which of the following factors would contribute to a planning variance in Birch Co?

○   A better negotiation of the material price with the supplier
○   An increase in wage costs due to unplanned overtime worked
○   An improvement in technology that led to an international reduction in sales price of Product X
○   A break in production due to a machine breakdown, which was caused by human error   (2 marks)

191 A manager in Birch Co asked for the market share variance. Which of the following variances was she looking for?

Select... ▼
The sales volume planning variance
The sales volume operational variance
The sales price planning variance
The sales price operational variance

(2 marks)

(Total = 10 marks)

Organic Bread Co (Sep/Dec 15 amended)   18 mins

The following scenario relates to questions 192 – 196.

The Organic Bread Company (OBC) makes a range of breads for sale direct to the public. The production process begins with workers weighing out ingredients on electronic scales and then placing them in a machine for mixing. A worker then manually removes the mix from the machine and shapes it into loaves by hand, after which the bread is placed into the oven for baking.

All baked loaves are then inspected by OBC's quality inspector before they are packaged up and made ready for sale. Any loaves which fail the inspection are donated to a local food bank.

The standard cost card for OBC's 'Mixed Bloomer', one of its most popular loaves, is as follows:

			$
White flour	450 grams	at $1.80 per kg	0.81
Wholegrain flour	150 grams	at $2.20 per kg	0.33
Yeast	10 grams	at $20 per kg	0.20
Total	610 grams		1.34

Budgeted production of Mixed Bloomers was 1,000 units for the quarter, although actual production was only 950 units. The total actual quantities used and their actual costs were:

	Kg	$ per kg
White flour	408.50	1.90
Wholegrain flour	152.0	2.10
Yeast	10.0	20.00
Total	570.5	

192 What is the favourable materials usage variance (to two decimal places)?

$ [   ]

(2 marks)

193 Select two boxes to indicate the material mix variance and whether it is favourable or adverse.

Value ($)	Sign
14.17	Favourable
16.51	Adverse

(2 marks)

194 Select two boxes to indicate the material yield variance and whether it is favourable or adverse.

Value ($)	Sign
3.30	Favourable
19.77	Adverse

(2 marks)

195   Indicate, by selecting the relevant boxes in the table below, whether each of the following statements would
       result in an adverse material yield variance in Organic Bread Company?

Not fully removing the mix out of the machine, leaving some behind.	YES	NO
Errors in the mix causing sub-standard loaves and rejections by the quality inspector.	YES	NO
An unexpected increase in the cost of flour introduced by the supplier.	YES	NO

                                                                                        (2 marks)

196   Indicate, by selecting the relevant boxes in the table below, whether each of the following statements would
       result in a material mix variance in Organic Bread Company?

The production manager in Organic Bread Co deviates from the standard mix.	YES	NO
The selling price of the Mixed Bloomer changes.	YES	NO
An inferior quality of flour or yeast is used unknowingly.	YES	NO

                                                                                        (2 marks)

                                                                               (Total = 10 marks)

Elm Co   18 mins

The following scenario relates to questions 197 – 201.

Elm Co is a company which operates in Sealand. Elm Co budgeted to sell 25,000 units of a new product during the
year. The budgeted sales price was $8 per unit, and the variable cost $4 per unit.

Actual sales during the year were 22,000 units and variable costs of sales were $88,000. Sales revenue was only $9
per unit. With the benefit of hindsight, it is realised that the budgeted sales price of $8 was too low, and a price of
$10 per unit would have been much more realistic.

Required

197   What is the favourable sales price planning variance?

       $ [   ]   (2 marks)

198   What is the adverse sales price operational variance?

       $ [   ]   (2 marks)

199   In a subsequent year, the cost of labour was $73,000. 4,000 hours were worked. The budgeted cost of
       labour was $15 per labour hour.

       What is the adverse labour rate variance for this subsequent year?

       $ [   ]   (2 marks)

200   Are the following statements about Elm Co true or false?

The sales manager of Elm Co should be held responsible if an unfavourable planning sales price variance is found.	TRUE	FALSE
It is possible for the revised price to be manipulated and revised to a level whereby a favourable operational sales price could be found.	TRUE	FALSE

                                                                                        (2 marks)

201　Are the following statements about Elm Co true or false?

The operational manager of Elm Co should examine each variance in isolation only.	TRUE	FALSE
A change in economic conditions in Sealand will result in operational variances.	TRUE	FALSE

(2 marks)

(Total = 10 marks)

Maple Co

18 mins

The following scenario relates to questions 202 – 206.

A company made a product called Bark. Bark had a standard direct material cost in the budget of:

2.5 kg of Material X at $4 per kg = $10 per unit.

The average market price for Material X during the period was $5 per kg, and it was decided to revise the material standard cost to allow for this.

During the period, 8,000 units of Bark were manufactured. They required 22,000 kg of Material X, which cost $123,000.

Required

202　What is the adverse material price planning variance?

$ [　　　　　]

(2 marks)

203　What is the adverse material price operational variance?

$ [　　　　　]

(2 marks)

204　What is the adverse material usage operational variance?

$ [　　　　　]

(2 marks)

205　Are the following possible reasons for a material price planning variance valid or invalid?

Maple Co failed to order a sufficient amount of Material X for production from the main supplier. They sourced the rest of the material from another supplier at a higher price to make up for this.	VALID	INVALID
There was a disruption to the supply of Material X to the market.	VALID	INVALID

(2 marks)

206　Are the following statements about variances in Maple Co true or false?

Any operational variances arising should be a realistic measure of what the causes of the variances have cost Maple Co.	TRUE	FALSE
The causes of the planning variances should not be investigated immediately by the operational manager in Maple Co.	TRUE	FALSE

(2 marks)

(Total = 10 marks)

Pine Co

18 mins

The following scenario relates to questions 207 – 211.

Pine Co makes a single product. At the beginning of the budget year, the standard labour cost was established as $45 per unit, and each unit should take 3 hours to make.

However, during the year, the standard labour cost was revised. The labour rate was reduced to $14 per hour, and the revised labour time was 4.5 hours per unit.

In the first month after revision of the standard cost, budgeted production was 10,000 units but only 8,000 units were actually produced. These took 24,300 hours of labour time, which cost $352,350.

Required

207   What is the favourable labour rate planning variance?

$ [   ]   **(2 marks)**

208   What is the adverse labour efficiency planning variance?

$ [   ]   **(2 marks)**

209   What is the adverse labour rate operational variance?

$ [   ]   **(2 marks)**

210   What is the favourable labour efficiency operational variance?

$ [   ]   **(2 marks)**

211   Are the following statements about labour variances in Pine Co true or false?

Production management's motivation is likely to increase if they know they will not be held responsible for poor planning and faulty standard setting.	TRUE	FALSE
Planning variances will provide a more realistic and fair reflection of actual performance.	TRUE	FALSE

(2 marks)

(Total = 10 marks)

Kiss Co

18 mins

The following scenario relates to questions 212 – 216.

Kiss Co has developed a new product. The first batch of 200 units will take 3,500 labour hours to produce. There will be a 75% learning curve that will continue until 4,800 units have been produced. Batches after this level will each take the same amount of time as the 24th batch. The batch size will always be 200 units.

Note. The learning index for a 75% learning curve is –0.415

Ignore the time value of money.

212   What is the time taken for the 24th batch (to the nearest hour)? [   ] hours   **(2 marks)**

213   The total time for the first 16 batches of units was 22,000 hours.

What was the actual learning rate, to the nearest %? [   ] %   **(2 marks)**

214   Kiss Co makes another product, the Lyco. The learning effect stopped after the 16th batch of product, and a 'steady state' was reached. Workers in Kiss Co received $15 per hour. The first batch of Lyco took 0.75 hours to produce. The 16th batch of Lyco took 0.5 hours, and the standard cost was revised to this figure once the 'steady state' was reached. Kiss Co produced 10,000 batches of Lyco during the year.

What is the favourable labour efficiency planning variance? $ [   ]   **(2 marks)**

215   Are the following statements about Kiss Co true or false?

Because of the learning effect, the labour efficiency planning variance of Lyco will always be favourable.	TRUE	FALSE
A standard labour cost should only be established when a 'steady state' is reached.	TRUE	FALSE

(2 marks)

216   In which of the following ways might an operational manager in Kiss Co try to improve labour efficiency and achieve favourable labour efficiency variances?

○   Increase output volumes
○   Increase inspection and testing of products
○   Provide workers with training
○   Arrange for overtime working

(2 marks)

(Total = 10 marks)

Section C questions

217 Mic Co (12/13)

36 mins

Mic Co produces microphones for mobile phones and operates a standard costing system. Before production commenced, the standard labour time per batch for its latest microphone was estimated to be 200 hours. The standard labour cost per hour is $12 and resource allocation and cost data were therefore initially prepared on this basis.

Production of the microphone started in July and the number of batches assembled and sold each month was as follows:

Month	No of batches assembled and sold
July	1
August	1
September	2
October	4
November	8

The first batch took 200 hours to make, as anticipated, but, during the first four months of production, a learning effect of 88% was observed, although this finished at the end of October. The learning formula is shown on the formula sheet and at the 88% learning rate the value of b is −0.1844245.

Mic Co uses 'cost plus' pricing to establish selling prices for all its products. Sales of its new microphone in the first five months have been disappointing. The sales manager has blamed the production department for getting the labour cost so wrong, as this, in turn, caused the price to be too high. The production manager has disclaimed all responsibility, saying that, 'as usual, the managing director prepared the budgets alone and didn't consult me and, had he bothered to do so, I would have told him that a learning curve was expected.'

Required

(a) Calculate the actual total monthly labour costs for producing the microphones for each of the five months from July to November. **(9 marks)**

(b) Discuss the implications of the learning effect coming to an end for Mic Co, with regard to costing, budgeting and production. **(4 marks)**

(c) Discuss the potential advantages and disadvantages of involving senior staff at Mic Co in the budget-setting process, rather than the managing director simply imposing budgets on them. **(7 marks)**

(Total = 20 marks)

218 ZBB (12/10)

36 mins

Some commentators argue that: 'With continuing pressure to control costs and maintain efficiency, the time has come for all public sector organisations to embrace zero-based budgeting. There is no longer a place for incremental budgeting in any organisation, particularly public sector ones, where zero-based budgeting is far more suitable anyway.'

Required

(a) Discuss the particular difficulties encountered when budgeting in public sector organisations compared with budgeting in private sector organisations, drawing comparisons between the two types of organisation.

(5 marks)

(b) Explain the terms 'incremental budgeting' and 'zero-based budgeting'. **(4 marks)**

(c) State the main stages involved in preparing zero-based budgets. **(3 marks)**

(d) Discuss the view that 'there is no longer a place for incremental budgeting in any organisation, particularly public sector ones', highlighting any drawbacks of zero-based budgeting that need to be considered.

(8 marks)

(Total = 20 marks)

219 Designit (12/12)

Designit is a small company providing design consultancy to a limited number of large clients. The business is mature and fairly stable, year on year. It has 30 employees and is privately owned by its founder. Designit prepares an annual fixed budget. The company's accounts department consists of one part-qualified accountant who has a heavy workload. They prepare the budget using spreadsheets. The company has a November year end.

Designit pays each of its three sales managers an annual salary of $150,000, plus an individual bonus based on sales targets set at the beginning of the year. There are always two levels of bonus that can be earned, based on a lower and an upper level of fee income. For the year ended 30 November 20X2, for example, each of the sales managers was given a lower target of securing $1.5m of fee income each, to be rewarded by an individual bonus equating to 20% of salary. If any of the managers secured a further $1.5m of fee income, their bonus would increase by 5% to the upper target of 25%. None of the managers achieved the upper target but all of them achieved the lower one.

This is the same every year and Designit finds that often the managers secure work from several major clients early in the year and reach the $1.5m target well before the year has ended. They then make little effort to secure extra fees for the company, knowing that it would be almost impossible to hit the second target. This, together with a few other problems that have arisen, has made the company consider whether its current budgeting process could be improved and whether the bonus scheme should also be changed.

Designit is now considering replacing the fixed budget with a monthly rolling budget, which Designit believes will make the budgeting process more relevant and timely and encourage managers to focus on the future rather than the past. It would also prevent the problem of targets being met too early on in the year by the sales managers, because the targets would be set for monthly performance rather than annual performance. For example, a manager could be given a target of securing $200,000 fee income in the first month for a reward of 2% of salary. Then, depending on what is happening both within the business and in the economy as a whole, at the end of the first month, a different target fee income could be set for the second month.

Required

(a) Explain what a monthly rolling budget is and how it would operate at Designit. **(4 marks)**

(b) Discuss the problems that may be encountered if Designit decides to introduce monthly rolling budgets together with a new bonus scheme, such as the one outlined above. **(6 marks)**

(c) Discuss the problems with the current bonus scheme and, assuming that the company decides against introducing rolling budgets, describe and justify an alternative, more effective bonus scheme that could be introduced. **(6 marks)**

(d) Discuss the risk of using the company accountant's own spreadsheets for budgeting. **(4 marks)**

(Total = 20 marks)

220 Crumbly Cakes (6/09 amended)

Crumbly Cakes makes cakes, which are sold directly to the public. The new production manager (a celebrity chef) has argued that the business should use only organic ingredients in its cake production. Organic ingredients are more expensive but should produce a product with an improved flavour and give health benefits for the customers. It was hoped that this would stimulate demand and enable an immediate price increase for the cakes.

Crumbly Cakes operates a responsibility-based standard costing system which allocates variances to specific individuals. The individual managers are paid a bonus only when net favourable variances are allocated to them.

The new organic cake production approach was adopted at the start of March 20X9, following a decision by the new production manager. No change was made at that time to the standard costs card. The variance reports for February and March are shown below (Fav = Favourable and Adv = Adverse).

Manager responsible	Allocated variances	February variance $	March variance $
Production manager	Material price (total for all ingredients)	25 Fav	2,100 Adv
	Material mix	0	600 Adv
	Material yield	20 Fav	400 Fav
Sales manager	Sales price	40 Adv	7,000 Fav
	Sales contribution volume	35 Adv	3,000 Fav

The production manager is upset that they seem to have lost all hope of a bonus under the new system. The sales manager thinks the new organic cakes are excellent and is very pleased with the progress made.

Crumbly Cakes operates a JIT inventory system and holds virtually no inventory.

Required

(a) Assess the performance of the production manager and the sales manager and indicate whether the current bonus scheme is fair to those concerned. **(7 marks)**

In April 20X9 the following data applied:

Standard cost card for one cake (not adjusted for the organic ingredient change)

Ingredients	Kg	$
Flour	0.10	0.12 per kg
Eggs	0.10	0.70 per kg
Butter	0.10	1.70 per kg
Sugar	0.10	0.50 per kg
Total input	0.40	
Normal loss (10%)	(0.04)	
Standard weight of a cake	0.36	

The budget for production and sales in April was 50,000 cakes. Actual production and sales was 60,000 cakes in the month, during which the following occurred:

Ingredients used	Kg	$
Flour	5,700	$741
Eggs	6,600	$5,610
Butter	6,600	$11,880
Sugar	4,578	$2,747
Total input	23,478	$20,978
Actual loss	(1,878)	
Actual output of cake mixture	21,600	

All cakes produced must weigh 0.36 kg, as this is what is advertised.

Required

(b) Calculate the material price, mix and yield variances for April. You are not required to make any comment on the performance of the managers. **(9 marks)**

With the benefit of hindsight the management of Crumbly Cakes realises that a more realistic standard cost for current conditions would be $0.40 per cake. The planned standard cost is unrealistically low.

Required

(c) Calculate the total cost planning and operational variances for April. Briefly comment on each variance. **(4 marks)**

(Total = 20 marks)

221 Secure Net (12/09 amended)

36 mins

Secure Net (SN) manufactures security cards that restrict access to government-owned buildings around the world.

The standard cost for the plastic that goes into making a card is $4 per kg and each card uses 40 g of plastic after an allowance for waste. In November 100,000 cards were produced and sold by SN and this was well above the budgeted sales of 60,000 cards.

The actual cost of the plastic was $5.25 per kg and the production manager (who is responsible for all buying and production issues) was asked to explain the increase. They said 'World oil price increases pushed up plastic prices by 20% compared to our budget and I also decided to use a different supplier who promised better quality and increased reliability for a slightly higher price. I know we have overspent but not all the increase in plastic prices is my fault. The actual usage of plastic per card was 35 g per card and again the production manager had an explanation. They said 'The world-wide standard size for security cards increased by 5% due to a change in the card reader technology; however, our new supplier provided much better quality of plastic and this helped to cut down on the waste.'

SN operates a just-in-time (JIT) system and hence carries very little inventory.

Required

(a)   Discuss the behavioural problems that can arise from using standard costs and ways to prevent them.

(4 marks)

(b)   Analyse the above total variances into component parts for planning and operational variances in as much detail as the information allows.   (8 marks)

(c)   Assess the performance of the production manager.   (8 marks)

(Total = 20 marks)

222 Noble (6/11)

36 mins

Noble is a restaurant that is only open in the evenings, on **six** days of the week. It has eight restaurant and kitchen staff, each paid a wage of $8 per hour on the basis of hours actually worked. It also has a restaurant manager and a head chef, each of whom is paid a monthly salary of $4,300. Noble's budget and actual figures for the month of May was as follows:

	Budget	$	Actual	$
Number of meals	1,200		1,560	
	$		$	
Revenue: Food	48,000		60,840	
Drinks	12,000		11,700	
		60,000		72,540
Variable costs:				
Staff wages	(9,216)		(13,248)	
Food costs	(6,000)		(7,180)	
Drink costs	(2,400)		(5,280)	
Energy costs	(3,387)		(3,500)	
		(21,003)		(29,208)
Contribution		38,997		43,332
Fixed costs:				
Manager's and chef's pay	(8,600)		(8,600)	
Rent, rates and depreciation	(4,500)	(13,100)	(4,500)	(13,100)
Operating profit		25,897		30,232

The budget above is based on the following assumptions:

(1) The restaurant is only open six days a week and there are four weeks in a month. The average number of orders each day is 50 and demand is evenly spread across all the days in the month.

(2) The restaurant offers two meals: Meal A, which costs $35 per meal and Meal B, which costs $45 per meal. In addition to this, irrespective of which meal the customer orders, the average customer consumes four drinks each at $2.50 per drink. Therefore, the average spend per customer is either $45 or $55 including drinks, depending on the type of meal selected. The May budget is based on 50% of customers ordering Meal A and 50% of customers ordering Meal B.

(3) Food costs represent 12.5% of revenue from food sales.

(4) Drink costs represent 20% of revenue from drinks sales.

(5) When the number of orders per day does not exceed 50, each member of hourly paid staff is required to work exactly six hours per day. For every incremental increase of five in the average number of orders per day, each member of staff has to work 0.5 hours of overtime for which they are paid at the increased rate of $12 per hour. You should assume that all costs for hourly paid staff are treated wholly as variable costs.

(6) Energy costs are deemed to be related to the total number of hours worked by each of the hourly paid staff, and are absorbed at the rate of $2.94 per hour worked by each of the eight staff.

Required

(a) Prepare a flexed budget for the month of May, assuming that the standard mix of customers remains the same as budgeted.
(12 marks)

(b) After preparation of the flexed budget, you are informed that the following variances have arisen in relation to total food and drink sales:

Sales mix contribution variance $1,014 Adverse
Sales quantity contribution variance $11,700 Favourable

BRIEFLY describe the sales mix contribution variance and the sales quantity contribution variance. Identify why each of them has arisen in Noble's case.
(4 marks)

(c) Noble's owner told the restaurant manager to run a half-price drinks promotion at Noble for the month of May on all drinks. Actual results showed that customers ordered an average of six drinks each instead of the usual four but, because of the promotion, they only paid half of the usual cost for each drink. You have calculated the sales margin price variance for drink sales alone and found it to be a worrying $11,700 adverse. The restaurant manager is worried and concerned that this makes their performance for drink sales look very bad.

Required

Briefly discuss **TWO** other variances that could be calculated for drinks sales or food sales in order to ensure that the assessment of the restaurant manager's performance is fair. These should be variances that **COULD** be calculated from the information provided above although no further calculations are required here.
(4 marks)

(Total = 20 marks)

223 Truffle Co (12/12)

36 mins

Truffle Co makes high quality, hand-made chocolate truffles which it sells to a local retailer. All chocolates are made in batches of 16, to fit the standard boxes supplied by the retailer. The standard cost of labour for each batch is $6.00 and the standard labour time for each batch is half an hour. In November, Truffle Co had budgeted production of 24,000 batches; actual production was only 20,500 batches. 12,000 labour hours were used to complete the work and there was no idle time. All workers were paid for their actual hours worked. The actual total labour cost for November was $136,800. The production manager at Truffle Co has no input into the budgeting process.

At the end of October, the managing director decided to hold a meeting and offer staff the choice of either accepting a 5% pay cut or facing a certain number of redundancies. All staff subsequently agreed to accept the 5% pay cut with immediate effect.

At the same time, the retailer requested that the truffles be made slightly softer. This change was implemented immediately and made the chocolates more difficult to shape. When recipe changes such as these are made, it takes time before the workers become used to working with the new ingredient mix, making the process 20% slower for at least the first month of the new operation.

The standard costing system is only updated once a year, in June, and no changes are ever made to the system outside of this.

Required

(a) Calculate the total labour rate and total labour efficiency variances for November, based on the standard cost provided above. **(4 marks)**

(b) Analyse the total labour rate and total labour efficiency variances into component parts for planning and operational variances in as much detail as the information allows. **(8 marks)**

(c) Assess the performance of the production manager for the month of November. **(8 marks)**

(Total = 20 marks)

224 Block Co (6/13)

36 mins

Block Co operates an absorption costing system and sells three types of product – Commodity 1, Commodity 2 and Commodity 3. Like other competitors operating in the same market, Block Co is struggling to maintain revenues and profits in face of the economic recession which has engulfed the country over the last two years. Sales prices fluctuate in the market in which Block Co operates. Consequently, at the beginning of each quarter, a market specialist, who works on a consultancy basis for Block Co, sets a budgeted sales price for each product for the quarter, based on their expectations of the market. This then becomes the 'standard selling price' for the quarter. The sales department itself is run by the company's sales manager, who negotiates the actual sales prices with customers. The following budgeted figures are available for the quarter ended 31 May 20X3.

Product	Budgeted production and sales units	Standard selling price per unit	Standard variable production costs per unit
Commodity 1	30,000	$30	$18
Commodity 2	28,000	$35	$28.40
Commodity 3	26,000	$41.60	$26.40

Block Co uses absorption costing. Fixed production overheads are absorbed on the basis of direct machine hours and the budgeted cost of these for the quarter ended 31 May 20X3 was $174,400. Commodities 1, 2 and 3 use 0.2 hours, 0.6 hours and 0.8 hours of machine time respectively.

BPP
LEARNING MEDIA

Questions 63

The following data shows the actual sales prices and volumes achieved for each product by Block Co for the quarter ended 31 May 20X3 and the average market prices per unit.

Product	Actual production and sales units	Actual selling price per unit	Average market price per unit
Commodity 1	29,800	$31	$32.20
Commodity 2	30,400	$34	$33.15
Commodity 3	25,600	$40.40	$39.10

The following variances have already been correctly calculated for Commodities 1 and 2:

Sales price operational variances

Commodity 1: $35,760 Adverse
Commodity 2: $25,840 Favourable

Sales price planning variances

Commodity 1: $65,560 Favourable
Commodity 2: $56,240 Adverse

Required

(a) Calculate, for Commodity 3 only, the sales price operational variance and the sales price planning variance.

(4 marks)

(b) Using the data provided for Commodities 1, 2 and 3, calculate the total sales mix variance and the total sales quantity variance.

(11 marks)

(c) Briefly discuss the performance of the business and, in particular, that of the sales manager for the quarter ended 31 May 20X3.

(5 marks)

(Total = 20 marks)

225 Newtown School (6/13)

36 mins

Newtown School's head teacher has prepared the budget for the year ending 31 May 20X4. The government pays the school $1,050 for each child registered at the beginning of the school year, which is June 1, and $900 for any child joining the school part-way through the year. The school does not have to refund the money to the government if a child leaves the school part-way through the year. The number of pupils registered at the school on 1 June 20X3 is 690, which is 10% lower than the previous year. Based on past experience, the probabilities for the number of pupils starting the school part-way through the year are as follows:

Probability	No of pupils joining late
0.2	50
0.3	20
0.5	26

The head teacher admits to being 'poor with numbers' and does not understand probabilities so, when calculating budgeted revenue, he just calculates a simple average for the number of pupils expected to join late. His budgeted revenue for the year ending 31 May 20X4 is therefore as follows:

	Pupils	Rate per pupil	Total income
Pupils registered at beginning of school year	690	$1,050	$724,500
Average expected number of new joiners	32	$900	$28,800
			$753,300

The head teacher uses incremental budgeting to budget for his expenditure, taking actual expenditure for the previous year as a starting point and simply adjusting it for inflation, as shown below.

	Note	Actual cost for y/e 31 May 20X3 $	Inflationary adjustment	Budgeted cost for y/e 31 May 20X4 $
Repairs and maintenance	1	44,000	+ 3%	45,320
Salaries	2	620,000	+ 2%	632,400
Capital expenditure	3	65,000	+ 6%	68,900
Total budgeted expenditure				746,620
Budget surplus				6,680

Notes

1   $30,000 of the costs for the year ended 31 May 20X3 related to standard maintenance checks and repairs that have to be carried out by the school every year in order to comply with government health and safety standards. These are expected to increase by 3% in the coming year. In the year ended 31 May 20X3, $14,000 was also spent on redecorating some of the classrooms. No redecorating is planned for the coming year.

2   One teacher earning a salary of $26,000 left the school on 31 May 20X3 and there are no plans to replace her. However, a 2% pay rise will be given to all staff with effect from 1 December 20X3.

3   The full $65,000 actual costs for the year ended 31 May 20X3 related to improvements made to the school gym. This year, the canteen is going to be substantially improved, although the extent of the improvements and level of service to be offered to pupils is still under discussion. There is a 0.7 probability that the cost will be $145,000 and a 0.3 probability that it will be $80,000. These costs must be paid in full before the end of the year ending 31 May 20X4.

The school's board of governors, who review the budget, are concerned that the budget surplus has been calculated incorrectly. They believe that it should have been calculated using expected income, based on the probabilities provided, and using expected expenditure, based on the information provided in notes 1 to 3. They believe that incremental budgeting is not proving a reliable tool for budget setting in the school since, for the last three years, there have been shortfalls of cash despite a budget surplus being predicted. Since the school has no other source of funding available to it, these shortfalls have had serious consequences, such as the closure of the school kitchen for a considerable period in the last school year, meaning that no hot meals were available to pupils. This is thought to have been the cause of the 10% fall in the number of pupils registered at the school on 1 June 20X3.

Required

(a)   Considering the views of the board of governors, recalculate the budget surplus/deficit for the year ending 31 May 20X4.   **(6 marks)**

(b)   Discuss the advantages and disadvantages of using incremental budgeting.   **(4 marks)**

(c)   Briefly outline the three main steps involved in preparing a zero-based budget.   **(6 marks)**

(d)   Discuss the extent to which zero-based budgeting could be used by Newtown School to improve the budgeting process.   **(4 marks)**

(Total = 20 marks)

226 Bedco (12/13)

36 mins

Bedco manufactures bed sheets and pillowcases, which it supplies to a major hotel chain. It uses a just-in-time system and holds no inventories.

The standard cost for the cotton which is used to make the bed sheets and pillowcases is $5 per m^2.

Each bed sheet uses 2 m^2 of cotton and each pillowcase uses 0.5 m^2. Production levels for bed sheets and pillowcases for November were as follows:

	Budgeted production levels Units	Actual production levels Units
Bed sheets	120,000	120,000
Pillow cases	190,000	180,000

The actual cost of the cotton in November was $5.80 per m^2. 248,000 m^2 of cotton was used to make the bed sheets and 95,000 m^2 was used to make the pillowcases.

The world commodity prices for cotton increased by 20% in the month of November. At the beginning of the month, the hotel chain made an unexpected request for an immediate design change to the pillowcases. The new design required 10% more cotton than previously. It also resulted in production delays and therefore a shortfall in production of 10,000 pillowcases in total that month.

The production manager at Bedco is responsible for all buying and any production issues which occur, although they are not responsible for the setting of standard costs.

Required

(a) Calculate the following variances for the month of November, for both bed sheets and pillow cases, and in total:

    (i)   Total material price planning variance   **(3 marks)**
    (ii)   Total material price operational variance   **(3 marks)**
    (iii)   Total material usage planning variance   **(3 marks)**
    (iv)   Total material usage operational variance   **(3 marks)**

(b) Assess the performance of the production manager for the month of November.   **(8 marks)**

(Total = 20 marks)

227 Valet Co (6/14)

36 mins

Valet Co is a car valeting (cleaning) company. It operates in the country of Strappia, which has been badly affected by the global financial crisis. Petrol and food prices have increased substantially in the last year and the average disposable household income has decreased by 30%. Recent studies have shown that the average car owner keeps their car for five years before replacing it, rather than three years as was previously the case. Figures over recent years also show that car sales in Strappia are declining, while business for car repairs is on the increase.

Valet Co offers two types of valet – a full valet and a mini valet. A full valet is an extensive clean of the vehicle, inside and out; a mini valet is a more basic clean of the vehicle. Until recently, four similar businesses operated in Valet Co's local area, but one of these closed down three months ago after a serious fire on its premises. Valet Co charges customers $50 for each full valet and $30 for each mini valet and this price never changes. Their budget and actual figures for the last year were as follows:

	Budget		Actual	
Number of valets:				
Full valets	3,600		4,000	
Mini valets	2,000		3,980	
	$	$	$	$
Revenue		240,000		319,400
Variable costs:				
Staff wages	(114,000)		(122,000)	
Cleaning materials	(6,200)		(12,400)	
Energy costs	(6,520)		(9,200)	
		(126,720)		(143,600)
Contribution		113,280		175,800
	$	$	$	$
Fixed costs:				
Rent, rates and depreciation		(36,800)		(36,800)
Operating profit		76,480		139,000

The budgeted contribution to sales ratios for the two types of valet are 44.6% for full valets and 55% for mini valets.

Required

(a) Using the data provided for full valets and mini valets, calculate:

(i) The total sales mix contribution variance **(4 marks)**
(ii) The total sales quantity contribution variance **(4 marks)**

(b) Briefly describe the sales mix contribution variance and the sales quantity contribution variance. **(2 marks)**

(c) Discuss the **SALES** performance of the business for the period, taking into account your calculations from part (a) **AND** the information provided in the scenario. **(10 marks)**

(Total = 20 marks)

228 Glove Co (Mar/Jun 16 amended) 36 mins

Glove Co makes high quality, hand-made gloves which it sells for an average of $180 per pair. The standard cost of labour for each pair is $42 and the standard labour time for each pair is three hours. In the last quarter, Glove Co had budgeted production of 12,000 pairs, although actual production was 12,600 pairs in order to meet demand. 37,000 hours were used to complete the work and there was no idle time. The total labour cost for the quarter was $531,930.

At the beginning of the last quarter, the design of the gloves was changed slightly. The new design required workers to sew the company's logo onto the back of every glove made and the estimated time to do this was 15 minutes for each pair. However, no-one told the accountant responsible for updating standard costs that the standard time per pair of gloves needed to be changed. Similarly, although all workers were given a 2% pay rise at the beginning of the last quarter, the accountant was not told about this either. Consequently, the standard was not updated to reflect these changes.

When overtime is required, workers are paid 25% more than their usual hourly rate.

Required

(a) Calculate the total labour rate and total labour efficiency variances for the last quarter. **(2 marks)**

(b) Analyse the above total variances into component parts for planning and operational variances in as much detail as the information allows. **(6 marks)**

(c) Explain what is meant by the controllability principle and assess the performance of the production manager for the last quarter. **(12 marks)**

(Total = 20 marks)

229 SU Co (Mar/Jun 17)

36 mins

The School Uniform Company (SU Co) manufactures school uniforms. One of its largest contracts is with the Girls' Private School Trust (GPST), which has 35 schools across the country, all with the same school uniform.

After a recent review of the uniform at the GPST schools, the school's spring/summer dress has been re-designed to incorporate a dropped waistband. Each new dress now requires 2.2 metres of material, which is 10% more material than the previous style of dress required. However, a new material has also been chosen by the GPST which costs only $2.85 per metre which is 5% cheaper than the material used on the previous dresses. In February, the total amount of material used and purchased at this price was 54,560 metres.

The design of the new dresses has meant that a complicated new sewing technique needed to be used. Consequently, all staff required training before they could begin production. The manager of the sewing department expected each of the new dresses to take 10 minutes to make as compared to 8 minutes per dress for the old style. SU Co has 24 staff, each of whom works 160 hours per month and is paid a wage of $12 per hour. All staff worked all of their contracted hours in February on production of the GPST dresses and there was no idle time. No labour rate variance arose in February.

Activity levels for February were as follows:

Budgeted production and sales (units)   30,000

Actual production and sales (units)   24,000

The production manager at SU Co is responsible for all purchasing and production issues which occur. SU Co uses standard costing and usually, every time a design change takes place, the standard cost card is updated prior to production commencing. However, the company accountant responsible for updating the standards has been off sick for the last two months. Consequently, the standard cost card for the new dress has not yet been updated.

Required

(a)   Calculate the material variances in as much detail as the information allows for the month of February.

(7 marks)

(b)   Calculate the labour efficiency variances in as much detail as the information allows for the month of February.

(5 marks)

(c)   Assess the performance of the production manager for the month of February.   **(8 marks)**

(Total = 20 marks)

PART D: PERFORMANCE MEASUREMENT AND CONTROL

Questions 230 to 320 cover Performance measurement and control, the subject of Part D of the BPP Study Text for PM.

Section A questions

MCQ bank – Performance measurement and control   90 mins

230   The following statements have been made about a transfer pricing system where Division A transfers output to Division B.

    (1)   Internal transfers should be preferred when there is an external market for the transferred item, because there will be more control over quality and delivery.

    (2)   The transfer price will determine how profits will be shared between the two divisions.

    Which of the above statements is/are true?

    O   1 only
    O   2 only
    O   Neither 1 nor 2
    O   Both 1 and 2   **(2 marks)**

231   The following statements have been made about performance measurements in not-for-profit organisations.

    (1)   Not-for-profit organisations do not have financial objectives.

    (2)   The outputs produced by not-for-profit organisations are easier to measure than output of commercial companies.

    Which of the above statements is/are true?

    O   1 only
    O   2 only
    O   Neither 1 nor 2
    O   Both 1 and 2   **(2 marks)**

232   Which of the following figures would be the most suitable for divisional profit for the purpose of performance measurement?

    O   Gross profit
    O   Profit before interest and tax
    O   Profit before tax
    O   Profit after tax   **(2 marks)**

233   A hospital wishes to establish a performance measurement for its 'quality of care', and in particular its adherence to appointment times for patients receiving medical checks.

    Which of the following performance measurements would be the most suitable for this purpose?

    O   Average length of appointments
    O   Average number of appointments per day
    O   Average number of days from making an appointment to the appointment date
    O   Average waiting time at the hospital   **(2 marks)**

234 A company that uses a balanced scorecard approach to performance measurement has recorded the following data for the previous financial year.

	Products made and sold for at least 2 years	Products introduced to market within the previous two years = 'new products'	Total
Number of products	16	4	
Annual sales	$3.0 million	$0.50 million	$3.50 million
Cost of sales	$2.4 million	$0.42 million	$2.82 million
Hours worked	27,500	4,500	
Research and development costs			$150,000

Which of the following would be the most suitable measure of performance from the innovation and learning perspective in a balanced scorecard?

- O   Development cost per new product
- O   Sales revenue per new product
- O   Sales revenue from new products as a percentage of total revenue
- O   Sales revenue per hour worked on new products   **(2 marks)**

235 Which of the following measures of performance for public sector services is a measure of efficiency?

- O   Number of patients treated per $1 spent on the state hospital service

- O   Percentage reduction in the spending budget of a government department compared with the previous year

- O   Proportion of reported crimes that are solved by the police service

- O   Proportion of students in a state-owned college achieving good pass grades in their examinations
                                                                                            (2 marks)

236 The following statements have been made about data and information.

(1) Automated systems for data capture are generally more reliable than data capture requiring input by individuals.

(2) As a general rule, secondary information is more expensive to collect than primary data.

Which of the above statements is/are true?

- O   1 only
- O   2 only
- O   Neither 1 nor 2
- O   Both 1 and 2   **(2 marks)**

237 When goods are transferred from one division in a company to another division, and there is an intermediate external market for the transferred item in which the goods could be sold, which of the following states the economic transfer pricing rule for what the maximum transfer price should be?

- O   Marginal cost of the transferring-out division minus any lost contribution of the transferring-out division from having to make the internal transfer

- O   The higher of the net marginal revenue for the transferring-in division and the external purchase price in the market for the intermediate product

- O   The lower of the net marginal revenue for the transferring-in division and the external purchase price in the market for the intermediate product

- O   None of the above   **(2 marks)**

238 A company has a call centre to handle queries and complaints from customers. The company is concerned about the average length of calls and the time that it takes to deal with customers. As part of its balanced scorecard, it has set a target for reducing the average time per customer call.

A target for reducing the average time per call would relate to which of the four balanced scorecard perspectives?

- ○ Customer perspective
- ○ Financial perspective
- ○ Innovation and learning perspective
- ○ Internal business (operational) perspective **(2 marks)**

239 The following statements have been made about management information and management information systems.

(1) Management information is often produced from transaction processing systems.

(2) The data used in management information systems comes mainly from sources within the organisation and its operations.

Which of the above statements is/are true?

- ○ 1 only
- ○ 2 only
- ○ Neither 1 nor 2
- ○ Both 1 and 2 **(2 marks)**

240 The following statements have been made about operational control.

(1) Budgeting is commonly associated with decision making at the operational planning level within a management hierarchy.

(2) Operational control decisions in general are more narrowly focused and have a shorter time horizon than management control decisions.

Which of the above statements is/are true?

- ○ 1 only
- ○ 2 only
- ○ Neither 1 nor 2
- ○ Both 1 and 2 **(2 marks)**

241 Which of the following terms is used to describe an information system that provides senior executives with online access to important information obtained from both internal and external sources?

- ○ Executive information system
- ○ Enterprise resource planning system
- ○ Management information system
- ○ Transaction processing system **(2 marks)**

242 In a balanced scorecard system of performance measurement, which of the following is most likely to be used as a measure of performance from the customer perspective?

- ○ Increase in size of product range
- ○ Percentage of customers making repeat orders
- ○ Number of orders won per sales representative
- ○ Speed of processing an order **(2 marks)**

243 The following statements have been made about performance measurements in not-for-profit organisations.

(1) Providing value for money (VFM) means providing a service that is cheap, efficient and effective.

(2) For the refuse collection department of a local government authority, the efficiency of operations can be measured by the proportion of collected refuse that is recycled.

Which of the above statements is/are true?

○ 1 only
○ 2 only
○ Neither 1 nor 2
○ Both 1 and 2   (2 marks)

244 The following statements have been made about divisionalisation and performance measurement systems.

(1) Residual income as a measure of performance enables fair comparisons to be made between the performances of different divisions in the company.

(2) When a transfer price is based on cost because there is no external market for the transferred item, at least one of the divisional managers is likely to consider the transfer price as 'unfair'.

Which of the above statements is/are true?

○ 1 only
○ 2 only
○ Neither 1 nor 2
○ Both 1 and 2   (2 marks)

245 Which of the following aspects of performance is measured by the average time between receipt of an order from a customer and the time the goods are despatched?

○ Quality
○ Quantity
○ Reliability
○ Speed   (2 marks)

246 In the Fitzgerald and Moon model of performance measurement in service businesses, which of the following dimensions of performance reflects past results or achievements, rather than provides a guide or determinant for future performance?

○ Competitiveness
○ Flexibility
○ Quality
○ Resource utilisation   (2 marks)

247 Which of the following is **NOT** usually a consequence of divisionalisation?

○ Duplication of some activities and costs
○ Goal congruence in decision making
○ Faster decision making at operational level
○ Reduction in head office control over operations   (2 marks)

248 The following statements have been made about the measurement of ROI and residual income.

(1) ROI is usually measured as divisional operating profit before deducting depreciation as a percentage of the division's capital employed.

(2) Residual income is calculated after deducting both depreciation on non-current assets and notional interest on the division's capital employed.

Which of the above statements is/are true?

○ 1 only
○ 2 only
○ Neither 1 nor 2
○ Both 1 and 2   (2 marks)

249 For which of the following reasons are controls needed over internally generated information?

(1) To prevent information overload
(2) To prevent unauthorised dissemination of information

○ 1 only
○ 2 only
○ Neither 1 nor 2
○ Both 1 and 2   (2 marks)

250 The following statements have been made about information systems.

(1) Feedback is information produced from a system that is used by management to take action to control further inputs to the system.

(2) Information for benchmarking purposes may be obtained from both internal and external sources.

Which of the above statements is/are true?

○ 1 only
○ 2 only
○ Neither 1 nor 2
○ Both 1 and 2   (2 marks)

251 The following statements have been made about transfer pricing.

(1) Transfer pricing is almost inevitably required when a business is structured as more than one division and some divisions provide goods or services to other divisions.

(2) Where a perfect external market price exists and unit variable costs and unit selling prices are constant, the opportunity cost of transfer will be external market price or external market price less savings in selling costs.

Which of the above statements is/are true?

○ 1 only
○ 2 only
○ Neither 1 nor 2
○ Both 1 and 2   (2 marks)

252 If the performance of a local fire service is judged in terms of its inputs rather than its outputs, which one of the following would be a suitable measure of performance?

○ Average response times to call-outs
○ Cost of the local fire service per member of the local population
○ Number of emergency calls answered per month
○ Average length of time between call-outs   (2 marks)

253 A typical balanced scorecard measures performance from four different perspectives. Which perspective is concerned with measuring 'What must we excel at?'

○ Customer satisfaction perspective
○ Financial success perspective
○ Growth perspective
○ Process efficiency perspective   (2 marks)

254 A company has a divisionalised structure in which Division A transfers its output to Division B. There is no external market for the transferred item and cost will be used as the basis for setting a transfer price. Which of the following will be the most appropriate basis for negotiating and agreeing a transfer price?

○ Actual cost
○ Actual cost plus a profit margin equal to a percentage of cost
○ Standard cost
○ Standard cost plus a profit margin equal to a percentage of cost   (2 marks)

(Total = 50 marks)

CBE style OTQ bank – Performance measurement and control

36 mins

255 In a company with a divisionalised structure, Division A transfers its output to Division B. Division A produces just one item, Component X. Division B makes and sells an end product that requires one unit of Component X.

	$ per unit of X
Marginal cost of production in Division A	8
Fixed overhead cost of production	3
Market price in the external market	16
Division B contribution from further processing Component X, before deducting the transfer cost	25

Division A is not working at full capacity, and can meet in full the external market demand and the demand from Division B for internal transfers.

What should be the minimum transfer price per unit and the maximum transfer price per unit for Component X in this situation?

minimum transfer price	$	
maximum transfer price	$	

(2 marks)

256 Which of the following is a dimension of performance in a service business, as identified by Fitzgerald and Moon?

- O   Controllability
- O   Innovation
- O   Rewards
- O   Standards

(2 marks)

257 In a company with a divisionalised structure, Division A transfers its output to Division B. Division A produces just one item, Component X. Division B makes and sells an end product that requires one unit of Component X.

	$ per unit of X
Marginal cost of production in Division A	8
Fixed overhead cost of production	3
Cost of selling in the external market	1
Market price in the external market	16
Division B contribution from further processing Component X, before deducting the transfer cost	25

Division A is working at full capacity.

What should be the minimum transfer price per unit of Component X in this situation?

$	

(2 marks)

258 On which **TWO** of the following matters would the manager of an investment centre make decisions?

- [ ] Granting credit to customers.
- [ ] Administration of centralised departments
- [ ] Settling inter-departmental disputes
- [ ] Inventory carrying decisions

(2 marks)

259 At the beginning of 20X2, a division has capital employed, consisting of non-current assets of $2 million (at net book value) and working capital of $0.2 million. These are expected to earn a profit in 20X2 of $0.5 million, after depreciation of $0.4 million. A new machine will be installed at the beginning of 20X2. It will cost $0.8 million and will require an additional $0.1 million in working capital. It will add $0.35 million to divisional profits before deducting depreciation. This machine will have a four-year life and no residual value: depreciation is by the straight-line method. When calculating ROI, capital employed is taken at its mid-year value.

What is the expected ROI of the division in 20X2?

- ○ 21.7%
- ○ 23.2%
- ○ 24.1%
- ○ 26.0%

(2 marks)

260 A company has two Divisions, A and B. Division A manufactures a component which is transferred to Division B. Division B uses two units of the component from Division A in every item of finished product that it makes and sells. The transfer price is $43 per unit of the component.

	$ per unit
Selling price of finished product made in Division B	154
Variable production costs in Division B, excluding the cost of transfers from Division A	32
Variable selling costs, chargeable to the division	1
	33

Fixed costs	$160,000
External sales in units	7,000
Investment in the division	$500,000

The company uses 16% as its cost of capital.

What is the residual income of Division B for the period?

$ [   ]

(2 marks)

261 An investment centre has prepared the following forecasts for the next financial year.

	$
Operating profit before depreciation	85,000
Depreciation	20,000
Net current assets at beginning of year	30,000
Carrying value of non-current assets at beginning of year	180,000

The centre manager is now considering whether to sell a machine that is included in these forecasts. The machine would add $2,500 to divisional profit next year after depreciation of $500. It has a carrying value of $6,000 and could be sold for this amount. They would use the proceeds from the sale plus additional cash from Head Office to purchase a new machine for $15,000. This new machine would add $5,200 to divisional profit next year after depreciation of $2,000.

What will be the expected return on investment (ROI) for the division next year, assuming that the manager acquires the new machine and that non-current assets are valued at the start of year carrying amount for the purpose of the ROI calculation?

[   ] %

(2 marks)

262 Classify the following into qualitative and quantitative aspects of non-financial performance.

Volume of customer complaints	☐ Quantitative	☐ Qualitative
Employee revenue	☐ Quantitative	☐ Qualitative
Defective products per batch	☐ Quantitative	☐ Qualitative
Customer needs	☐ Quantitative	☐ Qualitative
Employee morale	☐ Quantitative	☐ Qualitative
Brand recognition	☐ Quantitative	☐ Qualitative
Customer satisfaction	☐ Quantitative	☐ Qualitative
Repeat business	☐ Quantitative	☐ Qualitative **(2 marks)**

263 The 3Es are often used to assess performance in non-profit making organisations, especially in relation to value for money

Which **THREE** of the following Es are used?

☐ Efficiency
☐ Effectiveness
☐ Economy
☐ Enterprise
☐ Efficacy
☐ Expediency
☐ Endurance   **(2 marks)**

264 Organisations may need to develop performance measures to ensure that the needs of stakeholders are met.

Which **TWO** of the following measures are geared towards customer needs?

☐ Morale index
☐ Percentage of repeat customers
☐ Number of warranty claims
☐ Dividend yield   **(2 marks)**

(Total = 20 marks)

Section B questions

MCQ case questions

Cherry Co   18 mins

The following scenario relates to questions 265 – 269.

Cherry Co has two independent divisions, A and B. Division A produces product X. B is a new division which produces product Y. It requires units of product X to produce product Y. Last year, A sold X exclusively to the external market. Management at Cherry Co did not wish to disrupt the operations of A as B was an experimental division. However, due to the success of product Y, B is now a permanent division of Cherry Co. Management wants A to provide at least some units of product X to B.

The table below shows the contribution margin for each division when B purchases X from an outside supplier.

	B	A
	$	$
Selling price per unit	150	37
Variable cost per unit		
(Div B does not include the cost of X)	65	30
Cost of X purchased from outside suppliers	35	
Contribution margin per unit	50	7

265   What would the minimum transfer price per unit of product X be if A sold 12,000 units of X, assuming that A has capacity for 15,000 units?

   ○ $36
   ○ $30
   ○ $37
   ○ $35   **(2 marks)**

266   What would the minimum transfer price per unit of product X be if A sold 12,000 units of X, assuming that A has no spare capacity?

   ○ $36
   ○ $30
   ○ $37
   ○ $35   **(2 marks)**

267   If there was no external market for product X, which of the following approaches could be used to negotiate a transfer price?

   ○   Full cost
   ○   Management estimate of market cost
   ○   Scrap value of product X
   ○   All of the above   **(2 marks)**

268   The following two statements have been made about Cherry Co.

   (1)   Cherry Co's transfer pricing system should seek to establish a transfer price for X that will provide an incentive for the managers of A and B to make and sell quantities of products that will maximise sales of Product Y.

   (2)   The manager of division B is likely to be more motivated if she is given freedom in which to operate and is able to purchase from outside suppliers if prices are cheaper.

   Which of the above statements is/are correct?

   ○   1 only
   ○   2 only
   ○   Both 1 and 2
   ○   Neither 1 nor 2   **(2 marks)**

269 The following two statements have been made about Cherry Co.

(1) The performance of the managers of A and B will be easier to assess in an environment in which managers are able to control greater elements of the business.

(2) In a competitive market, it is likely that suppliers will offer product X to Division B significantly cheaper than Division A can, for a sustained period of time.

Which of the above statements is/are correct?

- ○ 1 only
- ○ 2 only
- ○ Both 1 and 2
- ○ Neither 1 nor 2   (2 marks)

(Total = 10 marks)

Jamair (12/14 amended)   18 mins

The following scenario relates to questions 270 – 274.

Jamair is one of a growing number of low-cost airlines in the country of Shania.

Jamair's strategy is to operate as a low-cost, high-efficiency airline.

The airline was given an 'on time arrival' ranking of seventh best by the country's aviation authority, which ranks all 50 of the country's airlines based on the number of flights which arrive on time at their destinations.

The average 'ground turnaround time' for airlines in Shania is 50 minutes, meaning that, on average, planes are on the ground for cleaning, refuelling, etc for 50 minutes before departing again.

The number of passengers carried by the airline has grown from 300,000 passengers on a total of 3,428 flights in 2007 to 920,000 passengers on 7,650 flights in 2013.

The overall growth of the airline has been helped by the limited route licensing policy of the Shanian government, which has given Jamair almost monopoly status on some of its routes. However, the government is now set to change this policy with almost immediate effect, and it has become more important than ever to monitor performance effectively.

270 The _____ perspective considers whether the management in Jamair meets the expectations of its shareholders and how it creates value for them.

Which of the following words is missing from the above statement?

- ○ Customer
- ○ Internal business
- ○ Innovation and learning
- ○ Financial   (2 marks)

271 The following performance measure has been suggested for Jamair:

Improve on the 'on time arrival' ranking of seventh best in the country's aviation authority ratings.

To which perspective of the balanced scorecard does this measure belong?

- ○ Customer perspective
- ○ Internal business perspective
- ○ Innovation and learning perspective
- ○ Financial perspective   (2 marks)

272 The following performance objective has been suggested for Jamair:

Improve the turnaround time on the ground

To which perspective of the balanced scorecard does this objective belong?

- ○ Customer perspective
- ○ Internal business perspective
- ○ Innovation and learning perspective
- ○ Financial perspective   (2 marks)

273 The following performance objective has been suggested for Jamair:

Increase seat revenue per plane

To which perspective of the balanced scorecard does this objective belong?

○   Customer perspective
○   Internal business perspective
○   Innovation and learning perspective
○   Financial perspective   **(2 marks)**

274 The following statements have been made about Jamair's performance measurement system.

(1) When performance is not quantified, it is difficult to target and monitor.

(2) Jamair is more likely to have a reliable and comprehensive system for collecting data about qualitative aspects of performance than a well-established system for measuring quantitative data.

Which of the above statements is/are correct?

○   1 only
○   2 only
○   Both 1 and 2
○   Neither 1 nor 2.   **(2 marks)**

(Total = 10 marks)

Stickleback Co   18 mins

The following scenario relates to questions 275 – 279.

Kingfisher is an investment centre within Stickleback Co. Kingfisher has an operating profit of $30,000, and operating assets of $150,000. The cost of capital is 15%. There is a proposed investment of $15,000 which will increase the operating income by $1,900.

275 What is the return on investment (ROI) for Kingfisher with and without the proposed investment?

○   Before investment: 20%, After investment 17%
○   Before investment: 17%, After investment 19.3%
○   Before investment: 19.3%, After investment 20%
○   Before investment: 20%, After investment 19.3%   **(2 marks)**

276 What is the residual income (RI) for Kingfisher with and without the proposed investment?

○   Before investment: $3,350, After investment $7,150
○   Before investment: $7,500, After investment $3,350
○   Before investment: $7,500, After investment $7,150
○   Before investment: $7,150, After investment $7,500   **(2 marks)**

277 The following statements have been made about the use of ROI as a performance measure in Stickleback Co.

(1) If a manager's performance is being evaluated, a portion of head office assets should be included in the calculation of ROI in Stickleback Co's investment centres.

(2) It may lead to short termism.

Which of the above statements is/are correct?

○   1 only
○   2 only
○   Both 1 and 2
○   Neither 1 nor 2   **(2 marks)**

278   The divisional manager for Kingfisher wants to increase the ROI for the next period.

The following options are available.

1   Increase payables
2   Reduce interest payments
3   Accept all projects with a positive NPV
4   Keep Kingfisher's old machinery

Which of the above would increase the ROI?

○   1 only
○   1, 2 and 4
○   1 and 4
○   3 and 4   **(2 marks)**

279   The following statements have been made about Stickleback Co's divisionalised structure.

(1)   There is a danger that managers in the divisions may use their decision-making freedom to make decisions that are not in the best interests of the overall company.

(2)   Stickleback Co's top management must have involvement in the day-to-day operations of the divisions.

Which of the above statements is/are correct?

○   1 only
○   2 only
○   Both 1 and 2
○   Neither 1 nor 2   **(2 marks)**

(Total = 10 marks)

Squarize (6/13 amended)   **18 mins**

The following scenario relates to questions 280 – 284.

Squarize is a large company which started as a pay-TV broadcaster and then started offering broadband and telephone services to its pay-TV customers. Customers could take advantage of discounts for 'bundle' packages of all three services.

All contracts to customers of Squarize are for a minimum three-month period. The pay-TV box is sold to the customer at the beginning of the contract; however, the broadband and telephone equipment is only rented to them.

In the first few years after product bundling was introduced, the company saw a steady increase in profits. Then, Squarize saw its revenues and operating profits fall. Several reasons were identified for the deterioration of results:

(1)   In a bid to save cash, many pay-TV customers were cancelling their contracts after the minimum three-month period as they were then able to keep the pay-TV box. The box comes with a number of free channels, which the customer can continue to receive free of charge, even after the cancellation of their contract.

(2)   Some bundle customers found that the broadband service that they had subscribed to did not work. As a result, they were immediately cancelling their contracts for all services within the 14-day cancellation period permitted under the contracts.

In a response to the above problems and in an attempt to increase revenues and profits, Squarize made the following changes to the business:

(i)   It made a strategic decision to withdraw the bundle package from the market and, instead, offer each service as a standalone product.

(ii)   It investigated and resolved the problem with customers' broadband service.

It is now one year since the changes were made and the finance director wants to use a balanced scorecard to assess the extent to which the changes have been successful in improving the performance of the business.

280 The following performance objective has been suggested for Squarize:

Reduce the number of contracts cancelled due to the broadband service not working

To which perspective of the balanced scorecard does this objective belong?

- ○ Customer perspective
- ○ Internal business perspective
- ○ Innovation and learning perspective
- ○ Financial perspective   **(2 marks)**

281 The following performance measure has been suggested for Squarize:

Volume of sales to new customers for each product/service

To which perspective of the balanced scorecard does this measure belong?

- ○ Customer perspective
- ○ Internal business perspective
- ○ Innovation and learning perspective
- ○ Financial perspective   **(2 marks)**

282 Which of the following would be the most suitable measure of performance from the innovation and learning perspective in Squarize's balanced scorecard?

- ○ Development cost per new standalone service
- ○ Sales revenue per new standalone service
- ○ Sales revenue from new standalone service as a percentage of total revenue
- ○ Sales revenue per hour worked on new standalone service   **(2 marks)**

283 Which of the following is most likely to be used as a measure of performance from the customer perspective in Squarize's balanced scorecard?

- ○ Increase in size of the product range
- ○ Percentage of customers renewing their subscription or making repeat orders
- ○ Number of orders won per sales representative
- ○ Speed of processing an order   **(2 marks)**

284 Squarize has been advised that it could also use the Fitzgerald and Moon building block model to attempt to overcome the problems associated with performance measurement of service businesses. Which of the following is not a building block included in this performance management system?

- ○ Rewards
- ○ Innovation
- ○ Standards
- ○ Dimensions of performance   **(2 marks)**

(Total = 10 marks)

CBE OT case questions

Alder Co

18 mins

The following scenario relates to questions 285 – 289.

An investment centre with capital employed of $750,000 is budgeted to earn a profit of $200,000 next year. A proposed non-current asset investment of $125,000, not included in the budget at present, will earn a profit next year of $20,000. The company's cost of capital is 15%.

285 What is the budgeted ROI for next year, both before and after the investment is made (to the nearest %)?

Before investment: [   ] %

After investment: [   ] %

(2 marks)

286 What is the residual income for next year, both before and after the investment is made?

Before investment: $ [   ]

After investment: $ [   ]

(2 marks)

287 Are the following statements about the divisionalised structure in Alder Co true or false?

The authority to act to improve performance motivates the divisional managers in Alder Co, more so than if the company was centralised.	TRUE	FALSE
Alder Co's top management must have involvement in the day-to-day operations of Alder Co.	TRUE	FALSE

(2 marks)

288 Are the following statements about the use of ROI in Alder Co true or false?

If a manager's performance is being evaluated, a portion of head office assets should be included in the calculation of ROI in Alder Co's investment centres.	TRUE	FALSE
If the performance of the investment centre is being appraised, head office assets or investment centre assets controlled by head office should not be included in the calculation of ROI.	TRUE	FALSE

(2 marks)

289 Are the following statements about the use of ROI in Alder Co true or false?

The profit figure for ROI should always be the amount before any interest is charged.	TRUE	FALSE
The asset base of the ratio can be altered by increasing/decreasing payables and receivables (by speeding up or delaying payments and receipts).	TRUE	FALSE

(2 marks)

(Total = 10 marks)

Apple Co

The following scenario relates to questions 290 – 294.

An investment centre in Apple Co generates a profit of $24,000. You have been given the following additional information about the investment centre.

Working capital		20,000
Non-current assets at cost	230,000	
Accumulated depreciation	170,000	
Net book value		60,000

290 What is the ROI for the investment centre? (to the nearest %) [   ] %   **(2 marks)**

291 An investment in a non-current asset could be made which would result in a capital employed figure of $100,000. The investment would result in a new profit figure of $35,000 for the division. If the investment is made, what would the residual income be for the investment centre if the cost of capital is 12%?

$ [   ]   **(2 marks)**

292 Are the following statements about the use of different performance measures in Apple Co true or false?

Residual income is more flexible, since a different cost of capital can be applied to investments with different risk characteristics.	TRUE	FALSE
Residual income does not facilitate comparisons between investment centres.	TRUE	FALSE

(2 marks)

293 Apple Co operates a transfer pricing system between two divisions based on market price. Are the following statements about this true or false?

The market price acts as an incentive to use up any spare capacity in the selling division of Apple Co.	TRUE	FALSE
Using the market price as the transfer price encourages selling and buying decisions which appear to be in the best interests of the division's performance. This leads to the company as a whole achieving optimal results as each division optimises its performance.	TRUE	FALSE

(2 marks)

294 Apple Co has two divisions which are set to begin buying and selling a product between themselves. It has been suggested that a cost-based approach to transfer pricing be used.

Are the following statements about this suggestion true or false?

A cost-based approach is suitable for Apple Co in this scenario if there is no external market for the product that is being transferred.	TRUE	FALSE
A cost-based approach is suitable for Apple Co in this scenario if an imperfect market exists.	TRUE	FALSE

(2 marks)

(Total = 10 marks)

Box Co

18 mins

The following scenario relates to questions 295 – 299.

Box Co has an operating profit of $20,000, and operating assets of $95,000. The cost of capital is 12%. There is a proposed investment of $10,000 which will increase the operating profit by $1,400.

295   What is the ROI with and without the proposed investment? (to one dp)

Without investment: [   ] %

With investment: [   ] %   **(2 marks)**

296   What is the RI with and without the proposed investment?

Without investment: $ [   ]

With investment: $ [   ]   **(2 marks)**

297   One of the managers in Box Co is critical of the performance measures used. She has said that they are too focused on financial performance and do not take into account any non-financial performance measures.

Are the following statements she has made true or false?

Financial performance measures do not necessarily provide sufficient information about ongoing problems with product quality. As a result, there is little attention paid to the generation of information on quality in Box Co.	TRUE	FALSE
Non-financial performance indicators can give a better indication of future prospects.	TRUE	FALSE

(2 marks)

298   Which of the following methods would encourage the managers of Box Co to take a short-term view?

   ○   Link managers' rewards to share price
   ○   Set quality-based targets as well as financial targets
   ○   Keep managers informed about the short-term budget targets
   ○   Make long-term targets realistic   **(2 marks)**

299   Are the following statements about Box Co's divisionalised structure true or false?

There is a danger that managers in Box Co may use their decision-making freedom to make decisions that are not in the best interests of the overall company.	TRUE	FALSE
A good performance measure for the divisional managers in Box Co should include a portion of head office costs in the calculations.	TRUE	FALSE

(2 marks)

(Total = 10 marks)

Willow Co

18 mins

The following scenario relates to questions 300 – 304.

An investment centre with capital employed of $600,000 is budgeted to earn a profit of $100,000 next year. A proposed fixed asset investment of $150,000, not included in the budget at present, will earn a profit next year of $23,000 after depreciation. The company's cost of capital is 13%.

Required

300 What is the budgeted return on investment (ROI) for next year, both before and after the investment is made (to the nearest %)?

	% before investment

| | % after investment **(2 marks)**

301 What is the residual income (RI) for next year, both before and after the investment is made?

$ | | before investment

$ | | after investment **(2 marks)**

302 Due to its size, Willow Co operates a divisionalised structure. One of the manager's área of responsibility is 'decisions over costs, revenues, and assets'. The typical financial performance measures used by this manager is return on investment and residual income.

Which of the following centres best describes the manager's responsibility area?

○ Profit centre
○ Responsibility centre
○ Cost centre
○ Investment centre **(2 marks)**

303 Two of the divisional managers in Willow Co disagree on the performance measure which should be used to determine their bonus for the year. Manager 1 is the manager of a large division, while manager 2 is manager of a small division. Manager 1 prefers to use residual income and has given the following examples of limitations of ROI to support this decision.

Which of the following is a valid reason for Willow Co choosing to use RI and not ROI?

○ ROI requires an estimate of the cost of capital, a figure which can be difficult to calculate.

○ ROI can over-emphasise short-term performance at the expense of long-term performance.

○ If assets are valued at net book value, ROI figures generally improve as assets get older. This can encourage managers to retain outdated plant and machinery.

○ ROI is a relative measure, therefore small investments with a high rate of return may appear preferable to a larger investment with lower ROI. However, the larger investment may be worth more in absolute terms. **(2 marks)**

304 Manager 2 wishes to use ROI as a performance measure.

Which of the following reasons is a valid reason for Willow Co choosing to use ROI and not RI?

○ Identifying controllable (traceable) profits and investment can be difficult.

○ RI attempts to measure divisional performance in a single figure.

○ ROI ties in with NPV, theoretically the best way to make investment decisions.

○ Manager 1 will show a higher RI because of the size of the division rather than superior managerial performance. **(2 marks)**

(Total = 10 marks)

Section C questions

305 Biscuits and Cakes (6/12)

36 mins

The Biscuits division (Division B) and the Cakes division (Division C) are two divisions of a large, manufacturing company. While both divisions operate in almost identical markets, each division operates separately as an investment centre. Each month, operating statements must be prepared by each division and these are used as a basis for performance measurement for the divisions.

Last month, senior management decided to recharge head office costs to the divisions. Consequently, each division is now going to be required to deduct a share of head office costs in its operating statement before arriving at 'net profit', which is then used to calculate return on investment (ROI). Prior to this, ROI has been calculated using controllable profit only. The company's target ROI, however, remains unchanged at 20% per annum. For each of the last three months, Divisions B and C have maintained ROIs of 22% per annum and 23% per annum respectively, resulting in healthy bonuses being awarded to staff. The company has a cost of capital of 10%.

The budgeted operating statement for the month of July is shown below:

	B	C
	$'000	$'000
Sales revenue	1,300	1,500
Less variable costs	(700)	(800)
Contribution	600	700
Less controllable fixed costs	(134)	(228)
Controllable profit	466	472
Less apportionment of head office costs	(155)	(180)
Net profit	311	292
Divisional net assets	$23.2m	$22.6m

Required

(a) Calculate the expected annualised return on investment (ROI) using the new method as preferred by senior management, based on the above budgeted operating statements, for each of the divisions. **(2 marks)**

The divisional managing directors are unhappy about the results produced by your calculations in (a) and have heard that a performance measure called 'residual income' may provide more information.

(b) Calculate the annualised residual income (RI) for each of the divisions, based on the net profit figures for the month of July. **(3 marks)**

(c) Discuss the expected performance of each of the two divisions, using both ROI and RI, and making any additional calculations deemed necessary. Conclude as to whether, in your opinion, the two divisions have performed well. **(6 marks)**

Division B has now been offered an immediate opportunity to invest in new machinery at a cost of $2.12 million. The machinery is expected to have a useful economic life of four years, after which it could be sold for $200,000. Division B's policy is to depreciate all of its machinery on a straight-line basis over the life of the asset. The machinery would be expected to expand Division B's production capacity, resulting in an 8.5% increase in contribution per month.

Required

(d) Recalculate Division B's expected annualised ROI and annualised RI, based on July's budgeted operating statement after adjusting for the investment. State whether the managing director will be making a decision that is in the best interests of the company as a whole if ROI is used as the basis of the decision.

(5 marks)

(e) Explain any behavioural problems that will result if the company's senior management insist on using solely ROI, based on net profit rather than controllable profit, to assess divisional performance and reward staff.

(4 marks)

(Total = 20 marks)

306 Story

Story is a well-established, global publishing conglomerate. The corporation is structured to allow each country of operation to function as an autonomous business unit, that reports back to head office. The data from each business unit is entered onto the mainframe computer at head office. Each business unit can make use of any service offered by other business units and can also offer services to the other units. The services include translation into different languages, typesetting, printing, storage and so forth. In each country of operation there is at least one, and usually several, retail outlets.

The core business was traditionally based upon the provision of fictional stories for the mass market. For the past decade Story has diversified into publishing textbooks and technical literature. The organisation currently enjoys a good reputation in both areas of the business and global sales are increasing annually at a rate of 5% for fictional books and 2% for textbooks. Last year 700 million fictional works and 25 million textbooks were sold.

The corporate management team wish to increase the growth in sales of textbooks but realise that they cannot afford to allocate significant resources to this task as the market, and profit margin, for textbooks is very much smaller than for fiction. They also wish to improve the sales performance of the fictional books.

Story is currently having trouble in maintaining a corporate image in some countries of operation. For example, several business units may be unaware of additions to the product range. Another example is that a price change in a book is not simultaneously altered by all the business units, leading to pricing discrepancies.

Some members of the corporate management team see possible advantages to upgrading the existing computer system to one that is fully networked. Other members are more sceptical and are reluctant to consider enhancing the system.

Required

(a)   Discuss the issues involved in upgrading the existing information system and the proposed changes, with reference to both the wider business environment and the decision-making process.   **(8 marks)**

(b)   Explain what is meant by the terms **open systems** and **closed systems** as applied to systems theory. Identify, with justification and, where possible, any examples of these from the information given in, or implied by, the case study.   **(7 marks)**

(c)   Management information systems (MIS) allow managers to make timely and effective decisions using data in an appropriate form. List three types of MIS and how they would be used in an organisation.   **(5 marks)**

(Total = 20 marks)

307 Hammer (6/10)

Hammer is a large garden equipment supplier with retail stores throughout Toolland. Many of the products it sells are bought in from outside suppliers but some are currently manufactured by Hammer's own manufacturing division 'Nail'.

The prices (a transfer price) that Nail charges to the retail stores are set by head office and have been the subject of some discussion. The current policy is for Nail to calculate the total variable cost of production and delivery and add 30% for profit. Nail argues that all costs should be taken into consideration, offering to reduce the mark-up on costs to 10% in this case. The retail stores are unhappy with the current pricing policy arguing that it results in prices that are often higher than comparable products available on the market.

Nail has provided the following information to enable a price comparison to be made of the two possible pricing policies for one of its products.

Garden shears

Steel: the shears have 0.4 kg of high quality steel in the final product. The manufacturing process loses 5% of all steel put in. Steel costs $4,000 per tonne (1 tonne = 1,000 kg)

Other materials: Other materials are bought in and have a list price of $3 per kg although Hammer secures a 10% volume discount on all purchases. The shears require 0.1 kg of these materials.

The labour time to produce shears is 0.25 hours per unit and labour costs $10 per hour.

Variable overheads are absorbed at the rate of 150% of labour rates and fixed overheads are 80% of the variable overheads.

Delivery is made by an outsourced distributor that charges Nail $0.5 per garden shear for delivery.

Required

(a) Calculate the price that Nail would charge for the garden shears under the existing policy of variable cost plus 30%. **(6 marks)**

(b) Calculate the increase or decrease in price if the pricing policy switched to total cost plus 10%. **(4 marks)**

(c) Discuss whether or not including fixed costs in a transfer price is a sensible policy. **(4 marks)**

(d) Discuss whether the retail stores should be allowed to buy in from outside suppliers if the prices are cheaper than those charged by Nail. **(6 marks)**

(Total = 20 marks)

308 Woodside (6/07 amended)   36 mins

Woodside is a local charity dedicated to helping homeless people in a large city. The charity owns and manages a shelter that provides free overnight accommodation for up to 30 people, offers free meals each and every night of the year to homeless people who are unable to buy food, and runs a free advice centre to help homeless people find suitable housing and gain financial aid. Woodside depends entirely on public donations to finance its activities and had a fundraising target for the last year of $700,000. The budget for the last year was based on the following forecast activity levels and expected costs:

Free meals provision: 18,250 meals at $5 per meal
Overnight shelter: 10,000 bed-nights at $30 per night
Advice centre: 3,000 sessions at $20 per session
Campaigning and advertising: $150,000

The budgeted surplus (budgeted fundraising target less budgeted costs) was expected to be used to meet any unexpected costs. Included in the above figures are fixed costs of $5 per night for providing shelter and $5 per advice session, representing fixed costs expected to be incurred by administration and maintaining the shelter. The number of free meals provided and the number of beds occupied each night depends on both the weather and the season of the year. The Woodside charity has three full-time staff and a large number of voluntary helpers.

The actual costs for the last year were as follows:

Free meals provision: 20,000 meals at a variable cost of $104,000
Overnight shelter: 8,760 bed-nights at a variable cost of $223,380
Advice centre: 3,500 sessions at a variable cost of $61,600
Campaigning and advertising: $165,000

The actual costs of the overnight shelter and the advice centre exclude the fixed costs of administration and maintenance, which were $83,000.

The actual amount of funds raised in the last year was $620,000.

Required

(a) Prepare an operating statement, reconciling budgeted surplus and actual shortfall and discuss the charity's performance over the last year. **(12 marks)**

(b) Discuss problems that may arise in the financial management and control of a not-for-profit organisation such as the Woodside charity. **(8 marks)**

(Total = 20 marks)

309 Ties Only Co (12/07) 36 mins

Ties Only Co is a new business, selling high quality imported men's ties through the internet. The managers, who also own the company, are young and inexperienced but they are prepared to take risks. They are confident that importing quality ties and selling through a website will be successful and that the business will grow quickly. This is despite the well-recognised fact that selling clothing is a very competitive business.

They were prepared for a loss-making start and decided to pay themselves modest salaries (included in administration expenses in Table 1 below) and pay no dividends for the foreseeable future.

The owners are so convinced that growth will quickly follow that they have invested enough money in website server development to ensure that the server can handle the very high levels of predicted growth. All website development costs were written off as incurred in the internal management accounts that are shown below in Table 1.

Significant expenditure on marketing was incurred in the first two quarters, to launch both the website and new products. It is not expected that marketing expenditure will continue to be as high in the future.

Customers can buy a variety of styles, patterns and colours of ties at different prices.

The business's trading results for the first two quarters of trade are shown below in Table 1.

Table 1

	Quarter 1		Quarter 2	
	$	$	$	$
Sales		420,000		680,000
Less cost of sales		(201,600)		(340,680)
Gross profit		218,400		339,320
Less expenses				
Website development	120,000		90,000	
Administration	100,500		150,640	
Distribution	20,763		33,320	
Launch marketing	60,000		40,800	
Other variable expenses	50,000		80,000	
Total expenses		(351,263)		(394,760)
Loss for quarter		(132,863)		(55,440)

Required

(a) Assess the financial performance of the business during its first two quarters, using only the data in Table 1 above. **(10 marks)**

(b) Briefly consider whether the losses made by the business in the first two quarters are a true reflection of the current and likely future performance of the business. **(3 marks)**

The owners are well aware of the importance of non-financial indicators of success and therefore have identified a small number of measures to focus on. These are measured monthly and then combined to produce a quarterly management report.

The data for the first two quarters' management reports is shown below:

Table 2

	Quarter 1	Quarter 2
Number of ties sold	27,631	38,857
On-time delivery	95%	89%
Sales returns	12%	18%
System downtime	2%	4%

The industry average for sales returns was 13%.

Required

(c) Comment on each of the non-financial data in Table 2 above, taking into account, where appropriate, the industry averages provided, providing your assessment of the performance of the business. **(7 marks)**

(Total = 20 marks)

310 The Accountancy Teaching Co (12/10)   36 mins

The Accountancy Teaching Co (AT Co) is a company specialising in the provision of accountancy tuition courses in the private sector. It makes up its accounts to 30 November each year. In the year ending 30 November 20X9, it held 60% of market share. However, over the last 12 months, the accountancy tuition market in general has faced a 20% decline in demand for accountancy training, leading to smaller class sizes on courses. In 20X9 and before, AT Co suffered from an ongoing problem with staff retention, which had a knock-on effect on the quality of service provided to students. Following the completion of developments that have been ongoing for some time, in 20Y0 the company was able to offer a far-improved service to students. The developments included:

- A new dedicated 24-hour student helpline

- An interactive website providing instant support to students

- A new training programme for staff

- An electronic student enrolment system

- An electronic marking system for the marking of students' progress tests. The costs of marking electronically were expected to be $4 million less in 20Y0 than marking on paper. Marking expenditure is always included in cost of sales

Extracts from the management accounts for 20X9 and 20Y0 are shown below:

	20X9		20Y0	
	$'000	$'000	$'000	$'000
Turnover		72,025		66,028
Cost of sales		(52,078)		(42,056)
Gross profit		19,947		23,972
Indirect expenses:				
Marketing	3,291		4,678	
Property	6,702		6,690	
Staff training	1,287		3,396	
Interactive website running costs	–		3,270	
Student helpline running costs	–		2,872	
Enrolment costs	5,032		960	
Total indirect expenses		(16,312)		(21,866)
Net operating profit		3,635		2,106

On 1 December 20X9, management asked all 'freelance lecturers' to reduce their fees by at least 10% with immediate effect ('freelance lecturers' are not employees of the company but are used to teach students when there are not enough of AT Co's own lecturers to meet tuition needs). All employees were also told that they would not receive a pay rise for at least one year. Total lecture staff costs (including freelance lecturers) were $41.663 million in 20X9 and were included in cost of sales, as is always the case. Freelance lecturer costs represented 35% of these total lecture staff costs. In 20Y0, freelance lecture costs were $12.394 million. No reduction was made to course prices in the year and the mix of trainees studying for the different qualifications remained the same. The same type and number of courses were run in both 20X9 and 20Y0 and the percentage of these courses that was run by freelance lecturers as opposed to employed staff also remained the same.

Due to the nature of the business, non-financial performance indicators are also used to assess performance, as detailed below.

	20X9	20Y0
Percentage of students transferring to AT Co from another training provider	8%	20%
Number of late enrolments due to staff error	297	106
Percentage of students passing exams first time	48%	66%
Labour turnover	32%	10%
Number of student complaints	315	84
Average number of employees	1,080	1,081

Required

Assess the performance of the business in 20Y0 using both financial performance indicators calculated from the above information **AND** the non-financial performance indicators provided.

Note. State any assumptions and show all workings clearly. Your answer should be structured around the following main headings: turnover; cost of sales; gross profit; indirect expenses; net operating profit. However, in discussing each of these areas you should also refer to the non-financial performance indicators, where relevant.

(Total = 20 marks)

311 Jump (6/10)   36 mins

Jump has a network of sports clubs which are managed by local managers reporting to the main board. The local managers have a lot of autonomy and are able to vary employment contracts with staff and offer discounts for membership fees and personal training sessions. They also control their own maintenance budget, but do not have control over large amounts of capital expenditure.

A local manager's performance and bonus is assessed relative to three targets. For every one of these three targets that is reached in an individual quarter, $400 is added to the manager's bonus, which is paid at the end of the year. The maximum bonus per year is therefore based on 12 targets (three targets in each of the four quarters of the year). Accordingly, the maximum bonus that could be earned is 12 × $400 = $4,800, which represents 40% of the basic salary of a local manager. Jump has a 31 March year end.

The performance data for one of the sports clubs for the last four quarters is as follows.

	Qtr to 30 June 20X1	Qtr to 30 September 20X1	Qtr to 31 December 20X1	Qtr to 31 March 20X2
Number of members	3,000	3,200	3,300	3,400
Member visits	20,000	24,000	26,000	24,000
Personal training sessions booked	310	325	310	339
Staff days	450	480	470	480
Staff lateness days	20	28	28	20
Days in quarter	90	90	90	90

Agreed targets are:

(1)   Staff must be on time over 95% of the time (no penalty is made when staff are absent from work).
(2)   On average 60% of members must use the clubs' facilities regularly, by visiting at least 12 times per quarter.
(3)   On average 10% of members must book a personal training session each quarter.

Required

(a)   Calculate the amount of bonus that the manager should expect to be paid for the latest financial year.

(6 marks)

(b)   Discuss to what extent the targets set are controllable by the local manager (you are required to make a case for both sides of the argument).

(9 marks)

(c)   Describe two methods as to how a manager with access to the accounting and other records could unethically manipulate the situation so as to gain a greater bonus.

(5 marks)

(Total = 20 marks)

312 Bridgewater Co (6/08 amended)

Bridgewater Co provides training courses for many of the mainstream software packages on the market.

The business has many divisions within Waterland, the one country in which it operates. The senior managers of Bridgewater Co have very clear objectives for the divisions and these are communicated to divisional managers on appointment and subsequently in quarterly and annual reviews. These are:

- Each quarter, sales should grow and annual sales should exceed budget
- Trainer (lecture staff) costs should not exceed $180 per teaching day
- Room hire costs should not exceed $90 per teaching day
- Each division should meet its budget for profit per quarter and annually

It is known that managers will be promoted based on their ability to meet these targets. A member of the senior management is to retire after Quarter 2 of the current financial year, which has just begun. The divisional managers anticipate that one of them may be promoted at the beginning of Quarter 3 if their performance is good enough.

The manager of the Northwest division is concerned that their chances of promotion could be damaged by the expected performance of their division. They are a firm believer in quality and they think that if a business gets this right, growth and success will eventually follow.

The current quarterly forecasts, along with the original budgeted profit for the Northwest division, are as follows:

	Q1	Q2	Q3	Q4	Total
	$'000	$'000	$'000	$'000	$'000
Sales	40.0	36.0	50.0	60.0	186.0
Less:					
Trainers	8.0	7.2	10.0	12.0	37.2
Room hire	4.0	3.6	5.0	6.0	18.6
Staff training	1.0	1.0	1.0	1.0	4.0
Other costs	3.0	1.7	6.0	7.0	17.7
Forecast net profit	24.0	22.5	28.0	34.0	108.5
Original budgeted profit	25.0	26.0	27.0	28.0	106.0
Annual sales budget					180.0
Teaching days	40	36	50	60	

Required

(a)   Assess the financial performance of the Northwest division against its targets and reach a conclusion as to the promotion prospects of the divisional manager. **(8 marks)**

The manager of the Northwest division has been considering a few steps to improve the performance of their division.

Voucher scheme

As a sales promotion, vouchers will be sold for $125 each, a substantial discount on normal prices. These vouchers will entitle the holder to attend four training sessions on software of their choice. They can attend when they want to but are advised that one training session per quarter is sensible. The manager is confident that, if the promotion took place immediately, they could sell 80 vouchers and that customers would follow the advice given to attend one session per quarter. All voucher holders would attend planned existing courses and all will be new customers.

Software upgrade

A new important software programme has recently been launched for which there could be a market for training courses. Demonstration programs can be bought for $1,800 in Quarter 1. Staff training would be needed, costing $500 in each of Quarters 1 and 2 but in Quarters 3 and 4 extra courses could be offered selling this training. Assuming similar class sizes and the usual sales prices, extra sales revenue amounting to 20% of normal sales are expected (measured before the voucher promotion above). The manager is keen to run these courses at the same tutorial and room standards as they normally provide. Software expenditure is written off in the income statement as incurred.

Delaying payments to trainers

The manager is considering delaying payment to the trainers. They think that, since their commitment to quality could cause them to miss out on a well-deserved promotion, the trainers owe them a favour. They intend to delay payment on 50% of all invoices received from the trainers in the first two quarters, paying them one month later than is usual.

Required

(b)   Revise the forecasts to take account of all three of the proposed changes.   **(6 marks)**

(c)   Comment on each of the proposed steps and reach a conclusion as to whether, if all the proposals were taken together, the manager will improve their chances of promotion.   **(6 marks)**

(Total = 20 marks)

313 Oliver's Salon (6/09)   36 mins

Oliver is the owner and manager of Oliver's Salon which is a quality hairdresser that experiences high levels of competition. The salon traditionally provided a range of hair services to female clients only, including cuts, colouring and straightening.

A year ago, at the start of his 20X9 financial year, Oliver decided to expand his operations to include the hairdressing needs of male clients. Male hairdressing prices are lower, the work simpler (mainly hair cuts only) and so the time taken per male client is much less.

The prices for the female clients were not increased during the whole of 20X8 and 20X9 and the mix of services provided for female clients in the two years was the same.

The latest financial results are as follows:

	20X8 $	$	*20X9* $	$
Sales		200,000		238,500
Less cost of sales:				
Hairdressing staff costs	65,000		91,000	
Hair products – female	29,000		27,000	
Hair products – male			8,000	
		94,000		126,000
Gross profit		106,000		112,500
Less expenses:				
Rent	10,000		10,000	
Administration salaries	9,000		9,500	
Electricity	7,000		8,000	
Advertising	2,000		5,000	
Total expenses		28,000		32,500
Profit		78,000		80,000

Oliver is disappointed with his financial results. He thinks the salon is much busier than a year ago and was expecting more profit. He has noted the following extra information.

Some female clients complained about the change in atmosphere following the introduction of male services, which created tension in the salon.

Two new staff were recruited at the start of 20X9. The first was a junior hairdresser to support the specialist hairdressers for the female clients. She was appointed on a salary of $9,000 per annum. The second new staff member was a specialist hairdresser for the male clients. There were no increases in pay for existing staff at the start of 20X9 after a big rise at the start of 20X8 which was designed to cover two years' worth of increases.

Oliver introduced some non-financial measures of success two years ago.

	20X8	20X9
Number of complaints	12	46
Number of male client visits	0	3,425
Number of female client visits	8,000	6,800
Number of specialist hairdressers for female clients	4	5
Number of specialist hairdressers for male clients	0	1

Required

(a) Calculate the average price for hair services per male and female client for each of the years 20X8 and 20X9.

(3 marks)

(b) Assess the financial performance of the salon using the data above. **(11 marks)**

(c) Analyse and comment on the non-financial performance of Oliver's business, under the headings of quality and resource utilisation. **(6 marks)**

(Total = 20 marks)

314 Web Co (12/12)   36 mins

Web Co is an online retailer of fashion goods and uses a range of performance indicators to measure the performance of the business. The company's management have been increasingly concerned about the lack of sales growth over the last year and, in an attempt to resolve this, made the following changes right at the start of Quarter 2.

Advertising: Web Co placed an advert on the webpage of a well-known online fashion magazine at a cost of $200,000. This had a direct link from the magazine's website to Web Co's online store.

Search engine: Web Co also engaged the services of a website consultant to ensure that, when certain key words are input by potential customers onto key search engines, such as Google and Yahoo, Web Co's website is listed on the first page of results. This makes it more likely that a customer will visit a company's website. The consultant's fee was $20,000.

Website availability: During Quarter 1, there were a few problems with Web Co's website, meaning that it was not available to customers some of the time. Web Co was concerned that this was losing them sales and the IT department therefore made some changes to the website in an attempt to correct the problem.

The following incentives were also offered to customers:

Incentive 1: A free 'Fast Track' delivery service, guaranteeing delivery within two working days, for all continuing customers who subscribe to Web Co's online subscription newsletter. Subscribers are thought by Web Co to become customers who place further orders.

Incentive 2: A $10 discount to all customers spending $100 or more at any one time.

The results for the last two quarters are shown below, Quarter 2 being the most recent. The results for Quarter 1 reflect the period before the changes and incentives detailed above took place and are similar to the results of other quarters in the preceding year.

	Quarter 1	*Quarter 2*
Total sales revenue	$2,200,000	$2,750,000
Net profit margin	25%	16.7%
Total number of orders from customers	40,636	49,600
Total number of visits to website	101,589	141,714
Conversion rate – visitor to purchaser	40%	35%
The percentage of total visitors accessing website through magazine link	0	19.9%
Website availability	95%	95%
Number of customers spending more than $100 per visit	4,650	6,390
Number of subscribers to online newsletter	4,600	11,900

Assess the performance of the business in Quarter 2 in relation to the changes and incentives that the company introduced at the beginning of this quarter. State clearly where any further information might be necessary, concluding as to whether the changes and incentives have been effective.

(Total = 20 marks)

315 PAF Co (12/13)   36 mins

Protect Against Fire Co (PAF Co) manufactures and sells fire safety equipment and also provides fire risk assessments and fire safety courses to businesses. It has been trading for many years in the country of Calana, where it is the market leader.

Five years ago, the directors of PAF Co established a similar operation in its neighbouring country, Sista, renting business premises at various locations across the country. The fire safety market in Sista has always been dominated by two other companies, and when PAF Co opened the Sista division, its plan was to become market leader there within five years. Both the Calana division (Division C) and the Sista division (Division S) usually restrict themselves to a marketing budget of $0.5 million per annum but in 20X3, Division S launched a $2 million advertising campaign in a final push to increase market share. It also left its prices for products and services unchanged in 20X3 rather than increasing them in line with its competitors.

Although the populations of both countries are similar, geographically, the country of Sista is twice as large as Calana and its customers are evenly spread across the country. The products and services offered by the two divisions to their customers require skilled staff, demand for which is particularly high in Sista. Following the appointment of a new government in Sista at the end of 20X2, stricter fire safety regulations were immediately introduced for all companies. At the same time, the government introduced a substantial tax on business property rents which landlords passed on to their tenants.

International shortages of fuel have led to a 20% increase in fuel prices in both countries in the last year.

Summary statements of profit or loss for the two divisions for the two years ended 30 November 20X2 and 30 November 20X3 are shown below.

	Division S 20X3 $'000	Division S 20X2 $'000	Division C 20X3 $'000	Division C 20X2 $'000
Revenue	38,845	26,937	44,065	40,395
Material costs	(3,509)	(2,580)	(4,221)	(3,385)
Payroll costs	(10,260)	(6,030)	(8,820)	(7,700)
Property costs	(3,200)	(1,800)	(2,450)	(2,320)
Gross profit	21,876	16,527	28,574	26,954
Distribution and marketing (D&M) costs	(10,522)	(7,602)	(7,098)	(5,998)
Administrative overheads	(7,024)	(6,598)	(12,012)	(11,974)
Operating profit	4,330	2,327	9,464	8,982
Employee numbers	380	241	420	385
Market share	30%	25%	55%	52%

Required

Using all the information above, assess the financial performance of Division S in the year ended 30 November 20X3. State clearly where further information might be required in order to make more reasoned conclusions about the division's performance.

Note. Up to 7 marks are available for calculations.   **(20 marks)**

316 CIM Co (Sep/Dec 15 amended)

36 mins

Cardale Industrial Metal Co (CIM Co) is a large supplier of industrial metals. The company is split into two divisions: Division F and Division N. Each division operates separately as an investment centre, with each one having full control over its non-current assets. In addition, both divisions are responsible for their own current assets, controlling their own levels of inventory and cash and having full responsibility for the credit terms granted to customers and the collection of receivables balances. Similarly, each division has full responsibility for its current liabilities and deals directly with its own suppliers.

Each divisional manager is paid a salary of $120,000 per annum plus an annual performance-related bonus, based on the return on investment (ROI) achieved by their division for the year. Each divisional manager is expected to achieve a minimum ROI for their division of 10% per annum. If a manager only meets the 10% target, they are not awarded a bonus. However, for each whole percentage point above 10% which the division achieves for the year, a bonus equivalent to 2% of annual salary is paid, subject to a maximum bonus equivalent to 30% of annual salary.

The following figures relate to the year ended 31 August 20X5:

	Division F $'000	Division N $'000
Sales	14,500	8,700
Controllable profit	2,645	1,970
Less apportionment of Head Office costs	(1,265)	(684)
Net profit	1,380	1,286
Non-current assets	9,760	14,980
Inventory, cash and trade receivables	2,480	3,260
Trade payables	2,960	1,400

During the year ending 31 August 20X5, Division N invested $6.8 million in new equipment, including a technologically advanced cutting machine, which is expected to increase productivity by 8% per annum. Division F has made no investment during the year, although its computer system is badly in need of updating. Division F's manager has said that they have already had to delay payments to suppliers (ie accounts payables) because of limited cash and the computer system 'will just have to wait', although the cash balance at Division F is still better than that of Division N.

Required:

(a) For each division, for the year ended 31 August 20X5, calculate the appropriate closing return on investment (ROI) on which the payment of management bonuses will be based. Briefly justify the figures used in your calculations.

   Note. There are 3 marks available for calculations and 2 marks available for discussion. **(5 marks)**

(b) Based on your calculations in part (a), calculate each manager's bonus for the year ended 31 August 20X5.

   (3 marks)

(c) Discuss whether ROI is providing a fair basis for calculating the managers' bonuses and the problems arising from its use at CIM Co for the year ended 31 August 20X5. **(7 marks)**

(d) Briefly explain steps that could be taken by CIM Co to encourage managers to take a long-term view in decision making. **(5 marks)**

(Total = 20 marks)

317 Man Co (Mar/Jun 16 amended)   36 mins

A manufacturing company, Man Co, has two divisions: Division L and Division M. Both divisions make a single standardised product. Division L makes component L, which is supplied to both Division M and external customers. Division M makes product M using one unit of component L and other materials. It then sells the completed product M to external customers. To date, Division M has always bought component L from Division L.

The following information is available:

	Component L $	Product M $
Selling price	40	96
Direct materials:		
Component L		(40)
Other	(12)	(17)
Direct labour	(6)	(9)
Variable overheads	(2)	(3)
Selling and distribution costs	(4)	(1)
Contribution per unit before fixed costs	16	26
Annual fixed costs	$500,000	$200,000
Annual external demand (units)	160,000	120,000
Capacity of plant	300,000	130,000

Division L charges the same price for component L to both Division M and external customers. However, it does not incur the selling and distribution costs when transferring internally.

Division M has just been approached by a new supplier who has offered to supply it with component L for $37 per unit. Prior to this offer, the cheapest price at which Division M could have bought component L from outside the group was $42 per unit.

It is head office policy to let the divisions operate autonomously without interference at all.

Required:

(a) Calculate the incremental profit/(loss) per component for the group if Division M accepts the new supplier's offer and recommend how many components Division L should sell to Division M if group profits are to be maximised.   **(3 marks)**

(b) Using the quantities calculated in (a) and the current transfer price, calculate the total annual profits of each division and the group as a whole.   **(6 marks)**

(c) Discuss the problems which will arise if the transfer price remains unchanged and advise the divisions on a suitable alternative transfer price for component L.   **(6 marks)**

(d) Discuss the advantages of allowing divisions to operate autonomously.   **(5 marks)**

                                                                                        (Total = 20 marks)

318 Rotech group (6/14)

The Rotech group comprises two companies, W Co and C Co.

W Co is a trading company with two divisions: The Design division, which designs wind turbines and supplies the designs to customers under licences, and the Gearbox division, which manufactures gearboxes for the car industry.

C Co manufactures components for gearboxes. It sells the components globally and also supplies W Co with components for its Gearbox manufacturing division.

The financial results for the two companies for the year ended 31 May 20X4 are as follows:

	W Co		C Co
	Design division $'000	Gearbox division $'000	C Co $'000
External sales	14,300	25,535	8,010
Sales to Gearbox division			7,550
			15,560
Cost of sales	(4,900)	(16,200)*	(5,280)
Administration costs	(3,400)	(4,200)	(2,600)
Distribution costs	–	(1,260)	(670)
Operating profit	6,000	3,875	7,010
Capital employed	23,540	32,320	82,975

* Includes cost of components purchased from C Co.

Required

(a) Discuss the performance of C Co and each division of W Co, calculating and using the following three performance measures:

   (i) Return on capital employed (ROCE)
   (ii) Asset turnover
   (iii) Operating profit margin

   Note. There are 4.5 marks available for calculations and 5.5 marks available for discussion.   **(10 marks)**

(b) C Co is currently working to full capacity. The Rotech group's policy is that group companies and divisions must always make internal sales first, before selling outside the group. Similarly, purchases must be made from within the group wherever possible. However, the group divisions and companies are allowed to negotiate their own transfer prices without interference from Head Office.

   C Co has always charged the same price to the Gearbox division as it does to its external customers. However, after being offered a 5% lower price for similar components from an external supplier, the manager of the Gearbox division feels strongly that the transfer price is too high and should be reduced. C Co currently satisfies 60% of the external demand for its components. Its variable costs represent 40% of revenue.

   Required

   Advise, using suitable calculations, the total transfer price or prices at which the components should be supplied to the Gearbox division from C Co.   **(10 marks)**

   (Total = 20 marks)

319 Bus Co (Sep/Dec 15 amended)

Bus Co is a large bus operator, operating long-distance bus services across the country. There are two other national operators in the country. Bus Co's mission is to 'be the market leader in long-distance transport providing a greener, cleaner service for passengers nationwide'. Last month, an independent survey of 40,000 passengers was carried out, the results of which are shown in the table below:

Table: Bus passenger satisfaction % by national operator

Operator	Overall satisfaction	Value for money	Punctuality	Journey time
Bus	*	67	80	82
Prime	*	58	76	83
Express	*	67	76	89

* denotes that the percentage has not yet been calculated.

The 'overall satisfaction' percentages, which have not yet been inserted into the table, are calculated using a weighted average which reflects the importance customers place on each of the other three criteria above. The weightings used are as follows:

Value for money	40%
Punctuality	32%
Journey time	28%

The managing director (MD) of Bus Co has said: 'Independent research has shown that our customers are the most satisfied of any national bus operator. We are now leading the way on what matters most to customers – value for money and punctuality.'

Required

(a) Calculate the 'overall satisfaction' percentage for each operator. **(2 marks)**

(b) Taking into account all the data in the table and your calculations from part (a), discuss whether the managing director's statement is true. **(4 marks)**

(c) When measuring performance using a 'value for money' approach, the criteria of economy, efficiency and effectiveness can be used.

Required

Briefly define 'efficiency' and 'effectiveness' and suggest one performance measure for **EACH**, which would help Bus Co assess the efficiency and effectiveness of the service it provides. **(4 marks)**

(d) Describe the balanced scorecard approach to performance measurement and suggest a performance measure for Bus Co for each perspective of the balanced scorecard. **(10 marks)**

(Total = 20 marks)

320 People's Bank (Mar/Jun 17)

The People's Bank is a bank based in the country of Nawkrei. It has a total of 65 branches across the country and also offers online banking (access to services via computer) and telephone banking (access to customer service agents over the telephone) to its customers. Recently, The People's Bank also began offering its customers a range of mobile banking services, which can be accessed from customers' smartphones and tablet computers. Its customer-base is made up of both private individuals and business customers. The range of services it offers includes:

Current accounts
Savings accounts
Credit cards
Business and personal loans
Mortgages (loans for property purchases)

The People's Bank's vision is to be 'the bank that gives back to its customers' and their purpose is 'to help the people and businesses of Nawkrei to live better lives and achieve their ambitions'. In order to achieve this, the bank's values are stated as:

(1) Putting customers' needs first, which involves anticipating and understanding customers' needs and making products and services accessible to as many customers as possible. The People' Bank has recently invested heavily in IT security to prevent fraud and also invested to make more services accessible to disabled and visually impaired customers

(2) Making business simple, which involves identifying opportunities to simplify activities and communicating clearly and openly

(3) Making a difference to the communities they serve, which involves primarily helping the disadvantaged and new homeowners but also supporting small and medium-sized businesses (SMEs) and acting fairly and responsibly at all times

Extracts from The People's Bank's balanced scorecard are shown below:

Performance measure	20X6 Actual	20X6 Target
Financial perspective		
Return on capital employed (ROCE)	11%	12%
Interest income	$7.5m	$7m
Net interest margin (margin achieved on interest income)	2.4%	2.5%
Amount of new lending to SMEs	$135m	$150m
Customer perspective		
Number of first-time homebuyers given a mortgage by The People's Bank	86,000	80,000
Number of complaints (per 1,000 customers)	1.5	2
Number of talking cashpoints installed for the visually impaired	120	100
Number of wheelchair ramps installed in branches	55	50
Internal processes		
Number of business processes within The People's Bank re-engineered and simplified	110	100
Number of new services made available through 'mobile banking'	2	5
Incidences of fraud on customers' accounts or credit cards (per 1,000 customers)	3	10
Total carbon dioxide emissions (tonnes)	430,000	400,000
Learning and growth		
Number of colleagues trained to provide advice to SMEs	1,300	1,500
Number of hours (paid for by The People's Bank) used to support community projects	1,020,000	1,000,000
Number of trainee positions taken up by candidates from Nawkrei's most disadvantaged areas	1,990	2,000
Number of community organisations supported (either through funding or by volunteers from The People's Bank)	7,250	7,000

Required

(a)   Explain why the balanced scorecard approach to performance measurement is more useful to measure performance for The People's Bank than a traditional approach using solely financial performance measures.

(4 marks)

(b)   Using all of the information provided, including The People's Bank's vision and values, discuss the performance of The People's Bank in 20X6. **Note.** Use each of the four headings of the balanced scorecard to structure your discussion.

(16 marks)

(Total = 20 marks)

Section A questions

MCQ bank – mixed bank

321 A company has entered two different new markets.

In market A, it is initially charging low prices so as to gain rapid market share while demand is relatively elastic.

In market B, it is initially charging high prices so as to earn maximum profits while demand is relatively inelastic.

Which price strategy is the company using in each market?

O   Penetration pricing in market A and price skimming in market B
O   Price discrimination in market A and penetration pricing in market B
O   Price skimming in market A and penetration pricing in market B
O   Price skimming in market A and price discrimination in market B   **(2 marks)**

322 Which of the following statements is NOT consistent with the theory of constraints?

O   There is no inventory of work in progress or finished goods held
O   Raw materials are converted into sales as quickly as possible
O   Operations prior to the bottleneck operate at the same level as the bottleneck
O   Conversion costs and investment costs are kept to a minimum   **(2 marks)**

323 At the start of the year, a company has non-current assets amounting to $6 million and by the end of the year this figure has risen to $8 million after depreciation of $600,000 has been charged at the end of the year. Working capital at the start of the year has been reported at $0.5 million and by the year end had increased by $0.2 million. Profit for the same period is $1.6 million before any depreciation charges had been deducted.

What was the ROI of the company for the year, based on average capital employed?

O   11.49%
O   13.16%
O   14.29%
O   21.05%   **(2 marks)**

324 A budget that is continuously updated by adding a further accounting period (a month or quarter) when the earlier accounting period has expired is known as which of the following?

O   Zero-base budget
O   Rolling budget
O   Periodic budget
O   Flexible budget   **(2 marks)**

325 Division X and Division Y are profit centres in the same company. Division X makes a single component product. It has a fixed contract to supply an external customer with 5,000 units each month at a price of $35 per unit. All other sales are to Division Y at $30 per unit. Budgeted monthly profits for Division X are as follows:

	$
Sales: External	350,000
Sales to Division Y	150,000
	500,000
Variable costs	(270,000)
Fixed costs	(170,000
Profit	60,000

An external supplier offers to sell 4,000 units of the component to Division Y at a price of $25 per unit, for one month only. Division X would not be able to sell additional components externally.

If Division Y chooses to buy the components from the external supplier, how will profits for the month be affected?

- ○ Division X profit will be $0. The company's profit will be $20,000 lower.
- ○ Division X profit will be $0. The company's profit will be $28,000 lower.
- ○ Division X profit will be $12,000. The company's profit will be $20,000 lower.
- ○ Division X profit will be $12,000. The company's profit will be $28,000 lower. **(2 marks)**

326   The following are types of management accounting techniques.

(i)   Flow cost accounting
(ii)   Input/output analysis
(iii) Life cycle costing
(iv)   Activity-based costing

Which of the above techniques could be used by a company to account for its environmental costs?

- ○ i only
- ○ i and ii
- ○ ii and iii
- ○ All of the above **(2 marks)**

327   Which of the following statements describes target costing?

- ○ It allocated the expected cost of a product and then adds a margin to it to arrive at the target selling price

- ○ It allocates overhead costs to products by collecting the costs into pools and sharing them out according to each product's usage of the cost-driving activity

- ○ It identifies the market price of a product and then subtracts a desired profit margin to arrive at the target cost

- ○ It identifies different markets for a product and then sells that same product at different prices in each market **(2 marks)**

328   S Company is a manufacturer of multiple products and uses target costing. It has been noted that Product P currently has a target cost gap and the company wishes to close this gap.

Which of the following may be used to close the target cost gap for Product P?

- ○ Use overtime to complete work ahead of schedule
- ○ Substitute current raw materials with cheaper versions
- ○ Raise the selling price of P
- ○ Negotiate cheaper rent for S Company's premises **(2 marks)**

329   Tree Co is considering employing a sales manager. Market research has shown that a good sales manager can increase profit by 30%, an average one by 20% and a poor one by 10%. Experience has shown that the company has attracted a good sales manager 35% of the time, an average one 45% of the time and a poor one 20% of the time. The company's normal profits are $180,000 per annum and the sales manager's salary would be $40,000 per annum.

Based on the expected value criterion, which of the following represents the correct advice which Tree Co should be given?

- ○ Do not employ a sales manager as profits would be expected to fall by $1,300
- ○ Employ a sales manager as profits will increase by $38,700
- ○ Employ a sales manager as profits are expected to increase by $100
- ○ Do not employ a sales manager as profits are expected to fall by $39,900 **(2 marks)**

330   Which of the following may be used to study possible future outcomes when there are many different variables in the situation and the relationships between variables are not predictable?

- ○ Sensitivity analysis
- ○ Stress testing
- ○ Pay-off table
- ○ Simulation model **(2 marks)**

331   The following costs arise in relation to production of a new product.

    (i)   Research and development costs
    (ii)   Design costs
    (iii)   Testing costs
    (iv)   Advertising costs
    (v)   Production costs

In calculating the lifetime costs of the product, which of the above items would be **EXCLUDED**?

    ○   i, ii, and iii
    ○   ii and iii
    ○   iv and v
    ○   None of the above   **(2 marks)**

332   A company has two divisions. The divisions are identical in terms of the number and type of machines they have and the operations they carry out. However, one division was set up four years ago and the other was set up one year ago. Head office appraises the division using both the return on investment (ROI) and residual income (RI).

Which of the following statements is correct in relation to the outcome of the appraisal for each division?

    ○   Both ROI and RI will favour the older division
    ○   ROI will favour the older division, but RI will treat each fairly
    ○   RI will favour the newer division and ROI will favour the older division
    ○   Both RI and ROI will favour the newer division   **(2 marks)**

333   Which of the following is the best definition of a traceable divisional cost?

    ○   A variable cost incurred in a division

    ○   A cost incurred in a division over which the divisional manager has control

    ○   A cost attributable directly to a division over which the manager may or may not have control

    ○   Costs charged to a division, including both directly attributable costs and a share of general overheads   **(2 marks)**

334   A company makes and sells Product P. At the current selling price of $6 per unit, weekly demand is 4,000 units. It is estimated that for every $0.50 increase in price, sales demand will fall by 200 units, and for every $0.50 reduction in price, sales demand will increase by 200 units.

What is the formula for the sales demand curve for this product, where P is the sales price and Q is the quantity demanded?

    ○ $P = 6 - 0.0025Q$
    ○ $P = 16 - 0.0025Q$
    ○ $P = 6 - 0.005Q$
    ○ $P = 16 - 0.005Q$ **(2 marks)**

335   The following statements have been made about activity-based costing.

    (1)   There may be more than one cost driver for an activity.
    (2)   ABC involves some arbitrary allocation or apportionment of overhead costs.

Which of the above statements is/are true?

    ○   1 only
    ○   2 only
    ○   Neither 1 nor 2
    ○   Both 1 and 2   **(2 marks)**

(Total = 30 marks)

CBE style OTQ bank – mixed bank

72 mins

336 The following statements have been made when making comparisons between traditional absorption costing and activity-based costing. Are they true or false?

ABC has evolved as a response to the increase in support activities in modern organisations.	TRUE	FALSE
Absorption costing uses volume as a basis for cost allocation, and so tends to allocate too great a proportion of overheads to low volume products.	TRUE	FALSE

(2 marks)

337 A company makes a single product which it sells for $2 per unit.

Fixed costs are $13,000 per month.

The contribution/sales ratio is 40%.

Sales revenue is $62,500.

What is the margin of safety (in units)?

[   ] units

(2 marks)

338 The following statements have been made about the balanced scorecard. Are they true or false?

It focuses solely on non-financial performance measures.	TRUE	FALSE
It looks at both internal and external matters concerning the organisation.	TRUE	FALSE

(2 marks)

339 The following statements have been made about changing budgetary systems. Are they true or false?

The costs of implementation may outweigh the benefits.	TRUE	FALSE
Employees will always welcome any new system which improves planning and control within the organisation.	TRUE	FALSE

(2 marks)

340 C Co uses material B, which has a current market price of $0.80 per kg. In a linear program, where the objective is to maximise profit, the shadow price of material B is $2 per kg. Are the following statements true or false?

Contribution will be increased by $2 for each additional kg of material B purchased at the current market price.	TRUE	FALSE
The maximum price which should be paid for an additional kg of material B is $2.	TRUE	FALSE
Contribution will be increased by $1.20 for each additional kg of material B purchased at the current market price	TRUE	FALSE
The maximum price which should be paid for an additional kg of material B is $2.80	TRUE	FALSE

(2 marks)

341 The following budgeted data for Period 1 was available for a division selling two products, which are sold in a standard mix:

	Sales price per unit	Variable cost per unit	Sales volume in units
Product X	$40	$16	41,400
Product Y	$46	$20	10,350

The actual results for Period 1 were as follows:

	Sales price per unit	Variable cost per unit	Sales volume in units
Product X	$45	$16	38,800
Product Y	$48	$20	12,400

Select two boxes to indicate the total sales quantity contribution variance for Period 1 and whether it is favourable or adverse.

Value ($)	Sign
13,420	Favourable
15,840	Adverse

(2 marks)

342 Indicate, by selecting the relevant boxes, whether each of the following of the controls help to ensure the security of highly confidential information.

Logical access controls	YES	NO
Database controls	YES	NO
Hierarchical passwords	YES	NO
Range checks	YES	NO

(2 marks)

343 Total production costs for 900 units of output are $58,200 and total production costs for 1,200 units are $66,600.

The variable cost per unit is constant up to a production level of 2,000 units per month, but a step up of $6,000 in the monthly total fixed cost occurs when production reaches 1,100 units per month.

What is the total cost for a month when 1,000 units are produced?

$ _____

(2 marks)

344 The following circumstances may arise in relation to the launch of a new product. Which **TWO** of the circumstances favour a penetration pricing policy?

☐ Demand is relatively inelastic

☐ There are significant economies of scale

☐ The firm wishes to discourage new entrants to the market

☐ The product life cycle is particularly short

(2 marks)

345 Are the following statements about management information systems true or false?

They are designed to report on existing operations.	TRUE	FALSE
They have an external focus.	TRUE	FALSE

(2 marks)

346 The following are some of the areas which require control within a division.
Indicate, by selecting the relevant boxes, which areas the manager has control over in an investment centre.

Generation of revenues	YES	NO
Investment in non-current assets	YES	NO
Investment in working capital	YES	NO
Apportioned head office costs	YES	NO

(2 marks)

347 An investment centre in a manufacturing group produced the following results in the previous financial year:

	$'000
Operating profit	360
Capital employed: non-current assets	1,500
current assets	100

For the purpose of performance measurement, non-current assets are valued at cost. The investment centre is considering a new investment that will increase annual operating profit by $25,000, and will require an investment of $100,000 in a non-current asset and an additional $30,000 in working capital.

Will the performance measurement criteria of (1) return on investment (ROI) and (2) residual income (RI) motivate the centre manager to undertake the investment? Assume a notional capital charge of 18% on divisional capital.

	Yes	No
ROI	○	○
RI	○	○

(2 marks)

348 T Co makes and sells two products X and Y. The two products are sold in a product mix ratio of X:Y = 3:2. T Co's fixed costs per month amount to $30,000 and details of both products are as follows.

	X	Y
Selling price per unit	$58	$28
Marginal costs per unit	$26	$16

T Co wishes to earn a profit of $3,600 next month.

Using the given product mix, what total volume of sales units would be needed to achieve a target profit of $3,600?

☐ units

(2 marks)

349 A company introduced Product C to the market 12 months ago and is now about to enter the maturity stage of its life cycle. The maturity stage is expected to last for three months. The Director of Sales and Marketing has suggested four possible prices that the company could charge during the next three months. The following table shows the results of some market research into the level of weekly demand at alternative prices:

Selling price per unit	$300	$255	$240	$225
Weekly demand (units)	1,800	2,400	3,600	4,200

Each unit of product C has a variable cost of $114 and takes one standard hour to produce.

Which selling price will maximise the weekly profit during this stage of the product life cycle (to two decimal places)?

$ [   ]

(2 marks)

350 A company has received a special order for which it is considering the use of material B, which it has held in its inventory for some time. This inventory of 945 kg was bought at $4.50 per kg. The special order requires 1,500 kg of material B. If the inventory is not used for this order, it would be sold for $2.75 per kg. The current price of material B is $4.25 per kg.

What is the total relevant cost of material B for the special order (to two decimal places)?

$ [   ]

(2 marks)

351 Are the following statements about zero-based budgeting true or false?

Employees will focus on eliminating wasteful expenditure.	TRUE	FALSE
Short-term benefits could be emphasised over long-term benefits.	TRUE	FALSE

(2 marks)

352 An education department has a statutory obligation to report on the number of students on site throughout the day. In order to produce this information, a swipe card system has been introduced.

The following table details the costs of the swipe card system in its first year:

	$	Notes
Purchase price of the swipe system (vendor list price)	100,000	Invoiced and paid
Installation costs of the system (negotiated with vendor)	20,000	Invoiced and paid
Pre-launch testing costs (in-house)	17,000	Salaries time spent on testing
Cost per 100 swipe cards	5,000	1,000 cards purchased in the first year
Apportionment of the technology insurance cost	9,000	Fixed cost
Salary of clerk employed to collate and distribute swipe card system information	36,000	Fixed cost

What is the indirect cost of producing the information required in the first year of the swipe card system?

$ [   ]

(2 marks)

353 A company is making product P with the following cost card:

	$	$
Selling price		100
Marginal	25	
Labour	30	
Variable overheads	20	
Fixed overheads	10	
		(85)
Profit		15

Each unit of P takes one hour to make and the available labour and machinery are fully used in its current production of P. The company is considering making a new product, Q, but would have to divert labour and machine use from product P.

What is the relevant total cost per hour for labour and variable overheads which should be included in the cost of product q?

$ [   ]

(2 marks)

354 B Co operates a production process which generates a contribution of $4 per hour. Wages are paid at $7 per hour and labour is fully utilised. During busy periods workers are offered the chance to work overtime, which is paid $10 per hour. However, workers are currently refusing to work overtime because of an industrial dispute.

B Co has just received an additional order which must be fulfilled immediately and which will require 10 hours of labour to fulfil.

What is the total relevant cost of labour for the additional order?

$ [   ]

(2 marks)

355 Mabel Co manufactures and sells tables and chairs in a standard mix of one table to four chairs. The following information is available:

Product	Table	Chair
Variable cost per unit ($)	120	16
Contribution to sales ratio	0.4	0.6

Annual fixed costs are $100,000.

What is the breakeven point in sales revenue (to the nearest hundred dollars)?

$ [   ]

(2 marks)

(Total = 40 marks)

Answers

Part A answers

MCQ bank – Specialist cost and management accounting techniques

1   The correct answer is: All of the above.

   A product's life cycle costs are incurred from its design stage through development to market launch, production and sales, and finally to its eventual decline and withdrawal from the market.

   (Syllabus area A3(a))

2   The correct answer is: 2 only

   Financial returns can be improved over the life cycle of a product by minimising the breakeven time, minimising the time to get a new product to market and maximising the length of the product life cycle.

   (Syllabus area A3(c))

3   The correct answer is: $3.41

   Throughput per unit of Product X = $(40 − 10) = $30
   Throughput per bottleneck hour = $30/0.01 hours = $3,000
   Factory costs per year = $2,920,000 + (50,000 × $12) = $3,520,000
   Factory cost per bottleneck hour = $3,520,000/4,000 hours = $880
   Throughput accounting ratio = $3,000/$880 = 3.41

   (Syllabus area A4(b))

4   The correct answer is: Both 1 and 2

   In MFCA, a distinction is made between good finished output (positive output) and waste and emissions (negative output). Both types of output are given a cost. Performance can be improved by finding ways to reduce the amount of negative output – and so achieve the same amount of output with less input materials.

   (Syllabus area A5(b))

5   The correct answer is: The cost driver for materials handling and despatch costs is likely to be the number of orders handled.

   'The cost driver for quality inspection is likely to be batch size' is incorrect. The cost driver for quality inspection costs is likely to be either the number of units produced or the number of batches produced, depending on whether quality inspection is linked to batches produced or total production output. The batch size is not a factor that drives total inspection costs.

   'In the short run, all the overhead costs for an activity vary with the amount of the cost driver for the activity' is incorrect. Some costs of activities may vary with the volume of the activity, but other costs of the activity will be fixed costs. ' A cost driver is an activity based cost' is incorrect. A cost driver is not the cost itself; it is a measure of the volume or quantity of an activity.

   (Syllabus area A1 (a))

6   The correct answer is: $50.95

Variable costs	$
Year 1: $(30 + 6 + 4) × 25,000	1,000,000
Year 2: $(25 + 5 + 3) × 100,000	3,300,000
Year 3: $(20 + 4 + 2) × 75,000	1,950,000
R&D costs	940,000
Other fixed costs	3,000,000
Total life cycle costs	10,190,000
Total units made and sold	200,000
Average life cycle cost per unit	$50.95

   (Syllabus area A3 (b))

7   The correct answer is: Neither 1 nor 2

In throughput accounting, all inventory, including work in progress and finished goods, should be valued at the cost of their materials. They should not include any other costs (labour or overhead costs). The aim should not be to maximise the use of all available resources, because this will simply create unwanted inventory. The aim should be to maximise the use of the bottleneck resource and efficiency is achieved by meeting production schedules and delivery dates to customers.

(Syllabus area A4 (a))

8   The correct answer is: Contingent cost

The US Environment Protection Agency in 1998 suggested classifying environmental costs into four types: conventional costs, hidden costs (costs hidden because they are included in general overheads and not identified separately), contingent costs and image and relationship costs.

(Syllabus area A5 (a))

9   The correct answer is: Both 1 and 2

Factory labour costs are always treated as a part of the factory cost/conversion cost of a product. Throughput accounting does not make a distinction between direct and indirect costs. It is also assumed that labour costs are a fixed cost, so if machine time is the bottleneck resource, nothing is gained by improving labour efficiency, because this will not increase throughput.

(Syllabus area A4 (a))

10   The correct answer is: 3 only

ABC can be used for cost-plus pricing. Traditional absorption costing tends to allocate insufficient overhead costs to low-volume products that use up a disproportionate amount of time for order handling, production runs and set-ups. ABC is expensive and time-consuming to implement. It is therefore important to assess whether the benefits will outweigh the costs before implementing ABC.

(Syllabus area A1 (c))

11   The correct answer is: Products should be discontinued if there is a target cost gap.

If there is a target cost gap that cannot be eliminated, management may consider whether or not to continue with the product, since it will not be achieving the required profit margin. However, a decision to discontinue a product, or whether to continue making it, should not be based on target costs or profit margins alone. Therefore the statement 'Products should be discontinued if there is a target cost gap' is NOT true and this is the correct answer.

For services that have a large fixed cost base, other methods of cost control may be more appropriate, such as activity-based management, and a key to reducing costs is often increasing sales volumes rather than reducing expenditure. To achieve a target cost, one approach is to remove design features from a product specification that do not add value for customers (so do not affect the price that customers are willing to pay).

(Syllabus area A2(a/b))

12   This question appeared in the September 2017 exam.

The correct answer is: 1, 2 and 3

Environmental failure costs are costs incurred as a result of environmental issues being created either internally or outside the company. These can be financial or societal costs. Compensation, penalties and air pollution are all environmental failure costs.

(Syllabus area A1 (c))

13   The correct answer is: Output flows

Flow cost accounting divides the material flows into three categories: material, system and delivery and disposal.

(Syllabus area A1 (c))

14   The correct answer is: Method 1 and Method 2

The aim should be to improve the output capacity of the binding constraint. This can be done by achieving more output per unit of binding resource (improving efficiency) or obtaining more of the resource that is the binding constraint.

By increasing output through the binding constraint, a point will eventually be reached where it ceases to be the binding constraint, and another resource becomes the binding constraint.

(Syllabus area A1 (c))

15   The correct answer is: Reducing the machine time per unit to make the product

Reducing material costs or increasing the sales price will increase throughput per machine hour. Reducing factory costs will reduce the factory cost per machine hour. These will increase the TA ratio. Reducing the machine time per unit will increase throughput per hour and factory cost per hour by the same proportion, leaving the TA ratio unchanged.

(Syllabus area A1 (c))

CBE style OTQ bank – Specialist cost and management accounting techniques

16   The correct answer is: Both are true

A system of environmental management accounting provides environmental information for internal use by management, but not for external reporting. It is distinct from environmental accounting, which is concerned with external reporting (as well as internal reporting). Environmental management accounting systems typically make use of life cycle costing, given that there may be substantial clean-up and disposal costs at the end of the life of an activity or operation.

(Syllabus area A5(a))

17   The correct answers are: 'Unless output capacity is greater than sales demand, there will always be a binding constraint' and 'The production capacity of a bottleneck resource should determine the production schedule for the organisation as a whole'.

Output from a binding constraint should be used immediately, not built up as inventory, because it is the factor that constrains output and sales. Some inventory may build up before the binding constraint, but the general principle in throughput accounting is that any inventory is undesirable.

The production capacity of a bottleneck resource should determine the production schedule for the organisation as a whole. This means inevitably that there will be idle time in other parts of production where capacity is greater.

(Syllabus area A4(a))

18   The correct answer is: Capping.

Operation	Wash Units	Fill Units	Cap Units	Label Units
(a) Capacity in mins	(1,200 × 60)	(700 × 60)	(250 × 60)	(450 × 60)
	72,000	42,000	15,000	27,000
(b) Time in minutes per 12 units	6	3	1.5	2
Capacity in groups of 12 units ((a)/(b))	12,000	14,000	10,000	13,500

Therefore capping is the bottleneck as it is the process which determines the maximum number of units which can be produced.

(Syllabus area A1 (c))

19   The correct answers are: 'In a system of ABC, for costs that vary with production levels, the most suitable cost driver is likely to be direct labour hours or machine hours' and 'Activity based costing is a form of absorption costing'.

Implementation of ABC is likely to be cost effective when variable production costs are a low proportion of total production costs; and when overhead costs, traditionally assumed to be fixed costs, are a large proportion of total production costs.

At a unit level, the cost driver for production-related overheads is likely to be direct labour hours or machine hours.

It is a mistake to associate activity-based costs with the variable costs of an activity. Some of the costs may be variable in the short run, but others are not. So ABC costs should **not** be treated as relevant costs for the purpose of short-term decision making. It is more appropriate to think of ABC as a form of absorption costing, where overheads are allocated to activities and products on a more meaningful basis than with traditional absorption costing.

(Syllabus area A1 (a/c))

20   The correct answers are: 'Target costing may be applied to services that are provided free of charge to customers' is false and the others are true.

Cost reduction measures may reduce the perceived value of a product to customers, so that the target selling price becomes unachievable for the sales volume required. The projected cost of a new product may be reduced by simplifying the design (such as using more standard components, fewer components in total and removing design features that do not add value), but simplification of the design should not reduce the value of the product for customers.

Overhead costs are usually a large proportion of total costs; therefore it is important to have reliable estimates of sales demand at a given target sales price in order to establish a target cost. Target costing is dependent on identifying a target selling price for an item, so it is not appropriate for costing services provided free of charge. Call centre costs, for example, should be managed using other methods of cost control.

(Syllabus area A2 (b/c))

21   The correct answers are: 'An important use of life cycle costing is to decide whether to go ahead with the development of a new product' and 'Life cycle costing encourages management to find a suitable balance between investment costs and operating expenses'.

A product is usually most profitable during the maturity phase of its life cycle. Life cycle costing is not particularly useful for deciding the selling price for a product, because the appropriate selling price changes over the life of a product.

By looking at the costs over the entire life cycle of a product, and comparing these with expected sales revenues, a decision can be taken at an early stage, before too much cost has been committed, about whether to go ahead with developing a new product. Life cycle costing also helps management to consider the merits of investing more money at the design stage for a new product if this will reduce operating costs over the product life cycle.

(Syllabus area A3 (c)/A4(a))

22   The correct answer is: $362.50

Required return: $500,000 × 30% = $150,000
Total sales revenue: $550 × 800 units = $440,000
Therefore total cost = $440,000 − $150,000 = $290,000
Unit cost = $290,000/800 = $362.50

(Syllabus area A2(a))

23   The correct answers are: 'The majority of environmental costs are already captured within a typical organisation's accounting system. The difficulty lies in identifying them' is **true**. 'Input/output analysis divides material flows within an organisation into three categories: material flows; system flows; and delivery and disposal flows' is **false**.

Statement 2 refers to flow cost accounting rather than input/output analysis. Under the flow cost accounting technique, material flows within an organisation are divided into three categories: material flows; system flows; and delivery and disposal flows.

(Syllabus area A5(a))

24   The correct answer is: 500 units.

	A	B	C	D
Maximum sales demand	1,000	500	2,000	1,000
Selling price per unit	$15	$21	$18	$25
Material cost per unit	$6	$10	$9	$16
Throughput per unit	$9	$11	$9	$9
Machine hours per unit	0.1	0.2	0.3	0.2
Throughput per machine hour	$90	$55	$30	$45
Priority for manufacture	1st	2nd	4th	3rd

In the 750 hours available, the company should make 1,000 units of A (100 hours), then 500 units of B (100 hours), then 1,000 units of D (200 hours) leaving 350 hours available to make 1,166 units of Product C.

(Syllabus area A4(d))

25   The correct answer is: $92.00

(Syllabus area A3 (b))

	Year 1	Year 2	Year 3	Year 4	Total
	$'000	$'000	$'000	$'000	$'000
R&D costs	900	300			1,200
Marketing	300	300	100	100	800
Production	400	400	750	300	1,850
Customer services	100	150	250	50	550
Disposal				200	200
Total					4,600

Units	50,000
Life cycle cost per unit	$92.00

26   The correct answer is: $80

The return per factory hour is measured using the bottleneck resource as a measure of factory hours. Return = Throughput

Return per machine hour = $(30 − 10)/0.25 hours = $80.

(Syllabus area A1 (c))

27   The correct answer is: 2.4

Throughput per unit of Product X = $(50 − 14) = $36.

Throughput per bottleneck hour = $36/0.05 hours = $720

Factory costs per year = $1,620,000 + (18,000 × $10) = $1,800,000

Factory cost per bottleneck hour = $1,800,000/6,000 hours = $300

Throughput accounting ratio = $720/$300 = 2.40.

(Syllabus area A1 (c))

28 The correct answers are:

- ABC recognises the complexity of modern manufacturing by the use of multiple cost drivers
- ABC establishes separate cost pools for support activities

Reapportionment of service centre costs is not done via ABC specifically. It would instead be done via the direct, step or reciprocal method under traditional absorption costing. If ABC is used to allocate costs it uses the cost driver approach, where costs are allocated to a cost pool and a cost driver is used to allocate to a product.

ABC is an appropriate system if overheads are high relative to prime costs and when there is significant diversity in the product range. If overheads could be allocated based solely on production time then traditional AC would be fine.

(Syllabus area A1 (a))

29 The correct answers are:

- Labour costs are a relatively minor proportion of total costs
- Overheads vary with many different measures of activity

That overheads are difficult to predict, and cost drivers difficult to identify, are not reasons to prefer ABC.

(Syllabus area A1 (a))

30 The correct answers are:

- Set up costs
- Raw material handling costs

These two costs are likely to increase, as batch sizes get smaller.

Remember, the whole aim of JIT is to hold no inventory. Thus raw material storage costs should fall, not rise. Customer order costs will not be changed by the introduction of JIT.

(Syllabus area A1 (a))

Linacre Co

31 The correct answer is: Production set up $350 per set up, product testing $200 per test.

ABC recovery rates for production set ups and product testing

Cost Pool	Cost ($)	Cost driver	Number of drivers	ABC recovery rate ($)
Production set ups	105,000	Set-ups	300	350 per set-up
Product testing	300,000	Tests	1,500	200 per test

32 The correct answer is: Component supply and storage $50 per order, customer orders and delivery $112.50 per order.

ABC recovery rates for component supply and storage, and customer orders and delivery

Cost Pool	Cost ($)	Cost driver	Number of drivers	ABC recovery rate ($)
Component supply and storage	25,000	Component orders	500	50 per order
Customer orders and delivery	112,500	Customer orders	1,000	112.50 per order

33   The correct answer is: General overhead $0.50 per unit, Direct labour cost $1.30 per unit

General overhead per unit of Product ZT3

General overhead = 0.50 per unit

$900,000/300,000 = $3/direct labour hour

9,000/6 or 1,500 direct labour hours spent on manufacture (10 minutes per unit)

1,500 hours/9,000 units × $3/unit = $0.50/unit

Direct labour per unit of Product ZT3

10 minutes per unit at $7.80 per hour = 10/60 × 7.80 = $1.30 per unit

34   The correct answer is: Both 1 and 2

Statement 1 is true. This is one of the main flaws associated with a mark-up approach to costing. The product's price is based on its cost, but no one might want to buy at that price.

Statement 2 is true. There is an emphasis on the planning and design stage with target costing. This becomes very important to the cost of the product because if something is designed such that it is needlessly expensive to make, it does not matter how efficient the production process is: it will always be a struggle to make satisfactory profits.

35   The correct answer is: 2 only.

ABC is a method of absorption costing that uses cost drivers to calculate absorption rates per unit of overhead activity, and then apportion overhead costs to products. It is not a technique for identifying variable overhead costs.

ABC can be used as a basis for preparing budgets. This approach to budgeting is called activity-based budgeting (ABB).

Triple

36   The correct answer is: **$65 per unit**

Traditional cost per unit

	Product D
	$
Material	20
Labour @ $6 per hour	3
Direct costs	23
Production overhead @ $28 per machine hour	42
Total production cost per unit	65

37   The correct answer is: **$7,000**.

Product C uses 1,250 machine hours (W1) × $5.60 per hour (W2) = $7,000

Workings

(1)   Total machine hours (needed as the driver for machining overhead)

Product	Hours/unit	Production units	Total hours
D	1½	750	1,125
C	1	1,250	1,250
P	3	7,000	21,000
Total machine hours			23,375

(2)

Type of overhead	Driver	%	Total overhead	Level of driver activity	Cost/driver
Machining	Machine hours	20	$130,900	23,375 (W1)	$5.60

38   The correct answer is: **$9,818**.

Type of overhead	Driver	%	Total overhead	Level of driver activity	Cost/driver
Materials handling	Material movements	15	98,175	120	818.13

Product D:

Activity	Level of activity	Cost
Material handling	12	818.13 × 12 = 9,818

39   The correct answer is: Number of inspections

The number of inspections per product is likely to be the main driver of quality control costs. The number of set ups is unlikely to have an effect on the quality control costs. Some product lines may require more inspections than others, therefore 'number of units produced' is not sufficient to use as the cost driver. Labour hours will not reflect the quality control aspect of individual products.

40   The correct answer is: The benefits obtained from ABC might not justify the costs.

Some companies find the costs of implementing ABC to be prohibitive. If Triple Co believes that the difference in cost per unit of each product under ABC and traditional based costing systems is not material, it should not adopt ABC.

Distracters:

- ABC can be applied to all overheads, not just production overheads.
- The cost per unit provided under ABC principles will be more accurate.
- ABC costing will provide much better insight into what drives overhead costs.

Brick by Brick

41   The correct answer is: $3,000

Overhead absorption rate is calculated as $400,000/40,000hrs = $10/hr

A GC takes 300 labour hours to complete.

300 × $10/hr = $3,000

42   The correct answer is: GC: $180

Supervisor costs of the **GC using ABC**.

1   **Cost drivers**

	Costs $	Number of drivers	Cost per driver $
Supervisor	90,000	500	180

2   **Cost per product**

	Supervisor
Cost per driver (W1)	$180
GC	180 × 1 = 180

43   The correct answer is: EX: $1,400

Planning costs of the **EX using ABC**.

1   **Cost drivers**

	Costs $	Number of drivers	Cost per driver $
Planning	70,000	250	280

2   **Cost per product**

	Planning
Cost per driver (W1)	$280
EX	280 × 5 = 1,400

44   The correct answer is: 'Changing to a system of ABC costing should lead to a more competitive price being charged for the GC' is **true**. 'Using ABC would cause total overhead costs to increase' is **false**.

ABC leads to more competitive pricing of the GC because it is allocated a fairer proportion of the total overheads. This will reflect the reality of the overheads that the GC is actually generating. Traditional absorption costing is more arbitrary which can lead to uncompetitive pricing.

Total overhead costs will be the same no matter which method of allocation is used, therefore 'Using ABC would cause total overhead costs to increase' is false.

45   The correct answer is: ABC improves pricing decisions.

It is ABC which gives a better indication of where cost savings can be made. BBB uses cost-plus pricing and so more accurate costs will lead to better pricing decisions.

ABC is expensive to implement and BBB currently has an absorption costing system set up.

ABC does not eliminate the need for cost apportionment. It may still be required at the cost pool stage for shared items such as rent.

Jola Publishing Co

46   The correct answer is: $2.57 per unit

Number of units produced per year = 1,000,000 + (12 × 10,000) = 1,120,000 units

Overhead absorption rate is calculated as $2,880,000/1,120,000 units = $2.57/unit

47   The correct answer is:

	Correct order
Step 1	Identify major activities within each department which creates cost.
Step 2	Create a cost centre/cost pool for each activity – the 'activity cost pool'.
Step 3	Determine what causes the cost of each activity – the 'cost driver'.
Step 4	Calculate the absorption rate for each 'cost driver'.
Step 5	Calculate the overhead cost per unit of CB and TJ.

48   The correct answer is: $1,800,000

Production of CB takes a total of 100,000 hours at **$18 per machine hour**

Cost per driver

Cost pool	Cost $'000	Quantity of cost drivers	Rate per cost driver $	
Production costs	2,160	120,000*	18	per machine hour

* Number of machine hours

CB
1,000,000 units × 6 mins/60 = 100,000 hours

TJ
(10,000 × 12) units × 10 mins/60 = 20,000 hours

49   The correct answer is: $66,800

Quality control of the TJ : $3,340 per inspection × 20 inspections

Cost per driver

Cost pool	Cost $'000	Quantity of cost drivers	Rate per cost driver $	
Quality control	668	180 + 20 = 200	3,340	per inspection

50   The correct answer is: More accurate costs per unit.

Distracters:

There will not be a reduction in overhead costs as a result of the adoption of ABC. However, management of Jola Publishing Co may benefit from improved decision making regarding cost control, if they understand the cost drivers better.

ABC tends to be a more expensive approach to absorption costing

ABC is a more complex form of costing

Corrie

51   The correct answer is: $360,000.

Profit per day = throughput contribution − conversion cost

= [($80 × 6,000) + ($80 × 4,500) + ($200 × 1,200)] − $720,000 = $360,000

52   The correct answer is: 125%.

Product	Minutes in alpha per unit	Minutes in alpha per day
X	60/1,200 = 0.05	6,000 × 0.05 = 300
Y	60/1,500 = 0.04	4,500 × 0.04 = 180
Z	60/600 = 0.10	1,200 × 0.10 = 120
		600

Total hours = 600 minutes ÷ 60 = 10 hours

Hours available = 8, hours produced = 10, ∴ **Efficiency** = 10/8 × 100% = 125%

53   The correct answer is: $90,000

Conversion cost per factory hour = $720,000/8 = $90,000

54   The correct answer is:

X 1.2

Y 1.5

Z 1.5

TA ratio = throughput contribution per factory hour/conversion cost per factory hour

Product	Throughput contribution per factory hour	Cost per factory hour	TA ratio
X	$80 × (60 ÷ 0.05 mins) = $96,000	$80,000	1.2
Y	$80 × (60 ÷ 0.04 mins) = $120,000	$80,000	1.5
Z	$200 × (60 ÷ 0.10 mins) = $120,000	$80,000	1.5

55   The correct answers are:

'TA assumes that labour costs are largely fixed' and 'TA assumes that material costs can be controlled in the short term'. There is a technical article on ACCA's website called 'Throughput accounting and the theory of constraints' which explains this.

'The TA ratio for each product should be less than 1' is incorrect. The TA ratio should be greater than 1.

'Corrie Co's priority, using TA, should be given to products with the highest throughput contribution per unit' is incorrect. Priority should be given to products with the highest throughput contribution per unit of bottleneck resource.

A Co

56   The correct answers are:

    B1 Department 1   40 units

    B1 Department 2   42 units

    B2 Department 1   30 units

    B2 Department 2   56 units

	Maximum number of B1 units	Maximum number of B2 units
Department 1	480/12 = 40	480/16 = 30
Department 2	840/20 = 42	840/15 = 56

57   The correct answer is: $1.93.

The question requires us to use **traditional contribution analysis**:

We need to calculate the contribution (sales less direct materials, labour and variable overheads) per unit of the bottleneck resource, which is time in Department 1. The contribution maximising output is found by dividing contribution per unit by the time in minutes required in Department 1.

		B1
	$	$
Sales price		50.00
Less variable costs		
Direct materials	10.00	
Direct labour	10.40	
Variable overheads	6.40	
		(26.80)
Contribution		23.20

	$
Contribution per unit of limiting factor	$\dfrac{23.20}{12} = \$1.933$

58   The correct answer is: $3.13

The **throughput approach** is based on throughput maximisation. Throughput is defined as **sales less direct materials**.

	B2
	$
Sales price	65
Less direct materials	(15)
	50

Throughput per minute of bottleneck resource is:

	B2
	$
	50/16 = 3.125

59   The correct answer is: The throughput accounting approach is more suitable for short-term decision making than limiting factor analysis

The fundamental belief in throughput accounting is that all costs except direct material costs are largely fixed; therefore to work on the basis of maximising contribution is flawed because to do so is to take into account costs that cannot be controlled in the short term anyway. In most businesses, it is simply not possible to hire workers on a daily basis and lay workers off if they are not busy.

Distracters:

- In throughput accounting idle time must be accepted. To do otherwise can lead to non-bottleneck activities being falsely identified as bottleneck activities, and possibly obsolescence if products need to be stored for a period of time

- Bottlenecks cannot be eliminated, only the activity identified as the bottleneck can change

- A certain amount of buffer material may need to be held in order to maximise throughput through the bottleneck activity

60   The correct answer is:

Correct order	
Step 1	Identify A Co's bottlenecks.
Step 2	Decide how to exploit the system's bottlenecks.
Step 3	Subordinate everything else to the decisions made about exploiting the bottlenecks.
Step 4	Elevate the system's bottlenecks.

Step 1   Identify A Co's bottlenecks

Before any other work can be carried out, the bottleneck must first be identified.

Step 2   Decide how to exploit the system's bottlenecks

This involves making sure that the bottleneck resource is actively being used as much as possible and is producing as many units as possible.

Step 3   Subordinate everything else to the decisions made about exploiting the bottlenecks

The production capacity of the bottleneck resource should determine the production schedule for the organisation as a whole

Step 4   Elevate the system's bottlenecks

It is important that an organisation does not ignore Step 2 and jump straight to Step 4, which often happens. This ensures that no unnecessary capital investment occurs.

Cam Co

61   The correct answer is: $130

Target selling price per unit $200
Profit margin 35%
Target cost $200 − ($200 × 35%) = $130

62   The correct answer is: $21.60

Direct material cost

Parts to be replaced by standard parts = $40 × 80% = $32
New cost of standard parts at 45% (100% − 55%) = $14.40
Unique irreplaceable parts (original cost) = $40 × 20% = $8
New cost = $8 × 90% = $7.20
Revised direct material cost = $14.40 + $7.20 = $21.60

63   The correct answer is: $10.98.

Direct labour

$Y = ax^b$

b = − 0.152 (given in question)

The question states that a learning curve of 90% is expected to occur until the 100th unit has been completed.

Total labour time for first 100 units

x = 100

The question states that the first unit is expected to take 45 minutes (a = 45)

$Y = 45 × 100^{-0.152}$
   = 45 × (1/2.0137)
   = 22.3469 minutes

Therefore, labour time for 100 units = 22.3469 × 100 = 2,234.69 minutes

Labour time for the 100th unit

Time for 99 units

$Y = 45 × 99^{-0.152}$
   = 45 × (1/2.01065)
   = 22.38082 minutes

Therefore, labour time for 99 units = 22.38082 × 99 = 2,215.70 minutes

Therefore, time for 100th unit = 2,234.69 − 2,215.70 = 18.99 minutes, say 19 minutes

Labour time for remaining 49,900 units × 19 = 948,100 minutes
Total labour time for 50,000 units = 2,234.69 + 948,100 = 950,334.69 minutes

Therefore, total labour cost = (950,334.69/60) × $34.67 per hour = $549,135
Average labour cost per unit = $549,135/50,000 = $10.98

64   The correct answer is: Both statements are false.

Cam Co's target costing system may take product development costs into consideration, but recovery of product design and development costs is associated more with life cycle costing. Even with life cycle costing, recovery of design and development costs is not assured: much depends on whether customers will buy enough webcams at the target price.

In target costing, a cost gap is the difference between the current estimate of the cost per webcam and the target cost that Cam Co wants to achieve.

65   The correct answer is: Redesign the webcam

Changes to selling price will have no effect upon target cost. The remaining options (employ more specialist staff; increase the number of bespoke components) would serve to increase the target cost gap rather than decrease it. If a product cannot be made within the target cost, so that a cost gap exists, the targets must be reduced, or the product redesigned.

Yam Co

66   The correct answer is:

    Product A: 450,000 metres
    Product B: 450,000 metres
    Product C: 562,500 metres

Output capacity for each process

Total processing hours for the factory = 225,000

	Product A Metres	Product B Metres	Product C Metres
Pressing	225,000/0.50 = 450,000	225,000/0.50 = 450,000	225,000/0.40 = 562,500

67   The correct answer is: $90

Conversion cost	= Labour costs + factory costs
	= (225,000 hours × $10) + $18,000,000
	= $20,250,000

Conversion cost per factory hour   = $20,250,000/225,000 hours = $90

68   The correct answer is: $115

Return per factory hour = Sales − direct costs/usage of bottleneck resource in hours

	Product B $
Selling price per metre	60.00
Raw material cost per metre	2.50
Return	57.50
Usage of bottleneck resource in hours	0.50
Return per factory hour	115.00

69   The correct answer is: 1.41

Throughput accounting ratios

TPAR = Return per factory hour/total conversion cost per factory hour

Return per factory hour = Sales − direct costs/usage of bottleneck resource in hours

	Product A $
Return per factory hour	134.00
Conversion cost per factory hour	95.00
TPAR	1.41

70   The correct answer is: Both statements are true.

The theory of constraints is based on the view that the focus should be on elevating a bottleneck resource to the level where it ceases to be a bottleneck, and at this time a new bottleneck will 'take over'. The throughput accounting ratio is the ratio of return per factory hour divided by cost per factory hour. If this ratio is less than 1, the commercial viability of Yam Co's product should be questioned.

Part B answers

MCQ bank – Decision-making techniques

71   The correct answer is: 2 only.

The decision options are given expected values, not the various different possible outcomes from each decision option. Each possible outcome is given a value, but not an expected value (EV).

(Syllabus area B6(e))

72   The correct answer is: 1 only.

In circumstances of inelastic demand, prices should be increased because revenues will increase and total costs will reduce (because quantities sold will reduce).

Price elasticity of demand is measured as the amount of change in quantity demanded (measured as a percentage of the current sales volume) divided by the amount of change in sales price (measured as a percentage of the current sales price).

$$\frac{\text{The change in quantity demanded, as a \% of demand}}{\text{The change in price, as a \% of the price}}$$

(Syllabus area B4(b))

73   The correct answer is: 2 only

A price in excess of full cost per unit will not necessarily ensure that a company will cover all its costs and make a profit. Making a profit with cost plus pricing also depends on working at a sufficient capacity level, so that all fixed costs are covered by sales revenue.

Cost plus pricing is an appropriate pricing strategy when there is no comparable market price for the product or service.

(Syllabus area B4(g))

74   The correct answer is: 1 only

Expected value is a more reliable guide to the outcome from a situation that will occur many times over than for an outcome that will happen only once. A risk-averse decision maker makes decisions on the basis that the worst outcome will occur, but no one can avoid risk entirely in decision making.

(Syllabus area B6(b))

75   The correct answer is: Price discrimination

Price discrimination involves charging different prices in two or more different markets. This is only effective when the markets can be kept entirely separate – such as charging different prices for different age groups (children and old age pensioners), or charging a different price for a product or service at different times of the day or week.

(Syllabus area B4(g))

76   The correct answer is: $2,802,000

When sales revenue is $1.5 million, total contribution is 45% × $1.5 million = $675,000.

This leaves a further $625,000 of fixed costs to cover. To achieve breakeven, sales in excess of $1.5 million need to be $625,000/0.48 = $1.302 million.

Total sales to achieve breakeven = $1.5 million + $1.302 million = $2.802 million.

(Syllabus area B2(b))

77   The correct answer is: $7,500

EV of Project 1 = (0.1 × 70,000) + (0.4 × 10,000) − (0.5 × 7,000) = $7,500
EV of Project 2 = (0.1 × 25,000) + (0.4 × 12,000) + (0.5 × 5,000) = $9,800
EV of Project 3 = (0.1 × 50,000) + (0.4 × 20,000) − (0.5 × 6,000) = $10,000

Project 3 would be chosen on the basis of EV without perfect information. With perfect information, this decision would be changed to Project 1 if market research indicates strong demand and Project 2 if market research indicates weak demand.

EV with perfect information: (0.1 × 70,000) + (0.4 × 20,000) + (0.5 × 5,000) = $17,500

Value of perfect information = $(17,500 − 10,000) = $7,500 − ignoring the cost of obtaining the information.

(Syllabus area B6(f))

78   The correct answer is: $2,750

	FP1	FP2	Total
Input to further processing (kg)	5,500	4,000	
Finished output (kg)	4,950	3,800	
	$	$	$
Revenue from sales of FP1/FP2	44,550	34,200	
Relevant further processing costs	(11,000)	(12,000)	
Revenue from sales of CP1/CP2	(33,000)	(20,000)	
	550	2,200	2,750

(Syllabus area B5(d))

79   The correct answer is: There are two breakeven points: $5.64 million and $6.36 million

	$
Total cost at sales of $6.8 million	6,560,000
Deduct step increase in fixed costs	(400,000)
Total cost excluding step cost increase	6,160,000
Total cost at sales of $5.2 million	5,440,000
Therefore variable cost of sales of $1.6 million	720,000

Variable cost = 720,000/1,600,000 = 45% of sales. Contribution/sales ratio is 55%.

	$
Total cost at sales of $6.8 million	6,560,000
Variable cost (45%)	(3,060,000)
Fixed cost	3,500,000

If fixed costs are $3.5 million at the higher sales level and $3.1 million at the lower sales level.

When fixed costs are $3.1 million, breakeven sales = $3.1 million/0.55 = $5.636 million

When fixed costs are $3.5 million, breakeven sales = $3.5 million/0.55 = $6.363 million

(Syllabus area B2(b))

80   The correct answer is: Simulation modelling

A unique feature of simulation modelling using the Monte Carlo method is the use of random numbers to determine the value of input variables to the model.

(Syllabus area B6(a))

81   The correct answer is: $1.968 million

Breakeven sales = $(2.4 million − 400,000) = $2,000,000

Contribution at this level of sales = $360,000. Therefore contribution/sales ratio = 360,000/2,000,000 = 18%

Variable costs = 82% of sales. At a sales level of $2.4 million, variable costs = 82% × $2.4 million = $1.968 million

(Syllabus area B2(c))

82   The correct answer is: Up to but not including $12.50

The shadow price of a limiting resource is the amount above the normal variable cost that will be added to the objective function (total contribution) if one extra unit of the resource is made available. This means that the company would increase contribution by paying up to $(8 + 4.50) = $12.50 per hour for additional labour time. However, it would not pay exactly $12.50, as this would leave it no better and no worse off than if it did not have the extra labour hour.

(Syllabus area B3(d))

83   The correct answer is: Statements 1 and 2 only

When the price elasticity of demand is elastic, a reduction in price by x% will increase the quantity demanded by more than x% and as a result total sales revenue will increase. Without knowing about marginal costs, it is not possible to determine whether profits would increase or fall.

(Syllabus area B4(b))

84   The correct answer is: $1.50 per hour for the next 38,000 direct labour hours

If one extra direct labour hour is available, the optimal solution will change to the point where:

(1): sales demand for X	x	=	10,000
(2): direct labour	5x + 4y	=	60,001
Multiply (1) by 5			
(3)	5x	=	50,000
Subtract (3) from (2)	4y	=	10,001
	y	=	2,500.25

Total contribution = $(10,000 × $8) + $(2,500.25 × $6) = $80,000 + $15,001.15 = $95,001.50

Total contribution in original solution = $(10,000 × $8) + $(2,500 × $6) = $95,000

The shadow price per direct labour hour is therefore $1.50

The solution is changing because each additional labour hour allows the company to produce an additional 0.25 units of Product Y, to increase total contribution by $1.50.

This shadow price will cease to apply when the direct labour hours constraint is replaced in the optimal solution by the sales demand for Product Y constraint. At this level of output, total labour hours would be (10,000 units of X at 5 hours) + (12,000 units of Y at 4 hours) = 98,000 hours.

The shadow price of $1.50 per hour therefore applies for an additional 38,000 hours above the current limit.

(Syllabus area B3(d))

85   The correct answer is: $4.00

If one extra direct labour hour is available, the optimal solution will change to the point where:

(1): direct labour hours	2x + 4y	=	10,001
(2): materials	4x + 2y	=	14,000
Multiply (1) by 2			
(3)	4x + 8y	=	20,002
Subtract (2) from (3)	6y	=	6,002
	y	=	1,000.333
Substitute in (2)	4x + 2,000.667	=	14,000
	x	=	2,999.8333

Total contribution = $(2,999.833 × $12) + $(1,000.333 × $18) = $35,998 + $18,006 = $54,004

Total contribution in original solution = $(3,000 × $12) + $(1,000 × $18) = $54,000

The shadow price per direct labour hour is therefore $54,004 - $54,000 = $4

(Syllabus area B3(d))

CBE style OTQ bank – Decision-making techniques

86 The correct answer is: Z3 1st   Z2 2nd   Z1 3rd

	Z1	Z2	Z3
Materials per unit	7 kg	4 kg	2 kg
	$	$	$
Profit per unit	40	35	30
Add back fixed overheads	30	25	20
Contribution per unit	70	60	50
Contribution per kg	10	15	25
Ranking	3rd	2nd	1st

87 The correct answer is: Total revenue will fall and profit will fall.

If demand is price-inelastic, a reduction in price will result in a fall in total sales revenue. At the lower price, there will be some increase in sales demand, so total costs will increase. With falling revenue and increasing costs, profits will fall.

(Syllabus area B4(b))

88 The correct answer is: W, Y, X then Z

Product	W	X	Y	Z
Extra cost of external purchase	$1	$2.1	$2	$1
Direct labour hours per unit	0.1	0.3	0.25	0.2
Extra cost per hour saved by purchasing	$10	$7	$8	$5
Priority for external purchasing	4th	2nd	3rd	1st
Priority for making in-house	1st	3rd	2nd	4th

(Syllabus area B5(b))

89 The correct answer is: 200%

Breakeven point = $20,000 = 500 × (selling price – $20)
$20,000/500 = $40
$40 = selling price – $20
$60 = selling price
Profit mark up on marginal cost = ($60 – $20) / $20 × 100% = 200%

Note. Fixed overheads ($40) are omitted, as only marginal costs are included in the calculation of the profit or 'contribution' to the recovery in the fixed costs of $20,000.

(Syllabus area B2(b) and B4(h))

90 The correct answer is: Sensitivity analysis

The 'What if' refers to the type of question used in sensitivity analysis. For example, what if the volume of sales is 10% less than expected? What if variable unit costs are 5% more than expected?

(Syllabus area B6(b))

91 The correct answers are:

- Identify all possible outcomes and their probabilities
- Assume the investor is risk neutral

Using EV for decision making is more appropriate when the decision will often be repeated, because an EV is an estimate of the long-run average outcome. However, EV can be used as the basis for making a one-off decision, even though this has severe limitations.

(Syllabus area B6(b))

92 The correct answer is: Opportunity cost

The question provides a definition of opportunity cost. An opportunity cost is a relevant cost for the purpose of decision making, but the definition in the question is too narrow to fit the term 'relevant cost'.

(Syllabus area B1(c))

93 The correct answer is: $376

	$
Additional purchases (5 tonnes × $50)	250
Relevant cost of material M already held: higher of	
$126 and (3 × $35)	126
Relevant cost total	376

(Syllabus area B1(b))

94 The correct answer is: P1

	Weekly contribution			
	Price P1	Price P2	Price P3	Price P4
	$	$	$	$
Best possible	30,000	31,500	32,000	31,500
Most likely	24,000	26,250	28,000	27,000
Worst possible	18,000	17,500	16,000	13,500

The maximin decision rule is to select the price offering the maximum possible benefit under the worst of circumstances. (It is similar to the minimax rule for decisions on minimising cost.) Price P1 will provide the biggest weekly contribution under the worst of circumstances, which is a contribution of $18,000 if the worst possible demand occurs. Only the bottom line of the above table needs to be calculated for your answer. The full table is shown here for the sake of completeness.

(Syllabus area B6(d))

95 The correct answer is: Choice 4

EV of Choice 1 = $9,500
EV of Choice 2 = (0.3 × 14,000) + (0.3 × 10,000) + (0.4 × 5,000) = $9,200
EV of Choice 3 = (0.4 × 10,000) + (0.6 × 9,000) = $9,400
EV of Choice 4 = (0.7 × 8,000) + (0.3 × 14,000) = $9,800

(Syllabus area B6(e))

96 The correct answer is: 4,000 units of W and 4,000 units of Z

Material	W	X	Y	Z
	$	$	$	$
Extra cost per unit of external purchase	1	6	3	2
Total extra cost of external purchase	4,000	12,000	9,000	8,000
Fixed costs saved by not making in-house	(5,000)	(8,000)	(6,000)	(7,000)
Difference	(1,000)	4,000	3,000	1,000

It would save $1,000 in cash to buy Material W externally. If full production can be achieved for the other materials, only W would be purchased externally. However, there is insufficient capacity to produce all three materials in-house.

Only 8,000 units can be produced in-house. If all the requirement for W is purchased externally (4,000 units), at least 1,000 units of X, Y or Z must be purchased externally too. The additional cost of buying Z externally is the least of these three.

If in-house production of Material Z is reduced to 3,000 units, the additional cost of external purchase would be only $6,000, so that $1,000 would be saved by purchasing all of Z externally.

(Syllabus area B5(b))

97 The correct answers are:

- Demand is 'perfectly inelastic'
- There is no change in the quantity demanded, regardless of any change in price

Demand is perfectly inelastic (that is, price elasticity is zero) when price changes have no impact upon demand.

The formula for the price elasticity of demand is percentage change in demand divided by percentage change in price; it will equal zero only if demand remains unchanged. A perfectly inelastic demand curve is a vertical straight line.

(Syllabus area B4(d))

98 The correct answer is: P2

Weekly contribution

	Price P1 $	Price P2 $	Price P3 $	Price P4 $
Best possible	30,000	31,500	32,000	31,500
Most likely	24,000	26,250	28,000	27,000
Worst possible	18,000	17,500	16,000	13,500

Regret

	Price P1 $	Price P2 $	Price P3 $	Price P4 $
Best possible	2,000	500	0	500
Most likely	4,000	1,750	0	1,000
Worst possible	0	500	2,000	4,500
Maximum regret	4,000	1,750	2,000	4,500

The maximum regret is minimised by selecting Price P2

(Syllabus area B6(d))

99 The correct answer is: $1,500

EV of Project 1 = (0.2 × 80,000) + (0.4 × 50,000) − (0.4 × 5,000) = $34,000
EV of Project 2 = (0.2 × 60,000) + (0.4 × 25,000) + (0.4 × 10,000) = $26,000

Project 1 would be chosen on the basis of EV without perfect information. With perfect information, this decision would be changed to Project 2 if market research indicates weak demand.

EV with perfect information: (0.2 × 80,000) + (0.4 × 50,000) + (0.4 × 10,000) = $40,000

Value of perfect information = $(40,000 − 34,000) − $4,500 cost = $1,500

(Syllabus area B6(f))

100 The correct answer is: $5.188 million

Weighted average sales price per unit = [(20 × 2) + (18 × 3) + (24 × 5)]/(2 + 3 + 5) = $21.40
Weighted average variable cost per unit = [(11 × 2) + (12 × 3) + (18 × 5)]/(2 + 3 + 5) = $14.80
Therefore weighted average contribution per unit = $(21.40 − 14.80) = $6.60
Weighted average C/S ratio = 6.60/21.40 = 0.3084112

Sales required to achieve target contribution of $1.6 million = $1.6 million/0.3084112 = $5.188 million.

(Syllabus area B2(d))

101 The correct answer is: To gain insight into which assumptions or variables in a situation are critical

Sensitivity analysis can be used to identify how much the outcome from a situation or decision would be different if the value of an input variable changes. In this way, the input variables that are most critical to the situation or decision can be identified. Sensitivity analysis can also be described as assessing how projected performance or outcome will be affected by changes in the assumptions that have been used.

(Syllabus area B6(a))

102   The correct answer is: $96

An increase in price of $25 will result in a fall in demand quantity by 6,250 units. Each $1 change in price therefore results in a change in demand by 6,250/25 = 250 units.

Demand Q will be 0 when the price P is $145 + $(5,000/250) = $165
Demand function = 165 − Q/250 = 165 − 0.004Q
Marginal revenue = 165 − 0.008Q

Profit is maximised when marginal revenue equals marginal cost:

When 27 = 165 − 0.008Q, so Q = 138/0.008 = 17,250

Price = 165 − (17,250/250) = $96   (Syllabus area B4(f))

103   The correct answer is: $914,000

Product	A	B	C	Total
	$'000	$'000	$'000	$'000
Sales revenue	360	720	200	1,280
Variable costs	90	240	110	440
Contribution	270	480	90	840
Fixed costs	180	360	60	600

Contribution/sales ratio = 840/1,280 = 0.65625

Breakeven point in sales revenue = $600,000/0.65625 = $914,286

With CVP analysis for a company that sells several products, a fixed sales mix has to be assumed.

(Syllabus area B2(b))

104   The correct answers are:

- The final sales value of the joint product
- The further processing cost of the joint product

When deciding whether or not to process further a joint product, the final sales value of the joint product is deducted from the sum of the further processing cost of the joint product and the opportunity cost of further processing (ie the sales value of the joint product at the separation point).

(Syllabus area B5(d))

105   The correct answers are:

- If the aim is to minimise costs, the solution is where the total cost line touching the feasible area at a tangent is as close to the origin as possible.

- If the aim is to maximise profit, the solution is where the total contribution line touching the feasible area at a tangent is as far away from the origin as possible.

If the aim is to minimise costs, the solution is where the total cost line touching the feasible area at a tangent, is as close to the origin as possible as this will allow the company to make as little as possible given constraints. If the aim is to maximise profit, the solution is where the total contribution line touching the feasible area at a tangent, is as far away from the origin as possible as this will allow the company to make as much as possible given contraints.

All other statements are false.   (Syllabus area B3(c))

Ennerdale

106   The correct answer is $30,870

Relevant cost – Material K

Since the material is regularly used by the company, the relevant cost of material K is the current price of the material.

Cost last month $= \dfrac{\$19,600}{2,000\,\text{kg}}$

$= \$9.80$

Revised cost (+5%) $= \$9.80 \times 1.05$
$= \$10.29$

∴ Relevant cost of material K $= 3,000 \text{ kg} \times \$10.29 \text{ per kg}$
$= \$30,870$

107   The correct answer is $2,200

Relevant cost – Material L

Since the material is not required for normal production, the relevant cost of this material is its net realisable value if it were sold.

∴ Relevant cost of material L $= 200 \text{ kg} \times \$11 \text{ per kg}$
$= \$2,200$

108   The correct answer is $15,600

Relevant cost – skilled labour

Skilled labour is in short supply and therefore the relevant cost of this labour will include both the actual cost and the opportunity cost of the labour employed.

	$
Cost of skilled labour (800 hours × $9.50)	7,600
Opportunity cost of skilled labour (see working)	8,000
Relevant cost – skilled labour	15,600

Working

Skilled labour cost per unit of Product P = $38

Cost per skilled labour hour = $9.50

∴ Number of hours required per unit of Product P $= \dfrac{\$38}{\$9.50}$
$= 4 \text{ hours}$

Contribution per unit of Product P $= \$40$

∴ Contribution per skilled labour hour $= \dfrac{\$40}{4 \text{ hours}}$
$= \$10 \text{ per hour}$

∴ Opportunity cost of skilled labour $= 800 \text{ hours} \times \$10 \text{ per hour}$
$= \$8,000$

109   The correct answer is: $120
$15 × 8 hours = $120

The cost of hiring an accountant is $25 × 75% × 8 hours = $150. As this cost is greater than if the work were done by the finance team, the finance team overtime cost of $120 is the relevant cost.

110   The correct answer is: Both 1 and 2

These are fundamental statements about relevant costing.

Pixie Pharmaceuticals

111   The correct answer is: $48,000

	Fairyoxide $'000	Spriteolite $'000	Goblinex $'000	Total $'000
Sales value	80	200	160	440
Variable costs	56	136	112	304
Contribution	24	64	48	136
Fixed costs	16	40	32	88
Profit	8	24	16	48

If we produce our three drugs in-house our total profits are $48,000.

112   The correct answer is: $0.05 per unit

	Fairyoxide $
Unit variable costs:	
direct material	0.80
direct labour	1.60
direct expense	0.40
Total variable cost	2.80
Imported price	2.75
Saving/(increased cost) of purchasing	0.05

113   The correct answer is: $(0.80) per unit

	Spriteolite $
Unit variable costs:	
direct material	1.00
direct labour	1.80
direct expense	0.60
Total variable cost	3.40
Imported price	4.20
Saving/(increased cost) of purchasing	(0.80)

114   The correct answer is: $(0.60) per unit

	Goblinex $
Unit variable costs:	
direct material	0.40
direct labour	0.80
direct expense	0.20
Total variable cost	1.40
Imported price	2.00
Saving/(increased cost) of purchasing	(0.60)

115   The correct answer is: 1 only.

Pixie Pharmaceutical should consider a number of other factors before making a final decision on whether to produce all of its products in house, or to purchase from the overseas supplier. Those factors include the reliability of the overseas supplier, customer reaction, and any legal implications.

BDU Co

116   The correct answer is: $500

The **maximin** decision rule involves choosing the outcome that offers the **least unattractive worst outcome**, in this instance choosing the outcome which **maximises the minimum contribution**.

Demand/price	Minimum contribution
1,000/$425	$165,000
730/$500	$175,200
420/$600	$142,800

BDU would therefore set a price of **$500**.

117   The correct answer is: $425

The **minimax regret** decision rule involves choosing the **outcome that minimises the maximum regret** from making the wrong decision, in this instance choosing the outcome which **minimises the opportunity loss** from making the wrong decision.

We can draw up an **opportunity loss table**.

Variable cost	Price		
	$425	$500	$600
$170	–	$14,100	$74,400 (W1)
$210	–	$3,300	$51,200 (W2)
$260	$10,200	–	$32,400 (W3)
Minimax regret	$10,200	$14,100	$74,400

Minimax regret strategy (price of $425) is that which minimises the maximum regret ($10,200).

Workings

(1)   At a variable cost of $170 per day, the best strategy would be a price of $425. The opportunity loss from setting a price of $600 would be $(255,000 – 180,600) = $74,400.

(2)   At a variable cost of $210 per day, the best strategy would be a price of $425. The opportunity loss from setting a price of $600 would be $(215,000 – 163,800) = $51,200.

(3)   At a variable cost of $260 per day, the best strategy would be a price of $500. The opportunity loss from setting a price of $600 would be $(175,200 – 142,800) = $32,400.

118   The correct answer is: $425

Expected values calculations:

$425: (255,000 × 0.4) + (215,000 × 0.25) + (165,000 × 0.35) = $213,500

$500: (240,900 × 0.4) + (211,700 × 0.25) + (175,200 × 0.35) = $210,605

$600: (180,600 × 0.4) + (163,800 × 0.25) + (142,800 × 0.35) = $163,170

119   The correct answers are: Market research and focus groups

Market research is used to obtain data about customer/consumer attitudes and preferences to products or markets, and the quantitative or qualitative information obtained from market research can help to reduce uncertainty for some elements of decision making, such as pricing and product design decisions.

Like market research, focus groups reduce uncertainty by providing information and the information will influence decisions such as pricing decisions.

120   The correct answer is: Both statements are incorrect.

Statement 1 is incorrect. Expected values are used to support the risk-neutral decision maker, who will ignore any variability or extremities in the range of possible outcomes and be interested only in the overall average expected value. By contrast, a risk-averse decision maker is likely to be more interested in those extreme outcomes, and so an overall average will not give enough information. Statement 2 is incorrect. The average profit calculated may not correspond to any of the possible outcomes, and this is a limitation of expected value analysis.

Metallica Co

121   The correct answers are: Product P4 $70 Product P6 $100

	Product P4	Product P6
	$	$
Selling price	125	175
Opportunity cost		
Direct materials:		
M1	15	10
M2	10	20
Direct labour	20	30
Variable overhead	10	15
Total variable costs	55	75
Contribution/unit	70	100

122   The correct answer is: The contribution per limiting factor of P4 and P6 is $113.33 and $190 respectively, therefore P6 should be produced first.

The most profitable course of action can be determined by ranking the products and components according to **contribution per unit of the limiting factor**. Direct material M1 is the limiting factor in this case, therefore the highest rank will be given to the product/component with the greatest contribution per m^2 of this material.

Contribution/unit	85	95
m^2 of M1/unit	0.75	0.5
Contribution/m^2	$113.33	$190
Ranking	2	1

123   The correct answers are:

Selling price	YES	
Direct materials	YES	
Direct labour		NO

In throughput accounting, a very similar calculation to limiting factor analysis is performed. However, in throughput accounting, it is not contribution per unit of scarce resource which is calculated, but throughput return per unit of bottleneck resource. Throughput is calculated as 'selling price less direct material cost'. This is different from the calculation of 'contribution', in which both labour costs and variable overheads are also deducted from selling price.

124   The correct answers are:

Limited demand for P4 or P6.	YES
Limited M1 or M2.	YES
Limited labour.	YES

Firms face many constraints on their activities and have to plan accordingly.

125   The correct answer is:

Step 1: Calculate the contribution per unit for each product

Step 2: Calculate the contribution per unit of the scarce resource for each product

Step 3: Rank the products in order of the contribution per unit of the scarce resource

Step 4: Allocate resources using the ranking

T Co

126   The correct answer is: $500

One of the three engineers has spare capacity to complete the installation and their salary will be paid regardless of whether they work on the contract for Push Co. The relevant cost is therefore $Nil.

The other two engineers are currently fully utilised and earn a contribution of $200 per week each on Contract X. The engineers could be temporarily taken off of Contract X to work on the contract for Push Co. Work on Contract X would recommence in one week's time when there is no other scheduled work for the engineers.

Delaying the work on Contract X would result in T Co missing the contractual completion deadline and having to pay a one-off penalty of $500.

Relevant cost = $500

127   The correct answer is: $2,184

120 handsets would need to be supplied to Push Co. Though 80 handsets are already in inventory, the handsets are frequently requested by T Co's customers and so would need to be replaced if supplied to Push Co. The current cost of a handset is $18.20.

Relevant cost = $18.20 × 120 handsets = $2,184

128   The correct answer is: $7,600

The current market price of Swipe 2 is $10,800.

The original cost of Swipe 1 ($5,400) is a sunk cost and not relevant to the decision.

The current market price of Swipe 1 ($5,450) is also not relevant to the decision as T Co has no intention of replacing Swipe 1.

The company could sell Swipe 1 for $3,000 if it does not use it for this contract. This represents an opportunity cost.

In addition to the $3,000, Swipe 1 could be modified at a cost of $4,600, bringing the total cost of converting Swipe 1 to $7,600.

129   The correct answer is: Both statements are false

An opportunity cost is the benefit forgone taking one course of action instead of the next most profitable course of action.

The effect that the decision to accept the Push Co contract has on profit or cost is an important factor in decision making, but non-financial factors should also be taken into consideration.

130   The correct answer is: Sunk cost

The cost of the demonstration has already been incurred and cannot be recovered. It is, therefore, a sunk cost and is not relevant to the decision about whether or not to accept the Push Co contract.

Rotanola Co

131   The correct answer is: P = 210 − 0.005Q

Find the price at which demand would be nil: Each price increase of $10 results in a fall in demand of 2,000 phones. For demand to be nil, the price needs to rise by as many times as there are 2,000 units in 20,000 units (20,000/2,000 = 10) ie to $110 + (10 × $10) = $210.

So a = 210 and b = change in price/change in quantity = 10/2,000 = 0.005

The demand equation is therefore P = 210 − 0.005Q

132   The correct answer is: $TC = 460,000 + 62Q$

Cost behaviour can be modelled using equations. These equations can be highly complex but in this case are quite simple.

b = variable cost = $30 + 18 + 14 = \$62$
a = fixed cost = $\$23 \times 20,000 = 460,000$
$TC = 460,000 + 62Q$ where Q = number of units

133   The correct answer is: $TC = 460,000 + 59Q$

With the **volume-based discount**:

$b = 27 + 18 + 14 = 59$
$TC = 460,000 + 59Q$

134   The correct answer is $969,000.

Materials

Probability	Forecast material cost	Expected value
	$	$
0.6	50	30
0.3	60	18
0.1	40	4
		52

Sales units

Probability	Forecast sales units	Expected value
	$	$
0.5	25,000	12,500
0.4	22,500	9,000
0.1	26,250	2,625
		24,125

Expected profit

		$	$
Sales	$(24,125 \times \$150)$		3,618,750
Materials	$(24,125 \times \$52)$	1,254,500	
Labour	$(24,125 \times \$18)$	434,250	
Variable overheads	$(24,125 \times \$16)$	386,000	
			2,074,750
Attributable fixed overheads			575,000
Expected profit			969,000

135   The correct answer is: 'Rotanola Co can use market research to reduce uncertainty and monitor performance' is **true** and 'Rotanola Co could use market research to estimate by how much costs and revenues would need to differ from their estimated values before the decision would change' is **false**.

Decision makers need data to reduce uncertainty and risk when planning for the future and to monitor business performance. Market researchers provide the data that helps them to do this.

Sensitivity analysis could be used by Rotanola to estimate by how much costs and revenues would need to differ from their estimated values before the decision would change.

136 RB Co

(a) **Managing director's pricing strategy**

The managing director has adopted what is known as a **full cost plus** pricing strategy, which means that a profit margin (in this case, of 50%) is added to the budgeted full cost of the product.

Given the information in the question, the **selling price used by RB Co** is calculated as follows.

	$
Full cost	400
50% mark up	200
Selling price	600

Disadvantages of this pricing strategy

Its **focus** is **internal** – internal costs and internal targets. It therefore takes **no account of the market conditions** faced by RB Co, which is why the company's selling price bears little resemblance to those of its competitors. By adopting a fixed mark-up, **it does not allow the company to react to competitors'** pricing decisions.

Absorption bases used when calculating the full cost are **decided arbitrarily**. The current basis of absorption is based on the budgeted level of production, which is lower than the current capacity. **Depending on the absorption basis** used in the calculation of total cost, the strategy can **produce different selling prices**.

Advantages of this pricing strategy

It is **quick**, **cheap** and relatively **easy** to apply. Pricing can therefore be delegated to more junior management if necessary.

It ensures that **all costs are covered** and that the organisation **makes a profit**, provided budget figures used in the pricing calculation are reasonably accurate. This was the case in the first two years for RB Co.

The **costs of collecting market information** on demand and competitor activity are **avoided**.

(b) **Alternative pricing strategies**

(1) **Market penetration pricing**

Market penetration pricing is a policy of **low prices** when a product is first launched in order to achieve **high sales volumes** and hence gain a **significant market share**. If RB Co had adopted this strategy it might have discouraged competitors from entering the market.

(2) **Market skimming**

This pricing strategy involves charging **high prices** when a product is first launched and **spending heavily on advertising and promotion** to obtain sales so as to exploit any price insensitivity in the market. Such an approach would have been particularly suitable for RB's circumstances: demand for the software would have been relatively inelastic, customers being prepared to pay high prices for the software given its novelty appeal. As the product moves into later stages of its life cycle, prices can be reduced in order to remain competitive.

(c) When demand is linear the equation for the demand curve is:

$$P = a - bQ$$

where P = the price

Q = the quantity demanded

a = the price at which demand would be nil

$$b = \frac{\text{change in price}}{\text{change in quantity}}$$

a = $750

$$b = \frac{\$10}{1,000}$$

= 0.01

∴ P = 750 − 0.01Q

(d) **Cost behaviour** can be modelled using a **simple linear equation** of the form y = a + bx where 'a' represents the fixed costs, which for RB are $1,200,000 (15,000 × $80), and 'b' represents the variable costs per unit, ie $320 (400 − 80) per unit for RB. This cost model assumes fixed costs remain unchanged over all ranges of output and a constant unit variable cost.

(e) **Price elasticity of demand**

Price elasticity of demand is a measure of the extent of change in market demand for a good in response to a change in its price. It is measured as:

$$\frac{\text{The change in quantity demanded, as a \% of demand}}{\text{The change in price, as a \% of the price}}$$

Since the demand goes up when the price falls, and goes down when the price rises, the elasticity has a negative value, but it is usual to ignore the minus sign.

The value of demand elasticity may be anything from zero to infinity.

Elastic and inelastic demand

Demand is referred to as **inelastic** if the absolute value is less than 1. Where demand is **inelastic**, the **quantity demanded falls by a smaller percentage than the percentage increase in price**.

Where demand is **elastic, demand falls** by a **larger percentage than the percentage rise in price.** The absolute value is greater than 1.

Pricing decisions

An awareness of the concept of elasticity can assist management with **pricing decisions**.

In circumstances of **inelastic demand**, **prices should be increased** because revenues will increase and total costs will reduce (because quantities sold will reduce).

In circumstances of **elastic demand**, increases in prices will bring decreases in revenue and decreases in price will bring increases in revenue. Management therefore have to **decide** whether the **increase/decrease in costs will be less than/greater than the increase/decrease in revenue**.

In situations of **very elastic demand**, overpricing can lead to a massive drop in quantity sold and hence a massive drop in profits; whereas underpricing can lead to costly stock outs and, again, a significant drop in profits. **Elasticity must therefore be reduced by creating a customer preference which is unrelated to price** (through advertising and promotional activities).

In situations of **very inelastic demand**, customers are **not sensitive to price. Quality, service, product mix and location** are therefore **more important** to a firm's pricing strategy.

Cost-plus pricing

Cost-plus pricing is based on the **assumption** that demand for the company's software is **inelastic** and prices should be increased in order to increase total revenue and hence profit. The market research information for RB Co does not support this view, however. It suggests that increasing prices will lead to a drop in demand and hence a reduction in profit.

137 The Cosmetic Co

Text reference. Graphical linear programming is covered in Chapter 4.

Top tips. Perhaps the biggest challenge in this question is time management. There is a lot to do in the time allowed.

Use the step-by-step approach in part (a), clearly labelling your workings to make it easy for the marker to follow. Make sure you read the question scenario very carefully as it is easy to miss an element.

Easy marks. There are plenty of easy marks available throughout for establishing the constraints and clearly drawing and labelling each line on the graph.

Examining team's comments. Much of this question could have been examined in the lower level MA (Management Accounting) exam. Why then, was it in the PM exam? It is becoming more and more apparent that the assumed MA knowledge for PM simply isn't there and it is therefore necessary to make candidates realise that it is examinable under PM and that, if they don't know the subject matter, they need to go away and study it!

Candidates who had revised this area made a decent attempt at this question, with many of them scoring full marks in part (a) at least. It is important, when answering a linear programming question like this, to set out your workings clearly, with a logical progression in steps from defining the variables and constraints, through to drawing the graph and finding the solution. This makes it easier to mark. The recommended approach is to use the iso-contribution line to find the optimum solution; it is the quickest way to do it. Candidates weren't penalised if they used the simultaneous equations method, because they were not told which method to use, but they penalised themselves because it took them longer to do it.

It is essential to show all of your workings. So, for example, the iso-contribution line needs to be worked out and then drawn onto the graph. If you didn't show how you worked it out, you stood to lose some marks.

Where you are asked to work to 2 decimal places, you should do it. In this question, it was necessary in order to keep a level of accuracy required to answer part (b) as well. While we gave follow-on marks for part (b) wherever possible, if fundamental mistakes had been made in part (a) so that, for example, there was no slack for amino acids, it was hard to award marks.

	Marks
(a) Optimum production plan:	
Assigning letters for variables	½
Defining constraint for silk powder	½
Defining constraint for amino acids	½
Defining constraint for labour	½
Non-negativity constraint	½
Sales constraint: x	½
Sales constraint: y	½
Iso-contribution line worked out	1
The graph:	
Labels	½
Silk powder	½
Amino acids	½
Labour line	½
Demand for x line	½
Demand for y line	½
Iso-contribution line	½
Vertices a–e identified	½
Feasible region shaded	½
Optimum point identified	1
Equations solved at optimum point	3
Total contribution	1
	14
(b) Shadow prices and slack:	
Shadow price	4
Slack	2
	6
	20

(a) **Define variables**

Let x = number of jars of face cream to be produced
Let y = number of bottles of body lotion to be produced
Let C = contribution

Establish objective function

The objective is to maximise contribution (C).

Face cream contribution (x) = $9.00 per unit

Body lotion contribution (y) = $8.00 per unit

Maximise C = 9x + 8y, subject to the constraints below.

Establish constraints

Silk powder:	$3x + 2y \leq 5,000$
Silk amino acids:	$1x + 0.5y \leq 1,600$
Skilled labour:	$4x + 5y \leq 9,600$
Non-negativity constraints:	$x, y \geq 0$
Maximum demand for body lotion:	$y \leq 2,000$

Establish coordinates to plot lines representing the inequalities

Silk powder:	$3x + 2y \leq 5,000$
	If $x = 0$, $y = 2,500$
	If $y = 0$, $x = 1,666.7$
Silk amino acids:	$1x + 0.5y \leq 1,600$
	If $x = 0$, $y = 3,200$
	If $y = 0$, $x = 1,600$
Skilled labour:	$4x + 5y \leq 9,600$
	If $x = 0$, $y = 1,920$
	If $y = 0$, $x = 2,400$

Also plot the line $y = 2,000$ (maximum weekly demand for body lotion).

Draw the graph

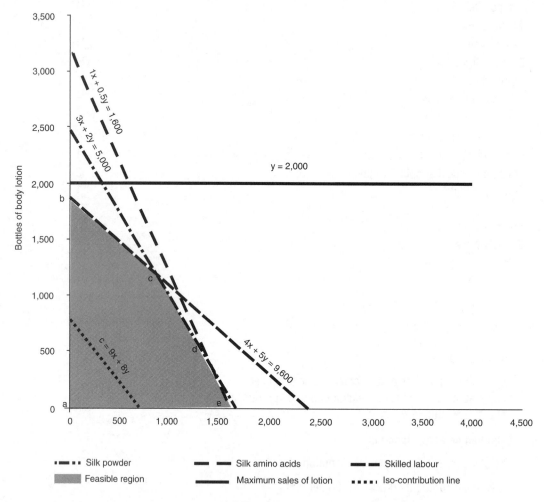

Find the optimal solution using an iso-contribution line

$C = 9x + 8y$

If $C = (8 \times 800) = 6,400$, then:

If $y = 0$, $9x = 6,400$

Therefore $x = 711.11$

By moving the iso-contribution line out across the graph, it is clear that the optimal solution lies as point C, the intersection of the constraints for skilled labour and silk powder.

Solving the simultaneous equations for these constraints:

$4x + 5y = 9,600 \qquad \times 3$
$3x + 2y = 5,000 \qquad \times 4$

$12x + 15y = 28,800 \quad (1)$
$12x + 8y = 20,000 \quad (2)$

Subtract (2) from (1):
$7y = 8,800$
$y = 1,257.14$

If y = 1,257.14 and
$4x + 5y = 9,600$

Then $5 \times 1,257.14 + 4x = 9,600$
Therefore x = 828.58

The **optimal solution** is therefore to make 828.58 jars of face cream and 1,257.14 bottles of body lotion.

Maximum profit

Contribution		$
Face cream:	828.58 units × unit contribution of $9.00	7,457.22
Body lotion:	1,257.14 units × unit contribution of $8.00	10,057.12
		17,514.34

(b)   **Shadow price for silk powder**

The shadow price for silk powder can be found by solving the two simultaneous equations that intersect at point C on the graph in part (a). The **shadow price** is the **increase in value which would be created by having one additional unit** of limiting factor. For this reason, we must add one more hour to the equation for silk powder.

$4x + 5y = 9,600 \qquad \times 3$
$3x + 2y = 5,001 \qquad \times 4$

$12x + 15y = 28,800 \quad (1)$
$12x + 8y = 20,004 \quad (2)$

Subtract (2) from (1):
$7y = 8,796$
$y = 1,256.57$

$3x + (2 \times 1,256.57) = 5,001$
$x = 829.29$

$C = (9 \times 829.29) + (8 \times 1,256.57) = \$17,516.17$

Original contribution = $17,514.34

The **shadow price for silk powder** is therefore $1.83 per gram.

Slack for amino acids

Each unit of face cream requires 1 gram of silk amino acids and each unit of body lotion requires 0.5 grams of amino acids.

$(828.58 \times 1) + (0.5 \times 1,257.14) = 1,457.15$ grams used.

Grams available = 1,600 grams.

Therefore slack = 142.85 grams.

138 Bits and Pieces

Marking scheme

		Marks	
(a)	Existing total sales	1	
	Existing total gross profit	1	
	New sales	1	
	New gross profit	1	
	Incremental gross profit	1	
	Existing purchasing	1	
	Discount allowed for	1	
	Incremental Sunday purchasing costs	1	
	Staff cost	1	
	Lighting cost	1	
	Heating cost	1	
	Manager's bonus	1	
			12
(b)	Time off at normal rate not time and a half	1	
	Lack of flexibility	1	
	Bonus per day worked calculation and comment	1	
	Risk	1	
			4
(c)	Changing customer buying pattern	2	
	Complaints risk	2	
	Quality link	2	
	Maximum		4
			20

(a) Incremental revenue

	Sales $	Gross profit %	Gross profit $
Average	10,000	70	
Sunday (60% more than average)	16,000	50	8,000
Annual Sunday sales (50 weeks)	800,000	50	400,000

Purchasing costs

Current annual spending = 50 weeks × 6 days × 10,000 × 30%
$$= \$900,000$$

New annual spending with discount   = (900,000 + 400,000) × 95%
                                       = $1,235,000

Incremental purchasing cost   = $(1,235,000 − 900,000)
                                = $335,000

Staff costs

Additional staff costs on a Sunday = 5 sales assistants × 6 hours × 50 weeks × 1.5 × $20
                                     = $45,000

Manager's costs

The salary of the manager is a sunk cost and there will be no additional costs for their time.

They will be entitled to an extra bonus of 1% × $800,000 = $8,000

Lighting costs

50 weeks × 6 hours × $30 = $9,000

Heating costs

25 weeks × 8 hours × $45 = $9,000

Rent

The rent of the store is a sunk cost so is not relevant to this decision.

Net incremental revenue

Net incremental revenue = 800,000 − (335,000 + 45,000 + 9,000 + 9,000 + 8,000)
                        = **$394,000**

Conclusion

Incremental revenue exceeds incremental costs by $394,000 so Sunday opening is **financially justifiable**.

(b) **Manager's pay deal**

Time off

If the manager works on a Sunday they will take the equivalent **time off** during the week. They are not entitled to extra pay in the same way as the sales assistants and this does not seem fair. Weekend working is disruptive to most people's family and social life and it is reasonable to expect **extra reward** for giving up time at weekends. It is unlikely that time off in lieu during the week will motivate the manager.

Bonus

The bonus has been calculated as $8,000 which equates to an extra $160 per day of extra work. The sales assistants will be paid $180 per day (6 × $20 × 1.5) so again the manager is **not getting a fair offer**.

The bonus is based on **estimated sales** so could be higher if sales are higher than predicted. However, there is a **risk** that sales and therefore the bonus could be lower. It is therefore again unlikely that this bonus will motivate the manager.

(c) **Price discounts and promotions**

B & P plans to offer substantial discounts and promotions on a Sunday to attract customers. This may indeed be a good **marketing strategy** to attract people to shop on a Sunday, but it is not necessarily good for the business.

Customer buying pattern

B & P wants to attract **new** customers on a Sunday but customers may simply **change the day** they do their shopping in order to take advantage of the discounts and promotions. The effect of this would be to **reduce the margin** earned from customer purchases and not increase revenue.

Customer dissatisfaction

Customers who buy goods at full price and then see their purchases for sale at lower prices on a Sunday may be disgruntled. They could then complain or switch their custom to another shop.

The **reputation** of B & P could be damaged by this marketing policy, especially if customers associate lower prices with **lower quality**.

139 Robber Co

Text reference. Make/buy decisions and relevant costs are covered in Chapter 6.

Top tips. This question tests relevant costing within a 'make or buy context'. There are a number of calculations required for parts (a) and (b) so present your answer clearly and show all of your workings to maximise your score.

Part (c) asks you to discuss **non-financial** factors, so do not waste time discussing financial factors!

Easy marks. There are easy marks available in part (c) for discussing the non-financial factors the company should consider when making a decision about outsourcing.

Examining team's comments. It was pleasing to see many candidates making a decent attempt at part (a). In the suggested solution, the $4k and $6k machine costs are treated as **specific** fixed costs and are therefore included in the relevant cost of manufacturing in-house, together with the depreciation. However, it is acceptable to assume these costs to be **general** fixed costs and therefore exclude them for their manufacture cost together with the depreciation.

Part (b) produced weaker answers but many candidates were at least able to work out the shortage of hours and the number of units that needed to be bought in (without going through the process of ranking the two components), for which they could earn nearly half of the total marks available.

Part (c) was a straightforward knowledge requirement and the majority of candidates scored full marks.

		Marks	
(a)	Incremental cost of buying in:		
	Direct materials	½	
	Direct labour	½	
	Heat and light	½	
	Set-up costs	3	
	Depreciation and insurance	1	
	Total cost of making	½	
	Total cost of buying	½	
	Saving	½	
	Conclusion	1	
			8
	Method 2:		
	Direct materials	½	
	Direct labour	½	
	Heat and power	½	
	Avoidable fixed costs	½	
	Activity related costs	3	
	Avoidable depreciation and insurance	½	
	Total relevant manufacturing costs	½	
	Relevant cost per unit	½	
	Incremental cost of buying in	½	
	Conclusion	1	
			8

(b) If 100,000 control panels made:

Variable cost of making per unit	1
Saving from making	1
Saving per labour hour	1
Ranking	1
Make 100,000 keypads	1
Make 66,666 display screens	1
Buy 33,334 display screens	1
	7

(c) Non-financial factors:

1–2 marks per factor	Max 5
	20

(a) **Incremental costs of making in-house compared to cost of buying**

	Keypads (K) $	Display screens (D) $
Variable costs		
Materials:		
K = ($160k × 6/12) + ($160k × 1.05 × 6/12) : D = ($116k × 1.02)	164,000	118,320
Direct labour	40,000	60,000
Machine set-up costs:		
K = ($26k – $4k) × 500/400 : D = ($30k – $6k) × 500/400	27,500	30,000
	231,500	208,320
Attributable fixed costs		
Heat and power: K = ($64k – $20k) : D = ($88k – $30k)	44,000	58,000
Fixed machine costs	4,000	6,000
Depreciation and insurance: K = ($84k × 40%) : D = ($96k × 40%)	33,600	38,400
	81,600	102,400
Total incremental costs of making in-house	313,100	310,720
Cost of buying: K = (80,000 × $4.10) : D = (80,000 × $4.30)	328,000	344,000
Total saving from making	14,900	33,280

Robber Co should therefore make all of the keypads and display screens in-house.

Note: The above calculations assume that the fixed set-up costs only arise if production takes place.

Alternative approach (Relevant costs)

	Keypads (K) $	Display screens (D) $
Direct materials:		
K = ($160k/2) + ($160k/2 × 1.05) : D = $116k × 1.02	164,000	118,320
Direct labour	40,000	60,000
Heat and power		
K = $64K – (50% × $40K) : D = $88k – (50% × $60k)	44,000	58,000
Machine set-up costs:		
Avoidable fixed costs	4,000	6,000
Activity related costs (W1)	27,500	30,000
Avoidable depreciation and insurance costs:		
K = ($84k × 40%) : D = ($96k × 40%)	33,600	38,400
Total relevant manufacturing costs	313,100	310,720
Relevant cost per unit	3.91375	3.884
Cost per unit of buying in	4.10	4.30
Incremental cost of buying in	0.18625	0.416

As each of the components is cheaper to make in-house than to buy in, the company should continue to manufacture both products in-house.

Working
Current no. of batches produced = 80,000/500 = 160
New no. of batches produced = 80,000/400 = 200
Current cost per batch for keypads = ($26,000 − $4,000)/160 = $137.50
Therefore new activity related batch cost = 200 × $137.50 = $27,500
Current cost per batch for display screens = ($30,000 − $6,000)/160 = $150
Therefore new activity related batch cost = 200 × $150 = $30,000

(b) **Note.** Attributable fixed costs are not included in the following calculation. Attributable fixed costs remain unaltered irrespective of the level of production of keypads and display screens, because as soon as one unit of either is made, the costs rise. We know that we will make at least one unit of each component as both are cheaper to make than buy. They are therefore an irrelevant common cost.

Plan to minimise costs

	Keypads (K)	Display screens (D)
	$	$
Buy-in price	4.10	4.30
Variable cost of making:		
K = ($231,500 / 80,000): D = ($208,320 / 80,000)	2.89	2.60
Saving from making (per unit)	1.21	1.70
Labour hours per unit	0.50	0.75
Saving from making (per unit of limiting factor)	2.42	2.27
Priority of making	1	2

Total labour hours available = 100,000 hours

Make maximum keypads ie 100,000 using 50,000 labour hours (100,000 × 0.5 hours per unit)

Use remaining 50,000 labour hours to make 66,666 display screens (50,000/0.75 hours per unit)

Therefore buy in 33,334 display screens (100,000 − 66,666).

(c) Robber Co should consider the following non-financial factors when making a decision about outsourcing the manufacture of keypads and display screens.

Supplier performance

Robber Co would need to establish whether the supplier is reliable in meeting **delivery dates** and delivering components of a **high quality**.

If the components delivered are not of the required quality Robber risks damaging its **reputation** and losing sales as well as incurring **high repair costs** for control panels under warranty. This is particularly significant given that the supplier is based overseas – Robber therefore has less control over quality and continuity of supply than if it were dealing with a locally based supplier.

Information to support the supplier's record in meeting delivery dates may be hard to come by, especially as the supplier is a newly established company. Late delivery of components could disrupt Robber's production schedule and its ability to supply control panels to meet market demand.

New company

The potential supplier is a **newly formed company**. There is no guarantee the company will be able to operate at the level required to supply the desired level of components at the right quality.

BPP LEARNING MEDIA

Robber Co should consider whether there are any other potential suppliers of the components. This would enable Robber to compare prices and get the best deal. It could also provide the company with an **alternative supplier** should the new supplier go out of business.

Pricing

The new supplier has only guaranteed the current price for **two years**. After this, the supplier could increase prices significantly. Robber Co should negotiate **a price fix** for a longer period of time as part of the agreement or seek out **alternative suppliers** to ensure that the company is not forced to accept a significant increase in component prices at the end of the two-year period.

140 Gam Co

Text reference. Risk and uncertainty is covered in Chapter 7.

Top tips. Part (a) is straightforward provided you read the information carefully and use a clear layout and workings. Make sure you make a recommendation in your answer in part (b). Know the difference between maximin, minimax and maximax for part (c).

Examining team's comments. This was a very well answered question. Where mistakes were made it was through inaccurate reading of the question, incorrectly applying probabilities to profit figures (part (b)), or failure to recommend which option Gam Co would choose (part (b)). In part (c), some candidates mixed up maximin with minimax regret or maximax and consequently gave the wrong explanation and recommendation.

Marking scheme

			Marks
(a)	Profit calculations:		
	Unit contribution up to 100,000 units	1	
	Unit contribution above 100,000 units	1	
	Each line of table for price of $30 (3 in total)	3	
	Each line of table for price of $35 (3 in total)	3	
			8
(b)	Expected values		
	Expected value for $30	1	
	Expected value for $35	1	
	Recommendation	1	
			3
(c)	Maximin		
	Explanation	2	
	Decision	1	
			3
(d)	Uncertainty		
	Each point made	1	
			6
			20

(a) **Profit outcomes**

	$30	$35
Price per unit		
Contribution to 100,000 units ($30/$35 – $12)	$18	$23
Contribution above 100,000 units ($30/$35 – $12)	$19	$24

	1	2	3	4	5	6
	$	$	$	$	$	$
Sales price	30	30	30	35	35	35
Sales volume (units)	120,000	110,000	140,000	108,000	100,000	94,000
Unit contribution	19	19	19	24	23	23
Total contribution	2,280,000	2,090,000	2,660,000	2,592,000	2,300,000	2,162,000
Fixed costs	(450,000)	(450,000)	(450,000)	(450,000)	(450,000)	(450,000)
Advertising costs	(900,000)	(900,000)	(900,000)	(970,000)	(970,000)	(970,000)
Profit	930,000	740,000	1,310,000	1,172,000	880,000	742,000

(b) **Expected values**

	1	2	3	4	5	6
Sales price	$30	$30	$30	$35	$35	$35
Sales volume (units)	120,000	110,000	140,000	108,000	100,000	94,000
Profit	$930,000	$740,000	$1,310,000	$1,172,000	$880,000	$742,000
Probability	0.4	0.5	0.1	0.3	0.3	0.4
EV of profit ($)	$372,000	$370,000	$131,000	$351,600	$264,000	$296,800
Totals			$873,000			$912,400

Using the expected value of profit as the basis for decision, a sales price of $35 should be chosen as it gives the highest expected value.

(c) **Maximin decision rule**

The maximin decision rule involves choosing the outcome that offers the least unattractive worst outcome, in this instance choosing the outcome which maximises the minimum profit. Management would therefore choose a selling price of $35, which has a lowest possible profit of $742,000. This is better than the worst possible outcome from a selling price of $30, which would provide a profit $740,000.

(d) **Reasons for uncertainty arising in the budgeting process**

Uncertainty arises largely because of changes in the external environment over which a company will sometimes have little control. Reasons include:

- Customers may decide to buy more or less goods or services than originally forecast. For example, if a major customer goes into liquidation, this has a huge effect on a company and could also cause them to go into liquidation.

- Competitors may strengthen or emerge and take some business away from a company. On the other hand, a competitor's position may weaken leading to increased business for a particular company.

- Technological advances may take place which lead a company's products or services to become out-dated and therefore less desirable.

- The workforce may not perform as well as expected, perhaps because of time off due to illness or maybe simply because of lack of motivation.

- Materials may increase in price because of global changes in commodity prices.

Inflation can cause the price of all inputs to increase or decrease.

- If a company imports or exports goods or services, changes in exchange rates can cause prices to change.

- Machines may fail to meet production schedules because of breakdown.

- Social/political unrest could affect productivity, eg the workforce goes on strike.

Note. This list is not exhaustive, nor would candidates be expected to make all the points raised in order to score full marks.

141 Cardio Co

Marking scheme

			Marks
(a)	Weighted average C/S ratio:		
	Variable labour cost	1	
	Total revenue	1	
	Total contribution	1	
	WA C/S ratio	1	
			4
(b)	Margin of safety		
	Fixed costs	1	
	Breakeven sales	1	
	Margin of safety	1	
			3
(c)	Breakeven chart		
	Point A	0.5	
	Length B	1	
	Length C	1	
	Line D	0.5	
	Line E	1	
	Line F	0.5	
	Axis labels	1	
	Graph name (breakeven chart)	0.5	
			6
(d)	Discussion		
	Each point made	1	
			2
(e)	Limitations		
	Each point made	1-2	
			5
			20

(a) **Weighted average C/S ratio**

Weighted average contribution to sales ratio (WA C/S ratio) = total contribution/total sales revenue.

Per unit		T		C		R
	$	$	$	$	$	$
Selling price		1,600		1,800		1,400
Material	(430)		(500)		(360)	
Variable labour (40%)	(88)		(96)		(76)	
Variable overheads	(110)		(120)		(95)	
Total variable costs		(628)		(716)		(531)
Contribution		972		1,084		869
Sales units		420		400		380
Total sales revenue		$672,000		$720,000		$532,000
Total contribution		$408,240		$433,600		$330,220

WA C/S ratio = ($408,240 + $433,600 + $330,220)/($672,000 + $720,000 + $532,000)

= $1,172,060/$1,924,000 = 60.92%.

(b) **Margin of safety**

Margin of safety = budgeted sales – breakeven sales

Budgeted sales revenue = $1,924,000

Fixed labour costs = ((420 × $220) + (400 × $240) + (380 × $190)) × 0.6 = $156,360k.

Therefore total fixed costs = $156,360 + $55,000 = $211,360.

Breakeven sales revenue = fixed costs/weighted average C/S ratio

= $211,360/60.92% = $346,947

Therefore margin of safety = $1,924,000 – $346,947 = $1,577,053.

(c)   The chart is a multi-product breakeven chart

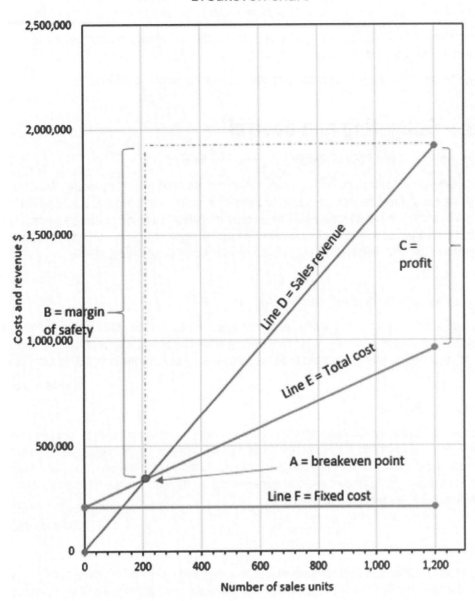

Breakeven chart

(d)   **BEP if products sold in order of profitability**

If the more profitable products are sold first, this means that the company will cover its fixed costs more quickly. Consequently, the breakeven point will be reached earlier, ie fewer sales will need to be made in order to break even. So, the breakeven point will be lower.

(e)   The limitations of CVP analysis are the unrealistic assumptions required.

(i)   It is assumed that fixed costs are the same in total and variable costs are the same per unit at all levels of output. This assumption is a great simplification.

• Fixed costs will change if output falls or increases substantially (most fixed costs are step costs).

• The variable cost per unit will decrease where economies of scale are made at higher output volumes, but the variable cost per unit will also eventually rise when diseconomies of scale begin to appear at even higher volumes of output (for example, the extra cost of labour in overtime working).

The assumption is only correct within a normal range or relevant range of output. It is generally assumed that both the budgeted output and the breakeven point lie within this relevant range.

(ii)   It is assumed that sales prices will be constant at all levels of activity. This may not be true, especially at higher volumes of output, where the price may have to be reduced to win the extra sales.

(iii)   Production and sales are assumed to be the same, so that the consequences of any increase in inventory levels or of 'de-stocking' are ignored.

(iv)   Uncertainty in the estimates of fixed costs and unit variable costs is often ignored.

MCQ bank – Budgeting and control

142   The correct answer is: It is difficult to identify a standard item for costing

With road haulage and distribution, drivers' times on the road are measured automatically. Variable costs can be high (labour and fuel, for example). Standard costing is more common in manufacturing but in principle can be applied to service industries. The problem is to identify a standard item for which a cost can be measured and variances subsequently calculated. In road haulage, for example, a standard measure may be cost per tonne/kilometre delivered: this does not lend itself easily to variance analysis.

(Syllabus area C6(b))

143   The correct answer is: Material usage operational variance

Material usage is within the control of a production manager, whereas material price variances are usually the responsibility of the purchasing manager. Line managers are responsible for operational variances, but planning variances are commonly assumed to be the responsibility of someone in senior management.

(Syllabus area C6(c))

144   The correct answer is: 2 only.

Mix variances should only be calculated when a product contains two or more materials that can be mixed together in different proportions. For example, calculating a mix variance for the production of a bicycle out of its component parts would be meaningless. It is important to be aware of the interdependence between variances: a favourable mix variance – meaning a cheaper mix of materials in a product – may result in adverse total output of the product (adverse yield).

(Syllabus area C4(b))

145   The correct answer is: Both 1 and 2

Flexible budgets enable actual results to be compared with expected results for the same volume of activity, such as production and sales. To reconcile an original budgeted profit to actual profit with variances there must be a sales volume variance (measured in terms of either budgeted/standard contribution or profit, depending on the type of costing system used).

(Syllabus area C3(c))

146   The correct answer is: Sales mix variance

The loss of the advertising campaign means that sales of Product Y will be less than budgeted, which should lead us to expect adverse sales volume variance for Y and an adverse sales quantity variance for both products together. The price discounting for Product Y should lead us to expect an adverse sales price variance. The increase in the proportion of Product X units sold in the total sales mix should lead us to expect a favourable sales mix variance, because Product X has a bigger standard contribution, both per unit and per $1 of standard sales price, than Product Y.

(Syllabus area C5(a))

147   The correct answer is: Managers should be held accountable only for costs and revenues over which they have some influence or control

This should be a fundamental principle of management control, but it is not always applied in practice.

(Syllabus area C3(d))

148   The correct answer is: Neither 1 nor 2

Mix and yield variances measure costs and output quantities, not quality. A potential problem is that persistent **favourable** mix variances may have an adverse effect on sales volume variances and direct labour efficiency variances, because the cheaper materials mix may affect the quality of the product sold to customers and also make the product more difficult to handle. These consequences could lead to adverse sales volume and labour efficiency variances.

(Syllabus area C5(a))

149   The correct answer is: 2 only

Standard costing systems are not compatible with a Total Quality Management approach to operations. With standard costing, the aim is to achieve standard cost or, perhaps, obtain some favourable variances. With TQM, guiding principles are 'continuous improvement' and 'zero defects'. Existing standards and methods of operating are always unsatisfactory and improvements should always be sought. This is not compatible with a standard costing 'philosophy'.

Standard costing tends to be of little value in a rapidly changing environment, because products are not standardised for a sufficient length of time to make the preparation of standard costs worthwhile.

(Syllabus area C7(e))

150   The correct answer is: Neither 1 nor 2

Learning curves are more difficult to apply in teams with a high labour turnover, as it can affect efficiency and knowledge significantly. Learning rates are affected by time gaps between the production of additional units of a product, because acquired learning may be forgotten with the passage of time unless the work continues regularly.

(Syllabus area C3(c))

151   The correct answer is: 1 only

If an EV is used as a value in a budget, it represents a weighted average value that may not be expected to occur. If so, comparing actual results against the budget for control purposes would have limited value. The use of expected values and probabilities in budgeting is most useful when there is some, but a limited, amount of uncertainty about the future. When uncertainty is very high, the use of probabilities becomes little more than guesswork.

(Syllabus area C2(d))

152   The correct answer is: Dimensions, standards and rewards

In the Fitzgerald and Moon model, there are three building blocks. Dimensions are the bases for measuring performance, such as financial performance and quality. For each dimension of performance there must be standards or targets for achievement. And there should be a reward system to provide incentives to managers and other employees to achieve the targets or standards.

(Syllabus area C4(a))

153   The correct answer is: It is easier to put public sector activities into decision packages because they are more easily definable than in the private sector

In an article in *Student Accountant* on incremental budgeting and zero-based budgeting, the ACCA examining team described two reasons why ZBB is often considered more suitable for public sector service organisations than for private sector companies. One is that ZBB is more suited to costs where there is a lot of discretionary spending, as in the public sector services. The second reason is that activities of public sector organisations are more easily definable and so can usually be put into decision packages. (For example, the activities of a local authority can be grouped into packages for local housing, local education, local refuse collection and waste disposal, and so on.)

(Syllabus area C1(d))

154 The correct answer is: Both 1 and 2

The advantages of spreadsheets in budgeting include time-saving in preparing figures, and the ability to carry out sensitivity analysis by analysing the effect of alterations to the value of key variables. It is also relatively easy to prepare alternative draft budgets or new draft budgets, simply by altering the value of variables in the spreadsheet budget model.

(Syllabus area C2(e))

155 The correct answer is: Rolling budget

If it is difficult to forecast or plan costs and revenues accurately for more than three months ahead, it would be appropriate to prepare new annual budgets every three months, giving most emphasis to the budget for the next three-month period. The disadvantage is that this would require four annual budgets in every 12-month period.

(Syllabus area C1(d))

156 The correct answer is: 1.442 hours

$Y = ax^b$

$b = \log 0.75 / \log 2 = -0.1249/0.3010 = -0.415$

When $x = 6$, $x^{-0.415} = 1/6^{-0.415} = 0.4754$

Average time for six jobs:

$Y = 5 \times 0.4754 = 2.377$ hours

Total time required for six jobs = 6×2.377 hours = 14.262 hours

Average time for five jobs: $5 \times 5^{-0.415} = 2.564$ hours

Total time required for five jobs = 5×2.564 hours = 12.820 hours

Time required to perform the 6th job = Total time required for six jobs – Total time required for five jobs.

Therefore, time required to perform the 6th job = 14.262 hours – 12.820 hours = 1.442 hours

(Syllabus area C1(d))

CBE style OTQ bank– Budgeting and control

157 The correct answer is: $1,248 (F)

Standard yield from actual input of materials at standard cost: $19,552

Actual yield at standard materials cost: $20,800

Mix variance (19,552 – 20,800): $1,248 (F)

(Syllabus area C3(a))

158 The correct answers are:

- This standard makes allowances for expected wastage and inefficiencies.
- This standard should give employees a realistic, but challenging target of efficiency.

The least useful, and most rarely used, type of standard is the basic standard, which is kept unaltered over a long period of time and may be out of date. The standard that is based on perfect operating conditions is the ideal standard which makes no allowances for wastage or inefficiencies.

(Syllabus area C4(a))

159   The correct answer is: $645 Adverse

When Y = ax^b, b = log 0.90/log 2 = −0.0457575/0.30103 = −0.1520031

Average labour time for first 49 batches = 2,000 × 49$^{-0.1520031}$ = 2,000 × 0.5534584 = 1,106.916731 hours

Average labour time for first 50 batches = 2,000 × 50$^{-0.1520031}$ = 2,000 × 0.5517614 = 1,103.522743

	Hours
Total labour time for first 50 units (× 1,103.522743)	55,176.14
Total labour time for first 49 units (× 1,106.916731)	54,238.92
Labour cost for the 50th batch	937.22

Standard time = 937 hours. Actual time = 980 hours.

Labour efficiency variance for this unit = 43 hours (A) × $15 = $645 (A).   (Syllabus area C2(b))

160   The correct answer is: $880 (F)

	Actual mix	Standard mix	Mix variance	Std price	Mix variance
	kg	kg	kg	$	$
P	820	750	70 (A)	3.0	210 (A)
Q	1,740	1,500	240 (A)	2.5	600 (A)
R	2,300	2,250	50 (A)	4.0	200 (A)
S	2,640	3,000	360 (F)	5.25	1,890 (F)
	7,500	7,500	0		880 (F)

(Syllabus area C4(a))

161   The correct answer is: −$1,475 (A)

Product	Actual sales	Actual sales in std mix	Sales mix variance	Std profit	Sales mix variance
	Units	Units	Units	$	$
X	700	750.0	50.0 (A)	10	500 (A)
Y	1,200	937.5	262.5 (F)	6	1,575 (F)
Z	350	562.5	212.5 (A)	12	2,550 (A)
	2,250	2,250.0	0		1,475 (A)

(Syllabus area C4(a))

162   The correct answers are:

•   For standard costing to be useful for control purposes, it requires a reasonably stable environment.

•   The ethos behind a system of standard costing is that performance is satisfactory if it meets predetermined standards.

In a standard costing environment, products or processes must be standardised and repetitive, so that standards can be established for budgeting and control. In a TQM environment, the objective is continuous improvement, which may involve continuous changes in procedures, input quantities and prices. A stable standard is never achieved.

Standard costing assumes that there is a target level of performance and achieving that target represents success. With TQM the view is that performance can be improved continually. There is no 'target'.

(Syllabus area C3(a))

163   The correct answer is: $40 (F)

	Kg
120 units of product should use (× 3.50)	420
They did use	410
Operational usage variance in kg	10 (F)

Operational usage variance in $ (× Standard price per kg $4) = $40 (F)

(Syllabus area C6(c))

164   The correct answer is: –$1,325 (A)

	Budgeted sales Units	Std profit $ per unit	Budgeted profit $
X	800	10	8,000
Y	1,000	6	6,000
Z	600	12	7,200
	2,400		21,200

Weighted average standard profit per unit = $21,200/2,400 = $8.8333

Quantity variance in units = 2,400 – 2,250 = 150 units (A)

Quantity variance in $ (standard profit) = 150 (A) × $8.8333 = $1,325 (A)

(Syllabus area C5(a))

165   The correct answers are:

- Control reports are provided too late
- Targets are not communicated

If targets are too easy, they cannot provide an incentive, but they cannot be a disincentive either.

If targets are set at high levels that cannot realistically be achieved, this can be demotivating. Demotivation can also occur if targets are imposed by senior management however this can be overcome if budgets are prepared on a bottom-up basis. Management will also be demotivated if control reports are provided late so that the manager responsible is unable to take prompt action to deal with problems that may arise.

(Syllabus area C2(b))

166   The correct answers are:

- It can result in much reduced inventory holding costs
- It requires suppliers to operate sound quality control procedures

The aim of JIT is to increase efficiency of inventory control systems in order to reduce company costs, principally by minimising inventory levels and thus stockholding costs. This is achieved by using local, reliable suppliers who can deliver goods of the right quality in the right quantity at the right time. The burden of quality control is generally passed back to the supplier to cut costs of the company.

JIT works best when a tied supplier relationship is formed, where the orders form a large part, if not the entirety, of the supplier's business. This precludes the use of many different suppliers. In a JIT system, steps will also be taken to improve customer relations and communications, so that demand can be more accurately determined. This means that reorder levels, and thus safety inventories, can be minimised without necessarily increasing the risks (and thus costs) of stock outs.

(Syllabus area C8(g))

167   The correct answers are:

- There is often no measurable output from service functions
- The activities of many service functions are of a non-standard nature

The output of services functions is not as easily measurable as it is with goods which are physically manufactured. This makes it difficult to establish standard unit rates, because there are no easily available standard times or usages.

(Syllabus area C4(a))

168   The correct answer is:

- The quantity of work achievable at standard performance in an hour

(Syllabus area C4(a))

169   The correct answer is: Rolling budget.

If it is difficult to forecast or plan costs and revenues accurately for more than two or three months ahead, it would be appropriate to prepare new annual budgets every two or three months, giving most emphasis to the budget for the next three-month period. The disadvantage is that this would require four or six annual budgets in every 12-month period.

(Syllabus area C4(a))

170   The correct answer is: A standard which can be attained if production is carried out efficiently, machines are operated properly and/or materials are used properly. Some allowance is made for waste and inefficiencies.

Attainable standards may provide an incentive to work harder as they represent a realistic but challenging target of efficiency

(Syllabus area C4(a))

171   The correct answer is: Current standard.

Budgeted capacity is associated with current standards. Budgeted capacity is not associated with basic standards. Practical capacity is associated with attainable standards.

Full capacity is associated with ideal standards.   (Syllabus area C4(a))

Crush Co

172   The correct answer is: 565.6 hours

Cumulative average time per batch for the first 64 batches

$Y = ax^b$

Where Y = the cumulative average time per unit to produce x units

       x = the cumulative number of units

       a = the time taken for the first unit of output

       b = the index of learning (logLR/log2)

The cumulative average time per batch, with a learning curve of 85%, is therefore

$Y = aX^{-0.2345}$

where a = the time for the first batch (1,500 hours) and X is the number of the batch. For the 64th batch, X = 64.

$Y = 1,500 \times 64^{-0.2345}$

    $= 1,500 \times 0.37709 = 565.6$

The cumulative average time per batch for the first 64 batches is 565.6 hours.

173   The correct answer is: 78%

Batches	Total time	Average time/unit
1	1,500	1,500
2		$1,500 \times r$
4		$1,500 \times r2$
8		$1,500 \times r3$
16	9,000	$1,500 \times r4$

$9,000 = 16 \times 1,500\ r^4$

$9,000/(16 \times 1,500) = r^4$

$r = 0.78$ or 78%

174 The correct answer is: 1 only

Decisions about allocating resources and costing of the new product should be based on the time taken to produce the 64th batch because this is when the learning effect stops. After this point, the product will reach a point of steady state production. Using information regarding labour costs from a point prior to steady state level will result in too high a price being assigned to labour costs. The learning process starts when the first batch comes off the production line.

175 The correct answer is: Both 1 and 2

Statement 1 is one of the main assumptions of the learning effect. Employees must have some motivation to improve and learn, otherwise the learning effect will not appear. The second statement is also true.

176 The correct answer is: All of the above.

They are all conditions which allow the learning curve to flourish.

BBB Co

177 The correct answer is: 330.75 hours

Cumulative average time per batch for the first 71 batches

$Y = ax^b$

Where Y = the cumulative average time per unit to produce x units
x = the cumulative number of units
a = the time taken for the first unit of output
b = the index of learning (logLR/log2)

The cumulative average time per batch, with a learning curve of 90%, is therefore

$Y = aX^{-0.152}$

where a = the time for the first batch (750 hours) and X is the number of the batch. For the 71st batch, X = 71.

$Y = 750 \times 71^{-0.152}$
$= 750 \times 0.5231 = 392.35$

The cumulative average time per batch for the first 71 batches is 392.35 hours.

Time taken for the 71st batch

The cumulative average time per batch for the first 70 batches is Y $= 750 \times 70^{-0.152}$
$= 750 \times 0.5243 = 393.23$

	Hours
Total time for 1st 71 batches (71 × 392.35)	27,856.85
Total time for 1st 70 batches (70 × 393.23)	27,526.10
Time for the 71st batch	330.75

178 The correct answer is: 92%

Batches	Total time	Average time/unit
1	750	750
2		750 × r
4		750 × r^2
8		750 × r^3
16	8,500	750 × r^4

$8,500 = 16 \times 750\ r^4$

$8,500/(16 \times 750) = r^4$

r = 0.92 or 92%

179 The correct answer is: Neither 1 nor 2

The learning curve will eventually come to an end in all cases.

The use of the learning curve is not restricted to the manufacturing industries that it is traditionally associated with. It is also used in other less-traditional sectors, such as professional practice, financial services, publishing and travel.

180 The correct answer is: Lower labour costs

The learning effect leads to a reduction in labour hours per batch, which therefore lowers the labour costs. The other factors are not affected by the learning rate.

181 The correct answer is: Increasing the level of staff training

Increasing staff training could lead to an extension of the learning curve as the higher skilled employees should demonstrate an even greater improvement than if they were not trained.

Spinster Co

182 The correct answer is: 83.07 hours

Cumulative average time per batch for the first 54 batches

$Y = ax^b$

Where Y = the cumulative average time per unit to produce x units
x = the cumulative number of units
a = the time taken for the first unit of output
b = the index of learning (logLR/log2)

The cumulative average time per batch, with a learning curve of 80%, is therefore

$Y = aX^{-0.3219}$

where a = the time for the first batch (300 hours) and X is the number of the batch. For the 54th batch, X = 54
$Y = 300 \times 54^{-0.3219}$
$= 300 \times 0.2769 = 83.07$

The cumulative average time per batch for the first 54 batches is 83.07 hours.

183 The correct answer is: 91%

Batches	Total time	Average time/unit
1	300	
2		$300 \times r$
4		$300 \times r^2$
8		$300 \times r^3$
16	3,300	$300 \times r^4$

$3,300 = 16 \times 300\, r^4$

$3,300/(16 \times 300) = r^4$

$r = 0.91$ or 91%

184 The correct answer is: A standard which can be achieved if production is carried out efficiently, machines are properly operated and/or materials are properly used.

Distracters:

'A standard which can be attained under perfect operating conditions.' This is an ideal standard.
'A standard based on current working conditions.' This is a current standard.
'A long-term standard which remains unchanged over the years and is used to show trends.' This is a basic standard.

185 The correct answer is: Ideal

It is likely that management at Spinster Co have applied an ideal standard. Their view may have been that this created an incentive to be more efficient, even though it is highly unlikely that the standard will be achieved. However, the differences between standards and actual results will always be adverse. It appears that the employees feel that the goals are unattainable, so they are unmotivated to improve their performance.

186 The correct answer is: Direct labour rate

This rate will be governed by legislation and market conditions. It is therefore out of the control of the production department manager.

Birch Co

187 The correct answer is: $3,750 Adverse

The sales volume planning variance compares the revised budget with the original budget. It may be called a market size variance.

Revised sales volume	17,500 units
Original budgeted sales volume	20,000 units
Sales volume planning variance in units of sales	2,500 units (A)
× standard contribution per unit	$1.5
Sales volume planning variance in $	3,750 (A)

188 The correct answer is: $2,250 Adverse

The operational variance is calculated in a similar way to the planning variance, except that actual results are compared with the revised standard or budget.

Actual sales volume	16,000 units
Revised sales volume	17,500 units
Operational sales volume variance in units	1,500 units (A)
× standard contribution per unit	$1.5
Operational sales volume variance in $ contribution	2,250 (A)

189 The correct answer is: $440 Adverse

Fixed production overhead total variance:
Units produced × standard fixed costs per unit – actual cost

$[18,000 × ($3,000/17,500 units)] – $3,500$
$[18,000 × ($3,000/17,500 units)] – $3,500$
$[18,000 × 0.17] – $3,500$
$$3,060 – $3,500$
$= 440 (A)

190 The correct answer is: An improvement in technology led to an international reduction in sales price of Product X.

The improvement in technology is outside the control of the managers in Birch Co, and would therefore give rise to a planning variance. All of the other distracters are examples of operational issues.

191 The correct answer is: The sales volume operational variance

A sales volume operational variance, or market share variance, is caused by the difference between actual sales volume and the sales volume in the revised budget.

Organic Bread Co

192   The correct answer is: $3.30

Usage variance

	Std usage for actual output 950 units 'Should have used' kg	Actual usage 'Did use' kg	Variance kg	Standard cost per kg $	Variance $
White flour	427.50	408.50	19.00 (F)	1.80	34.20 (F)
Wholegrain flour	142.50	152.00	9.50 (A)	2.20	20.90 (A)
Yeast	9.50	10.00	0.50 (A)	20.00	10.00 (A)
	579.50	570.50			3.30 (F)

193   The correct answer is: $16.51 Adverse

Mix variance

	Actual usage kg	Actual usage in std mix (W1) kg	Mix Variance kg	Standard cost per kg $	Mix variance $
White flour	408.50	420.86	12.36 (F)	1.80	22.25 (F)
Wholegrain flour	152	140.29	11.71 (A)	2.20	25.76 (A)
Yeast	10	9.35	0.65 (A)	20.00	13.00 (A)
	570.50	570.50			16.51 (A)

Workings

$$\frac{450}{610} \times 570.50 = 420.86$$

$$\frac{150}{610} \times 570.50 = 140.29$$

$$\frac{10}{610} \times 570.50 = 9.35$$

194   The correct answer is: $19.77 Favourable

Yield variance

	Units
570.50 kg should produce (÷ 0.610)	935.25
They did produce	950.00
Yield variance in units of output	14.75 (F)
Standard material cost per unit	$1.34
Yield variance in $	$19.77 (F)

195   The correct answers are:

Not fully removing the mix out of the machine, leaving some behind.	YES	
Errors in the mix causing sub-standard loaves and rejections by the quality inspector.	YES	
An unexpected increase in the cost of flour introduced by the supplier.		NO

A material yield variance arises because there is a difference between what the input should have been for the output achieved and the actual input. Therefore an increase in the price of flour will not affect the yield; it would affect the material price variance.

196 The correct answers are:

The production manager in Organic Bread Co deviates from the standard mix.	**YES**	
The selling price of the Mixed Bloomer changes.		**NO**
An inferior quality of flour or yeast is used unknowingly.		**NO**

A change in the selling price of the Mixed Bloomer may influence the behaviour of the production manager, eg if the price has to be lowered, and cost savings made, so the mix may be reviewed. However, it will not lead directly to a mix variance.

An inferior quality of flour or yeast used unknowingly may lead to a yield variance, however, it will not lead to a mix variance.

Elm Co

197 The correct answer is: $44,000

Planning (selling price) variance

	$ per unit
Original budgeted sales price	8
Revised budgeted sales price	10
Sales price planning variance	2 (F)
× actual units sold	22,000
Planning variance for sales price	44,000 (F)

198 The correct answer is: $22,000

Operational (selling price) variance

	$
Actual sales revenue	198,000
Should have sold for (× $10)	220,000
Operational (selling price) variance	**22,000** (A)

199 The correct answer is: $13,000

Labour rate variance

	$
4,000 hours should have cost (× $15)	60,000
But did cost	73,000
Labour rate variance	**13,000** (A)

200 The correct answer is: 'The sales manager of Elm Co should be held responsible if an unfavourable planning sales price variance is found' is **false** and 'It is possible for the revised price to be manipulated and revised to a level whereby a favourable operational sales price could be found' is **true**.

The first statement is false because operational variances are the only variances within the control of the managers, so performance must be assessed with only operational variances in mind.

The second statement is true. One might question the validity of the revised price. The person responsible for the revised price should have sufficient evidence to support setting the revised price at that level to ensure that there is no manipulation of figures.

201 The correct answer is: Both statements are false.

An operational manager cannot appraise variances in isolation from each other. A favourable material price variance from using lower quality material may result in a much larger adverse usage variance, reaching the overall conclusion that the performance is poor.

Statement 2 is false because a change in the economic circumstances in Sealand is clearly outside of the control of the managers of Elm Co and will therefore not result in operational variances.

Maple Co

The original standard cost was 2.5 kg × $4 = $10. The revised standard cost is 4 kg × $5.50 = $22.

202 The correct answer is: $22,000 (A)

Material price planning variance

This is the difference between the original standard price for Material X and the revised standard price.

	$ per kg
Original standard price	4
Revised standard price	5
Material price planning variance	1 (A)
× Actual quantity of material used (22,000 kg)	$22,000 (A)

203 The correct answer is: $13,000 (A)

Material price operational variance

This compares the actual price per kg of material with the revised standard price. It is calculated using the actual quantity of materials used.

	$
22,000 kg of Material X should cost (revised standard $5)	110,000
They did cost	123,000
Material price operational variance	13,000 (A)

204 The correct answer is: $8,000 (A)

Material usage operational variance

This variance is calculated by comparing the actual material usage with the standard usage in the revised standard, but is then converted into a monetary value by applying the original standard price for the materials, not the revised standard price.

	kg of X
8,000 units of Bark should use (× 2.5kg)	20,000
They did use	22,000
Material usage (operational) variance in kg of X	2,000 (A)
Original standard price per kg of Material X	$4
Material usage (operational) variance in $	$8,000 (A)

205 The correct answer is: 'Maple Co failed to order a sufficient amount of Material X for production from the main supplier. They sourced the rest of the material from another supplier at a higher price to make up for this' is **invalid** and 'There was a disruption to the supply of Material X to the market' is **valid**.

Statement 1 is an example of a controllable variance, and would therefore give rise to an operational variance. The second statement is outside the control of management and is therefore a planning variance.

206 The correct answer is: 'Any operational variances arising should be a realistic measure of what the causes of the variances have cost Maple Co' is **true** and 'The causes of the planning variances should not be investigated immediately by the operational manager in Maple Co' is **false**.

Operational variances compare actual performance with a realistic standard cost or budget, and so should provide a realistic reflection of what the causes of the variances have cost Maple Co.

Planning variances are not the responsibility of operational managers, therefore there is no need for operational managers to immediately investigate their causes. However, their causes could be investigated by someone in Maple Co, since lessons may be learned for the future.

Pine Co

207 The correct answer is: $24,300 (F)

Labour rate planning variance

This is the difference between the original standard rate per hour and the revised standard rate per hour.

	$ per hour
Original standard rate	15
Revised standard rate	14
Labour rate planning variance	1 (F)
× actual no of hours worked	24,300
	24,300 (F)

208 The correct answer is: $180,000 (A)

Labour efficiency planning variance

This is the difference between the original standard time per unit and the revised standard time for the quantity of units produced.

	Hours
8,000 units of product should take: original standard (× 3)	24,000
8,000 units of product should take: revised standard (× 4.5)	36,000
Labour efficiency planning variance in hours	12,000 (A)
Original standard rate per hour	$15
Labour efficiency planning variance in $	$180,000 (A)

209 The correct answer is: $12,150 (A)

Labour rate operational variance

This is calculated using the actual number of hours worked and paid for.

	$
24,300 hours should cost (revised standard $14)	340,200
They did cost	352,350
Labour rate operational variance	12,150 (A)

210 The correct answer is: $175,500 (F)

Labour efficiency operational variance

	Hours
8,000 units of product should take (× 4.5 hours)	36,000
They did take	24,300
Labour efficiency (operational variance in hours)	11,700 (F)
Original standard rate per hour	$15
Labour efficiency (operational variance in $)	$175,500 (F)

211 The correct answers are: 'Production management's motivation is likely to increase if they know they will not be held responsible for poor planning and faulty standard setting' is **true** and 'Planning variances will provide a more realistic and fair reflection of actual performance' is **false**.

The second statement is false because it is operational variances which provide a more realistic and fair reflection of actual performance, since these are within the control of management.

Kiss Co

212   The correct answer is: 552 hours

Time taken for the 24th batch

Cumulative average time per batch for the first 24 batches

$Y = ax^b$

Where Y   =   the cumulative average time per unit to produce x units
       x   =   the cumulative number of units
       a   =   the time taken for the first unit of output
       b   =   the index of learning (logLR/log2)

The cumulative average time per batch, with a learning curve of 75%, is therefore

$Y = aX^{-0.415}$

where a = the time for the first batch (3,500 hours) and X is the number of the batch. For the 24th batch, X = 24.

$Y = 3,500 \times 24^{-0.415}$
$= 3,500 \times 0.2674 = 936$

The cumulative average time per batch for the first 24 batches is 936 hours.

The cumulative average time per batch for the first 23 batches is $Y = 3,500 \times 23^{-0.415} = 3,500 \times 0.2722 = 952.7$

	Hours
Total time for 1st 24 batches (24 × 936)	22,464.0
Total time for 1st 23 batches (23 × 952.7)	21,912.1
Time for the 24th batch	551.9

213   The correct answer is: 79%

Batches		Hours
1		3,500
2	Doubled once	
4	Doubled twice	
8	Doubled three times	
16	Doubled four times	22,000

Cumulative average time per batch = 22,000 / 16 = 1,375

$1,375 = 3,500 \, r^4$

r = 0.79 or 79%

214   The correct answer is: $37,500 (F)

Labour efficiency planning variance

	Hours
10,000 batches of product should take: original standard (× 0.75)	7,500
10,000 batches of product should take: revised standard (× 0.5)	5,000
Labour efficiency planning variance in hours	2,500 (F)
Original standard rate per hour	$15
Labour efficiency planning variance in $	$37,500 (F)

215   The correct answer is: Both statements are true.

The learning effect has the effect of reducing the labour time per unit. Therefore, the labour efficiency planning variance will always be favourable.

Standards should be as accurate as possible. Therefore, it is not advisable to set standards before 'steady state' production is reached. However, it is possible to combine standard costing with the learning curve to calculate planning and operational variances.

216   The correct answer is: Provide workers with training

Training may help employees to improve their efficiency in a job. Overtime working should increase output, but there is no reason why it should improve efficiency (output per hour worked). Extra inspection and testing may reduce efficiency by taking up more time: they will not improve efficiency, because they do not test efficiency, only quality. Output capacity relates to potential output volume, not efficiency of working: for example, output capacity may be increased by hiring extra workers, but this does not affect productivity.

217 Mic Co

Text reference. The learning curve is covered in Chapter 9 of the BPP Study Text.

Top tips. There are quite a few calculations in this question, so you need to organise your presentation clearly and in a way that helps you to prepare your answer. Remember that every time output doubles, the cumulative average time per unit falls to the learning curve percentage figure of what the cumulative average time per unit was previously. You don't need the learning curve factor of –0.1844245 for most of your calculations.

The potential trick in the question is that the learning curve no longer applies in November, when the average time per batch is the same as the time required to produce the eighth batch in October. To calculate this time per batch, you need to calculate the average and total times for the seventh and eighth batches. The time for the 8th batch is the difference between the total times for the first seven and the first eight batches.

Easy marks. There are some easy marks to be won if you remember that every time output doubles the cumulative average time per unit is x% of what it was previously, where x is the learning curve percentage. If you can write your points reasonably quickly, there should be easy marks in the answer to part (b) too.

Marking scheme

		Marks
(a)	Cost each month: July and August (1.5 mark per month)	3
	Cost each month: September and October (1.5 marks per month)	3
	Cost in November	3
		9
(b)	**End of learning period**	
	Each point discussed –maximum	2
	Maximum	4
(c)	**Advantages and disadvantages**	
	Each advantage	1
	Each disadvantage	1
	Maximum	7
	Total marks	20

(a) Every time output doubles, the average time per batch is 88% of what it was previously. The learning curve effect ends in October and does not apply in November, when the average time per unit is the same as the time required to make the eighth batch in October.

Month	Cumulative batches	Average time per batch Hours	Total time Hours	Incremental time in the month Hours	Labour cost per month at $12 per hour $
July	1	200.00	200.00	200.00	2,400
August	2	176.00	352.00	152.00	1,824
September	4	154.88	619.52	267.52	3,210
October	8	136.294	1,090.35	470.83	5,650

Average time to produce first 7 batches = 200 × 7 −0.1844245 = 200 × 1/1.4317157 = 139.6925 hours

Total time for first 7 batches = 7 × 139.6925 = 977.85 hours

Average time to produce first 8 batches = 200 × 8 −0.1844245 = 200 × 1/1.4674115 = 136.2944 hours

Total time for first 8 batches = 8 × 136.2944 = 1,090.35 hours

Time to make the 8th batch = 1,090.35 − 977.85 = 112.50 hours

Total labour cost in November = 8 batches × 112.50 per batch × $12 per hour = $10,800.

(b) The company sets selling prices on a cost plus basis, but in the first few months the cost per unit falls due to the 88% learning curve effect. The average time per batch was 200 hours for the first batch in July, but falls to 112.5 hours per batch from November onwards.

If cost plus pricing is used, and if the company wants to charge a stable price for its product, it should consider a cost plus price based on the longer-term unit cost from November onwards.

The company appears to have used actual cost plus to set the selling price on its initial batches, with the result that the price was high. This probably explains the disappointing initial sales.

Budgeting for labour time and labour costs should also take the learning curve into effect, because of the reduction in incremental labour time per batch in the months July – October.

(c) Involving senior staff at Mic Co in the budget-setting process

Advantages

- Since they are based on information from staff who are most familiar with the department, they are more likely to improve the accuracy of the budget. In Mic Co's case, the selling price could have been set more accurately and sales may have been higher if the production manager had been consulted.

- Staff are more likely to be motivated to achieve any targets as it is 'their' budget and they therefore have a sense of ownership and commitment. The production manager at Mic Co seems resigned to the fact that they are not consulted on budgetary matters.

- Morale amongst staff is likely to improve as they feel that their experience and opinions are valued.

- Knowledge from a spread of several levels of management is pooled.

- Co-ordination is improved due to the number of departments involved in the budget-setting process.

Disadvantages

- The whole budgeting process is more time consuming and therefore costly.

- The budgeting process may have to be started earlier than a non-participative budget would need to start because of the length of time it takes to complete the process

218 ZBB

Marking scheme

			Marks
(a)	Explanation:		
	Difficulty setting objectives quantifiably	2	
	Difficulty in saying how to achieve them	1	
	Outputs difficult to measure	2	
	No relationship between inputs and outputs	2	
	Value for money issue	2	
			max 5
(b)	Incremental and zero-based budgeting:		
	Explaining 'incremental budgeting'	2	
	Explaining 'zero-based budgeting'	2	
			4
(c)	Stages involved in zero-based budgeting:		
	1 mark per stage		3
(d)	Any disadvantage of incremental budgeting that supports the statement	1	
	Incremental budgeting is quick and easy	1	
	Any disadvantage of ZBB that refutes the statement	1	
	Easier to define decision packages in public sector	2	
	More appropriate for discretionary costs	2	
	Conclusion	1	
			8
			20

(a) **Difficulties when budgeting in the public sector**

The main objective for most companies is to **maximise profit**. Effective budgeting can assist in meeting this objective by focussing efforts on reducing certain costs and increasing revenues by a certain amount or percentage. The **objectives of public sector organisations** are more **difficult to define in a quantifiable way**.

The **objectives of public sector organisations** such as hospitals are likely to **be largely qualitative**. For example, ensuring that ambulances reach patients within 20 minutes from an emergency call being received. Such objectives are difficult to define in a quantifiable way, while identifying how the objective is actually achieved can also be problematic.

Another problem why budgeting is so difficult in public sector organisations is that outputs in the public sector can seldom be measured in a way that is generally agreed to be meaningful. While outputs for private companies can be measured in terms of sales revenue, outputs in the public sector are harder to pin down. For example in the education sector, are good exam results alone an adequate measure of the quality of teaching? In the public sector, **comparisons are often made between the funds available and the funds actually required**. Therefore, public sector budgeting naturally focuses on inputs, rather than the relationship between inputs and outputs.

Public sector organisations are under constant pressure to prove that they are economical, efficient and effective (offering value for money). **Resources are always kept to a minimum and each item of expenditure must be justified**. This makes the budgeting process more difficult.

(b) **Incremental budgeting**

Incremental budgeting **bases the budget on the current year's results plus an extra amount for estimated growth or inflation next year**. This form of budgeting is a reasonable procedure if current operations are as effective, efficient and economical as they can be.

Zero-based budgeting (ZBB)

ZBB rejects the assumption that underpins the concept of incremental budgeting; that next year's budget can be based on this year's costs plus an extra amount for estimated growth or inflation. ZBB involves **preparing a budget for each cost centre from a zero base**. Every item of **expenditure must be justified** in its entirety in order to be included in next year's budget.

(c) **Stages in zero-based budgeting**

ZBB involves three main stages.

Define activities (decision packages)

At the first stage, management identify the **key activities** within the organisation. These activities are described within a decision package. The decision package is originally **prepared at a base level** which shows the minimum level of resource required to meet the organisation's objectives. **Incremental packages** may be prepared to show any **additional work** that could be done, at what cost and for what benefit.

Evaluate and rank each activity

Management will then rank each activity (decision package) on the basis of its benefit to the organisation. Minimum work requirements (those that are essential to get the job done) will be given high priority and so too will work which meets legal obligations. This process will **help management to decide what to spend and where to spend it**.

Allocate resources

At the final stage, management allocate resources in the budget **according to the funds available and the evaluation and ranking of the competing packages**.

(d) **No longer a place for incremental budgeting and the drawbacks of ZBB**

Incremental budgeting can encourage **slack** and **wasteful spending** as past inefficiencies are perpetuated because cost levels are rarely subjected to close scrutiny. However, the view that there is no longer a place for it in any organisation is rather misleading. While inappropriate for public sector organisations where all expenditure must be justified, to say that it is of no use in any organisation effectively ignores the limitations of zero-based budgeting (ZBB). These limitations are analysed below.

The limitations of ZBB

The major limitation of ZBB is the volume of **extra paperwork** created. Assumptions about costs and benefits in each package must be continually updated and new packages must be developed as new activities occur within the organisation.

ZBB is likely to require **management skills both in constructing decision packages and in the ranking process**. If management do not possess such skills they will require training in ZBB techniques, which takes time and money.

The ranking process can also prove problematic. It can be difficult **to rank packages which appear to be equally vital**, for legal or operational reasons. Furthermore, it is difficult to rank activities which have **qualitative rather than quantitative benefits**.

ZBB can **give the impression that all decisions have to be made in the budget**. As a result, management may feel unable to carry out new ideas because they were not approved by a decision package and did not pass through the ranking process.

ZBB in practice

As all costs need to justified under a ZBB system, it would seem inappropriate to use it as the sole system within a private sector organisation where **certain costs will always be incurred in order to meet basic production requirements**. In such a scenario, incremental budgeting is likely to prove more efficient as it is quick and easily understood.

ZBB could be considered more **appropriate for public sector organisations**. The majority of costs in such organisations are **discretionary** and emphasis is placed on obtaining **value for money**. This objective is directly linked to the decision package ranking process within a ZBB system. Furthermore, it is easier to put activities into decision packages in organisations which undertake a number of set definable activities. Hospitals, for example, have set activities including outpatient wards, children's wards and A&E departments.

Conclusion

Whilst ZBB is more suitable for public sector organisations – particularly in the current economic climate – its limitations should not be overlooked. Incremental budgeting can still be of use to organisations.

219 Designit

Text reference. Budgetary systems are covered in Chapter 9. The use of spreadsheets in budgeting is covered in Chapter 10.

Top tips. There are easy marks available throughout this question so ensure you allocate enough time to each requirement. Refer to the scenario throughout your answer and, as a guide, aim for 1 mark per well explained point.

Easy marks. You should be able to score well in part (a) by briefly explaining what a rolling budget is and how it would operate in Designit.

		Marks
(a)	Explanation:	
	Updated after one month elapsed	1
	Always 12 months	1
	Example given	1
	First month in detail	1
	Later month less detail	1
	Need to revisit earlier months	1
		max 4

(b) Problems:

More time	1
Lack of experience	1
Too regular	2
Managers' resistance	2
Work harder	1
Holding back work	2
	max 6

(c) Simpler incentive scheme:

Current target too easy	1
Second target too hard	1
Other valid point re current scheme	1
New scheme outlined	3
	6

(d) Using spreadsheets:

Errors entering data	1
Rolling budgets more complex	1
Formulae may be wrong	1
Corruption of model	1
No audit trail	1
	max 4
	20

(a) **Rolling budget**

A **monthly rolling** budget is a budget which is **continuously updated** by adding a further month when the earliest month has passed.

For example, Designit would begin by preparing a 12-month budget covering the period 1 December 20X2 to 30 November 20X3. At the end of December 20X2, a budget for December 20X3 would be prepared, so that the **unexpired period covered by the budget is always 12 months**.

When the budget is initially prepared for the year ending 30 November 20X3, the budget for December 20X2 (the first month in the budget) should be prepared in detail. The later months will contain a lot **less detail** as there will be greater uncertainty regarding **internal resources** and **market conditions**.

When the budget for December 20X2 has elapsed and the budget for December 20X3 is prepared, the budget for January 20X3 should be **revised in greater detail**.

(b) **Problems**

Monthly rolling budgets **take time to prepare** and can be **complex**. The company's accounts department consists of a single part-qualified accountant who already has a **heavy workload**. As such it is unlikely that they have the **time or experience** required to successfully implement a system of monthly rolling budgets.

Rolling budgets are best suited to organisations that operate in **rapidly changing environments**. Designit is a **mature business and trading is fairly stable** year on year. A rolling budget updated on a **quarterly basis** (as opposed to a monthly basis) would probably be sufficient.

A monthly rolling budget will require **input from many staff**, reducing the time they have to dedicate to other tasks.

Sales managers are unlikely to embrace the new budgeting and incentive system. They will have become accustomed to **knowing their target for the whole year in advance** and will **be used to working to targets that are easily achievable**.

Under the proposed system, sales managers may hold back work once they have achieved their monthly target and let it run into the following month to increase their chances of meeting next month's target. This is **not in the best interests of the business**.

(c)   **Problems with the current bonus scheme**

The current bonus scheme consists of **two targets**. The first target ($1.5 million of fee income) is **too easily reached**, while the second target (a further $1.5 million of fee income) appears **unrealistic** and has not been achieved by any of the sales managers.

Due to the above, sales managers are **not motivated to earn additional fees** once they have reached the first target of $1.5 million.

Alternative bonus scheme

The company is currently paying each sales manager a bonus of $30,000 each year (20% of $150,000). This is 2% of $1.5 million. Changing the bonus to **2% commission on all sales** as opposed to a percentage of salary would motivate the sales managers to bring in fees throughout the year.

Alternatively, the company may consider **revising the current bonus scheme** to include smaller bonuses paid out at more regular intervals. For example, a bonus equivalent to 5% of salary for every $500,000 of fee income.

(d)   **Using the company accountant's own spreadsheets for budgeting**

The company should ensure that the accountant has the **necessary skills** to operate the budget spreadsheet. Even a minor error in the design of a budgeting model can **affect the validity of data throughout the spreadsheet**.

Even if the accountant does have the necessary skills, they are likely to have **to input large amounts of data** from the company's systems into the spreadsheet. The **opportunity for error is high**, especially if nobody is available to check their work.

It is **very easy to corrupt a model** by accidentally changing a cell or inputting data in the wrong place. The accountant is unlikely to spot this, due to their **lack of experience** and the **time pressure** on them.

Finally, when data is input from a company's system into a spreadsheet, the **audit trail is lost**. This can make it difficult to trace/check the numbers.

220 Crumbly Cakes

Text references. Variance analysis is covered in Chapters 12 and 13.

Top tips. You may find part (a) quite tricky. You need to plan a structured answer using the headings suggested by the question. Make some sensible, common sense suggestions and if you run out of ideas, move on to parts (b) and (c) where easier marks are available. Read the information very carefully and layout your workings clearly.

Easy marks. There are some easy variance calculations in parts (b) and (c) as well as some trickier mix and yield variances.

Examining team's comments. Many candidates completely missed the point in part (a). If a business fundamentally changes its business process without altering the standard costs of the process, it renders the variances that are produced meaningless. Some candidates tried to discuss each variance in turn rather than carry out a performance assessment of each manager. This is not as effective a method. Motivation is a complex topic and credit was given for any sensible comments.

Part (b) was well done with many candidates scoring good marks.

			Marks
(a)	Production manager assessment	2	
	Sales manager assessment	2	
	Bonus scheme comment	3	
			7
(b)	Price variance	3	
	Mix variance	3	
	Yield variance	3	
			9
(c)	Planning variance and comment	2	
	Operational variance and comment	2	
			4
			20

(a) **Production manager**

The production manager instigated the new organic cake production approach and this has **fundamentally changed** the nature of the business. Before the new system started, there were **favourable material variances** for price and yield and the production manager would have received a bonus as a result.

Organic ingredients are **more expensive** and this results in **adverse** material price and mix variances in March. The **material yield** variance is favourable but not by enough to compensate for the adverse variances. This means that the production manager would not receive a bonus under the current scheme.

Sales of the cakes have improved significantly so customers presumably appreciate the new flavour and mix of ingredients. The production manager does not receive any credit for the favourable sales variances and that does not seem fair.

Sales manager

In contrast, the **sales variances** that the sales manager is responsible for have moved from adverse in February to favourable in March. The new organic approach has, therefore, been a **success** with customers. The sales manager will have had to sell the new organic cakes to customers and is therefore **partly responsible** for the improvement, but the original impetus came from the production manager.

Bonus scheme

The bonus scheme does not seem to be fair as it will **not reward** the two managers fairly for their efforts. They are both responsible for the improved sales but it is very difficult to **fairly allocate responsibility** in this situation. Some form of **sharing** of responsibility and reward is required.

The **standards** that the variances are based on need to be changed to reflect the new approach that the business is taking. For example, the standard price of the materials needs to be increased.

(b) **Material price variances**

	$
5,700 kg of flour should have cost (× $0.12)	684
but did cost	741
Material price variance	57 (A)

	$
6,600 kg of eggs should have cost (× $0.70)	4,620
but did cost	5,610
Material price variance	990 (A)

		$
6,600 kg of butter should have cost (× $1.70)		11,220
but did cost		11,880
Material price variance		660 (A)

		$
4,578 kg of sugar should have cost (× $0.50)		2,289
but did cost		2,747
Material price variance		458 (A)

		$
Total material price variance		2,165 (A)

Material mix variances

Total quantity used = 5,700 + 6,600 + 6,600 + 4,578 = 23,478 kg

Standard mix of actual use of each ingredient is in equal proportions = 23,478/4 = 5,869.5 kg

	Actual quantity Actual mix	Actual quantity Standard mix	Variance	Standard cost per kg	Variance
	Kg	Kg	Kg	$	$
Flour	5,700	5869.5	169.5 (F)	0.12	20.34 (F)
Eggs	6,600	5869.5	730.5 (A)	0.70	511.35 (A)
Butter	6,600	5869.5	730.5 (A)	1.70	1,241.85 (A)
Sugar	4,578	5869.5	1,291.5 (F)	0.50	645.75 (F)
	23,478	23,478			1,087.11 (A)

Material yield variance

Standard cost of a cake

		$
Flour	0.1 kg × $0.12	0.012
Eggs	0.1 kg × $0.70	0.070
Butter	0.1 kg × $1.70	0.170
Sugar	0.1 kg × $0.50	0.050
		0.302

	Cakes
The actual quantity of inputs are expected to yield (23,478/0.4)	58,695
Actual output	60,000
Yield variance in cakes	1,305 (F)
× standard cost per cake ($0.302)	$394.11 (F)

Alternative method

	Standard quantity Standard mix	Actual quantity Standard mix	Variance	Standard cost per kg	Variance
	Kg	Kg	Kg	$	$
Flour	6,000	5869.5	130.5	0.12	15.66
Eggs	6,000	5869.5	130.5	0.70	91.35
Butter	6,000	5869.5	130.5	1.70	221.85
Sugar	6,000	5869.5	130.5	0.50	65.25
	24,000	23,478			394.11 (F)

(c) **Total operational variance**

	$
Revised standard cost of actual production (60,000 × $0.40)	24,000
Actual cost	20,978
Total operational variance	3,022 (F)

The variance is **favourable** because the actual cost was lower than the expected cost using the revised basis.

Total planning variance

	$
Revised standard cost (60,000 × $0.40)	24,000
Original standard cost (60,000 × $0.302)	18,120
Total planning variance	5,880 (A)

The planning variance reveals the extent to which the original standard was at fault. It is an **adverse variance** because the original standard was too optimistic, overestimating the expected profits by understating the standard cost. More simply, it is adverse because the revised standard cost is much higher than the original standard cost.

221 Secure Net

Text reference. Planning and operational variances are covered in Chapter 13.

Top tips. Part (a) should not cause any problems. In part (b) the ACCA examining team has stated that any methods applied consistently would score full marks. This answer shows the BPP approach and the approach used in the article previously written by the ACCA examining team. If you get stuck on the details of which numbers to use where, make an attempt at something sensible and move on.

Part (c) is a straightforward discussion of the production manager's performance. Even if you struggled with the calculations in part (b), you should be able to pick up on the clues given in the scenario for factors that would have been controllable and uncontrollable.

Easy marks. Part (a) should be an easy 4 marks and there are easy marks available in part (c) just from describing factors in the scenario.

Examining team's comments. Answers for part (b) could have been better. As we know from articles that have been written on operational and planning variances in the past, there are often different approaches to calculating some of them. Candidates should remain assured that, whichever approach they adopted, full credit would be given if they were consistent.

Part (c) produced some mixed answers. Candidates need to be reminded to state the obvious points: operational variances are deemed to be within the control of the production manager, planning variances are not; the net effect of usage and price variances must be considered when assessing the production manager's performance.

Marking scheme

			Marks
(a)	Behavioural problems with standard costing – 1 mark per point	Max 2	
	Ways to reduce problems – ½ mark per point	Max 2	
			4
(b)	Planning price variance	2	
	Planning usage variance	2	
	Operational price variance	2	
	Operational usage variance	2	
			8
(c)	Explanation of external problems beyond control of manager	4	
	Assessment of factors within the control of the manager	4	
	Conclusion	1	
	Maximum		8
			20

(a) **Behavioural problems that may arise from using standard costs**

Standard costing is principally used to value inventories, to prepare budgets and to act as a **control device**. The focus in using a standard cost system should not be to attribute blame, but to influence behaviour through **positive support** and **appropriate motivation**.

The perception of a standard costing system can affect its success or failure. A **negative perception** is often the consequence of unreasonable standards, lack of transparency in setting standards, poor communication or uneven reward systems. Such situations can make a good standard cost system a failure.

Ways to reduce negative perceptions/motivation

Organisations should set **understandable** and **achievable** standards, otherwise it neither motivates nor rewards employees. Complex financial measures and reports mean nothing to most employees.

Employees should be **involved** in setting standards and developing performance measures. This should result in realistic targets and increase **employee motivation**.

Standards should be **well defined** and **communicated** to all employees so that operational efficiency can be achieved. Management should ensure that any performance-related scheme does not reward behaviour that goes against the best interests of the organisation.

Finally, **performance pay plans** should be **reviewed and updated** on a regular basis to meet the changing needs of employees and the business as a whole.

(b)   **Planning price variance**

	$
Original standard price per kg	4.00
Revised standard price per kg	4.80
Planning price variance per kg	0.80 (A)
Quantity used = 100,000 × 0.035	3,500 kg
Planning price variance in $	$2,800 (A)

Planning usage variance

	kg
Original standard: 100,000 units should use (× 0.04)	4,000
Revised standard: 100,000 units should use (× 0.042)	4,200
Planning usage variance in kg	200 (A)
Original standard price per kg	$4
Planning usage variance in $	$800 (A)

Operational price variance

	$
Actual price of actual materials (3,500 kg)	18,375
Revised standard price of actual materials ($4.80 × 3,500 kg)	16,800
Operational price variance	1,575 (A)

Operational usage variance

Actual quantity should have been	4,200 kg
but was	3,500 kg
Operational usage variance in kg	700 kg (F)
× original standard cost per kg	× $4
Operational usage variance in $	$2,800 (F)

Check:	$	$
Actual cost of materials: 3,500 kg × $5.25		18,375
Original standard cost: 100,000 units × 40 g × $4 per kg		16,000
Total materials cost variance		2,375 (A)
Variances:		
Price planning	2,800 (A)	
Usage planning	800 (A)	
Price operational	1,575 (A)	
Usage operational	2,800 (F)	
		2,375 (A)

(c) **Worldwide standard size**

The size of the security card has to fit the reader of that card and if the **industry specification changes** there is nothing that the production manager can do about it. This is **beyond their control** and therefore a planning error and should not be used to assess their performance.

Oil prices

Worldwide oil prices have increased, which have **increased plastic prices** and again the production manager **cannot control** that. This is another planning error and should be ignored in an assessment of their performance.

New supplier

The decision to use a new supplier cost an extra $1,575 which is the **operational price variance** and could be regarded as **poor performance** by the production manager. However, the manager seems to have agreed to the higher price on the promise of **better quality** and **reliability**.

The **operational usage variance** is $2,800 favourable and this could be as a result of improved quality.

Increase in production and sales

Production levels increased significantly from 60,000 to 100,000 which could potentially have caused problems for the production manager. However, the ability to increase production suggests that the new supplier's reliability was good.

The total materials operational variance shows a favourable variance, which reflects well on the performance of the production manager. The ability to react and be flexible can often form a part of a performance assessment.

In **conclusion** the manager could be said to have performed well.

222 Noble

Text references. Flexed budgets are covered in Chapter 9. Sales mix and quantity variances are covered in Chapter 12. Planning and operational variances are covered in Chapter 13.

Top tips. When you prepare a flexed budget, remember its format should replicate the original budget to which it relates. For example, if the original budget totals up variable costs, so should the flexed budget. This makes it easier to compare like with like.

Easy marks. There are 12 marks available for preparing a flexed budget in part (a). The steps involved in preparing a flexed budget should be familiar to you from your earlier studies.

Examining team's comments. Many candidates answered part (a) well and easily scored 9 out of the 12 marks available, tripping up only on staff wages and energy costs calculations.

Many candidates confused the sales mix variance with the materials mix variance and talked about the latter in part (b). Also many candidates could not describe the quantity variance or identify why it had arisen. There is clearly a lack of understanding about variances, with candidates perhaps learning formulae in order to churn out calculations but not really understanding what variances mean to a business. This area needs more work by the majority of students.

In part (c) only a few candidates were able to show that planning and operational variances needed to be calculated, so that the manager would only be assessed on results that were within their control.

Marks

(a)   Flexed budget:
      Food sales   1
      Drink sales   1
      Total revenue   1
      Staff wages   1½
      Food costs   1
      Drink costs   1
      Energy costs   1½
      Variable costs total   1
      Contribution   1
      Manager's and chef's pay   ½
      Rent & rates   ½
      Operating profit   1
                                                     12

(b)   Explanation of variances   2
      Suggestions of reason for variances   2
                                                    4

(c)   Discussion of variance 1   Max 2
      Discussion of variance 2   Max 2
                                                       4
                                                   20

(a)   **Flexed budget**

Number of meals   1,560

	$	$
Revenue:		
Food sales (W1)	62,400	
Drink sales (W1)	15,600	
		78,000
Variable costs:		
Staff wages (W2)	(12,672)	
Food costs (W3)	(7,800)	
Drink costs (W4)	(3,120)	
Energy costs (W5)	(4,234)	
		(27,826)
Contribution		50,174
Fixed costs:		
Manager's and chef's pay	(8,600)	
Rent, rates and depreciations	(4,500)	
		(13,100)
Operating profit		37,074

Workings

1   *Revenue*
    Food revenue = 1,560 × (($45 + $35)/2) = $62,400
    Drinks revenue = 1,560 × ($2.50 × 4) = $15,600

2   *Staff wages*

Average number of orders per day = 1,560/(6 days × 4 weeks) = 65 orders per day
Therefore extra orders = 15 per day (65 − 50). 15/5 = 3 therefore, 3 × 0.5 hours (1.5 hours) of
overtime must be paid.
8 staff × 1.5 hours × 6 days × 4 weeks = 288 extra hours
Extra wages = 288 extra hours × $12 = $3,456 extra wages
Total flexed wages = $9,216 + $3,456 = $12,672

3   *Food costs*
Food costs = 12.5% × $62,400 = $7,800

4   *Drink costs*
Drink costs = 20% × $15,600 = $3,120

5   *Energy costs*
Standard total hours worked = (8 staff × 6 hours) × 6 days × 4 weeks = 1,152 hours
Extra hours worked = 288 (W2)
Total hours = 1,152 + 288 = 1,440
Total energy costs = 1,440 hours × $2.94 per hour = $4,234

(b)   **Sales mix contribution variance**

The sales mix contribution variance measures the effect on profit when the proportions of products sold are
different from those in the standard mix.

The sales mix variance is adverse. Meal B generates a higher contribution than meal A. This means that
more of meal A must have been sold, relative to meal B, than budgeted.

Sales quantity contribution variance

The sales quantity contribution variance shows the difference in contribution/profit because of a change in
sales volume from the budgeted number of sales.

The sales quantity variance is favourable. This means that the total number of meals sold (in the standard
mix) was higher than expected. Indeed, 1,560 meals were sold (budget was 1,200 meals).

(c)   **Food sales**

The half-price drinks promotion has attracted more customers to the restaurant. Calculating variances such
as the sales volume variance for food sales would help to show how the promotion on drinks has impacted
upon the number of meals sold.

Drink sales

The sales volume variance could also be calculated for drinks sales. This will compare the standard number
of drinks sold (1,560 × 4 drinks) to the actual number of drinks sold as a result of the drinks promotion
(1,560 × 6 drinks). The sales volume variance will be favourable as the variance is calculated by applying the
increase in volume to the standard margin per unit.

The restaurant manager should only be held accountable for matters within their control. As such, the total
sales margin price variance could be split into a planning and an operational variance.

The restaurant manager is only accountable for any operational variance and should not be held accountable
for any part of the sales margin price variance that relates to bad planning.

223 Truffle Co

Marking scheme

		Marks
(a)	Rate and efficiency variances:	
	Rate variance	2
	Efficiency variance	2
		4
(b)	Planning and operational variances:	
	Labour rate planning variance	2
	Labour rate operational variance	2
	Labour efficiency planning variance	2
	Labour efficiency operational variance	2
		8
(c)	Discussion:	
	Only operational variances controllable	1
	No labour rate operating variance	1
	Planning variance down to company, not manager	2
	Labour efficiency total variance looks bad	2
	Manager has performed well as regards efficiency	2
	Standard for labour time was to blame	2
	Conclusion	2
		max 8
		20

(a) **Labour variances**
Standard cost per labour hour = $6.00 / 0.5 = $12.00

Labour rate variance

	$
12,000 hours of work should have cost (× $12 per hr)	144,000
but did cost	136,800
Labour rate variance	7,200 (F)

Labour efficiency variance

20,500 batches should have taken (× 0.5 hrs)	10,250 hrs
but did take	12,000 hrs
Efficiency variance in hours	1,750 hrs (A)
× standard rate per hour	× $12
Efficiency variance	$21,000 (A)

(b)   **Planning and operational variances**

Labour rate planning variance

	$
Standard rate	12.00
Revised rate ($12 × 0.95)	11.40
Variance	0.60 (F)
× actual hours paid (12,000)	× 12,000
Labour rate planning variance	$7,200 (F)

Labour rate operational variance

	$
Revised cost of actual hours (12,000 × $12 × 95%)	136,800
Actual cost of actual hours	136,800
Labour rate operational variance	$nil

Labour efficiency planning variance

Standard hours for actual production (20,500 × 0.5 hrs per batch)	10,250 hrs
Revised hours for actual production (20,500 batches × 0.5 hrs per batch × 1.2)	12,300 hrs
Variance	2,050 hrs (A)
× original standard rate per hour	× $12
Labour efficiency planning variance	$24,600 (A)

Labour efficiency operational variance

20,500 batches should have taken (20,500 × 0.5 × 1.2)	12,300 hrs
but did take	12,000 hrs
Variance	300 hrs (F)
× original standard rate per hour	× $12
Labour efficiency operational variance	$3,600 (F)

Alternative solution

The following solution, calculating the **labour efficiency operational variance** using the **revised standard rate per hour**, and the **labour rate planning variance** based on **revised hours for actual production** also scored full marks.

Note that while this approach does not reconcile to the labour rate and efficiency variances calculated in part (a), it does **reconcile to the total labour variance ($13,800 adverse).**

Labour rate planning variance

	$
Standard rate	12.00
Revised rate ($12 × 0.95)	11.40
Variance	0.60 (F)
× revised hours for actual production (12,300)	× 12,300
Labour rate planning variance	$7,380 (F)

Labour rate operational variance

	$
Revised cost of actual hours (12,000 × $12 × 95%)	136,800
Actual cost of actual hours	136,800
Labour rate operational variance	$nil

Labour efficiency planning variance

Standard hours for actual production (20,500 × 0.5 hrs per batch)	10,250 hrs
Revised hours for actual production (20,500 batches × 0.5 hrs per batch × 1.2)	12,300 hrs
Variance	2,050 hrs (A)
× standard rate per hour	× $12
Labour efficiency planning variance	$24,600 (A)

(c)   **Performance of the production manager for the month of November**

The total labour rate variance calculated in part (a) suggests that the production manager has managed to secure **labour at a lower rate** than budgeted (favourable variance of $7,200). However, the total labour efficiency variance (adverse variance of $21,000) would appear to indicate that they have been extremely poor at controlling their **staff's efficiency**.

These variances should be split into **planning and operational variances** to give a truer indication of performance. Planning variances arise due to **inaccurate** planning and/or faulty standards (factors that are outside the control of the production manager). Therefore, the production manager should only be assessed on operational variances.

Labour rate

The labour rate operational variance was $nil. This means that the workforce were paid the **agreed reduced rate** of $11.40 per hour. It is unlikely that the production manager paid anyone for overtime, as this would have increased the hourly rate.

The production manager cannot take credit for the favourable total labour rate variance. The labour rate planning variance of $7,200 indicates that the reduced labour rate was beyond the production manager's control and was **secured by the company**.

Labour efficiency

The total labour efficiency variance is $21,000 adverse.

The planning variance is **$24,600 adverse**. This is because the standard labour time per batch was not updated in November to reflect the fact that it would take **longer to produce the truffles** as a result of the retailer requesting the truffles to be made slightly softer. The production manager cannot be held responsible for this variance.

In contrast, the operational variance is **$3,600 favourable**. When the truffle recipe changed in November, it was expected that the production process would take 20% longer for the first month, as the workers became used to working with the **new ingredient mix**. The workers actually took less than the 20% extra time predicted, yielding a **favourable operational variance**. The production manager can take credit for this variance.

In summary, the production manager **performed well** in the month of November.

224 Block Co

┌───┐
│ **Text reference.** Sales mix and quantity variances are covered in Chapter 11 of the BPP Study Text. Sales planning │
│ and operational variances are covered in Chapter 12.   │
│   │
│ **Top tips.** You may have been surprised that this question focussed on sales variances rather than cost variances, │
│ but the principles are very similar. In part (a), the planning and operational variances for Commodity 1 and 2 have │
│ already been calculated and the information is available to calculate the variances for both commodities, so you can │
│ check your logic as you calculate the variances for Commodity 3.   │
│   │
│ The use of a proforma layout in part (b) is essential for clarity of presentation. │
│   │
│ **Easy marks.** There are easy marks available in part (c) providing you understand what the variances you have │
│ calculated in parts (a) and (b) mean for the business and refer to the scenario throughout your answer. │
└───┘

BPP
LEARNING MEDIA

Marking scheme

			Marks
(a)	Planning and operational variances:		
	Operational variance	2	
	Planning variance	2	
			4
(b)	Mix and quantity variances:		
	Standard profit per unit	4	
	Mix variance	4	
	Quantity variance	3	
			11
(c)	Discussion:		
	1 mark per valid comment	max	5
			20

(a) **Sales price operational variance for Commodity 3**

	$
Actual sales (25,600 units × $40.40)	1,034,240
Revised budget at market price (25,600 units × $39.10)	1,000,960
Sales price operational variance	33,280 (F)

Sales price planning variance for Commodity 3

	$
Revised 'standard' sales price budget	39.10
Original standard sales price	41.60
Sales price planning variance per unit	2.50 (A)
Units sold	25,600
Sales price planning variance in total	$64,000 (A)

(b) **Total sales mix variance**

	Actual total sales in actual mix	Actual total sales in standard mix (W1)	Sales mix variance in units	× Standard profit margin (W2)	Variance $
Commodity 1	29,800 units	30,643 units	843 (A)	× $11.20	9,442 (F)
Commodity 2	30,400 units	28,600 units	1,800 (F)	× $4.20	7,560 (A)
Commodity 3	25,600 units	26,557 units	957 (A)	× $12.00	11,484 (A)
	85,800 units	85,800 units			13,366 (A)

Total sales quantity variance

Budgeted total sales units (30,000 + 28,000 + 26,000)	84,000
Actual total sales units	85,800
Total sales quantity variance in units	1,800 (F)
Average standard profit per unit (W3)	$9.11
Total sales quantity variance	$16,406 (F)

Workings

1   Actual sales quantity in standard mix

Product	Actual quantity in standard mix
Commodity 1: 85,800 × 30/84 =	30,643
Commodity 2: 85,800 × 28/84 =	28,600
Commodity 3: 85,800 × 26/84 =	26,557
	85,800

2   Standard profit margins per unit

$$\text{Overhead absorption rate (OAR)} = \frac{\$174,400}{\left[(0.2 \times 30,000) + (0.6 \times 28,000) + (0.8 \times 26,000)\right]} = \$4 \text{ per hour}$$

Product	Commodity 1 $	Commodity 2 $	Commodity 3 $
Standard selling price	30.00	35.00	41.60
Variable production costs	(18.00)	(28.40)	(26.40)
Fixed production overheads ($4 per hr)	(0.80)	(2.40)	(3.20)
Standard profit margin	11.20	4.20	12.00

3   Average standard profit per unit

	Budgeted sales units	Standard profit per unit $	Budgeted profit $
Commodity 1	30,000	11.20	336,000
Commodity 2	28,000	4.20	117,600
Commodity 3	26,000	12.00	312,000
	84,000		765,600

Budgeted average profit per unit = $765,600/84,000 = $9.11

(c)   The calculations above have shown that, as regards the sales price, there is a $23,360 favourable operational variance and a $54,680 adverse planning variance. In total, these net off to a sales price variance of $31,320 adverse. The sales manager can only be responsible for a variance to the extent that they control it. Since the standard selling prices are set by a consultant, rather than the sales manager, the sales manager can only be held responsible for the operational variance. Given that this was a favourable variance of $23,360, it appears that they have performed well, achieving sales prices which, on average, were higher than the market prices at the time. The consultant's predictions, however, were rather inaccurate, and it is these that have caused an adverse variance to occur overall in relation to sales price.

As regards sales volumes, the mix variance is $13,366 adverse and the quantity variance is $16,406 favourable, meaning that the total volume variance is $3,040 favourable. This is because total sales volumes were higher than expected, although it is apparent that the increased sales related to the lower margin Commodity 2, with sales of Commodity 1 and Commodity 3 actually being lower than budget.

The total variance relating to sales is $28,280 adverse. This looks poor but, as identified above, it is due to the inaccuracy of the sales price forecasts made by the consultant. We know that Block Co is facing tough market conditions because of the economic recession and therefore it is not that surprising that market prices were actually a bit lower than originally anticipated. This could be due to the recession hitting even harder in this quarter than in previous ones.

225 Newtown School

Marking scheme

			Marks
(a)	Budgeted costs:		
	Budgeted income	2	
	Repairs and maintenance	1.0	
	Teachers' salaries	1.5	
	Capital expenditure	1.0	
	Deficit	0.5	
			6
(b)	Advantages and disadvantages:		
	Two advantages	2.0	
	Two disadvantages	2.0	
			4
(c)	Zero-based budgeting:		
	Explanation of ZBB process	max 4.0	
	Relevance to the school: 1 mark for each point made	max 4.0	
	Total for part (c)		max 6
(d)	Use of ZBB to Newtown School		
	Each point made	1.0	max 4
			20

(a)

	$
Budgeted income	
Income from pupils registered on 1 June Year 1 (given in question)	724,500
Expected income from new joiners (W1)	26,100
Total expected income	750,600
Budgeted expenditure	
Repairs and maintenance ($30,000 × 1.03)	30,900
Salaries (W2)	599,940
Expected capital expenditure [(0.7 × $145,000) + (0.3 × $80,000)]	125,500
Total expected expenditure	756,340
Budget deficit	**5,740**

Workings

1   *Expected income from new joiners*

    Expected number of new joiners = $(0.2 \times 50) + (0.3 \times 20) + (0.5 \times 26) = 29$

    $900 income from each new joiner $\times 29 = \$26,100$

2   *Salaries*

    $[(\$620,000 - \$26,000)/2] + [(\$620,000 - \$26,000 \times 1.02)/2]$

    $= \$297,000 + \$302,940 = \$599,940$

(b) Incremental budgeting bases the budget on the results for the current period plus an amount for estimated growth or inflation in the next period. It is therefore suitable for organisations that operate in a **stable environment** where historical figures are a reliable guide to the future.

Advantages

Incremental budgeting is very **quick** compared to other methods of budgeting such as zero-based budgeting.
The information required to prepare a budget under this approach is also **readily available**.

For the above reasons, incremental budgeting is very **easy to perform**. This makes it possible for an employee with little accounting training to prepare a budget.

Disadvantages

Incremental budgeting is a reasonable procedure if current operations are as **effective, efficient and economical** as they can be. In general, however, it is an inefficient form of budgeting as it encourages **slack** and **wasteful spending** to creep into budgets. Past inefficiencies are perpetuated because cost levels are rarely subjected to close scrutiny.

There is also a risk that **errors** from one year are carried to the next, since the previous year's figures are not questioned.

(c) **Zero-based budgeting**

The three main steps involved in preparing a zero-based budget are as follows:

1   Activities are identified by managers. Managers are then forced to consider different ways of performing the activities.

    These activities are then described in what is called a 'decision package', which:

    •   Analyses the cost of the activity

    •   States its purpose

    •   Identifies alternative methods of achieving the same purpose

    •   Establishes performance measures for the activity

    •   Assesses the consequence of not performing the activity at all or of performing it at different levels

    As regards this last point, the decision package may be prepared at the base level, representing the minimum level of service or support needed to achieve the organisation's objectives. Further incremental packages may then be prepared to reflect a higher level of service or support.

2   Management will then rank all the packages in the order of decreasing benefits to the organisation. This will help management decide what to spend and where to spend it. This ranking of the decision packages happens at numerous levels of the organisation.

3   The resources are then allocated, based on order of priority up to the spending level.

(d) The principle behind **zero-based budgeting** is that the budget for each cost centre should be prepared from 'scratch' or zero. Every item of expenditure must be justified, to be included in the budget for the forthcoming period.

The ZBB process involves identifying decision packages, which are activities or items of expenditure about which a decision should be made about cost. There are two types of decision package.

Mutually exclusive packages are alternative ways of getting the same job done. The best option among the packages must be selected by comparing costs and benefits and the other packages are then discarded.

Incremental packages analyse an activity into different levels of effort. The 'base' package will describe the minimum amount of work that must be done to carry out the activity and the other incremental packages describe what additional work could be done, at what cost and for what benefits.

Packages are ranked in order of priority, and given a limited budget (limited cash and other resources); the preferred mutually exclusive and incremental packages are selected for the budget.

Use of ZBB at Newtown School

Implementing ZBB would enable the school to distinguish between **necessary** and **discretionary expenditure**, and allocate resources accordingly.

For example, although some level of sports education is needed, the extent of the different activities offered is discretionary. As a bare minimum, it is essential that children have somewhere safe and secure to exercise. ZBB could be used to put together **decision packages** which reflect the **different levels of sports facilities** available to the children. For example, the most basic level could be to continue to hold all sports classes inside in the existing gym. The next level would be to offer a combination of indoor and outdoor sports classes which would require the sports field to be maintained. Finally, the highest level would be a state-of-the-art gym and sports pitches. At Newtown School the sports staff could **prepare the decision packages** and they would be decided upon by the head teacher, who would **rank them accordingly**.

ZBB can take a long time to implement however, and would **not be appropriate for all categories of expenditure** at the school. Incremental budgeting could still be **used as a basis for essential expenditure** such as repairs and maintenance, since the costs of the checks and repairs needed to comply with health and safety standards seem to stay largely the same year on year, with an inflationary increase.

226 Bedco

Text reference. Planning and operational variances are covered in Chapter 12 of the BPP Study Text.

Top tips. To answer this question within the allocated time, you need to be familiar with planning and operational variances. You should identify that the planning variance for material usage applies to pillow cases only.

Remember that when calculating an operational variance for usage, the standard cost to apply is the standard cost per unit of material in the original standard cost.

If you have time, comment on the usage operational variances for bed sheets and pillow cases separately.

Part (b) of the question is worth eight marks, so make sure that you allocate the right amount of time to this part of your answer.

Easy marks. When answering a question on planning and operational variances, calculate the original standard cost and the revised standard cost. This should indicate what the planning variances are, per unit or price or usage. Having done this, the task is then to convert the planning variance as a price per unit of material or a quantity used of material into a total variance.

			Marks
(a)	For each variance: 3 marks		12
(b)	Each valid point	2	
			8
			20

(a)

Original standard cost

Sheets	2m² × $5 per m²	$10 per unit
Pillow cases	0.5m² × $5 per m²	$2.50 per unit

Revised standard cost

Sheets	2m² × $6 per m²	$12 per unit
Pillow cases	0.55m² × $6 per m²	$3.30 per unit

(i) **Material price planning variance**

	$
Original standard price of materials per m²	5.0
Revised standard price	6.0
Material price planning variance per m²	1.0 (A)
Actual quantity used/purchased (248,000 + 95,000)	343,000
Material price planning variance in $	$343,000 (A)

(ii) **Material price operational variance**

	$
Revised standard price of materials per m²	6.0
Actual price paid	5.8
Material price operational variance per m²	0.2 (F)
Actual quantity used/purchased (248,000 + 95,000)	343,000
Material price operational variance in $	$68,600 (F)

(iii) **Material usage planning variance**

This applies to pillow cases only

	m²
180,000 pillow cases should use: original standard (× 0.5)	90,000
180,000 pillow cases should use: revised standard (× 0.55)	99,000
Material usage planning variance in m²	9,000 (A)
Original standard price per m²	$5
Material usage planning variance in $	$45,000 (A)

(iv) **Material usage operational variance**

This applies to pillow cases only

	m²
180,000 pillow cases should use: revised standard (× 0.55)	99,000
120,000 sheets should use (× 2)	240,000
Together they should use	339,000
They did use	343,000
Material usage operational variance in m²	4,000 (A)
Original standard price per m²	$5
Material usage planning variance in $	$20,000 (A)

	$	$
Check:		
Actual cost of materials: 343,000 m² × $5.80		1,989,400
Original standard cost: (120,000 sheets × $10) + (180 pillow cases × $2.50)		1,650,000
Total materials cost variance		339,400 (A)
Variances:		
Price planning	343,000 (A)	
Usage planning	45,000 (A)	
Price operational	68,600 (F)	
Usage operational	20,000 (A)	
		339,400 (A)

(b) The production manager is not responsible for setting the standard costs and is therefore not responsible for any planning variances. They are responsible, however, for the operational variances (including the price variance, since they have responsibility for materials purchasing).

The manager is also not responsible for the production shortfall of 10,000 pillow cases in the month, since this was caused by the change in customer requirements. However, this did not affect the materials variances. (It is much more likely to have affected labour efficiency or idle time variances in the month.)

Assessing performance on operational variances only, it would appear that the production manager has performed well. Although the expected material price rose to $6 per m^2, they were able to purchase materials at $5.80 per m^2, which 'saved' $68,600 in purchase costs.

The materials usage operational variance was adverse in total, by 4,000 m^2. The usage of materials on bed sheets (248,000m^2) was more than the expected 240,000 m^2 for 120,000 sheets produced (120,000 × 2). On the other hand, materials usage for pillow cases (95,000m^2) was 4,000 m^2 less than the expected usage of 99,000 m^2 for the 180,000 pillow cases produced (180,000 × 0.55). The production manager should therefore be asked to explain the adverse usage of materials in producing the bed sheets.

The large favourable variance for materials usage on pillow cases should also be explained, to make sure that the pillow cases are being made properly to the new standard requirement.

227 Valet Co

Text references. Mix and yield variances are covered in Chapter 11.

Top tips. If you know how to calculate mix and quantity variances then part (a) should be straightforward. Make sure you set out your answer clearly and label each variance. You must learn what the variances mean as part (b) of a variance question will often ask you to explain what the variances mean. For part (c) you must read the question carefully. It states that your discussion should be on the sales performance. This means that calculating and discussing costs will give no marks.

Examining team's comments. This is a very popular PM topic. Students either knew how to calculate the variances and scored full marks, or did not and scored zero. Part (b) was not answered well, even though it only asked for a brief description of the variances calculated in part (a). It really is a case of revising this area, learning the method and performing the calculations.

Marking scheme

			Marks
a)	Calculations		
	Sales mix contribution variance		4
	Sales quantity contribution variance		4
(b)	Description		
	One mark per description		2
(c)	Discussion on sales performance		
	Calculations – each one 0.5, max 2	2	
	Maximum for each point made	2	10
			20

(a) **Variances**

(i) *Sales mix contribution variance*

	Should mix Actual qty Std mix	Did mix Actual qty Actual mix	Difference	Std contribution $	Variance $
Full	5,130 (W1)	4,000	1,130 (A)	22.30 (W2)	25,199 (A)
Mini	2,850 (W1)	3,980	1,130 (F)	16.50 (W2)	18,645 (F)
	7,980	7,980	0		6,554 (A)

Workings

1   *Actual sales quantity in standard mix*

Full	7,980	× (3,600/5,600)	=	5,130
Mini	7,980	× (2,000/5,600)	=	2,850

2   *Standard contributions per valet*

Full	$50	× 44.6%	=	$22.30 per valet
Mini	$30	× 55%	=	$16.50 per valet

(ii)   *Sales quantity contribution variance*

	Should mix Actual qty Std mix	Budgeted Std qty Std mix	Difference	Std contribution $	Variance $
Full	5,130 (W1)	3,600	1,530 (F)	22.30 (W2)	34,119 (F)
Mini	2,850 (W1)	2,000	850 (F)	16.50 (W2)	14,025 (F)
	7,980	5,600	2,380		48,144 (F)

(b)   **Description**

The sales mix variance occurs when the proportions of the various products sold are different from those in the budget.

The sales quantity variance shows the difference in contribution/profit because of a change in sales volume from the budgeted volume of sales.

(c)   **Sales performance of the business**

The sales performance of the business has been very good over the last year, as shown by the favourable sales quantity variance of $48,144. Overall, total sales revenue is 33% higher than budgeted (($319,400 – $240,000)/$240,000). This is because of a higher total number of valets being performed. When you look at where the difference in sales quantity actually is, you can see from the data provided in the question that it is the number of mini valets which is substantially higher. This number is 99% ((3,980 – 2,000)/2,000) higher than budgeted, whereas the number of full valets is only 11% ((4,000 –3,600)/3,600) higher. Even 11% is still positive, however.

The fact that the number of mini valets is so much higher, combined with the fact that they generate a lower contribution per unit than the full valet, led to an adverse sales mix variance of $6,554 in the year. This cannot be looked at in isolation as a sign of poor performance; it is simply reflective of the changes which have occurred in Strappia. We are told that disposable incomes in Strappia have decreased by 30% over the last year. This means that people have less money to spend on non-essential expenditure – such as car valeting. Consequently, they are opting for the cheaper mini valet rather than the more expensive full valet. At the same time, we are also told that people are keeping their cars for an average of five years now, as opposed to three years. This may be leading them to take more care of them and get them valeted regularly, because they know that the car has to be kept for a longer period. Thus, the total quantity of valets is higher than budgeted, particularly the mini valets.

Also, there is now one less competitor for Valet Co than there was a year ago, so Valet Co may have gained some of the old competitor's business. Together, all of these factors would explain the higher number of total valets being performed and, in particular, of the less-expensive type of valet.

Note. Other valid points will be given full credit.

228 Glove Co

Marking scheme

			Marks
(a)	Basic variances		
	Each variance	1	2
(b)	Operational and planning variances		
	Labour rate planning	1.5	
	Labour rate operational	1.5	
	Labour efficiency planning	1.5	
	Labour efficiency operational	1.5	
			6
(c)	Explanation of controllability principle		4
	Performance		
	Only operational variances	1	
	Adverse operational variance	2	
	Failure to update the standard	1	
	Overtime rate impacted	2	
	Favourable efficiency variance	2	
	Good overall	1	
	Maximum		8
	Total marks		20

(a) Basic variances

Labour rate variance

Standard cost of labour per hour = $42/3 = $14 per hour

	$
37,000 hours should have cost ($\times$ $14)	518,000
but did cost	531,930
Rate variance	13,930 (A)

Labour efficiency variance

12,600 units should have taken (× 3 hrs)	37,800 hrs
but did take	37,000 hrs
Efficiency variance in hours	800 (F)
× standard rate per hour	× $14
Efficiency variance in $	$11,200 (F)

(b) **Planning and operational variances**

Labour rate planning variance

	$ per hour
Original standard rate	14.00
Revised standard rate (14 × 1.02)	14.28
Labour rate planning variance	0.28 (A)

Labour rate planning variance = 37,000 hours × $0.28 (A) = $10,360 (A).

Labour efficiency planning variance

	Hours
12,600 units of product should take: original standard (× 3.00)	37,800
12,600 units of product should take: revised standard (× 3.25)	40,950
Labour efficiency planning variance in hours	3,150 (A)
Original standard rate per hour	$14
Labour efficiency planning variance in $	$44,100 (A)

Labour rate operational variance

	$
37,000 hours should cost (revised standard $14.28)	528,360
They did cost	531,930
Labour rate operational variance	3,570 (A)

Labour efficiency operational variance

	Hours
12,600 units of product should take (× 3.25 hours)	40,950
They did take	37,000
Labour efficiency (operational variance in hours)	3,950 (F)
Original standard rate per hour	$14
Labour efficiency (operational variance in $)	$55,300 (F)

(c) **Controllability principle**

The **controllability principle** is that managers of responsibility centres should only be held accountable for costs over which they have some influence. From a **motivation** point of view, this is important because it can be very demoralising for managers who feel that their performance is being judged on the basis of something over which they have no influence. It is also important from a **control** point of view in that control reports should ensure that information on costs is reported to the manager who is able to take action to control them.

The controllability principle can be **implemented** either by removing the uncontrollable items from the areas that managers are accountable for, or producing reports which calculate and distinguish between controllable and uncontrollable items.

For example, the controllability principle means that operational managers should only be held responsible for **excess** idle time, above that which is expected, based on realistic forecasts.

Analysis of performance

At a first glance, performance looks mixed because the total labour rate variance is adverse and the total labour efficiency variance is favourable. However, the operational and planning variances provide a lot more detail on how these variances have occurred.

The production manager should only be held accountable for variances which they can control. This means that they should only be held accountable for the operational variances. When these operational variances are looked at, it can be seen that the labour rate operational variance is $3,570 A. This means that the production manager did have to pay for some overtime in order to meet demand but the majority of the total labour rate variance is driven by the failure to update the standard for the pay rise that was applied at the start of the last quarter. The overtime rate would also have been impacted by that pay increase.

Then, when the labour efficiency operational variance is looked at, it is actually $55,300 F. This shows that the production manager has managed their department well, with workers completing production more quickly than would have been expected when the new design change is taken into account. The total operating variances are therefore $51,730 F and so overall performance is good.

The adverse planning variances of $10,360 and $44,100 do not reflect on the performance of the production manager and can, therefore, be ignored here.

229 SU Co

Text reference. Planning and operational variances are covered in Chapter 12. The controllability principle is covered in Chapter 18.

Top tips. Variance questions are frequently examined in PM so it is worthwhile learning how to do the calculations. If you know how to calculate planning and operational variances then parts (a) and (b) should be straightforward.

Easy marks. Easy marks could be gained for explaining that the materials usage and labour efficiency planning variances were due to the change in design and therefore not controllable, and the materials price planning variance was due to GPST's decision to change the material – again, not controllable.

Examining team's comments. This was a fairly typical variances question but unfortunately students found it difficult. The question didn't say which material variances were required and this was one of the key skills being tested. The main reason why scores were low was that only the basic variances were calculated. It is worth noting that the most common error when calculating variances of this type is to use budgeted production, instead of the actual production, to calculate standard usage.

Marking scheme

		Marks	
(a)	Standard price	1	
	Standard quantity	0.5	
	Standard quantity actual price	0.5	
	Revised quantity actual price	0.5	
	Price planning variance	1.5	
	Usage planning variance	1.5	
	Usage operational variance	1.5	
			7
(b)	Actual hours	1	
	Standard hours actual price	0.5	
	Revised hours actual price	0.5	
	Planning variance	1.5	
	Operational variance	1.5	
			5
(c)	Controllability principle	1	
	Variances/performance	6	
	Other/conclusion	1	
			8
	Total marks		20

(a) **Material price planning variance**

	$
Original standard price of materials per m ($2.85/0.95)	3.00
Revised standard price	2.85
Material price planning variance per m	0.15 (F)
Actual quantity used/purchased	54,560
Material price planning variance in $	8,184 (F)

Material price operational variance

	$
54,560m should cost (× $2.85)	155,496
Did cost	155,496
Material price operational variance	0

Total price variance = $8,184 (F) + $0 = $8,184 (F)

Material usage planning variance

	m
24,000 dresses should use: original standard (× 2.2m/1.1)	48,000
24,000 dresses should use: revised standard (× 2.2m)	52,800
Material usage planning variance in m	4,800 (A)
Original standard price per m	$3
Material usage planning variance in $	$14,400 (A)

Material usage operational variance

	m
24,000 dresses should use: revised standard (× 2.2m)	52,800
They did use	54,560
Material usage operational variance in m	1,760 (A)
Original standard price per m	$3
Material usage planning variance in $	$5,280 (A)

Total usage variance = $14,400 (A) + $5,280 (A) = $19,680 (A)

Total material variance = $8,184 (F) + $19,680 (A) = $11,496 (A)

(b) **Labour efficiency planning variance**

	Hours
24,000 dresses should take: original standard (× 8/60)	3,200
24,000 dresses should take: revised standard (× 10/60)	4,000
Labour efficiency planning variance in hours	800 (A)
Original standard rate per hour	$12
Labour efficiency planning variance in $	$9,600 (A)

Labour efficiency operational variance

	Hours
24,000 dresses should take (× 10/60 hours)	4,000
They did take (24 staff × 160 hours)	3,840
Labour efficiency (operational variance in hours)	160 (F)
Original standard rate per hour	$12
Labour efficiency (operational variance in $)	$1,920 (F)

Total labour efficiency variance = $9.600 (A) + $1,920 (F) = $7,680 (A)

(c) The production manager did not have any control over the change in the design of the dress as this change was requested by the client. Similarly, it was not their fault that the company accountant responsible for updating standard costs was off sick and therefore unable to update the standards. Therefore, the production manager should be judged only by those variances over which they have control, which are the operational variances.

Materials

No operational variance arose in relation to materials price, since the actual price paid was the same as the revised price. A planning variance of $8,184F does arise but the production manager cannot take the credit for this, as the material chosen by GPST for the new dresses just happens to be cheaper.

As regards usage, an adverse variance of $5,280 arose. This suggests that, even with the revised quantity of material being taken into account, staff still used more than 2.2 metres on average to produce each dress. This is probably because they had to learn a new sewing technique and they probably made some mistakes, resulting in some wastage. The manager is responsible for this as it may have been caused by insufficient training. However, the labour efficiency variances below shed some more light on this.

Labour

The labour efficiency operational variance was favourable, which suggests good performance by the production manager. Staff took less than the expected revised 10 minutes per dress. However, when looked at in combination with the material usage operational variance above, it could be inferred that staff may have rushed a little and consequently used more material than necessary.

When both of the operational variances are looked at together, the adverse materials usage $5,280 far outweighs the favourable labour efficiency variance of $1,920. Consequently, it could be concluded that, overall, the manager's performance was somewhat disappointing.

Part D answers

MCQ bank – Performance measurement and control

230   The correct answer is: Both 1 and 2

Internal transfers should be preferred to external purchases because the company will have better control over output quality from Division A and the scheduling of production and deliveries. Transfer prices determine how total profit will be shared between the divisions.

(Syllabus area D5(b))

231   The correct answer is: Neither 1 nor 2

Not-for-profit organisations do have financial objectives, which may sometimes be described as financial constraints. For example, a charity organisation may want to maximise its funding and a government department may seek to carry out its activities within the spending budget for the department.

The outputs produced by commercial organisations can be measured simply by profit, which is a measure of the value created by the organisation in a period. Outputs of not-for-profit organisations cannot be measured as easily because they often have many different objectives, each measured in different ways.

(Syllabus area D6(a))

232   The correct answer is: Profit before interest and tax

Gross profit ignores other expenses other than cost of sales. Profit before tax and profit after tax are after deducting items that do not relate to divisional performance (costs of interest on company debt and tax charges). Profit before interest and tax is the most appropriate measure of the four, and it will often be the same as operating profit.

(Syllabus area D5(d))

233   The correct answer is: Average waiting time at the hospital

Adherence to appointment times means starting an appointment at the scheduled time. One suitable measure might be the percentage of appointments that begin later than a certain amount of time, say 15 minutes. Of the performance measurements in the question, average waiting time on the appointment date would be the most appropriate.

(Syllabus area D6(b))

234   The correct answer is: Sales revenue from new products as a percentage of total revenue

R&D expenditure on its own is not a measure of performance, and costs in the previous year will not relate to all four products introduced to the market in the past two years.

The most appropriate of these measures as an indication of innovation within the organisation is revenue from new products as a percentage of total revenue. (This is more meaningful for comparison purposes than simply measuring average revenue per new product.)

(Syllabus area D4(e))

235   The correct answer is: Number of patients treated per $1 spent on the state hospital service

Number of patients treated per $1 spent relates outputs to inputs, and is a measure of efficiency. Reducing a departmental budget is a measure of economy. A crime clear-up rate and an examination pass rate are measures of effectiveness for the police force and the state-owned college, respectively.

(Syllabus area D6(b))

236   The correct answer is: 1 only

For example, systems for recording attendance times at work are more reliable when recorded automatically by a card reader system than if individuals sign in and sign out in a manual attendance record. However, time-recording systems (such as time sheets for recording time spent on different jobs) must sometimes rely on human records. Secondary information is usually much cheaper to collect than primary data.

(Syllabus area D2(b))

237   The correct answer is: The lower of the net marginal revenue for the transferring-in division and the external purchase price in the market for the intermediate product

For example, if the marginal cost of a transferred item is $5 and it has an external intermediate market of $7 but external selling costs of $0.50; and if the transferring-in division can use the transferred item to make an end product that earns a contribution of $10, the maximum transfer price should be the lower of $7 and $10. The minimum transfer price should be $5 + $(7 − 5 − 0.50) = $6.50.

(Syllabus area D5(a))

238   The correct answer is: Internal business (operational) perspective

The target is to improve the efficiency of dealing with customer calls. This may affect customer satisfaction and profitability, but its prime objective is to reduce call times and improve efficiency in the call centre.

(Syllabus area D4(e))

239   The correct answer is: Both 1 and 2

Management information, often of an operational nature, is often produced as summary data output from a transaction processing system. Management information systems are based mainly on internal data sources rather than sources that are external to the organisation.

(Syllabus area D1(b))

240   The correct answer is: 2 only

Budgeting is commonly associated with decision making at the tactical planning level (management control level) within a management hierarchy.

(Syllabus area D1(a))

241   The correct answer is: Executive information system

EIS systems often present key information in a 'visually friendly' format.

(Syllabus area D1(b))

242   The correct answer is: Percentage of customers making repeat orders

Making repeat orders is possibly a measure of customer satisfaction, and so might be used as a measure of performance from a customer perspective in a balanced scorecard. The growth in the product range is more relevant to innovation, and speed of order processing and orders per sales representative are measures of operational efficiency and effectiveness, rather than customer attitudes to the organisation and its products.

(Syllabus area D4(e))

243   The correct answer is: Neither 1 nor 2

Providing value for money (VFM) means providing a service that is economical, efficient and effective. 'Economical' means getting the best price, but this does not necessarily mean 'cheap'. Measuring the percentage of collected refuse that is recycled is a measure of effectiveness, if recycling refuse is an objective of the service. ('Efficiency' measures an amount of output or benefit per unit of resource input.)

(Syllabus area D6(d))

244   The correct answer is: 2 only

When divisional performance is measured by residual income, a fair comparison of divisional performances is not possible, because the divisional residual incomes are not related to the size and asset value of each division. For example, residual income of $50,000 when divisional assets are $10 million is not as impressive as residual income of $50,000 when divisional assets are only $100,000.

When a transfer price is based on cost, the size of the profit mark-up is a matter for negotiation, and one of the divisional managers (or even both of them) are likely to consider the agreed transfer price as 'unfair', favouring the other division.

(Syllabus area D5(c))

245   The correct answer is: Speed

Time between order and despatch is a measure of speed, which is an aspect of efficiency.

(Syllabus area D4(b))

246   The correct answer is: Competitiveness

In the Fitzgerald and Moon model there are six dimensions of performance. Two of these reflect past results and achievements: financial performance and competitiveness. The other four dimensions of performance are determinants of future performance: flexibility, innovation, quality and resource utilisation.

(Syllabus area D4(e))

247   The correct answer is: Goal congruence in decision making

There is a risk of dysfunctional decision making and a lack of goal congruence with divisionalisation. Divisional managers may base investment decisions on whether they will improve ROI, which is inappropriate. Transfer pricing disputes, too, may lead to bad decisions by divisional managers. However, the risk can be avoided or minimised if divisional management and head office management are aware of the potential problem.

Authority is delegated to divisional managers; therefore there is some loss of head office control over operations, but decision making at 'local' operational level should be faster, since the decision does not have to be referred to head office for a decision. There is likely to be some duplication of costs, since each division will have its own administration activities.

(Syllabus area D4(d))

248   The correct answer is: 2 only

ROI is measured as divisional operating profit: this is after deducting depreciation charges.

(Syllabus area D5(c))

249   The correct answer is: Both 1 and 2

Controls are needed over internally produced information to prevent excessive amounts of information being circulated – leading to waste of management time. Controls are also needed to ensure that unauthorised information is not circulated. Controls may extend to the use of emails containing 'off-the-record' comments which could, potentially, have legal implications for the organisation.

(Syllabus area D3(a))

250   The correct answer is: Both 1 and 2

Feedback is information produced by a system as control information for management. Benchmarking means comparing performance of an organisation, or part of an organisation, with a 'benchmark'. The benchmark may be an external organisation, such as a competitor company, or another department or division within the same organisation.

(Syllabus area D2(b))

251   The correct answer is: Both 1 and 2

When an organisation is structured into divisions, there will almost inevitably be some transfer of goods or services between divisions, for which transfer prices are required.

Statement 2 is one of the guiding rules for identifying the optimal transfer price.

(Syllabus area D5(a))

252   The correct answer is: Cost of the local fire service per member of the local population

The cost of resources (inputs) per member of the local community is a measure of the resources spent on the fire service, without providing any measure of outputs obtained from the resources. A measure of the cost of the service provides an indication of the resources committed to it, but does not measure the value or benefits obtained from them.

(Syllabus area D6(b))

253   The correct answer is: Process efficiency perspective

The growth perspective is concerned with: 'Can we continue to improve and create value?' The process efficiency perspective, also called the operational perspective, is concerned with operational efficiency and excellence.

(Syllabus area D4(e))

254   The correct answer is: Standard cost plus a profit margin equal to a percentage of cost

Transfers should not be at actual cost, because there is no incentive for the transferring division to control the costs of the transferred item. A transfer price based on actual cost plus would be even worse, since the transferring division (Division A) would make a profit on any overspending that it incurs. Standard cost plus is preferable to standard cost because the profit margin provides an incentive for Division A to make and transfer the item.

(Syllabus area D5(a))

CBE style OTQ bank – Performance measurement and control

255   The correct answer is: Minimum transfer price $8, maximum transfer price $16

The minimum transfer price is the marginal cost of production in Division A, because any transfer price in excess of this amount will add to the division's contribution and profit. The maximum transfer price is the external market price of Component X, because any price in excess of this amount will lead to Division B sourcing Product X externally.

(Syllabus area D5(a))

256   The correct answer is: Innovation

Fitzgerald and Moon identified six dimensions or aspects of performance in a service business: financial performance, competitiveness, quality, resource utilisation, flexibility and innovation.

(Syllabus area D4(e))

257   The correct answer is: $15

The minimum transfer price is a price that should be sufficient to make the manager of Division A wiling to transfer units of Component X to Division B. This is the marginal cost of manufacture plus the opportunity cost of not being able to sell the component in the external market.

This is $8 + $(16 − 8 − 1) = $15.

(Syllabus area D5(a))

258   The correct answers are:

- Granting credit to customers
- Inventory carrying decisions

The investment centre manager would have power to make decisions over granting credit to customers and the level of inventory carried. This affects the investment centre's level of working capital and hence is the responsibility of the investment centre manager.

(Syllabus area D5(c))

259   The correct answer is: 23.2%

Capital employed at start of 20X2 = $2 million + $0.2 million + $0.8 million + $0.1 million = $3.1 million

Capital employed at the end of 20X2 is the capital employed at the beginning of the year, minus depreciation of $0.4 million on the 'old' assets and $0.2 million on the 'new' asset.

Capital employed at end of 20X2 = $1.6 million + $0.2 million + $0.6 million + $0.1 million = $2.5 million

Mid-year capital employed = $(3.1 m + 2.5m)/2 = $2.8 million

Profit = $0.5 million + $0.35 million − depreciation $0.2 million = $0.65 million

ROI = 0.65/2.8 = 0.232 = 23.2%

(Syllabus area D5(c))

260   The correct answer is: $5,000

	$'000	$'000
Sales (7,000 units × $154)		1,078
Variable costs in Division B (7,000 × $33)	231	
Costs of transfers (14,000 × $43)	602	
		833
		245
Fixed costs		160
Operating profit		85
Notional interest (16% × $500,000)		80
Residual income		5

(Syllabus area D5(c))

261   The correct answer is: 30.9%

	Profit	Capital employed
	$	$
Original forecast	65,000	210,000
Effect of machine sale	(2,500)	(6,000)
Effect of machine purchase	5,200	15,000
	67,700	219,000

Revised ROI = 67,700/219,000 = 30.9%

(Syllabus area D5(c))

262 The correct answers are:

- Volume of customer complaints – Quantitative
- Employee revenue – Quantitative
- Defective products per batch – Quantitative
- Customer needs – Qualitative
- Employee morale – Qualitative
- Brand recognition – Qualitative
- Customer satisfaction – Qualitative
- Repeat business – Quantitative

Quantitative performance measures are something that can be actually measured and a value assigned.

Volume of customer complaints, employee revenue, defective products per batch and repeat business are all performance measures which can be regularly monitored, values assigned and benchmarks made.

Qualitative performance measures are more difficult to measure and are based on judgement. It is only possible to gain an opinion as opposed to a concrete value. They are still important as many decisions are swayed by the strength of the qualitative arguments rather than the cold facts presented as part of qualitative analysis.

Customer needs, customer satisfaction, employee morale and brand recognition are all examples of qualitative performance measures. They are very difficult to measure accurately and their rating tends to be based on judgement.

There are still ways to devise quantitative measures for these areas. For example, volume of repeat business may give an indication of customer satisfaction. Additionally, surveying a sample of customers may help to devise some measure of satisfaction.

(Syllabus area D7(d))

263 The correct answers are:

- Efficiency
- Effectiveness
- Economy

Effectiveness is the relationship between an organisation's outputs and its objectives (ie getting done what was supposed to be done). Efficiency is the relationship between inputs and outputs (ie getting out as much as possible for what goes in).

Economy is attaining the appropriate quantity and quality of inputs at lowest cost (ie spending money frugally). Enterprise, efficacy, expediency and endurance although perhaps relevant are all red herrings in this context.

(Syllabus area D6(b))

264 The correct answers are:

- Percentage of repeat customers
- Number of warranty claims

Dividend yield is a shareholder measure; morale index is an employee measure.

(Syllabus area D4(e))

Cherry Co

265   The correct answer is: $30

Division A has available capacity of 15,000 units. Division A does not want to lose its contribution margin of $7 per unit, and therefore the minimum price it would now accept is $30 as shown below.

$30 (variable cost) + $0 (opportunity cost) = $30

In this case Division A and B should negotiate a transfer price within the range of $30 and $35 (cost from outside supplier).

266   The correct answer is: $37

Division A charges $37 and derives a contribution margin of $7 per unit of Product X. Division A has no spare capacity.

Therefore, Division A must receive from Division B a payment that will at least cover its variable cost per unit plus its lost contribution margin per unit (the opportunity cost). If Division A cannot cover that amount (the minimum transfer price), it should not sell units of Product X to Division B.

The minimum transfer price that would be acceptable to Division A is $37, as shown below.

$30 (variable cost) + $7 (opportunity cost) = $37

267   The correct answer is: Full cost

Under this approach, the full cost (including fixed overheads absorbed) incurred by the supplying division in making the 'intermediate' product is charged to the receiving division. It can be used when there is no external marker for the product being transferred, or if an imperfect market exists.

268   The correct answer is: 2 only

Statement 1 is false. Cherry Co's transfer pricing system should seek to establish a transfer price for X that will provide an incentive for the managers of A and B to make and sell quantities of products that will maximise the company's total profit. Statement 2 is true.

269   The correct answer is: 1 only

Statement 1 is true. Statement 2 is false because Division A is likely to save money on selling and distribution expenses if they can sell product X to Division B.

Jamair

270   The correct answer is: Financial

The financial perspective considers whether the management in Jamair meets the expectations of its shareholders and how it creates value for them.

This perspective focuses on traditional measures such as growth, profitability and cost reduction.

271   The correct answer is: Customer perspective

The customer perspective considers how new and existing customers view Jamair. The objective is to ensure that flights land on time.

272   The correct answer is: Internal business perspective

The internal business perspective makes Jamair consider what processes it must excel at in order to achieve financial and customer objectives. The measure may be: Reduction in 'on the ground' time from 50 minutes.

273   The correct answer is: Financial perspective

The measure could be 'Revenue per available passenger mile'. The financial perspective considers whether the management in Jamair meets the expectations of its shareholders and how it creates value for them.

274 The correct answer is: 1 only

Statement 1 is true. By its very nature, qualitative data is not quantified. At best, qualitative measures are converted into quantitative measures using a subjective scoring system.

Statement 2 is false. An organisation is much more likely to have a well-established system for measuring quantitative data, especially in the areas of accounting and sales statistics.

Stickleback Co

275 The correct answer is: Before investment: 20%, After investment 19.3%.

	Before investment $	After investment $
Divisional profit	30,000	31,900
Capital employed	150,000	165,000
ROI	20%	19.3%

276 The correct answer is: Before investment: $7,500, After investment $7,150.

	Before investment $	After investment $
Divisional profit	30,000	31,900
Imputed interest (15% of $150,000)	(22,500)	
Imputed interest (15% of $165,000)		(24,750)
Residual income	7,500	7,150

277 The correct answer is: 2 only.

Statement 1 is false because, if a manager's performance is being evaluated, only those assets which can be traced directly to the division and are controllable by the manager should be included.

The second statement is true. Short-termism is when there is a bias towards short-term rather than long-term performance. It is often due to the fact that a manager's performance is measured on short-term results such as ROI.

278 The correct answer is: 1 and 4

'Increase payables' and 'Keep Kingfisher's old machinery'

One of the problems with using ROI as a performance measure is that it can be manipulated. Allowing non-current assets to depreciate (giving a lower NBV) and delaying payments to suppliers, both reduce the capital employed and therefore increase the ROI.

Accepting all projects with a positive NPV may not necessarily increase the ROI. Projects may have lower ROIs than Kingfisher's current ROI and this could cause Kingfisher's overall ROI to reduce.

ROI is calculated using profit before interest and so interest makes no difference to the ROI.

279 The correct answer is: 1 only

Statement 1 is a danger of decentralisation. Managers may make dysfunctional decisions.

Statement 2 is false. The divisional organisation frees top management from detailed involvement in day-to-day operations and allows them to devote more time to strategic planning.

Squarize

280   The correct answer is: Internal business perspective

This is measuring the effectiveness of improving the broadband service (an internal process) and is therefore part of the internal business perspective.

281   The correct answer is: Customer perspective

The performance objective associated with this measure would be to 'Increase number of new customers'. It measures whether customers are willing to pay the individual prices for each service.

282   The correct answer is: Sales revenue from new standalone service as a percentage of total revenue

The most appropriate of these measures as an indication of innovation within the organisation is revenue from new standalone services as a percentage of total revenue. (This is more meaningful for comparison purposes than simply measuring average revenue per new standalone service.)

283   The correct answer is: Percentage of customers renewing their subscription or making repeat orders

Renewing subscription or making repeat orders is possibly a measure of customer satisfaction, and so might be used as a measure of performance from a customer perspective in a balanced scorecard.

The growth in the product range is more relevant to innovation, and speed of order processing and orders per sales representative are measures of operational efficiency and effectiveness rather than customer attitudes to the organisation and its products.

284   The correct answer is: Innovation

Innovation is an element of the 'Dimensions of performance' building block, but it is not included as a standalone building block.

The three building blocks are:

- Dimensions of performance
- Standards
- Rewards

Alder Co

285   The correct answer is: Before investment 27%, after investment 25%.

	Before investment	After investment
	$	$
Controllable divisional profit	200,000	220,000
Capital employed	750,000	875,000
ROI	27%	25%

286   The correct answer is: Before investment: $87,500. After investment $88,750.

	Before investment	After investment
	$	$
Divisional profit	200,000	220,000
Imputed interest		
(750,000 × 0.15)	(112,500)	
(875,000 × 0.15)		(131,250)
Residual income	87,500	88,750

287   The correct answer is: 'The authority to act to improve performance motivates the divisional managers in Alder Co, more so than if the company was centralised' is **true** and 'Alder Co's top management must have involvement in the day-to-day operations of Alder Co' is **false**.

Statement 1 is said to be one of the key advantages of a divisionalised structure.

Statement 2 is false because the divisional organisation frees top management from detailed involvement in day-to-day operations and allows them to devote more time to strategic planning.

288   The correct answer is: Both statements are false.

Statement 1 is false because, if a manager's performance is being evaluated, only those assets which can be traced directly to the division and are controllable by the manager should be included.

Statement 2 is false because an investment centre could not operate without the support of head office assets and administrative backup.

289   The correct answer is: Both statements are true.

The first statement is true and is a key exam focus point that should be remembered for your exam.

The second statement is true, and it is a risk associated with the use of ROI. If the bonus of a manager in Alder Co depends on ROI being met, the manager may feel pressure to massage the measure.

Apple Co

290   The correct answer is: 30%

	Investment
	$
Divisional profit	24,000
Capital employed (20,000 + 60,000)	80,000
ROI	30%

291   The correct answer is: $23,000.

	Investment
	$
Divisional profit	35,000
Imputed interest (100,000 × 12%)	(12,000)
Residual income	23,000

292   The correct answer is: Both statements are true.

Statement 1 is a key advantage of working with RI.
Statement 2 is a key disadvantage of working with RI.

293   The correct answer is: 'The market price acts as an incentive to use up any spare capacity in the selling division of Apple Co' is **false** and 'Using the market price as the transfer price encourages selling and buying decisions which appear to be in the best interests of the division's performance. This leads to the company as a whole achieving optimal results as each division optimises its performance' is **true**.

Statement 1 is false. The market price can act as a disincentive to use up any spare capacity in the selling division of Apple Co, particularly if the market price does not provide a significant mark-up. A price based on incremental cost, in contrast, might provide an incentive to use up the spare resources in order to provide a marginal contribution to profit.

Statement 2 is true and is a key advantage of using market price as a basis for transfer pricing.

294   The correct answer is: Both statements are true

Both statements are examples of the conditions under which market-based transfer prices are not suitable, and therefore a cost-based approach would be preferable.

Box Co

295   The correct answers are: Before investment: 21%. After investment 20.4%.

	Before investment $	After investment $
Divisional profit	20,000	21,400
Capital employed	95,000	105,000
ROI	21.1%	20.4%

296   The correct answers are: Without investment: $8,600. With investment $8,800.

	Before investment $	After investment $
Divisional profit	20,000	21,400
Imputed interest (12% of $95,000)	(11,400)	
Imputed interest (12% of $105,000)		(12,600)
Residual income	8,600	8,800

297   The correct answer is: Both statements are true.

Both statements are reasons for the growing emphasis on NFPIs.

Traditional responsibility accounting systems fail to provide information on the quality of products, and therefore statement 1 is true.

Financial performance indicators tend to focus on the short term. They can give a positive impression of what is happening now but problems may be looming. Therefore statement 2 is true.

298   The correct answer is: Keep managers informed about the short-term budget targets

The other options are all methods to encourage managers to take a long-term view, so that the 'ideal' decisions are taken.

Providing sufficient management information to allow managers to see what trade-offs they are making is a method of encouraging managers to take a long-term view. Managers must be kept aware of the long-term aims as well as shorter-term (budget) targets.

299   The correct answer is: 'There is a danger that managers in Box Co may use their decision-making freedom to make decisions that are not in the best interests of the overall company' is **true** and 'A good performance measure for the divisional managers in Box Co should include a portion of head office costs in the calculations' is **false**.

Statement 1 is a danger of divisionalised structures. Managers may make dysfunctional decisions.

Statement 2 is false. Only factors for which the manager can be held accountable should be included in calculations, and therefore head office costs would not be included.

Willow Co

300   The answer is: Before investment: 17%. After investment 16%.

	Before investment $	After investment $
Divisional profit	100,000	123,000
Capital employed	600,000	750,000
ROI	17%	16%

301   The answer is: Before investment: $22,000. After investment $25,500.

	Before investment	After investment
	$	$
Divisional profit	100,000	123,000
Imputed interest		
(600,000 × 0.13)	78,000	
(750,000 × 0.13)		97,500
Residual income	22,000	25,500

302   The correct answer is: Investment centre

Distracters:

- Profit centre. The manager's area of responsibility is: 'Decisions over costs and revenues', and a typical financial performance measure is 'Controllable profit'.

- Responsibility centre. This is the overall name of the categories of centre or accounting unit that can exist within a divisionalised company.

- Cost centre. The manager's area of responsibility is: 'Decisions over costs', and a typical financial performance measure is 'Standard cost variances'.

303   The correct answer is: ROI is a relative measure, therefore small investments with a high rate of return may appear preferable to a larger investment with lower ROI. However, the larger investment may be worth more in absolute terms.

The distracters are all examples of limitations which are common to both ROI and RI

304   The correct answer is: Manager 1 will show a higher RI because of the size of the division rather than superior managerial performance.

The first two distracters are examples of limitations which are common to both ROI and RI. Distracter 3 is false, RI ties in with NPV.

305 Biscuits and Cakes

Text references. Return on investment and residual income are covered in Chapter 17.

Top tips. Parts (a) and (b) ask you to calculate the **annualised** return on investment and residual income. Remember to multiply the monthly net profit figure by 12, to reflect that there are 12 months in a year.

Part (c) asks you to conclude as to whether the two divisions have performed well, using additional calculations as necessary. In order to fairly assess performance, take time to recalculate ROI and/or RI using controllable profit.

Easy marks. There are 5 marks up for grabs in parts (a) and (b) for calculating the annualised ROI and RI.

Examining team's comments. This was a straightforward performance measurement question in a divisional context. Parts (a) and (b) were relatively straightforward.

In part (c), stronger candidates realised that, in order to discuss the performance of the divisions well, they needed to recalculate the ROI and/or RI using controllable profit. Where candidates did this, they generally accompanied it with some good discussion and scored full marks.

Weaker answers performed other calculations on the two divisions and gave some general commentary, even though the question asked for a discussion 'using both ROI and RI'.

In part (e) candidates were supposed to identify the fact that changing the basis for calculating ROI and using this for performance measurement without changing the target ROI would cause managers to be demotivated. Many candidates answered this well, although some simply discussed the general problems encountered when using ROI, which were relevant to a degree but shouldn't have been the sole answer.

			Marks
(a)	ROI/RI calculations:		
	ROI for B	1	
	ROI for C	1	
			2
(b)	ROI/RI discussion:		
	RI for B	1½	
	RI for C	1½	
			3
(c)	Discussion:		
	ROI discussion	2	
	RI discussion	2	
	Extra ROI calculation under old method	1	
	Valid conclusion drawn	1	
			6
(d)	ROI/RI after investment:		
	ROI calculation	2	
	RI calculation	1	
	Comments and conclusion	2	
			5
(e)	Behavioural issues:		
	ROI of investment – 1 mark per valid point		Max 4
			20

(a) **Annualised return on investment (ROI)**

ROI = (Net profit / Net assets) × 100%

Division B

Net profit = $311,000 × 12 months = $3,732,000
ROI = ($3,732,000 / $23,200,000) × 100%
= 16.09%

Division C

Net profit = $292,000 × 12 months = $3,504,000
ROI = ($3,504,000 / $22,600,000) × 100%
= 15.5%

(b) **Annualised residual income (RI)**

	Division B	Division C
	$'000	$'000
Net profit (part (a))	3,732	3,504
Less: imputed interest charge:		
$23.2m × 10%	(2,320)	nil
$22.6m × 10%	nil	(2,260)
	1,412	1,244

(c) **Performance based on ROI**

The ROIs calculated for each division in part (a) are both significantly below the company's **target ROI** (20%). This would suggest that both divisions are performing poorly.

However, both divisions are now required to deduct a share of **head office costs** in their respective operating statements before arriving at 'net profit' which is then used to calculate ROI. The company's target ROI has not been reduced to take account of these **uncontrollable costs**.

Using the old method (prior to head office costs being recharged to divisions), ROI for both divisions would have **exceeded the 20% target**, and increased on ROIs for the last three months (Division B: 22% pa, Division C: 23% pa) – showing that both divisions have actually **improved their performance**.

ROI using the old method

Division B net profit = ($311,000 + $155,000) × 12 = $5,592,000

Division B ROI = $5,592,000 / $23,200,000 × 100% = **24.1%**

Division C net profit = ($292,000 + $180,000) × 12 = $5,664,000

Division C ROI = $5,664,000 / $22,600,000 × 100% = **25.06%**

Performance based on RI

Division B and Division C both have healthy RI figures of $1.4 million and $1.2 million respectively. These figures are impressive when you consider that they are based on **net profits** as opposed to **controllable profits**.

However, the company's cost of capital of 10% is significantly lower than the target return on investment (20%). This makes the residual income figure show a more **positive position**.

(d) **Division B's revised annualised net profit and opening net assets after investment**

Depreciation = ($2,120,000 – $200,000) / 48 months = $40,000 per month

Net profit for July = $311,000 + ($600,000 × 8.5%) – $40,000 = $322,000

Annualised net profit = $322,000 × 12 = $3,864,000

Opening net assets after investment = $23,200,000 + $2,120,000 = $25,320,000

Division B ROI

ROI = (Net profit / Net assets) × 100%

= $3,864,000 / $25,320,000 × 100% = 15.26%

Division B will not proceed with the investment as it will cause a decrease in ROI.

Division B RI

	$'000
Net profit	3,864
Less: imputed interest charge:	
$25.32m × 10%	(2,532)
Residual income	1,332

Based on the above calculation, it is clear that RI is lower with the investment. This would suggest that the company should not proceed with the investment and shows that the use of ROI as a performance measure is likely to result in the manager of Division B making a decision that is **in the best interests** of the company as a whole.

(e) **Behavioural problems**

Staff in both divisions are used to exceeding the target ROI of 20% and being rewarded for doing so. As a result of including head office costs in the calculation of net profit, staff will see that their respective divisions are **no longer meeting the target ROI**, despite performance actually improving.

The target ROI should be revised to take account of the these **uncontrollable allocated costs**.

Staff are likely to become **demotivated** by the fact that they are no longer meeting the target ROI despite continuing to operate at the same level as before. They may feel that management have deliberately altered how performance is measured in order to **avoid paying staff bonuses** for exceeding targets.

Staff may deliberately work slowly and refuse to work overtime to show their opposition to the new system. The company should resolve the situation as soon as possible to avoid a decrease in **production output** and **product quality**.

306 Story

Text reference. Management information systems are discussed in Chapter 14.

Top tips. This is quite a long and complicated scenario. You'll improve your chances of writing a good answer by reading the scenario carefully and then planning your answer.

We suggest that you start by making notes as a rough sketch for your answer. Spend around ten minutes doing this. Then elaborate your notes into your answer, using headings and paragraphs, and picking out the main points from the question. So, for example, head up a paragraph 'open systems' and write a paragraph on open systems. This makes it much clearer to mark and uses the key phrases the ACCA examining team is looking for in a good answer.

Part (b) of this question illustrates the importance of being able to apply theory to the scenario. You may not be able to give any examples of closed systems as these rarely occur. Just make sure you put down an explanation so that you get credit for knowing what a closed system is.

We have put our answer to Part (c) in a table though you could also use headings and paragraphs to answer the question.

(a) **Issues in upgrading the existing information system**

The issues involved in an upgrade of the existing information system include achieving the potential advantages at minimum cost and anticipating and managing necessary changes.

(i) **Advantages of upgrade**

A networked system would allow the **transmission** of information both to and from the business units and head office at Story. As such it is likely that performance indicators, financial statistics and similar **information** could be **rapidly gathered, processed and disseminated**. **Improved communication** between units and head office should improve, leading to **rapid reaction** to changes both within the organisation and outside it. This should result in a responsive, evolving organisation capable of meeting the challenges of the market place. It would also get rid of the problems currently experienced where some countries do not have the most up-to-date information on products and prices.

(ii) **Costs**

The **costs** of providing a fully networked computer system, changeover costs and the costs of future maintenance and training must be evaluated and budgeted for. The development and implementation of **security measures** to prevent the misuse of corporate data, and to prevent fraud by unauthorised users (who may be employees or external to the organisation) have to be considered and costed. In addition, there may be a possible need to **recruit** specialised staff to implement the changes to the existing information system. All of these costs are foreseeable and can be planned.

(iii) **Changes**

Upgrading corporate information systems usually results in many unforeseen changes to the **culture** of the organisation and to the **working practices** of staff at all levels. For example, would greater efficiency be achieved by allowing staff to have more flexible hours of attendance? Can costs be reduced by allowing some staff to telecommute on a regular basis, thus allowing hot-desking to take place? Is it likely that morale will be adversely affected by staff who may be concerned about using new technology or staff who fear that they may lose their jobs through the changes?

The proposed changes are unlikely to change the **role and remit of management** in relation to the directing of staff, although it is likely that there will be some impact upon organising staff tasks as new needs arise. **Strategic and tactical planning** are likely to change in response to the improved, and more rapid, flow of information that the information system will provide.

Operational decisions can be taken at lower levels of the corporate hierarchy as information becomes available more rapidly and in an appropriate format. As well as providing a swift response to changes in the business environment, it is possible that the organisation will, in time, evolve into one with a **flatter hierarchy**. This would particularly suit the autonomous business unit structure in Story which already operates with devolved decision making. However, there is always the danger of 'information overload' which can reduce efficiency and morale within the organisation.

BPP
LEARNING MEDIA

(b) **Closed systems and open systems**

Closed system

A closed system is one that **does not react to external stimuli or allow communication from internal processes to interact with the outside environment**. They are seldom, if ever, found in naturally occurring situations. A typical example of a closed system would be a chemical reaction that takes place under controlled conditions within a laboratory. Closed systems can be created to eliminate external factors and then used to investigate the relationship between known variables in an experiment.

Open system

An open system is one that **interacts fully with its environment**. It accepts **inputs** from its surroundings, processes the inputs in some manner and then produces an **output**. The input parameters can be foreseen or be unpredictable. Similarly, outputs can either be predicted or unforeseen. For example, predictable inputs of a metal smelting works would include items like the raw materials and coal, while the predictable outputs would be ash, smoke and the smelted metal. If the raw material to be smelted became contaminated in some way, it is likely that an undesirable product would be produced. These are examples of unforeseen inputs and outputs.

Examples in the question

Turning to the question, we can see that Story is clearly an **open system**. It reacts, albeit imperfectly, to inputs from its environment and produces outputs. Sales figures are collated and analysed and predictions are made based upon this information. Hence the organisation responds to external stimuli and reacts appropriately.

The question also provides instances of **sub-systems** within the organisation that are themselves open systems. For example, the information system, the corporate management team, the business units and retail outlets are examples of sub-systems within the business that are all open.

(c) **Three types of MIS and how they would be used in an organisation**

Type of MIS	Detail
Transaction processing systems (TPS)	Collect, store, modify and retrieve the transactions of an organisation. A **transaction** is an event that generates or modifies data that is eventually stored on an information system. There are two types of TPS: **Batch transaction processing** (BTP) collects transaction data as a group and processes it later, after a time delay, as batches of identical data. **Real time transaction processing** (RTTP) is the immediate processing of data. It involves using a terminal or workstation to enter data and display results and provides instant confirmation.
Executive information systems (EIS)	Give executives a straightforward means of access to **key internal and external data**. They provide summary-level data, captured from the organisation's main systems (which might involve integrating the executive's desktop PC with the organisation's mainframe), data manipulation facilities (such as comparison with budget or prior year data and trend analysis) and user-friendly presentation of data.
Enterprise resource planning systems (ERP)	Integrate the **key processes** in an organisation so that a single system can serve the information needs of all functional areas. They primarily support business operations including Finance, HR, Marketing and Accounting and work in real time, meaning that the exact status of everything is always available to all users. ERP systems can be deployed at sites around the world; they can work in multiple languages and currencies. When they are used this way, you can immediately see, for example, exactly how much of a particular part is to hand at the warehouse in Japan and what its value is in yen or dollars.

307 Hammer

Text references. Transfer pricing is covered in Chapter 17.

Top tips. Do not forget to exclude fixed costs from your calculations in part (a). The question states that the current pricing policy is variable cost plus 30%.

Easy marks. Six marks are available in part (d) for discussing factors to consider when purchasing from outside suppliers.

Examining team's comments. The numerical parts to the question were quite well answered by most candidates. However, a disappointing number of answers included the fixed costs within part (a) and part (b) which defied the purpose of the whole question really. That having been said, most answers were good.

The quality of answers to part (c) was really poor. The question was looking for a couple of key points, for example, that including fixed costs guarantees a profit for the seller but invites manipulation of overheads and passes on inefficiencies from one part of the business to another. Also, that this strategy causes fixed costs of one division to be turned into a variable cost for another division.

Similarly, part (d) rarely produced answers scoring full marks. It asked whether retail stores should be allowed to buy in from outside suppliers. Key points in any answer should have been that the overall profitability of the company is key, as is goal congruence; these points were rarely made. Thankfully, many candidates did spot the more obvious points such as the fact that the quality and reliability of any external supplier would need to be assessed.

Marking scheme

			Marks
(a)	Steel	1	
	Other material	1	
	Labour	1	
	Variable overhead	1	
	Delivery	1	
	Margin	1	
			6
(b)	Fixed cost	2	
	Margin	2	
			4
(c)	Covers all cost	1	
	Risk	1	
	Fixed cost accounting	1	
	Converts a FC to VC	2	
			max 4
(d)	Market price may be temporary	1	
	Brand	1	
	Profitability	1	
	Flexibility	1	
	Control	1	
	Motivation	1	
	Performance assessment	1	
		max	6
			20

(a) **Price Nail would charge under existing policy (cost plus 30%)**

	$
Steel (0.4kg/0.95 (5% steel loss)) × $4.00	1.68
Other materials ($3.00 × 0.9 × 0.1)	0.27
Labour ($10 × 0.25)	2.50
Variable overhead ($15 × 0.25)	3.75
Delivery	0.50
Total variable cost	8.70
Mark-up (30%)	2.61
Transfer price	11.31

(b) **Price Nail would charged under total cost plus 10%**

	$
Total variable cost from part (a)	8.70
Extra fixed cost (0.25 × $15 × 0.8)	3.00
Total cost	11.70
Mark up (10%)	1.17
Transfer price	12.87

The increase in price if the pricing policy switches to total cost plus 10% is $1.56 per unit ($12.87 – $11.31).

(c) Fixed costs can be accounted for in a number of ways. As such, including the fixed cost within the transfer price could lead to **manipulation of overhead treatment**. For example, employing absorption costing or activity-based costing.

Including the fixed costs in the transfer price will benefit the manufacturer, who can ensure that **all costs** incurred during the manufacturing process are **covered**. Assuming the fixed overhead absorption calculations are accurate, the manufacturing division should be **guaranteed a profit**.

The main **problem** with this pricing strategy is **fixed costs** are **effectively treated as variable costs** from the perspective of the stores, as they are included within the variable buy-in price. This could lead to **poor decision making** from a **group perspective**.

(d) Managers of the retail stores are likely to be more **motivated** if they are given **freedom** in which to **operate** and are able to purchase from outside suppliers if prices are cheaper.

In addition, the performance of **store managers will be easier to assess** in an environment in which managers are able to control greater elements of the business.

Price differences are perhaps to be expected, given that products are rarely identical. There is a **risk** that store managers purchase cheaper shears of **inferior quality** to those produced internally (whilst claiming they are comparable) in order to achieve a greater margin. Such scenarios jeopardise the **reputation** of the brand for the benefit of individual stores.

Allowing store managers to purchase from cheaper suppliers could result in Hammer **losing control** of its business as retail stores could potentially stock different shears and other products from a range of different suppliers. On the other hand, **flexibility is increased** and profits could increase as store managers find bargain prices.

In a competitive market, it is unlikely that suppliers will offer products significantly cheaper to Hammer for a sustained period of time. Any cheap prices accessed by store managers are likely to be the result of a sale or special promotion. If this is the case, it would not be advisable for Hammer to grant store managers the power to purchase from cheaper external suppliers in the long term.

Overall profitability of the company is key. The retail stores and Nail should be working in a way that is best for the company overall. This is known as **goal congruence**.

308 Woodside

(a)   **Operating statement**

			$
Budgeted surplus (W1)			98,750
Funding shortfall (W3)			(80,000)
			18,750

	Favourable $	Adverse $	
Free meals (W4)			
Price variance		4,000	
Usage variance		8,750	
Overnight shelter (W5)			
Price variance		4,380	
Usage variance	31,000		
Advice centre (W6)			
Price variance		9,100	
Usage variance		7,500	
Campaigning and advertising (W7)			
Expenditure variance		15,000	
Fixed cost (W8)			
Expenditure variance		18,000	
	31,000	66,730	(35,730)
Actual shortfall (W2)			(16,980)

Workings

1   *Budgeted figures*

	$	
Free meals provision	91,250	(18,250 meals at $5 per meal)
Overnight shelter (variable)	250,000	(10,000 bed-nights at $30 – $5 per night)
Advice centre (variable)	45,000	(3,000 sessions at $20 – $5 per session)
Fixed costs	65,000	(10,000 × $5) + (3,000 × $5)
Campaigning and advertising	150,000	
	601,250	
Surplus for unexpected costs	98,750	
Fundraising target	700,000	

2   *Actual figures*

	$	
Free meals provision	104,000	(20,000 meals at $5.20 per meal)
Overnight shelter	223,380	(8,760 bed-nights $25.50 per night)
Advice centre	61,600	(3,500 sessions at $17.60 per session)
Fixed costs	83,000	
Campaigning and advertising	165,000	
	636,980	
Shortfall	16,980	
Funds raised	620,000	

3   Funding shortfall = 700,000 – 620,000 = $80,000 (A)

4   Free meals price variance = (5.00 – 5.20) × 20,000 = $4,000 (A)
     Free meals usage variance = (18,250 – 20,000) × 5.00 = $8,750 (A)

5   Overnight shelter price variance = (25.00 – 25.50) × 8,760 = $4,380 (A)
     Overnight shelter usage variance – (10,000 – 8,760) × 25 = $31,000 (F)

6   Advice centre price variance = (17.60 – 15.00) × 3,500 = $9,100 (A)
     Advice centre usage variance = (3,000 – 3,500) × 15.00 = $7,500 (A)

7   Campaigning and advertising expenditure variance = 150,000 – 165,000 = $15,000 (A)

8   Fixed cost expenditure variance = 65,000 – 83,000 = $18,000 (A)

There was a **fundraising shortfall** of $80,000 compared to the target and **costs were over budget** in all areas except overnight shelter provision.

Provision of free meals cost 14% (104,000 – 91,250/91,250) more than budgeted with most of the variance due to the extra 1,750 meals that were provided. However $4,000 of the variance was due to an increase of 20c (5.20 – 5.00) in the average cost of a meal.

Overnight shelter cost $26,620 (250,000 – 223,380) less than expected. $31,000 was saved because there were 1,240 bed nights less of the service used than expected, but the average unit cost of the provision increased by 50c, leading to an adverse price variance of $4,380.

Advice centre costs were also above budget by 37% (61,600 – 45,000/45,000). There were two factors contributing to this increase. **Usage of the service** increased by 17% (3,500 – 3,000/3,000) and **average costs** also increased by 17% (17.60 – 15/15).

Fixed costs of administration and centre maintenance were $18,000 (28%) above budget and **campaigning and advertising** were $15,000 (10%) above budget.

The shortfall identified in the operating statement may initially cause concern and individual adverse variances could be investigated to determine if **future cost increases could be controlled**. However, the **objective** of a charity such as Woodside is not to make money but to provide help to homeless people.

The figures demonstrate that this **objective was achieved** in terms of advice and free meals provided. It appears that the demand for overnight shelter has fallen, so resources could be switched from this area if it is believed that this is a long-term trend. Further investigation of the reason for the fall in demand would be useful.

(b) Financial management and control in a not-for-profit organisation (NFPO) such as the Woodside charity needs to recognise that such organisations often have **multiple objectives** that can be **difficult to define** and are usually **non-financial**.

Performance of such organisations is judged in terms of inputs and outputs and hence the **value for money** criteria of economy, efficiency and effectiveness.

Economy means that inputs should be obtained at the lowest cost. **Efficiency** involves getting as much as possible for what goes in: ie using the charity's resources as efficiently as possible to provide the services offered by the charity. **Effectiveness** means ensuring the outputs, ie the services provided, have the desired impacts and achieve the charity's objectives.

Performance measures to determine whether objectives have been achieved can be difficult to formulate for an organisation such as Woodside.

Measures such as the number of free meals served, number of advice sessions given and number of bed-nights used, show that quantitative measures can be used to demonstrate that the charity is meeting a growing need.

Financial management and control in this organisation will primarily be concerned with preparing budgets and controlling costs.

Preparing budgets

Budgets rely on **forecasting** and accurate forecasts can be difficult to prepare for a charity such as Woodside. The level of activity is driven by the needs of the homeless and therefore **difficult to predict**. A high degree of **flexibility** is required to meet changing demand, so provision needs to be built into budgets for this.

It is unlikely that Woodside has carried out a **detailed analysis of costs** and it has probably used an **incremental** approach to budgeting. This will limit the accuracy of its forecasts, but staff may not have the necessary financial skills to use more advanced techniques.

Controlling costs

This is a key area of financial management due to the need for efficiency and economy. Inputs such as food, drink, bedding etc can be sourced as cheaply as possible and expenses such as electricity and telephone usage can be kept to an absolute minimum through careful use.

The responsibility for cost control would probably be the responsibility of the full-time members of staff, but a culture of economy and efficiency can be encouraged amongst the volunteers.

Woodside will also need to provide **annual accounts** in order to retain charitable status and to show the providers of funds that their donations are being used as they intended.

309 Ties Only Co

Text reference. Performance analysis is covered in Chapter 16.

Top tips. In parts (a) and (c) you need to analyse and comment on each part of the given results. Make sure your percentages calculation technique can cope with this!

Part (b) simply requires a summary of the information in part (a) with a comment about future performance versus current performance.

Easy marks. Using your common sense will gain you easy marks throughout this question. Use headings to make your answer easy for the marker to identify where to award marks.

Examining team's comments. Calculating a ratio without real comment did not gain full marks. An opinion such as 'impressive growth' was required. Candidates should offer an opinion as to why the ratio has occurred.

Marking scheme

			Marks
(a)	Sales	2	
	Gross profit	2	
	Website development	2	
	Administration	2	
	Distribution	1	
	Launch marketing	2	
	Overall comment	2	
	Maximum		10
(b)	Future profits comment		3
(c)	Number of tie sales	1	
	Tie price calculation	2	
	On-time delivery	2	
	Returns	2	
	System downtime	1	
	Summary comment	1	
	Maximum		7
			20

(a) **Financial performance**

Sales growth

Ties Only Co appears to have made an excellent start with initial sales of $420,000 growing by 62% ((680,000 – 420,000)/420,000 × 100%) to Quarter 2. This is particularly impressive given the acknowledged competitiveness of this business sector.

Gross profit

The gross profit margin in Quarter 1 was 52% (218,400/420,000 × 100%) and 50% (339,320/680,000 × 100%) in Quarter 2. The level of margin may be as expected for this business sector but we would need industry average data for comparison.

However, a **fall in margin** needs to be investigated. It could be that Ties Only was initially able to source cheaper ties but the rapid growth meant that alternative, more expensive, suppliers had to be found. Alternatively, competitors quickly responded to this new entrant and lowered their prices in response. This pressure could have forced Ties Only to lower their prices.

Website development

All website development costs are being **written off as incurred** so we would expect costs to be higher in the initial quarters. The website costs are over a third of total expenses, so the initial loss is mostly explained by this write-off and does not therefore give any major cause for concern.

Administration costs

Although administration costs have risen in absolute terms, as a **percentage of sales** they have **fallen** from 23.9% (100,500/420,000 × 100%) to 22.2% (150,640/680,000 × 100%). Administration costs are the second biggest expense so very important to control.

This could indicate that administration costs are being **effectively controlled** which is good news. It could also be because fixed overheads are being **spread over a larger volume** and this will continue to improve as the business grows.

Distribution costs

These costs form the **smallest proportion** of total expenses (about 6%) and the proportion of distribution costs to sales has **remained constant** at 4.9% (20,763/420,000 × 100%). These costs will be subject to external influences, such as a general rise in postage costs.

Launch marketing

This is similar to the website costs as it is expected to fall once the business is established. Ties Only will need to **continue to market** its website but this is likely to be cheaper than the initial big launch marketing campaign. The negative impact on profitability will therefore reduce over time.

Other variable expenses

These have again increased in line with the sales volume and are 11.9% of sales (50,000/420,000 × 100%).

(b) **Current and future profits**

An initial look at the accounts would identify a worrying total loss of $188,303 in the first two quarters.

However, much of this loss is due to the website development costs which will not be incurred again. Websites do need to be maintained and continually improved, but this cost will be much lower. Launch marketing is another initial cost which will fall rapidly. If we deduct these expenses, the business made an **underlying profit** of $47,137 in Quarter 1 and $75,360 in Quarter 2, an encouraging **upward trend**.

The initial impact of the business has been very good. There is a threat from falling margins to consider but cost control looks effective so the future is promising.

These figures illustrate that a short-term view of a new business is not necessarily a good indicator of future performance.

Non-financial performance indicators

Average price of ties

Quarter 1: $420,000/27,631 = $15.20
Quarter 2: $680,000/38,857 = $17.50

In part (a) it was suggested that **the fall in gross profit margin** might be due to a price reduction. This data provides evidence that this is **not** the case. There must therefore be an alternative explanation.

On-time delivery

This has dropped significantly from 95% to 89% and this is worrying. The service provided to customers is a **key differentiator**, especially if the company is competing on quality, not price. Customers will go elsewhere if their expectations are not met. Action will need to be taken to remedy this problem.

Sales returns

This is again a key indicator of **quality** and whether **customers' expectations** are being met. Returns have risen from 12% to 18% and are now above the industry average of 13%. Returns are to be expected on internet sales where the product may look different in reality, but a higher than average rate means that the internet is **not adequately describing and illustrating** the products. Again, quality may be less than customers expect.

Alternatively, the **pressure to dispatch orders** may be resulting in **errors** or packaging problems. Either of these reasons does not bode well for the business and action must be taken to remedy the problem.

System downtime

Customers who use shopping websites are usually **time-pressured** individuals who will not react well to delays in loading pages. It is all too easy to immediately switch to a competitor's website so it is essential that system downtime is kept to an absolute minimum to **avoid lost sales**.

It would be useful to compare the figures with an **industry average** but the important point is that system downtime has **doubled**. This could be due to **pressure on the website** as a result of the volume of demand. As the website development has been such a costly and important part of the business set-up, the owners of Ties Only should have an urgent discussion with the website developers to come up with a solution.

Conclusion

Ties Only is doing well in terms of sales growth and potential profitability for a brand new business. However the owners need to focus their attention on the accuracy of order delivery, website reliability and the quality of the product. Further investigation needs to be made of the fall in gross profit margin.

310 The Accountancy Teaching Co

Text reference. Performance measurement is covered in Chapter 16.

Top tips. At first glance, you may not know where to begin with this question! Take care to structure your answer around the headings given in the requirement and set out your workings clearly to maximise your score in each area.

Be sure to explain what your calculations mean for AT Co, to add depth to your answer. Finally, do not forget to comment on each of the non-financial performance indicators.

Easy marks. There are easy marks available throughout this question (providing you spend enough time on each heading provided in the question requirement!)

Examining team's comments. This was a typical performance measurement question. There was quite a lot of information to absorb but I strongly believe that, unless you are given plenty of information to work with, it is only possible to make very generalised, insipid comments. This is not what PM is all about. I want candidates to be able to handle information and make some quality analysis about it. It requires common sense and ability to link information. Needless to say, answers were poor. Anyone who had read my article on this area, or indeed my predecessor's article on this area, would know that insipid comments such as 'turnover decreased by 8.3%, which is poor' will score only a calculation mark, for working out the 8.3%. Is this decrease in turnover poor? Well, it depends on the market in which the company is operating. You have to read the scenario. When you take into account the fact that there has been a 20% decline in the demand for accountancy training, AT Co's 8.3% looks relatively good. You must link information; this is an essential skill for any accountant. Nothing is ever what it seems...ask any auditor!

Let me also take the opportunity to distinguish between an acceptable comment, which might earn one mark, compared to a good point, which might earn two marks. Cost of sales fell by $10.014m in the year. Part of this reduction was down to a fall in freelance lecture costs. A good candidate would have commented that, while the company requested that freelance lecturers reduce their fees by 10%, the actual fee reduction gained was 15%, a strong performance. A comment such as this would have earned two marks. A less observant comment, earning one mark, would have been that the reduction in cost of sales was partly due to the fact that the company requested freelance lecturers to reduce their fees by 10%.

I hope that this question will serve as a good revision question to future examinees of PM. The information given is there to help you make worthwhile comments. When planning the question, you should annotate it carefully, cross-referencing different parts of the question, linking financial and non-financial information etc.

Marking scheme

		Marks
Turnover:		
8.3% decrease	½	
Actual turnover 14.6% higher	½	
Performed well compared to market conditions	1	
Transfer of students	1	
		3
Cost of sales:		
19.2% decrease	½	
63.7% of turnover	½	
15% fee reduction from freelance staff	2	
Other costs of sale fell by $3.555m	2	
Online marking did not save as much as planned	1	
		Max 5
Gross profit – numbers and comment	1	
Indirect expenses:		
Marketing costs:		
42.1% increase	½	
Increase necessary to reap benefits of developments	1	
Benefits may take more than one year to be felt	½	
Property costs – stayed the same	½	
Staff training:		
163.9% increase	½	
Necessary for staff retention	1	
Necessary to train staff on new website etc	1	
Without training, staff would have left	1	
Less student complaints	1	
Interactive website and student helpline:		
Attracted new students	1	
Increase in pass rate	1	
Enrolment costs:		
Fall of 80.9%	½	
Result of electronic system being introduced	1	
Reduced number of late enrolments	1	
		Max 9

Net operating profit:

Fallen to $2.106m	½
Difficult market	1
Staff training costs should decrease in the future	1
Future increase in market share	1
Lower advertising cost in future	1
Charge for website	1
	Max **3**
	20

Turnover

Turnover has decreased by 8.3% from $72.025 million in 20X9 to $66.028 million in 20Y0. Given the 20% **decline in demand for accountancy training**, AT Co's turnover would have been expected to fall to $57.62 million in line with market conditions. As such, it would appear that **AT has performed well in a tough market as its actual turnover is 14.6% higher than expected**.

Non-financial performance indicators show that the number of students who transferred to AT from an alternative training provider has increased to 20% in 20Y0 (from 8% in 20X9). This **increase in market share** is likely to be directly linked to **the improved service provided to students** as a result of the new student helpline and interactive website, as well as other developments.

Cost of sales

Cost of sales has decreased by 19.2% from $52.078m in 20X9 to $42.056m in 20Y0. In 20X9, cost of sales represented 72.3% of turnover and in 20Y0 this figure was 63.7%. The reasons for this substantial decrease are considered below.

Freelance costs in 20X9 were $14.582m. Given that a minimum 10% reduction in fees had been requested to freelance lecturers and the number of courses run by them was the same year on year, the expected cost for freelance lecturers in 20Y0 was $13.124m. The **reduction in costs was successful** as actual costs were $12.394m (a reduction of 15%).

Prior to any cost cuts and **assuming a consistent cost of sales to turnover ratio**, costs of sales for 20Y0 were expected to be $47.738m. The actual cost of sales was $5.682m lower at $42.056m. Freelance lecturer costs fell by $2.188m, meaning that the remaining $3.494m is made up of decreases in other costs of sale.

Employees were told they would not receive a pay rise for at least one year and the average number of employees hardly changed year on year. As such, **the decreased costs are unlikely to be related to staff costs**.

The introduction of the **electronic marking system was expected to save the company $4m**. It is possible that the system did not save as much as predicted, hence the $3.494m fall. Alternatively, the saved marking costs may have been partially counteracted by an increase in another cost included in cost of sales.

Gross profit

As a result of the increased market share and cost savings discussed above, the **gross profit margin has increased** in 20Y0 from 27.7% to 36.3%.

Indirect expenses

Marketing costs

AT Co has increased spend on marketing campaigns to make students aware of the improved service and the range of facilities that the company offers. As such, marketing costs have increased by 42.1% in 20Y0. It would appear that the marketing campaigns have been a success, with higher student numbers relative to the competition in 20Y0. It is important to recognise the time lag between the cost outlay and the benefit received from such campaigns. It is likely that many of the benefits will not be felt until 20Y1.

Property costs

Property costs have remained in line with 20X9, indicating no significant investment in company premises.

Staff training

Training costs have increased dramatically from $1.287m in 20X9 to $3.396m in 20Y0, an increase of 163.9%. In 20X9 and before, AT Co had experienced problems with staff retention which resulted in a lower quality service being provided to students.

Considerable time and money is likely to have been spent on training staff to use the new interactive website as well as the electronic enrolment and marking systems. If the company had not spent this money on essential training, the quality of service would have deteriorated further and more staff would have left as they became increasingly dissatisfied with their jobs.

The number of student complaints has fallen dramatically in 20Y0, to 84 from 315, indicating that the staff training appears to have improved the quality of service being provided to students.

Interactive website and the student helpline

Interactive website and student helpline costs have not been incurred in previous years and have arisen from the drive towards providing students with an improved service and to increase pass rates. The percentage of students passing exams first time increased from 48% in 20X9 to 66% in 20Y0, which would suggest that the developments have improved the student learning environment.

Enrolment costs

Enrolment costs have fallen by $4.072m (80.9%), largely due to the new electronic enrolment system that was launched in 20Y0. It is likely that the new system has contributed to the reduction in late enrolments from 297 in 20X9 to 106 in 20Y0.

Net operating profit

Net operating profit has fallen from $3.635m to $2.106m (42%). While this is a significant decrease, AT Co has been operating in tough market conditions in 20Y0. The company may have considered charging students a fee to use the interactive website in order to recoup some of the funds invested. This would have increased net operating profit.

Going forward, staff training costs are likely to decrease as staff become familiar with the new developments and staff retention improves. Higher pass rates are likely to attract more students in the coming years, which will further increase market share.

As the AT brand becomes established in the market, it is likely that fewer advertising campaigns will take place, resulting in lower marketing costs.

Workings (**Note.** All workings are in $'000)

1   *Turnover*

Decrease in turnover = $72,025 − $66,028/$72,025 = 8.3%

Expected 20Y0 turnover given 20% decline in market = $72,025 × 80% = $57,620

Actual 20Y0 turnover compared to expected = $66,028 − $57,620/$57,620 = 14.6% higher

2   *Cost of sales*

Decrease in cost of sales = $42,056 − $52,078/$52,078 = 19.2%

Cost of sales as percentage of turnover: 20X9 = $52,078/$72,025 = 72.3%

20Y0 = $42,056/$66,028 = 63.7%

3   *Freelance staff costs*

In 20X9 = $41,663 × 35% = $14,582

Expected cost for 2010 = $14,582 × 90% = $13,124

Actual 20Y0 cost = $12,394

$12,394 − $14,582 = $2,188 decrease

$2,188/$14,582 = 15% decrease in freelancer costs

4   *Expected cost of sales for 20Y0*

Before costs cuts = $66,028 × 72.3% = $47,738

Actual cost of sales = $42,056

Difference = $5,682, of which $2,188 relates to freelancer savings and $3,494 relates to other savings.

5   *Gross profit margin*

20X9: $19,947/$72,025 = 27.7%

20Y0: $23,972/$66,028 = 36.3%

6   *Increase in marketing costs*

$4,678 – $3,291/$3,291 = 42.1%

7   *Increase in staff training costs*

$3,396 – $1,287/$1,287 = 163.9%

8   *Decrease in enrolment costs*

$960 – 5,032/5,032 = 80.9%

9   *Net operating profit*

Decreased from $3,635 to $2,106. This is a fall of 1,529/3,635 = 42.1%

311 Jump

Text references. Performance measurement is covered in Chapter 16.

Top tips. Ensure that your answer to part (b) supports both arguments. Use headings in your answer, one for each target.

Easy marks. Part (c) is relatively straightforward and is worth five marks.

Examining team's comments. Answers to part (a) were good on the whole. For a narrative requirement, part (b) was fairly well answered overall. Part (c) asked for a description of ways in which the manager could manipulate the situation in order to make sure they get their bonus.

Again, there were some good answers here, with only a minority of candidates talking about manipulating profits, which wasn't relevant to a business where profit-based targets weren't being used.

Marking scheme

			Marks
(a)	Per target	2	
			6
(b)	For each target – supporting controllability	1½	
	For each target – denying controllability	1½	
			9
(c)	For each idea of manipulation	2½	
			5
			20

(a) **Bonus calculation**

	Qtr to 30 June 20X9	Qtr to 30 September 20X9	Qtr to 31 December 20X9	Qtr to 31 March 20Y0	Bonus hits
Staff on time?					
On-time %	95.5%	94.2%	94.0%	95.8%	
	(430/450)	(452/480)	(442/470)	(460/480)	
Bonus earned?	Yes	No	No	Yes	2

	Qtr to 30 June 20X9	Qtr to 30 September 20X9	Qtr to 31 December 20X9	Qtr to 31 March 20Y0	Bonus hits
Member visits					
Target visits	21,600	23,040	23,760	24,480	
	(60% × 3,000 × 12)	(60% × 3,200 ×12)	(60% × 3,300 × 12)	(60% × 3,400 × 12)	
Actual visits	20,000	24,000	26,000	24,000	
Bonus earned?	No	Yes	Yes	No	2

	Qtr to 30 June 20X9	Qtr to 30 September 20X9	Qtr to 31 December 20X9	Qtr to 31 March 20Y0	Bonus hits
Personal training					
Target visits	300	320	330	340	
	(10% × 3,000)	(10% × 3,200)	(10% × 3,300)	(10% × 3,400)	
Actual visits	310	325	310	339	
Bonus earned?	Yes	Yes	No	No	2

Total number of bonus hits from table above = 6

The bonus earned by the manager is 6 × $400 = $2,400. This represents 50% of the total bonus available.

(b) It is essential that the targets set are based on elements of the job that the local managers are able to control. Targets that are based on elements that local managers are unable to influence will be seen as pointless and unrealistic and could **demotivate staff** at the local manager level.

Staff on time

Individual members of staff may be late for work as a result of external factors, including home pressures or delayed public transport. Such factors cannot be controlled by the local manager. However if such problems occur on a regular basis to certain members of staff, the local manager does have the power **to amend their contract of employment**.

The way in which the local manager manages staff will impact upon how **motivated** they are to work and to arrive on time. The **local manager** has the power to **devise shift patterns** that best suit their team and can **reward** them accordingly, through their ability to amend employment contracts.

In summary, **lateness** to work **can be controlled** by the local manager.

Personal training sessions

The local manager has control over prices charged to customers. If demand for personal training sessions falls they can reduce prices or make special offers in a bid to increase customer numbers.

A number of potential customers may view personal training sessions as a luxury, particularly in the current economic climate. Also, the personal training market is particularly competitive, which may make it difficult for the local managers to increase sales. Local managers can take steps to improve the service offered by the sports club but any significant expenditure requires approval at Board level.

In summary, the local manager can only **partly control** the number of **personal training sessions** that are booked.

Member use of facilities

The local manager controls the staff and hence the level of customer service. It is likely that a **high level of customer service** could encourage some **members to use** the facilities **more often**. The local manager also has the ability to influence member numbers by **adjusting membership prices**.

However, external factors such as **work pressures** and level of **health** may prevent some members from visiting the club as often as they would like.

In summary, the local manager can only **partly control** the **number of member visits**.

(c) **Reduce prices**

The targets are largely volume-driven and local managers have the power to **adjust membership fees** and **prices for personal training sessions**. Local managers could therefore reduce prices to ensure that they meet the targets and therefore obtain their bonus. Such a scenario would **harm** Jump's **overall profitability**.

Recording of transactions

A local manager with access to the accounting records could deliberately record visits to the club in the **incorrect period** in order to ensure that they achieve a bonus. For example, in Q2 the target for personal training sessions was not met by 5 sessions. The manager could record the first 5 transactions of Q3 in Q2 to ensure that they obtain an extra $400 bonus.

312 Bridgewater Co

Text references. Performance measurement is covered in Chapter 16.

Top tips. The key to success in this type of question is reading the information in the question very carefully and making full use of it. When the ACCA examining team asks for 'comment', an opinion is required, not simply a re-statement of the proposals.

Easy marks. For half marks in part (a) all that was expected was a statement (with simple supporting calculations) of whether or not the manager would meet each of the targets.

Examining team's comments. Candidates must be able to assess performance, which means interpret financial and other data and make sensible comments on it. Few candidates realised that the division's improving performance in Quarters 3 and 4 came too late for the promotion at the end of Quarter 2. Many only commented on the profits of the division and ignored all the other targets. Many also assessed the performance more generally, calculating among other things % margins and ignored the targets altogether. This was very disappointing.

Part (b) was also poorly performed and misreading the question was common. Candidates must learn to read performance management questions more carefully.

For Part (c) candidates answers primarily consisted of a re-statement of the different steps being proposed with little or no comment at all. A comment requires opinion and anything sensible scored marks.

Candidates should prepare themselves to assess the performance of a business, both financially and non-financially, if they want to pass.

Marking scheme

			Marks
(a)	Per target discussed	2	
			8
(b)	Revised forecasts		
	Voucher sales effect	1	
	Vista sales effect	2	
	Extra trainer cost	1	
	Extra room hire cost	1	
	Staff training increase	½	
	Software cost	½	
	Overall revised profit calculation	1	
	Maximum		6
(c)	Per idea commented on	2	
			Max 6
			20

(a)   **Each quarter, sales should grow and annual sales should exceed budget**

In the Northwest division, sales are forecasted to fall by 10% (4/40 × 100%) from Quarter 1 to Quarter 2 but then start to grow. Average growth per quarter over the year is 14.5% $(\sqrt[3]{(60/40)} - 1)$. Annual sales are forecast to exceed the sales budget by $6,000 (186 – 180).

It would therefore appear that the annual **target will be met**. However, the promotion decision is to be taken in Quarter 3 and the **slow start** to the year may not reflect well on the manager of the Northwest division.

Trainer costs should not exceed $180 per teaching day

The manager is paying $200 (8,000/40) per teaching day in trainer costs, which **exceeds the target**. They believe in quality and therefore appear to be paying more to attract better teaching staff. This may well improve sales in the long term as the reputation for quality delivery becomes known, but it is at the expense of increased costs in the short term.

Room hire costs should not exceed $90 per teaching day

The manager of this division is also **spending more** on room hire costs than the target. They are spending $100 per teaching day rather than $90. This could be again part of their quality improvement policy as they are hiring better facilities, but it could also be due to poor negotiation and buying strategy.

Each division should meet its budget for profit per quarter and annually

The achievement of this target suffers from the same problem as the sales target. The manager will meet the target for the year by $2,500, but is **below target** in the first two quarters.

This again will impact on their promotion prospects which, overall, are not looking good. They are failing to meet any of the targets in the first two quarters and will have to hope that the senior managers agree with their **long-term** rather than **short-termist** approach.

(b)   **Revised forecasts**

	Q1 $'000	Q2 $'000	Q3 $'000	Q4 $'000	Total $'000
Existing sales	40.0	36.0	50.0	60.0	186.0
Voucher sales ($125 × 80/4)	2.5	2.5	2.5	2.5	10.0
Software training			10.0	12.0	22.0
	42.5	38.5	62.5	74.5	218.0
Less:					
Existing trainer costs	8.0	7.2	10.0	12.0	37.2
Additional training costs ($200 × teaching days)			2.0	2.4	4.4
Room hire	4.0	3.6	5.0	6.0	18.6
Additional room hire ($100 × teaching days)			1.0	1.2	2.2
Staff training	1.0	1.0	1.0	1.0	4.0
Additional staff training	0.5	0.5			1
Other costs	3.0	1.7	6.0	7.0	17.7
Software	1.8				1.8
Forecast net profit	24.2	24.5	37.5	44.9	131.1
Original budget profit	25.0	26.0	27.0	28.0	106.0

(c)   **Voucher scheme**

The voucher scheme looks like a good idea as the manager is confident that the take-up would be good and customers would follow their advice to attend one session per quarter. This will **increase revenue** without incurring additional costs, as customers would attend existing planned courses. However, some additional unforeseen costs may still be incurred.

The additional revenue and profit will help, but targets for Quarters 1 and 2 will still not be met so the voucher scheme will not necessarily improve the manager's promotion prospects.

There is always the danger with offering a discount that **existing customers** will be disgruntled, particularly if they have already paid a higher price for a course that is now being offered at a discount. The vouchers are, however, only being offered to **new** customers so the manager should be able to offer this promotion without upsetting existing customers.

Software upgrade

It is essential that a software training company uses the **latest software technology** on its courses. The investment in software and staff training is therefore a **necessity** and cannot be avoided.

The courses will generate **extra revenue** but not until Quarters 3 and 4. This software upgrade will therefore further damage the achievement of targets in Quarters 1 and 2, as costs will rise but the extra revenue will be too late for the promotion assessment.

It is to be hoped that the senior managers will recognise the essential long-term planning being undertaken.

Delaying payments to trainers

This is not a good idea. None of the performance targets will be affected, as the plan will not affect costs or profits. The only positive impact will be on **cash flow**. The worrying aspect is the negative impact it may have on **relationships with trainers**. Software training is a competitive market and good trainers will be in demand by a number of training providers. If the company is to offer quality training, it must have the best trainers and this is not the way to retain them.

In conclusion, if all the proposals were taken together, they will **not improve** the manager's chance of promotion as any benefits will accrue after Quarter 2.

313 Oliver's Salon

Text references. Performance measurement is covered in Chapter 16.

Top tips. This is quite a long scenario with lots of information to deal with. In part (a) you need to use the sales value and the number of client visits to calculate the average price. Part (b) relates only to financial performance so a range of ratios need to be calculated and explained. The approach to use is to calculate a ratio (½ mark), make a qualitative statement (1 mark) and suggest a cause or some other comment (1 mark).

Part (c) gives you the headings to give a structure to your answer. Quality and resource utilisation are two of the dimensions in the Building Block model. The question does not ask for recommendations for Oliver, so make sure you stick to the requirements of the question.

Easy marks. The ratio analysis in part (b) has plenty of easy marks available – but make sure you do more than just calculate the ratios.

Examining team's comments. A significant number of candidates could not calculate the prices for female and male clients in the two years in question. In part (b) there was some improvement in candidates' ability to assess performance. There were problems, however: mathematical descriptions are not performance assessments; simply stating the % increases in numbers is not enough; indicating the absolute change in a cost is rarely that useful; too narrow a range of figures considered, as virtually all the numbers in the question carry marks.

In part (c) answers on quality dealt with the complaints issue well, but very few talked about the new members of staff and how their performance might be suspect. The lack of a pay rise can be demotivating and so quality might suffer; this, too, was rarely picked up.

On resource utilisation candidates had a mixed result. The male throughput per specialist was very high but this was perhaps due to the fact that male hair tends to be easier (quicker) to cut. The female situation was different, with fewer clients for more staff. Many candidates recognised this. Very few talked about the property utilisation at all.

			Marks
(a)	Average price for male customers	1	
	Average price for female customers	2	
			3
(b)	Sales growth	3	
	Gross margin	3	
	Rent	1½	
	Advertising spend	1	
	Staff costs	1½	
	Electricity	1	
			11
(c)	Quality – single gender	1	
	Quality – wage levels	1	
	Quality – other	1	
	Resource utilisation – property	1	
	Resource utilisation – staff	1	
	Resource utilisation – other	1	
			6
			20

(a) **Average price for hair services per female client**

20X8: Sales   = $200,000
     Number of female client visits = 8,000
     Average price   = 200,000/8,000
                            = $25

20X9: Prices were not increased so average price is still $25

Average price for hair services per male client

20X8: No male clients

20X9: Sales = $238,500

     Female sales   = $25 × 6,800 visits
                               = $170,000

     Male sales   = 238,500 – 170,000
                               = $68,500

     Average price   = 68,500/3,425
                               = $20

(b) **Financial performance**

Sales growth

Sales have grown by 19.25% ((238,500 – 200,000)/200,000 × 100%) from 20X8 to 20X9. This is particularly impressive as Oliver's Salon experiences high levels of competition.

This growth has come from the new **male hairdressing** part of the business, as female sales have fallen by 15% ((200,000 – 170,000)/200,000 × 100%). There was **no price increase** during this time, so this fall is due to fewer female client visits.

Gross profit

The gross profit margin in 20X8 was 53% (106,000/200,000 × 100%) and in 20X9 had **fallen** to 47.2% (112,500/238,500 × 100%). This is predominantly due to a 40% increase ((91,000 − 65,000)/65,000 × 100%) in **staff costs** as a result of the recruitment of two new staff.

The new specialist hairdresser for male clients is on a salary of $17,000 (91,000 − 65,000 − 9,000) whereas the female hairdressers were paid an average of $16,250 (65,000/4) in 20X8.

However it is the **female client** business which has been responsible for the drop in gross profit margin.

	20X8 Female $	20X9 Female $	20X9 Male $
Sales	200,000	170,000	68,500
Less cost of sales:			
Hairdressing staff	(65,000)	(74,000)	(17,000)
Hair products – female	(29,000)	(27,000)	
Hair products – male			(8,000)
Gross profit	106,000	69,000	43,500
Gross profit margin	106/200 × 100% = 53%	69/170 × 100% = 40.6%	43.5/68.5 × 100% = 63.5%

The gross profit margin from male clients is higher than for female clients.

Rent

This has not changed so is a **fixed cost** at the moment.

Administration salaries

These have increased by only 5.6% ((9,500 − 9,000)/9,000 × 100%) which is impressive given the expansion in the business.

Electricity

This has increased by 14.3% ((8,000 − 7,000)/7,000 × 100%. More clients would involve more electricity so it is a **semi-variable cost**. There may also have been a **general increase** in electricity prices, which would be beyond the control of Oliver.

Advertising

This has increased by 150% ((5,000 − 2,000)/2,000 × 100%) which could be expected at the **launch of a new service**. Provided the advertising has generated new clients, it should not be a cause for concern.

Net profit

Net profit has only increased by 2.6% ((80,000 − 78,000/78,000 × 100%) which is disappointing compared to a 19.25% increase in sales.

(c) **Non-financial performance**

Quality

The number of complaints has increased significantly by 283% ((46 − 12)/12 × 100%). This is not just due to the increase in client numbers.

Complaints per customer visit have increased from 0.15% (12/8,000 × 100%) to 0.44%. This is a cause for concern in a service business, especially as many customers will not actually complain but will just not come back.

The complaints could be from the new male clients who are not happy with the new hairdresser, or they could be from female clients who do not like having men in the salon. More information is needed and action to be taken to reduce the complaints.

Resource utilisation

The resources in Oliver's Salon are the **salon** itself and the **staff**. The salon is being utilised more as a result of the increase in clients from 8,000 in 20X8 to 10,225 (6,800 + 3,425) in 20X9. This is a 27.8% ((10,225 − 8,000)/8,000 × 100%) increase. This increase in utilisation has not however resulted in a proportionate increase in profit.

The **female specialist hairdressers** served 2,000 (8,000/4) clients per specialist in 20X8 and this fell to 1,360 (6,800/5) in 20X9, following the recruitment of two new staff. Oliver may be prepared to accept this reduction in resource utilisation in order to boost service levels and reduce complaints.

This contrasts with the higher figure of 3,425 clients per **male specialist** in 20X9. The time taken per male client is much less, so this should be expected.

314 Web Co

Text reference. Performance measurement is covered in Chapter 16.

Top tips. This question may look daunting at first glance, given the 20 marks available for a single requirement. Use the information in the scenario as a framework when structuring your answer and address each performance indicator under a separate heading. Don't forget to highlight any instances where further information is required.

	Marks
Calculations	4
Missing info	3
Discussion and further analysis (2–3 marks per point)	18
Conclusion	2
	Max 20

Total sales revenue

Web Co's total **sales revenue has increased 25%** (W1) on Quarter 1 (Q1), from $2.2m to $2.75m. This is impressive given the decision to give a $10 discount to all customers who spend over $100. It is not possible to attribute the increase to any particular change or incentive without analysing the **performance indicators** below.

Net profit margin

The net profit margin has decreased from 25% to 16.7%. Net profit was $550,000 in Q1 and $459,250 in Q2 (W2). If the profit margin remained at 25%, net profit for Q2 would have been $687,500. Net profit for Q2 is therefore $228,250 **lower** than it would have been.

This significant decrease is largely due to the fee of $200,000 paid for an advert on **the webpage of a well known fashion magazine**. A further $20,000 is attributable to the fee paid to the **website consultant**.

The remaining $8,250 could be the costs of providing the **free 'Fast Track' delivery service**. Alternatively it could be the cost of offering a $10 discount to all customers who spent more than $100. More information would be required on **how the discounts are accounted for** (whether they are included in cost of sales or netted off against sales revenue). Further detail of the **costs of providing the 'Fast Track' service** would also be useful.

Number of orders from customers/customers spending over $100

The number of orders received from customers has increased by 22%, from 40,636 in Q1 to 49,600 in Q2 (W3). This 22% increase is **in line with the 25% increase in sales revenue**.

The number of customers spending more than $100 per visit has increased by 37%, from 4,650 in Q1 to 6,390 in Q2. This increase is likely to explain the 3% increase in sales revenue that is not due to increased order numbers, depending on **how the discounts are accounted for**.

Number of visits to website

The number of visits to the website has also increased significantly, from 101,589 to 141,714 (39.5% (W4)). Of this increase, 28,201 (W5) can be attributed to visitors coming through the **fashion magazine's website**. The remainder of the increase is likely to be due to the work of the website consultant.

It is clear that both changes have been effective in increasing the number of visitors to Web Co's online store. At a cost of $20,000, the work of the web consultant represents excellent **value for money**. However Web Co's sales are not really high enough to justify an outlay of $200,000 for the web magazine advert, hence the **significant fall in net profit margin** (detailed above).

Conversion rate – visitor to purchaser

The conversion rate has decreased by 5 percentage points, from 40% to 35%. This is to be expected, given the substantial increase in visitors to the website as a result of the **web magazine advert** and **search engine optimisation**.

Readers of the fashion magazine may have clicked on the advert link out of curiosity and may return to the site and purchase products at a **later date**.

Further information is required to confirm the above. For example, the total number of 'visitors to purchasers' split into (i) visitors who visited the site through the link on the online magazine, and (ii) visitors who did not.

Website availability

Website availability has remained at 95%. This indicates that the changes made by the IT department **have not corrected the problem(s)**.

Lack of availability **may have lost Web Co a significant number of sales**. Further information is required to quantify the impact. For example, the number of **aborted purchases** due to the website becoming unavailable.

Subscribers to online newsletter

The number of subscribers has increased by 159%, from 4,600 to 11,900 (W6). This huge increase is most likely due to the **free 'Fast Track' delivery service** offered to all subscribers.

As the fall in net profit has already been accounted for above, it appears that Web Co has managed to offer this service **without incurring any extra cost**.

Further information is required to establish whether the company's view of subscribers is correct (that subscribers become customers who place further orders). For example, **has the number of repeat customers increased?**

Conclusion

In summary, **Web Co performed well in Q2**. With the exception of the work performed by the IT department to make the website more available, all other changes have increased sales and/or increased subscribers to the online newsletter.

Though further information is required in a number of areas, it is clear that the business has **responded well to the changes and incentives introduced**.

The cost of the web advert ($200,000) was so high that **profits have decreased substantially despite the incentives** and changes detailed above.

Workings

1   **Increase in sales revenue**
     $2.75m – $2.2m/$2.2m = 25% increase

2   **Net profit**

     Quarter 1 = $2.2m × 25% = $550,000

     Quarter 2 = $2.75m × 16.7% = $459,250

3   **Increase in orders**

     49,600 – 40,636/40,636 = 22%

4   **Increase in number of visits to website**

     141,714 – 101,589/101,589 = 39.5%

5 **Customers accessing website through magazine advert**

141,714 × 19.9% = 28,201

6 **Increase in subscribers to newsletter**

11,900 − 4,600/4,600 = 159%

315 PAF Co

Text reference. Performance measurement is covered in Chapter 16 of the BPP Study Text.

Top tips. This question allows you to analyse performance as much as you can within the available time. For every ratio or other performance measure that you calculate, be ready to comment on its significance. Even if a ratio does not seem significant, you can say so.

Some ratios for measuring performance might seem easy to identify, but remember to use the information given in the question. There are five items in particular you could use.

(1)   The aim five years ago was to become the market leader in Sista.

(2)   Division S left its prices for products and services unchanged in 20X3 rather than increasing them in line with its competitors – so increases in sales volume are down to sales volume entirely.

(3)   Skilled staff are in short supply – so it is worth looking at labour costs.

(4)   In Sista, fire safety regulations were introduced; this could have an impact on the requirement for labour.

(5)   In addition, the property tax has affected rental costs, so these should be looked at too.

And where possible, compare the relative performance of the two divisions.

There is a lot you could write about – but remember to keep your time discipline and do not exceed your allocated time for the question.

Easy marks. The question enables you to make as many ratio calculations as you can, and you should be able to calculate some quite easily – such as the increase in sales revenue and profit in each division, and the change in the ratio of operating profit to sales from one year to the next. However, there are twice as many marks available for discussion of performance as for calculation of ratios, so make sure that you comment on the measures you have calculated.

Marking scheme

	Marks
0.5 marks per calculation	Max 7
Per comment – 2 marks per point	13
	20

Workings

	Division S Year on year	Division C Year on year
Increase in sales revenue	44%	9%
Increase in material costs	36%	25%
Increase in payroll costs	70%	15%
Increase in property costs	78%	6%
Gross profit margin in 20X3	56%	65%
Gross profit margin in 20X2	61%	67%
Increase in D&M costs	38%	18%
Increase in administration costs	6%	0%
Net profit margin in 20X3	11%	21%
Net profit margin in 20X2	9%	22%
Revenue per employee in 20X3	$102,224	$104,917
Revenue per employee in 20X2	$111,772	$104,828
Payroll cost per employee in 20X3	$27,000	$21,000
Payroll cost per employee in 20X2	$25,020	$20,000
Total market size ($ revenue) in 20X3 (w1)	$129.48m	$80.12m
Total market size ($ revenue) in 20X2 (w1)	$107.75m	$77.61m

Working 1 for market size

Division S 20X3: $38,845m/30% = $129.48m   Division C 20X3: $44,065m/55% = $80.12m

Division S 20X2: $26,937/25% = $107,75m   Division C 20X2: $40,359m/52% = $77.61m

Note. Percentages have been calculated to the nearest 1%

Commentary

General overview

Overall, Division S has performed well in 20X3, although it has not managed to meet its objective of becoming market leader despite its $2m advertising campaign. Since it has 30% of the market in 20X3 and there are only two competitors holding 70% of the market between them, at least one of those competitors must hold 35% or more of the market.

Revenue and market share

This has increased by a huge 44% in the last year. This compares to an increase of only 9% in Division C. However, part of the reason that this has been achieved is because the changes in fire safety laws introduced by the government at the end of 20X2 have caused the market for fire products and services to increase from $107.75m to $129.48m. Part of Division S's success is therefore down to increased opportunity. However, Division S has also increased its market share by a further 5 percentage points compared to 20X2. Division C has only managed a 3 percentage point increase in its market share, so this is a good result by Division S. One can assume that this is at least partly as a result of the advertising campaign carried out by Division S. However, this did cost a large amount, $2m, and it did not quite enable the Division to achieve its aim of becoming market leader.

Materials costs

The increase in materials costs is 36%, compared to an increase in revenue of 44%. It is difficult to say whether this is good or bad since the increase in revenue includes revenue from services, for which no materials costs would be expected to arise. Further information is needed on the split of revenue between products and services.

Payroll costs, revenue per employee and cost per employee

Payroll costs have increased by a massive 70% and far more than Division C's 15% increase. This is largely due to the fact that Division S's employee numbers increased from 241 in 20X2 to 380 in 20X3. This is a really big increase in employee numbers and has been accompanied by a fall in revenue per employee from $111,772 in 20X2 to $102,224 in 20X3. It is possible that Division S over-recruited, as it hoped to secure a greater level of business than it did through its advertising campaign. Division S's payroll cost per employee also increased from $25,020 in 20X2 to $27,000 in 20X3. Presumably, this is because of the fact that there is high demand for staff skilled in this area and Division S has probably had to increase pay in order to attract the calibre of staff which it needs.

Increase in property costs

In percentage terms, the biggest increase in costs which Division S has suffered is in relation to its property costs. They have increased by 78%, compared to Division C's 6% increase. It would appear that this increase is due to the increased rent charged by Division S's landlords on its business premises, which in turn has risen because of the increased tax charges. However, it is not possible to quantify this precisely without further information on rent increases.

Gross profit margin

This has actually fallen from 61% to 56%. Division C has also seen a fall in its GPM, but only a 2 percentage point fall as opposed to Division S's 5 percentage point fall. The reasons for Division S's lower GPM are the higher material, payroll and property costs. Also, Division S did not try to pass on any of its increased costs to its customers in the form of higher prices.

Distribution and marketing costs

These have increased by 38% compared to Division C's 18%. However, when you take out the advertising costs in both years' figures and work out the cost increase without them ($8.522m − $7.102m/$7.102m), it leaves an increase of only 20%. This increase would be expected given the 20% increase in world fuel prices which occurred. Division S has to deliver to a wider geographical spread of customers than Division C, so it would be expected to feel the full brunt of fuel price increases.

Administrative costs

These have increased by 6% compared to Division C's less than 1% increase (0% when rounded down to the nearest percent).

Further information is needed about the items included in these cost figures to explain why this increase has arisen.

Net profit margin

Despite challenging cost increases in all categories, Division S has still managed to increase its NPM from 9% to 11%. However, this is substantially lower than the NPM in Division C, which has fallen slightly but is still 21%, almost twice that in Division S. As we have seen, Division S's GPM is lower than Division C's anyway and, on top of that, Division C has not suffered a big increase in advertising costs like Division S; nor have administrative costs risen inexplicably.

Head Office

There is no information given about Head Office. If the Calana Division is also the Head Office, there could be Head Office costs included in Calana's figures, which would affect the comparisons being made. Further information is required here.

316 CIM Co

> **Text reference.** Performance measurement is covered in Chapters 16 and 17 of the BPP Study Text.
>
> **Top tips.** For part (a) make sure you remember to justify the figures you've used in your calculation, otherwise you will lose 2 marks. For part (b), full credit is given for calculations which follow on from your answer in part (a).
>
> **Easy marks.** Part (d) is pure knowledge covered in the Study Text and provides easy marks.
>
> **Examining team's comments.** A number of students were not able to calculate ROI in part (a) and calculated profit margins instead. In part (b) many students didn't read the bonus calculation method carefully enough. Part (c) was generally well done.

(a)   **Division F**

Controllable profit = $2,645k.

Total assets less trade payables = $9,760k + $2,480k − $2,960k = $9,280k. ROI = 28.5%.

Division N

Controllable profit = $1,970k.

Total assets less trade payables = $14,980k + $3,260k − $1,400k = $16,840k. ROI = 11.7%.

In both calculations, controllable profit has been used to reflect profit, rather than net profit. This is because the managers do not have any control over the Head Office costs; responsibility accounting deems that managers should only be held responsible for costs which they control. The same principle is being applied in the choice of assets figures being used. The current assets and current liabilities figures have been taken into account in the calculation because of the fact that the managers have full control over both of these.

(b) **Bonus**

Bonus to be paid for each percentage point = $120,000 × 2% = $2,400. Maximum bonus = $120,000 × 0.3 = $36,000.

Division F: ROI = 28.5% = 18 whole percentage points above minimum ROI of 10%.

18 × $2,400 = $43,200.

Therefore manager will be paid the maximum bonus of $36,000.

Division N: ROI = 11.7% = 1 whole percentage point above minimum.

Therefore bonus = $2,400.

(c) Discussion

- The manager of Division N will be paid a far smaller bonus than the manager of Division F. This is because of the large asset base on which the ROI figure has been calculated. Total assets of Division N are almost double the total assets of Division F. This is largely attributable to the fact that Division N invested $6.8m in new equipment during the year. If this investment had not been made, net assets would have been only $10.04m and the ROI for Division N would have been 19.62%. This would have led to the payment of a $21,600 bonus (9 × $2,400) rather than the $2,400 bonus. Consequently, Division N's manager is being penalised for making decisions which are in the best interests of their division. It is very surprising that they did decide to invest, given that they knew that they would receive a lower bonus as a result. They have acted totally in the best interests of the company. Division F's manager, on the other hand, has benefitted from the fact that they have made no investment – even though it is badly needed. This is an example of sub-optimal decision making.

- Division F's trade payables figure is much higher than Division N's. This also plays a part in reducing the net assets figure on which the ROI has been based. Division F's trade payables are over double those of Division N. In part, one would expect this because sales are over 50% higher (no purchases figure is given). However, it is clear that it is also because of low cash levels at Division F. The fact that the manager of Division F is then being rewarded for this, even though relationships with suppliers may be adversely affected, is again an example of sub-optimal decision making.

- If the controllable profit margin is calculated, it is 18.24% for Division F and 22.64% for Division N. Therefore, if capital employed is ignored, it can be seen that Division N is performing better. ROI is simply making the division's performance look worse because of its investment in assets. Division N's manager is likely to feel extremely demotivated by their comparatively small bonus and, in the future, they may choose to postpone investment in order to increase their bonus. Managers not investing in new equipment and technology will mean that the company will not keep up with industry changes and affect its overall future competitiveness.

- To summarise, the use of ROI is leading to sub-optimal decision making and a lack of goal congruence, as what is good for the managers is not good for the company and vice versa. Luckily, the manager at Division N still appears to be acting for the benefit of the company but the other manager is not. The fact that one manager is receiving a much bigger bonus than the other is totally unfair here and may lead to conflict in the long run. This is not good for the company, particularly if there comes a time when the divisions need to work together.

(d)   Steps that could be taken to encourage managers to take a **long-term view**, so that the 'ideal' decisions are taken, include the following.

   (i)   **Making short-term targets realistic**. If budget targets are unrealistically tough, a manager will be forced to make trade-offs between the short and long term.

   (ii)   **Providing sufficient management information** to allow managers to see what trade-offs they are making. Managers must be kept aware of long-term aims as well as shorter-term (budget) targets.

   (iii) **Evaluating managers' performance** in terms of contribution to long-term as well as short-term objectives.

   (iv)   **Link managers' rewards to share price**. This may encourage goal congruence.

   (v)   **Set quality-based targets** as well as financial targets. Multiple targets can be used.

317 Man Co

Text reference. Transfer pricing is covered in Chapter 17 of the BPP Study Text.

Top tips. Part (a) is fairly straightforward, so don't fall into the trap of thinking that's more complicated than it is. It's only worth 3 marks. Make sure that you read the question again carefully before attempting part (c).

Easy marks. Part (d) is pure knowledge covered in the Study Text and provides easy marks.

Examining team's comments. Most students got part (a) wrong, perhaps because they expected it to be more difficult than it was. Part (b) was attempted by most students. In part (c) some students failed to notice that the divisions had autonomy.

(a)   **Maximising group profit**

Division L has enough capacity to supply both Division M and its external customers with component L.

Therefore, incremental cost of Division M buying externally is as follows:

Cost per unit of component L when bought from external supplier: $37

Cost per unit for Division L of making component L: $20.

Therefore incremental cost to group of each unit of component L being bought in by Division M rather than transferred internally: $17 ($37 – 20).

From the group's point of view, the most profitable course of action is therefore that all 120,000 units of component L should be transferred internally.

(b)   **Calculating total group profit**

Total group profits will be as follows:

Division L:

Contribution earned per transferred component = $40 – $20 = $20
Profit earned per component sold externally = $40 – $24 = $16

	$
120,000 × $20	2,400,000
160,000 × $16	2,560,000
	4,960,000
Less fixed costs	(500,000)
Profit	4,460,000

Division M:

Profit earned per component sold externally = $27 - $1 = $26

	$
120,000 × $26	3,120,000
Less fixed costs	(200,000)
Profit	2,920,000
Total profit	7,380,000

(c) **Problems with current transfer price and suggested alternative**

The problem is that the current transfer price of $40 per unit is now too high. While this has not been a problem before, since external suppliers were charging $42 per unit, it is a problem now that Division M has been offered component L for $37 per unit. If Division M now acts in its own interests rather than the interests of the group as a whole, it will buy component L from the external supplier rather than from Division L. This will mean that the profits of the group will fall substantially and Division L will have significant unused capacity.

Consequently, Division L needs to reduce its price. The current price does not reflect the fact that there are no selling and distribution costs associated with transferring internally, ie the cost of selling internally is $4 less for Division L than selling externally. So, it could reduce the price to $36 and still make the same profit on these sales as on its external sales. This would therefore be the suggested transfer price, so that Division M is still saving $1 per unit compared to the external price. A transfer price of $37 would also presumably be acceptable to Division M since this is the same as the external supplier is offering.

(d) (i) Divisionalisation can **improve** the **quality of decisions** made because divisional managers (those taking the decisions) know local conditions and are able to make more informed judgements. Moreover, with the personal incentive to improve the division's performance, they ought to take decisions in the division's best interests.

(ii) **Decisions should be taken more quickly** because information does not have to pass along the chain of command to and from top management. Decisions can be made on the spot by those who are familiar with the product lines and production processes and who are able to react to changes in local conditions quickly and efficiently.

(iii) The authority to act to improve performance should **motivate divisional managers**.

(iv) Divisional organisation **frees top management** from detailed involvement in day-to-day operations and allows them to devote more time to strategic planning.

(v) Divisions provide **valuable training grounds for future members of top management** by giving them experience of managerial skills in a less complex environment than that faced by top management.

(vi) In a large business organisation, the **central head office will not have the management resources or skills to direct operations closely enough itself**. Some authority must be delegated to local operational managers.

Note that you would probably need to have discussed 3 of the above points to get 5 marks.

318 Rotech group

Marking scheme

	Marks
Ratios	
Calculating ROCE	1.5
Calculating asset turnover	1.5
Calculating operating profit margin	1.5
Marks per valid comment (max 5.5)	5.5
	10
Transfer pricing	
Each valid comment/calculation	1/2
	10
	20

(a) Financial ratios

		W Co Design	W Co Gearbox	C Co
Return on capital employed	$\dfrac{\text{Profit before interest and tax}}{\text{Capital employed}}$ %	$6,000/$23,540 = 25.49%	$3,875/$32,320 = 11.99%	$7,010/$82,975 = 8.45%
Asset turnover	$\dfrac{\text{Sales}}{\text{Capital employed}}$	$14,300/$23,540 = 0.61 times	$25,535/$32,320 = 0.79 times	$15,560/$82,975 = 0.19 times
Operating profit margin	$\dfrac{\text{Profit before interest and tax}}{\text{Sales}}$ %	$6,000/$14,300 = 41.96%	$3,875/$25,535 = 15.18%	$7,010/$15,560 = 45.05%

Return on capital employed:

ROCE shows how much profit has been made in relation to the amount of resources invested. C Co and both divisions of W Co are profitable. The Design division of W Co has the highest ROCE, at over 25%, while the Gearbox division and C Co are significantly lower at 11.99% and 8.45% respectively. This is primarily due to the nature of the design business which derives its profits from personnel rather than physical assets. Employees generate profits by designing products, rather than by using expensive machinery. Therefore the Design division's capital employed (asset) figure is significantly lower.

C Co has the largest asset base, and this is reflected in a relatively low ROCE. The Gearbox division is closer to this than to the Design division, but this is as a result of similarities in the nature of the business rather than division performance alone.

Asset turnover:

Asset turnover is a measure of how well the assets of a business are being used to generate sales. The Gearbox division has the highest level at 79%, while C Co has the lowest at 19%. This is probably due in part to the fact that the Gearbox division buys from C Co, therefore C Co must hold a large asset base to produce the relevant components. Both divisions of W Co do not have the same requirement and this is reflected in the higher asset turnover figures.

Operating profit margin:

C Co comes out on top in the final profitability measure, which is the operating profit margin at just over 45%, while the Gearbox division is the lowest at 15.18%. The Design division performs well at 41.96%, as it did in asset turnover. This was to be expected from the ROCE of 25%, which is a combination of the other two ratios. The Design division has both high unit profitability and generates sales at a high level compared to its asset base.

There are limitations to these types of comparisons due to the differing nature of the businesses. It would be more useful to compare each business unit to an industry average for similar businesses, as well as comparing year-on-year figures to monitor the units on an ongoing basis.

(b)   **Transfer prices**

From C Co's perspective

C Co transfers components to the Gearbox division at the same price as it sells components to the external market. However, if C Co were not making internal sales then, given that it already satisfies 60% of external demand, it would not be able to sell all of its current production to the external market. External sales are $8,010,000, therefore unsatisfied external demand is ([$8,010,000/0.6] – $8,010,000) = $5,340,000.

From C Co's perspective, of the current internal sales of $7,550,000, $5,340,000 could be sold externally if they were not sold to the Gearbox division. Therefore, in order for C Co not to be any worse off from selling internally, these sales should be made at the current price of $5,340,000, less any reduction in costs which C Co saves from not having to sell outside the group (perhaps lower administrative and distribution costs).

As regards the remaining internal sales of $2,210,000 ($7,550,000 – $5,340,000), C Co effectively has spare capacity to meet these sales. Therefore, the minimum transfer price should be the marginal cost of producing these goods. Given that variable costs represent 40% of revenue, this means that the marginal cost for these sales is $884,000. This is therefore the minimum price which C Co should charge for these sales.

In total, therefore, C Co will want to charge at least $6,224,000 for its sales to the Gearbox division.

From the Gearbox division's perspective

The Gearbox division will not want to pay more for the components than it could purchase them for externally. Given that it can purchase them all for 95% of the current price, this means a maximum purchase price of $7,172,500.

Overall

Taking into account all of the above, the transfer price for the sales should be somewhere between $6,224,000 and $7,172,500.

319 Bus Co

Marking scheme

			Marks
(a)	Calculations		2
(b)	Accuracy of statement		
	First part untrue, Express higher percentage	1	
	Correct re what customers value	1	
	Correct re punctuality	1	
	Incorrect re leader	1	
			4
(c)	Efficiency and effectiveness:		
	Definition of efficiency	1	
	Performance measure for efficiency	1	
	Definition of effectiveness	1	
	Performance measure for effectiveness	1	
			4
(d)	Balanced scorecard approach:		
	Stating what it is	2	
	Financial perspective	2	
	Customer perspective	2	
	Internal perspective	2	
	Learning and growth perspective	2	
			10
			20

(a) Calculations

Bus: $(0.4 \times 0.67) + (0.32 \times 0.8) + (0.28 \times 0.82) = 75.36\%$
Prime: $(0.4 \times 0.58) + (0.32 \times 0.76) + (0.28 \times 0.83) = 70.76\%$
Express: $(0.4 \times 0.67) + (0.32 \times 0.76) + (0.28 \times 0.89) = 76.04\%$

(b) Accuracy of statement

The MD's statement says that Bus Co's customers are the most satisfied of any national bus operator. However, this is not quite the case since, when the 'overall satisfaction' levels are calculated, Express's level is 76.04% compared to Bus Co's 75.36%. So, the first part of the MD's statement is untrue.

The MD then goes on to say that Bus Co is leading the way on what matters most to customers – value for money and punctuality. Given the weightings attached to these two criteria, it appears true to say that these are the factors which matter most to customers. Similarly, it is true to say that Bus Co is leading as regards punctuality, being 4 percentage points ahead of Prime and Express on this criterion. However, given that Express also has the same level of satisfaction as regards offering value for money, Bus Co is only leading ahead of Prime on this criterion, not ahead of Express. Therefore, while it can say that it is the leader on punctuality, it can only say that it is the joint leader on value for money.

(c)   **VFM**

'Efficiency' focuses on the relationship between inputs and outputs, considering whether the maximum output is being achieved for the resources used.

Performance measure:

Occupancy rate of buses
Utilisation rate for buses (utilisation rate = hours on the road/total hours available)
Utilisation rate for drivers

(Many others could be given too, but only one was asked for.)

'Effectiveness' focuses on the relationship between an organisation's objectives and outputs, considering whether the objectives are being met.

Possible performance measures:

Percentage of customers satisfied with cleanliness of buses
Percentage of carbon emissions relative to target set

(Many others could be given too, but only one was asked for.)

(d)   **Balanced scorecard**

The **balanced scorecard** approach to performance measurement emphasises the need to provide management with a set of information which covers all relevant areas of performance in an objective and unbiased fashion.

The information provided may be both financial and non-financial and cover areas such as profitability, customer satisfaction, internal efficiency and innovation.

The balanced scorecard focuses on **four different perspectives**, as follows.

Customer perspective

The customer perspective considers how new and existing customers view the organisation. This perspective should identify targets that matter to customers, such as cost, quality, delivery, inspection and so on.

The customer perspective is linked to revenue/profit objectives in the financial perspective. If customer objectives are achieved, it is likely that revenue/profit objectives will also be achieved.

Performance measure: number of repeat trips to measure customer retention.

Internal perspective

The internal perspective makes an organisation consider what processes it must excel at in order to achieve financial and customer objectives.

The perspective aims to improve internal processes and decision making.

Performance measure: costs saved after reassessing internal processes.

Innovation and learning perspective

The innovation and learning perspective requires the organisation to consider how it can continue to improve and create value.

Organisations must seek to acquire new skills and develop new products in order to maintain a competitive position in their respective market(s) and provide a basis from which the other perspectives of the balanced scorecard can be accomplished.

Performance measure: revenue generated from new routes introduced.

Financial perspective

The financial perspective considers whether the organisation meets the expectations of its shareholders and how it creates value for them.

This perspective focuses on traditional measures, such as growth, profitability and cost reduction.

Performance measure: increase in market share compared to Prime and Express.

320 People's Bank

Text references. The balanced scorecard approach to performance measurement is covered in Chapter 16.

Top tips. Part (a) is fairly straightforward but make sure you use the information in the scenario to help you answer the question. For part (b), make sure you structure your answer using the four headings of the balanced scorecard. This question requires you to analyse the information given and spot how factors affect one another. Don't forget to finish with a brief conclusion.

Easy marks. You should score highly in part (b) providing your answer covers all four perspectives of the balanced scorecard and picks out information from the scenario. There is not a great deal of technical knowledge required.

Examining team's comments. Performance on this question was reasonably strong, although poor exam technique in addressing the specific requirement did let some students down. A key skill in these questions is to identify linkages between measures – cause and effect relationships. For example, new lending to SMEs was down on target and this is not in line with the bank's third value (financial perspective). The drop in new lending is due to the fact that fewer colleagues have been trained to provide advice to SMEs (learning and growth perspective).

Marking scheme

			Marks
(a)	Discussion		4
(b)	Financial	4	
	Customer	4	
	Internal	4	
	Learning	_4_	
			16
			_20_

(a) The balanced scorecard approach looks not only at the financial performance but also non-financial performance. In order to maintain a competitive edge, organisations have to be very aware of the changing needs of their customers. In the case of The People's Bank, this has involved identifying specific categories of customers which have particular needs, like SMEs in a commercial context, or like the disabled or visually impaired in a non-commercial context. This permits these needs to be addressed.

The People's Bank has a vision and strategy which goes far beyond just making money. They want to help the community and disadvantaged people and give something back to customers also. Hence, by using the balanced scorecard, performance measures which address whether the Bank is being successful in pursuing their vision can be incorporated.

In addition, from a purely business perspective, if employees and customers are valued and internal processes are efficient, an organisation should have more chance of achieving long-term success anyway. So, even putting aside the social objectives The People's Bank has, the balanced scorecard can be useful to The People's Bank to measure these other aspects of future success too.

(b)   The performance of the bank will be considered under each of the headings used in the balanced scorecard:

Financial perspective

The People's Bank has had a year of mixed success when looking at the extent to which it has met its financial targets. Its return on capital employed (ROCE) shows how efficiently it has used its assets to generate profit for the business. The target for the year was 12% but it has only achieved an 11% return. The People's Bank's interest income, however, was in fact $0.5m higher than its target, which is good. This may have been achieved by offering slightly better interest rates to customers than competing banks, as the interest margin The People's Bank achieved is slightly lower than target. The most likely reason for the under target ROCE is therefore probably the investment which The People's Bank has made in IT security and facilities for the disabled and visually impaired. Whilst this may have reduced ROCE, this investment is essentially a good idea as it helps The People's Bank pursue its vision and will keep customers happy. It will also, in the case of the IT security investment, prevent the bank and its customers from losing money from fraud in the future.

The other performance measure, the amount of new lending to SMEs, is a little bit disappointing, given The People's Bank's stated value of making a difference to communities. The failure to meet this target may well be linked to the fact that an insufficient number of staff were trained to provide advice to SMEs and consequently, fewer of them may have been successful in securing additional finance.

Customer perspective

With regard to its customers, The People's Bank has performed well in the year. It has exceeded its target to provide mortgages to new homeowners by 6,000. This is helping The People's Bank pursue its vision of helping new homeowners. It has also managed to beat the target for customer complaints such that there are only 1.5 complaints for every 1,000 customers, well below the target of 2. This may be as a result of improved processes at the bank or improved security. It is not clear what the precise reason is but it is definitely good for The People's Bank's reputation.

The bank has also exceeded both of its targets to help the disabled and visually impaired, which is good for its reputation and its stated value of making services more accessible.

Internal processes

The number of processes simplified within the bank has exceeded the target, which is good, and the success of which may well be reflected in the lower customer complaints levels. Similarly, the investment to improve IT systems has been a success, with only three incidences of fraud per 1,000 customers compared to the target of 10. However, perhaps because of the focus on this part of the business, only two new services have been made available via mobile banking, instead of the target of five, which is disappointing. Similarly, it is possible that some of the new systems have prevented the business from keeping its CO_2 emissions to their target level.

Learning and growth

The People's Bank has succeeded in helping the community, exceeding both of its targets relating to hours of paid volunteer work and number of community organisations supported by volunteers or funding. These additional costs could have contributed to the fact that the bank did not quite meet its target for ROCE.

However, the bank has not quite met its targets for helping small businesses and helping the disadvantaged. As mentioned earlier, the shortfall in training of employees to give advice to SMEs may have had an impact on The People's Bank's failure to meet its target lending to SMEs. As regards the percentage of trainee positions, the target was only just missed and this may well have been because the number of candidates applying from these areas was not as high as planned and the bank has no control over this.

Overall, the bank has had a fairly successful year, meeting many of its targets. However, it still has some work to do in order to meet its stated values and continue to pursue its vision.

MCQ mixed bank

321 The correct answer is: Penetration pricing in market A and price skimming in market B

Charging low prices initially to gain a large market share is market penetration pricing. Charging high prices in order to maximise unit profits is market skimming. Market penetration pricing is most effective when demand for the product is elastic (sensitive to price) and market skimming can maximise profitability when demand is inelastic (fairly insensitive to price).

Price elasticity of demand can be reduced by trying to persuade customers to buy products for reasons other than price, such as quality or design features. Advertising and sales promotion can also have the effect of reducing price elasticity.

322 This question appeared in the June 2017 exam.

The correct answer is: There is no inventory of work in progress or finished goods held

Holding no inventory of work in progress or finished goods is **not** consistent with the theory of constraints as the theory of constraints specifies that a small amount of buffer inventory should be maintained prior to the bottleneck activity so that the bottleneck never has to be slowed down or delayed. The other three statements are all consistent with the theory of constraints.

323 The correct answer is: 13.16%

Opening capital employed: $6m + $0.5m = $6.5m
Closing capital employed: $8m + ($0.5m + $0.2m) = $8.7m
Average capital employed: ($6.5m + $8.7m)/2 = $7.6m
Profit after depreciation: $1.6m − $0.6m = $1m
Therefore ROI = $1m/$7.6m = 13.16%.

324 The correct answer is: Rolling budget

A rolling budget is also known as a continuous budget.

325 The correct answer is: Division X profit will be $12,000. The company's profit will be $28,000 lower

External sales are 10,000 units and internal transfers are 5,000 units. The marginal cost per unit produced in Division X is $270,000/(10,000 + 5,000) = $18.

The marginal cost of making the units is $18 and the cost of external purchase would be $25. By purchasing externally, the company as a whole would incur additional costs of $(25 − 18) × 4,000 units = $28,000.

Division profit	$
Sales: External	350,000
Sales to Division Y (1,000 units)	30,000
	380,000
Variable costs (11,000 × $18)	(198,000)
Fixed costs	(170,000)
Profit	12,000

Division Y profits would increase by $20,000, Division X profits would fall by $48,000 and the company as a whole would suffer a fall in profit of $28,000.

326 The correct answer is: All of the above

Material flow cost accounting (MFCA) and input-output analysis are environmental management accounting techniques. Life cycle costing is concerned with analysing costs of a product over its entire life cycle from initial development to eventual withdrawal from the market. However, as long as you are aware that activity-based costing is a management accounting technique, the answer to this question is straightforward.

327 This question appeared in the June 15 exam.

The correct answer is: It identifies the market price of a product and then subtracts a desired profit margin to arrive at the target cost

A target cost is arrived at by identifying the market price of a product and then subtracting a desired profit margin from it.

328   The correct answer is: Substitute current raw materials with cheaper versions

Reducing the target cost gap should focus on ways of reducing the direct or variable costs of the product. This can be achieved by using a substitute cheaper raw material, but without affecting product quality. Reducing fixed overhead costs is not a way of reducing the gap. Using overtime is likely to increase costs and the target cost gap. Raising the selling price does not affect the cost gap directly, although it may lead to a reassessment of the target cost. .

329   The correct answer is: Do not employ a sales manager as profits would be expected to fall by $1,300

Expected value of increase in profit of hiring a sales manager:

		$
Good manager:	$180,000 × 30% × 35% =	18,900
Average manager:	$180,000 × 20% × 45% =	16,200
Poor manager:	$180,000 × 10% × 20% =	3,600
Expected value		38,700
Less the sales manager's salary		(40,000)
Effect on profit of hiring sales manager		(1,300)

330   The correct answer is: Simulation model

Sensitivity analysis is a term used to describe any technique whereby decision options are tested for their vulnerability to changes in any 'variable' such as expected sales volume, sales price per unit, material costs or labour costs. It can be used in any situation so long as the relationships between the key variables can be established. Stress tests are used to test for extreme possible circumstances and what the outcome might then be.

Simulation models can be used to deal with decision problems involving a large number of uncertain variables, when the relationship between the variables is uncertain or unpredictable. In practice, simulation modelling is carried out using a computer model.

331   The correct answer is: None of the above

All the costs are included in the lifetime costs of a product.

332   This question appeared in the March 2017 exam.

The correct answer is: Both ROI and RI will favour the older division.

ROI is calculated as (divisional profit/capital employed) × 100%

RI is calculated as divisional profit – (capital employed × cost of capital)

To see how ROI and RI would treat each division, it's a fair assumption to assume they're both generating the same profit (as they're virtually identical).

Both divisions have the same assets – however the older division will have suffered more depreciation, as it is three years older – reducing its capital employed.

Looking at both calculations, the smaller capital employed will give the older division an artificially high ROI compared to the newer division.

Likewise, the 'imputed interest' (capital employed × cost of capital) for the older division will be smaller. Both divisions use the overall company's cost of capital, thus giving the older division a higher RI than the newer division.

If in doubt with questions like this, make up some numbers. If they both generate profits of $100k, but the older division's assets have a NBV of $500k compared to the newer division's $2,000k (for example), this gives ROI of 20% and 5% respectively. Similarly, if you use a cost of capital of 10% (keeping the numbers simple), this gives RI of $50k and ($100k) – both clearly favouring the older division.

333 The correct answer is: A cost attributable directly to a division over which the manager may or may not have control

A distinction can be made between controllable fixed costs of a division, which are fixed costs over which the divisional manager has some control or influence, and traceable fixed costs which are costs attributable to a division but over which the manager has no control. For example, if a division is located in separate premises, the rental cost or depreciation cost of the premises is a traceable cost to the division, but the divisional manager may have no control over the amount of the expense.

334 The correct answer is: $P = 16 - 0.0025Q$

If $P = a - bQ$, a is the price when $Q = 0$

$Q = 0$ when $P = 6 + [(4,000/200) \times 0.50] = 16$

Demand falls by 200 for every $0.5 change in the price, so the demand curve formula is:

$P = 16 - (0.5/200) \times Q$

$P = 16 - 0.0025Q$

335 The correct answer is: Both 1 and 2

There may be more than one cost driver for an activity, but in order to simplify the ABC system, it is usual to use just one cost driver per activity. ABC does involve some arbitrary apportionment of overhead costs to activities, such as factory rental and heating costs. Alternatively, general overheads are absorbed into costs on a direct labour hour or machine hour basis: this too is an arbitrary method of charging overheads.

OTQ mixed bank

336 The correct answer is:

ABC has evolved as a response to the increase in support activities in modern organisations.	**TRUE**	
Absorption costing uses volume as a basis for cost allocation, and so tends to allocate too great a proportion of overheads to low volume products.		**FALSE**

ABC involves the identification of factors known as cost drivers, which drive the costs of an organisation's major activities. Overhead costs relating to support services are then charged to products on the basis of their usage of an activity. Statement 1 is therefore true.

Absorption costing uses volume as a basis for cost allocation, and so tends to allocate too great a proportion of overheads to **high** volume products and too **low** a proportion of overheads to low volume products.

337 The correct answer is: 15,000

Sales = $62,500

Breakeven sales = $13,000/0.40 = $32,500

Margin of safety (sales revenue) = $62,500 − $32,500 = $30,000

Margin of safety (units) $30,000/$2 = 15,000 units

338 The correct answer is:

It focuses solely on non-financial performance measures.		**FALSE**
It looks at both internal and external matters concerning the organisation.	**TRUE**	

The balanced scorecard includes a financial perspective. It also has a customer perspective, which means that it is concerned with external as well as internal matters.

339 The correct answer is:

The costs of implementation may outweigh the benefits.	**TRUE**	
Employees will always welcome any new system which improves planning and control within the organisation.		**FALSE**

The costs of introducing a new system may exceed the benefits. Employees are often inclined to resist change, even though the planned changes may improve planning and control within the organisation.

340 This question appeared in the June 15 exam.

The correct answers are:

Contribution will be increased by $2 for each additional kg of material B purchased at the current market price.	**TRUE**	
The maximum price which should be paid for an additional kg of material B is $2.		**FALSE**
Contribution will be increased by $1.20 for each additional kg of material B purchased at the current market price		**FALSE**
The maximum price which should be paid for an additional kg of material B is $2.80	**TRUE**	

Statement 2 is wrong as it reflects the common misconception that the shadow price is the maximum price which should be paid, rather than the maximum extra over the current purchase price.

Statement 3 is wrong but could be thought to be correct if 2 was wrongly assumed to be correct.

341 The correct answer is: $13,420 Adverse

	Actual sales units in std mix	Standard sales units in std mix	Difference in units	Standard contribution	Variance
Product X	40,960	41,400	440(A)	$24	$10,560(A)
Product Y	10,240	10,350	110(A)	$26	$2,860(A)
Total	51,200	51,750	550(A)		$13,420(A)

342 The correct answers are:

Logical access controls	**YES**	
Database controls	**YES**	
Hierarchical passwords	**YES**	
Range checks		**NO**

A range check is a control within specific IT applications to check that an input item of data has a value within an acceptable range, and any input items with a value outside the range are reported as errors.

343 The correct answer is: $59,000

	$
Total cost at 1,200 units	66,600
Deduct step increase in fixed costs	(6,000)
Total cost at 1,200 units excluding step cost increase	60,600
Total cost of 900 units	58,200
Therefore variable cost of 300 units	2,400

Variable cost per unit = $8

	$
Total cost of 900 units	58,200
Variable cost of 900 units (at 8 each)	7,200
Therefore fixed costs at this level of output	51,000

Total costs of 1,000 units = $51,000 + $(8 × 1,000) = $59,000

344 The correct answer is: 'There are significant economies of scale' and 'The firm wishes to discourage new entrants to the market'.

'Demand is relatively inelastic' is incorrect because a penetration policy is favourable in circumstances where demand is relatively **elastic**. 'The product life cycle is particularly short' favours a market skimming policy.

345 The correct answer is:

They are designed to report on existing operations.	TRUE	
They have an external focus.		FALSE

Management information systems provide information to management about existing operations, and have an internal focus.

346 The correct answer is:

Generation of revenues	YES	
Investment in non-current assets	YES	
Investment in working capital	YES	
Apportioned head office costs		NO

The manager of an investment centre should have control over costs, revenues, and non-current assets and working capital of the centre, but does not have control over general head office costs.

347 The correct answer is: ROI: No   RI: Yes

Current ROI 360/1,600 = 22.5% Residual income (in \$'000) = 360 − (18% × 1,600) = \$72 ie \$72,000

The new project: ROI = 25,000/130,000 = 19.2%. This is less than 22.5%; therefore ROI will fall.

New project RI = 25,000 − (18% × 130,000) = + \$1,600. RI would increase.

348 The correct answer is: 1,400

Fixed costs + target profit required: \$30,000 + \$3,600 = \$33,600

Weighted average of contributions:

[(3 × \$32) + (2 × \$12)]/5 = \$24

\$33,600/\$24 = 1,400 units.

349 The correct answer is: \$225

Selling price/unit (\$)	300	255	240	225
Contribution/unit (\$)	186	141	126	111
Demand (units)	1,800	2,400	3,600	4,200
	\$334,800	\$338,400	\$453,600	\$466,200

350 The correct answer is: \$4,957.50

Incremental purchases = (1,500 − 945)kg × \$4.25 per kg = \$2,358.75

Opportunity cost of materials already purchased = 945 kg × \$2.75 = \$2,598.75

Total relevant cost = \$2,358.75 + \$2,358.75 = \$4,957.50

351 The correct answers are:

Employees will focus on eliminating wasteful expenditure.	TRUE	
Short-term benefits could be emphasised over long-term benefits.	TRUE	

Zero-based budgeting begins by looking at the minimum budgeted expenditure, and building a budget from this zero base. This encourages employees to focus on wasteful and unnecessary spending.

However the focus is on short-term savings and may give insufficient consideration to longer-term benefits of current spending.

352 This question appeared in the March 2017 exam.

The correct answer is: $9,000

There are two types of costs of producing information in this case – direct and indirect. A direct cost can be completely attributed to obtaining the information. An indirect cost is required in order to produce the information, but can't be completely attributed to it.

In this example, only the apportionment of the technology insurance cost is indirect – all of the others are solely related to producing the information.

353 This question appeared in the June 2017 exam.

The correct answer is: $75

The relevant cost of diverting labour away from existing production when the resource is being used at full capacity is the variable cost of a labour hour + opportunity cost. The opportunity cost in this case would be the contribution of product P lost for every hour diverted away from its production. As each unit of P takes one labour hour the opportunity cost per labour hour is $25 and the cost per labour hour must be $30 (from the cost card). Therefore the relevant cost of labour is $55. Note that the question asks for the total relevant cost of labour and variable overheads. As these overheads are variable they are incurred when production happens and so are relevant and the variable overheads cost per hour is $20 (from the cost card). The total relevant cost of labour and variable overheads is $75

354 The correct answer is: $110

This question appeared in the September 2015 exam and the examining team noted that it was not answered well by students.

Relevant cost = contribution lost + labour cost
        = $4 + $7
        = $11 per hour
$11 × 10 hours = $110

355 This question appeared in the September 2017 exam.

The correct answer is: $204,500

To calculate breakeven revenue in a multi-product situation requires the annual fixed costs to be divided by the weighted average contribution to sales ratio. To do this firstly the selling price of both products need to be determined.

The selling price of a table is calculated as the variable cost divided by 1 – the C/S ratio: $120/(1 – 0.4) = $200. The selling price of a chair is $16/(1 – 0.6) = $40. Once the selling prices are determined the contribution of each product can be calculated. For a table this will be $200 × 0.4 = $80 and for a chair this will be $40 × 0.6 = $24. Now we have the selling price and contribution for both products we can calculate the weighted average C/S ratio.

Sales revenue based on the sales mix will be (1 × $200) + (4 × $40) = $360 and contribution will be (1 × $80) + (4 × $24) = $176; this gives a C/S ratio of 0.489. Therefore the breakeven revenue is $100,000/0.489 = $204,499 and to the nearest hundred dollars is $204,500.

Mock exams

ACCA
Performance Management

Mock Exam 1
(September 2016 CBE)

Question Paper: 3 hours
ALL questions are compulsory and MUST be attempted

DO NOT OPEN THIS PAPER UNTIL YOU ARE READY TO START UNDER EXAMINATION CONDITIONS

Section A – ALL FIFTEEN questions are compulsory and MUST be attempted

Each question is worth 2 marks.

1 A manufacturing company which produces a range of products has developed a budget for the life cycle of a new product, P. The information in the following table relates exclusively to product P:

	Lifetime total	Per unit
Design costs	$800,000	
Direct manufacturing costs		$20
Depreciation costs	$500,000	
Decommissioning costs	$20,000	
Machine hours		4
Production and sales units	300,000	

The company's total fixed production overheads are budgeted to be $72 million each year and total machine hours are budgeted to be 96 million hours. The company absorbs overheads on a machine hour basis.

What is the budgeted life-cycle cost per unit for product P?

○ $24.40
○ $25.73
○ $27.40
○ $22.73

2 A company makes and sells product X and product Y. Twice as many units of product Y are made and sold as that of product X. Each unit of product X makes a contribution of $10 and each unit of product Y makes a contribution of $4. Fixed costs are $90,000.

What is the total number of units which must be made and sold to make a profit of $45,000 (to the nearest whole unit)?

[   ] units

3 Product GX consists of a mix of three materials, J, K and L. The standard material cost of a unit of GX is as follows:

		$
Material J	5 kg at $4 per kg	20
Material K	2 kg at $12 per kg	24
Material L	3 kg at $8 per kg	24

During March, 3,000 units of GX were produced, and actual usage was:

Material J 13,200 kg
Material K 6,500 kg
Material L 9,300 kg

What was the favourable materials yield variance for March (to the nearest whole $)?

$ [   ]

4 A manufacturer and retailer of kitchens introduces an enterprise resource planning system.

Which of the following is **NOT** likely to be a potential benefit of introducing this system?

○ Schedules of labour are prepared for manufacturing
○ Inventory records are updated automatically
○ Sales are recorded into the financial ledgers
○ Critical strategic information can be summarised

5   Different management accounting techniques can be used to account for environmental costs.

One of these techniques involves analysing costs under three distinct categories: material, system, and delivery and disposal.

What is this technique known as?

O   Activity-based costing
O   Life-cycle costing
O   Input-output analysis
O   Flow cost accounting

6   A government is trying to assess schools by using a range of financial and non-financial factors. One of the chosen methods is the percentage of students passing five exams or more.

Which of the three Es in the value-for-money framework is being measured here?

O   Economy
O   Efficiency
O   Effectiveness
O   Expertise

7   Which of the following techniques is **NOT** relevant to target costing?

O   Value analysis
O   Variance analysis
O   Functional analysis
O   Activity analysis

8   A government department generates information which should not be disclosed to anyone who works outside of the department. There are many other government departments working within the same building.

Which of the following would **NOT** be an effective control procedure for the generation and distribution of the information within the government department?

O   If working from home, departmental employees must use a memory stick to transfer data, as laptop computers are not allowed to leave the department.

O   All departmental employees must enter non-disclosed and regularly updated passwords to access their computers.

O   All authorised employees must swipe an officially issued, personal identity card at the entrance to the department before they can gain access.

O   All hard copies of confidential information must be shredded at the end of each day or locked overnight in a safe if needed again.

9   A jewellery company makes rings (R) and necklaces (N).

The resources available to the company have been analysed and two constraints have been identified:

Labour time $3R + 2N \leq 2,400$ hours
Machine time $0.5R + 0.4N \leq 410$ hours

The management accountant has used linear programming to determine that R = 500 and N = 400.

Indicate, by clicking on the relevant boxes in the table below, whether each of the following is a slack resource.

	Slack resource	
Labour time available	YES	NO
Machine time available	YES	NO

10   At the end of 20X1, an investment centre has net assets of $1m and annual operating profits of $190,000. However, the bookkeeper forgot to account for the following:

A machine with a net book value of $40,000 was sold at the start of the year for $50,000 and replaced with a machine costing $250,000. Both the purchase and sale are cash transactions. No depreciation is charged in the year of purchase or disposal. The investment centre calculates return on investment (ROI) based on closing net assets.

Assuming no other changes to profit or net assets, what is the return on investment (ROI) for the year?

○   18.8%
○   19.8%
○   15.1%
○   15.9%

11   A manufacturing company uses three processes to make its two products, X and Y. The time available on the three processes is reduced because of the need for preventative maintenance and rest breaks.

The table below details the process times per product and daily time available:

Process	Hours available per day	Hours required to make one unit of product X	Hours required to make one unit of product Y
1	22	1.00	0.75
2	22	0.75	1.00
3	18	1.00	0.50

Daily demand for product X and product Y is 10 units and 16 units respectively.

Which of the following will improve throughput?

○   Increasing the efficiency of the maintenance routine for Process 2
○   Increasing the demand for both products
○   Reducing the time taken for rest breaks on Process 3
○   Reducing the time product X requires for Process 1

12   PlasBas Co uses recycled plastic to manufacture shopping baskets for local retailers. The standard price of the recycled plastic is $0.50 per kg and standard usage of recycled plastic is 0.2 kg for each basket. The budgeted production was 80,000 baskets.

Due to recent government incentives to encourage recycling, the standard price of recycled plastic was expected to reduce to $0.40 per kg. The actual price paid by the company was $0.42 per kg and 100,000 baskets were manufactured using 20,000 kg of recycled plastic.

What is the materials operational price variance?

○ $2,000 Favourable
○ $1,600 Favourable
○ $400 Adverse
○ $320 Adverse

13 A profit centre manager claims that the poor performance of her division is entirely due to factors outside her control.

She has submitted the following table along with notes from a market expert, which she believes explains the cause of the poor performance:

Category	Budget this year	Actual this year	Actual last year	Market expert notes
Sales volume (units)	500	300	400	The entire market has decreased by 25% compared to last year. The product will be obsolete in four years
Sales revenue	$50,000	$28,500	$40,000	Rivalry in the market saw selling prices fall by 10%
Total material cost	$10,000	$6,500	$8,000	As demand for the raw materials is decreasing, suppliers lowered their prices by 5%

After adjusting for the external factors outside the manager's control, in which category/categories is there evidence of poor performance?

- O Material cost only
- O Sales volume and sales price
- O Sales price and material cost
- O Sales price only

14 Indicate, by clicking on the relevant boxes in the table below, whether each of the following statements regarding market penetration as a pricing strategy are correct or incorrect.

It is useful if significant economies of scale can be achieved	CORRECT	INCORRECT
It is useful if demand for a product is highly elastic	CORRECT	INCORRECT

15 A company makes two products using the same type of materials and skilled workers. The following information is available:

	Product A	Product B
Budgeted volume (units)	1,000	2,000
Material per unit ($)	10	20
Labour per unit ($)	5	20

Fixed costs relating to material handling amount to $100,000. The cost driver for these costs is the volume of material purchased.

General fixed costs, absorbed on the basis of labour hours, amount to $180,000. Using activity-based costing, what is the total fixed overhead amount to be absorbed into each unit of product B (to the nearest whole $)?

$ [   ]

Section B – All 15 questions are compulsory and MUST be attempted

Mylo

The following scenario relates to questions 16–20.

Mylo runs a cafeteria situated on the ground floor of a large corporate office block. Each of the five floors of the building are occupied and there are in total 1,240 employees.

Mylo sells lunches and snacks in the cafeteria. The lunch menu is freshly prepared each morning and Mylo has to decide how many meals to make each day. As the office block is located in the city centre, there are several other places situated around the building where staff can buy their lunch, so the level of demand for lunches in the cafeteria is uncertain.

Mylo has analysed daily sales over the previous six months and established four possible demand levels and their associated probabilities. He has produced the following payoff table to show the daily profits which could be earned from the lunch sales in the cafeteria:

		Supply level			
Demand level	Probability	450	620	775	960
		$	$	$	$
450	0.15	1,170	980	810	740
620	0.30	1,170	1,612	1,395	1,290
775	0.40	1,170	1,612	2,015	1,785
960	0.15	1,170	1,612	2,015	2,496

16 If Mylo adopts a maximin approach to decision making, which daily supply level will he choose?

[   ] lunches

17 If Mylo adopts a minimax regret approach to decision making, which daily supply level will he choose?

○ 450 lunches
○ 620 lunches
○ 775 lunches
○ 960 lunches

18 Which **TWO** of the following statements are true if Mylo chooses to use expected values to assist in his decision making regarding the number of lunches to be provided?

☐ Mylo would be considered to be taking a defensive and conservative approach to his decision.

☐ Expected values will ignore any variability which could occur across the range of possible outcomes.

☐ Expected values will not take into account the likelihood of the different outcomes occurring.

☐ Expected values can be applied by Mylo, as he is evaluating a decision which occurs many times over.

19 The human resources department has offered to undertake some research to help Mylo to predict the number of employees who will require lunch in the cafeteria each day. This information will allow Mylo to prepare an accurate number of lunches each day.

What is the maximum amount which Mylo would be willing to pay for this information (to the nearest whole $)?

○ $191
○ $359
○ $478
○ $175

20   Mylo is now considering investing in a speciality coffee machine. He has estimated the following daily results for the new machine:

	$
Sales (650 units)	1,300
Variable costs	(845)
Contribution	455
Incremental fixed costs	(70)
Profit	385

Indicate, by clicking on the relevant boxes in the table below, whether each of the following statements regarding the sensitivity of this investment are true or false.

The investment is more sensitive to a change in sales volume than sales price	TRUE	FALSE
If the variable costs increase by 44% the investment will make a loss	TRUE	FALSE
The investment's sensitivity to incremental fixed costs is 550%	TRUE	FALSE
The margin of safety is 84.6%	TRUE	FALSE

Corfe Co

The following scenario relates to questions 21–25.

Corfe Co is a business which manufactures computer laptop batteries and it has developed a new battery which has a longer usage time than batteries currently available in laptops. The selling price of the battery is forecast to be $45.

The maximum production capacity of Corfe Co is 262,500 units. The company's management accountant is currently preparing an annual flexible budget and has collected the following information so far:

Production (units)	185,000	200,000	225,000
	$	$	$
Material costs	740,000	800,000	900,000
Labour costs	1,017,500	1,100,000	1,237,500
Fixed costs	750,000	750,000	750,000

In addition to the above costs, the management accountant estimates that for each increment of 50,000 units produced, one supervisor will need to be employed. A supervisor's annual salary is $35,000.

The production manager does not understand why the flexible budgets have been produced as they have always used a fixed budget previously.

21   Assuming the budgeted figures are correct, what would the flexed total production cost be if production is 80% of maximum capacity?

- O $2,735,000
- O $2,770,000
- O $2,885,000
- O $2,920,000

22   The management accountant has said that a machine maintenance cost was not included in the flexible budget but needs to be taken into account.

The new battery will be manufactured on a machine currently owned by Corfe Co, which was previously used for a product which has now been discontinued. The management accountant estimates that every 1,000 units will take 14 hours to produce. The annual machine hours and maintenance costs for the machine for the last four years have been as follows:

	Machine time (hours)	Maintenance costs ($'000)
Year 1	5,000	850
Year 2	4,400	735
Year 3	4,850	815
Year 4	1,800	450

What is the estimated maintenance cost if production of the battery is 80% of maximum capacity (to the nearest $'000)?

- O $575,000
- O $593,000
- O $500,000
- O $735,000

23   In the first month of production of the new battery, actual sales were 18,000 units and the sales revenue achieved was $702,000. The budgeted sales units were 17,300.

Based on this information, which of the following statements is true?

- O   When the budget is flexed, the sales variance will include both the sales volume and sales price variances.

- O   When the budget is flexed, the sales variance will only include the sales volume variance.

- O   When the budget is flexed, the sales variance will only include the sales price variance.

- O   When the budget is flexed, the sales variance will include the sales mix and quantity variances and the sales price variance.

24   Which of the following statements relating to the preparation of a flexible budget for the new battery are true?

- (1)   The budget could be time-consuming to produce as splitting out semi-variable costs may not be straightforward

- (2)   The range of output over which assumptions about how costs will behave could be difficult to determine

- (3)   The flexible budget will give managers more opportunity to include budgetary slack than a fixed budget

- (4)   The budget will encourage all activities and their value to the organisation to be reviewed and assessed

- O   1 and 2
- O   1, 2 and 3
- O   1 and 4
- O   2, 3 and 4

25   The management accountant intends to use a spreadsheet for the flexible budget in order to analyse
      performance of the new battery.

      Which of the following statements are benefits regarding the use of spreadsheets for budgeting?

      (1)   The user can change input variables and a new version of the budget can be quickly produced

      (2)   Errors in a formula can be easily traced and data can be difficult to corrupt in a spreadsheet

      (3)   A spreadsheet can take account of qualitative factors to allow decisions to be fully evaluated

      (4)   Managers can carry out sensitivity analysis more easily on a budget model which is held in a
             spreadsheet

      O   1, 3 and 4
      O   1, 2 and 4
      O   1 and 4
      O   2 and 3

Helot Co

The following scenario relates to questions 26–30.

Helot Co develops and sells computer games. It is well known for launching innovative and interactive role-playing
games and its new releases are always eagerly anticipated by the gaming community. Customers value the
technical excellence of the games and the durability of the product and packaging.

Helot Co has previously used a traditional absorption costing system and full cost plus pricing to cost and price its
products. It has recently recruited a new finance director who believes the company would benefit from using target
costing. They are keen to try this method on a new game concept called Spartan, which has been recently
approved.

After discussion with the board, the finance director undertook some market research to find out customers'
opinions on the new game concept and to assess potential new games offered by competitors. The results were
used to establish a target selling price of $45 for Spartan and an estimated total sales volume of 350,000 units.
Helot Co wants to achieve a target profit margin of 35%.

The finance director has also begun collecting cost data for the new game and has projected the following:

Production costs per unit	$
Direct material	3.00
Direct labour	2.50
Direct machining	5.05
Set up	0.45
Inspection and testing	4.30

Total non-production costs	$'000
Design (salaries and technology)	2,500
Marketing consultants	1,700
Distribution	1,400

26 Which **TWO** of the following statements would the finance director have used to explain to Helot Co's board what the benefits were of adopting a target costing approach so early in the game's life cycle?

☐ Costs will be split into material, system, and delivery and disposal categories for improved cost reduction analysis.

☐ Customer requirements for quality, cost and timescales are more likely to be included in decisions on product development.

☐ Its key concept is based on how to turn material into sales as quickly as possible in order to maximise net cash.

☐ The company will focus on designing out costs prior to production, rather than cost control during live production.

27 What is the forecast cost gap for the new game (to two decimal places)?

$ [   ]

28 The board of Helot Co has asked the finance director to explain what activities can be undertaken to close a cost gap on its computer games.

Which **TWO** of the following would be appropriate ways for Helot Co to close a cost gap?

☐ Buy cheaper, lower grade plastic for the game discs and cases

☐ Using standard components wherever possible in production

☐ Employ more trainee game designers on lower salaries

☐ Use the company's own online gaming websites for marketing

29 The direct labour cost per unit has been based on an expected learning rate of 90% but now the finance director has realised that a 95% learning rate should be applied.

Which of the following statements is true?

○ The target cost will decrease and the cost gap will increase
○ The target cost will increase and the cost gap will decrease
○ The target cost will remain the same and the cost gap will increase
○ The target cost will remain the same and the cost gap will decrease

30 Helot Co is thinking about expanding its business and introducing a new computer repair service for customers. The board has asked if target costing could be applied to this service.

Which of the following statements regarding services and the use of target costing within the service sector is true?

○ The purchase of a service transfers ownership to the customer.
○ Labour resource usage is high in services relative to material requirements.
○ A standard service cannot be produced and so target costing cannot be used.
○ Service characteristics include uniformity, perishability and intangibility.

Section C – Both questions are compulsory and MUST be attempted

31 Jungle Co

Jungle Co is a very successful multinational retail company. It has been selling a large range of household and electronic goods for some years. One year ago, it began using new suppliers from the country of Slabak, where labour is very cheap, for many of its household goods. In 20X4, Jungle Co also became a major provider of 'cloud' computing services, investing heavily in cloud technology. These services provide customers with a way of storing and accessing data and programs over the internet rather than on their computers' hard drives.

All Jungle Co customers have the option to sign up for the company's 'Gold' membership service, which provides next day delivery on all orders, in return for an annual service fee of $40. In September 20X5, Jungle Co formed its own logistics company and took over the delivery of all of its parcels, instead of using the services of international delivery companies.

Over the last year, there has been worldwide growth in the electronic goods market of 20%. Average growth rates and gross profit margins for cloud computing service providers have been 50% and 80% respectively in the last year. Jungle Co's prices have remained stable year on year for all sectors of its business, with price competitiveness being crucial to its continuing success as the leading global electronic retailer.

The following information is available for Jungle Co for the last two financial years:

	Notes	31 August 20X6 $'000	31 August 20X5 $'000
Revenue	1	94,660	82,320
Cost of sales	2	(54,531)	(51,708)
Gross profit		40,129	30,612
Administration expenses	3	(2,760)	(1,720)
Distribution expenses		(13,420)	(13,180)
Other operating expenses		(140)	(110)
Net profit		23,809	15,602

Notes

1 **Breakdown of revenue**

	31 August 20X6 $'000	31 August 20X5 $'000
Household goods	38,990	41,160
Electronic goods	41,870	32,640
Cloud computing services	12,400	6,520
Gold membership fees	1,400	2,000
	94,660	82,320

2 **Breakdown of cost of sales**

	31 August 20X6 $'000	31 August 20X5 $'000
Household goods	23,394	28,812
Electronic goods	26,797	21,216
Cloud computing services	4,240	1,580
Gold membership fees	100	100
	54,531	51,708

3 **Administration expenses**

Included in these costs are the costs of running the customer service department ($860,000 in 20X5; $1,900,000 in 20X6). This department deals with customer complaints.

4 Non-financial data

	31 August 20X6 $'000	31 August 20X5 $'000
Percentage of orders delivered on time	74%	92%
No. of customer complaints	1,400,000	320,000
No. of customers	7,100,000	6,500,000
Percentage of late 'Gold' member deliveries	14.00%	2.00%

Required

Discuss the financial and non-financial performance of Jungle Co for the year ending 31 August 20X6.

Note. There are 7 marks available for calculations and 13 marks available for discussion.

(Total = 20 marks)

32 CSC Co

CSC Co is a health food company producing and selling three types of high-energy products – cakes, shakes and cookies – to gyms and health food shops. Shakes are the newest of the three products and were first launched three months ago. Each of the three products has two special ingredients, sourced from a remote part the world. The first of these, Singa, is a super-energising rare type of caffeine. The second, Betta, is derived from an unusual plant believed to have miraculous health benefits.

CSC Co's projected manufacture costs and selling prices for the three products are as follows:

	Cakes	Cookies	Shakes
Per unit	$	$	$
Selling price	5.40	4.90	6.00
Costs:			
Ingredients: Singa ($1.20 per gram)	0.30	0.60	1.20
Ingredients: Betta ($1.50 per gram)	0.75	0.30	1.50
Other ingredients	0.25	0.45	0.90
Labour ($10 per hour)	1.00	1.20	0.80
Variable overheads	0.50	0.60	0.40
Contribution	2.60	1.75	1.20

For each of the three products, the expected demand for the next month is 11,200 cakes, 9,800 cookies and 2,500 shakes.

The total fixed costs for the next month are $3,000.

CSC Co has just found out that the supply of Betta is going to be limited to 12,000 grams next month. Prior to this, CSC Co had signed a contract with a leading chain of gyms, Encompass Health, to supply it with 5,000 shakes each month, at a discounted price of $5.80 per shake, starting immediately. The order for the 5,000 shakes is not included in the expected demand levels above.

Required

(a) Assuming that CSC Co keeps to its agreement with Encompass Health, calculate the shortage of Betta, the resulting optimum production plan and the total profit for next month. **(6 marks)**

One month later, the supply of Betta is still limited and CSC Co is considering whether it should breach its contract with Encompass Health so that it can optimise its profits.

Required

(b) Discuss whether CSC Co should breach the agreement with Encompass Health.

Note. No further calculations are required. **(4 marks)**

Several months later, the demand for both cakes and cookies has increased significantly to 20,000 and 15,000 units per month respectively. However, CSC Co has lost the contract with Encompass Health and, after suffering from further shortages of supply of Betta, Singa and of its labour force, CSC Co has decided to stop making shakes at all. CSC Co now needs to use linear programming to work out the optimum production plan for cakes and cookies for the coming month. The variable 'x' is being used to represent cakes and the variable 'y' to represent cookies.

The following constraints have been formulated and a graph representing the new production problem has been drawn:

Singa: $0.25x + 0.5y \leq 12,000$
Betta: $0.5x + 0.2y \leq 12,500$
Labour: $0.1x + 0.12y \leq 3,000$
$x \leq 20,000$
$y \leq 15,000$
$x, y \geq 0$

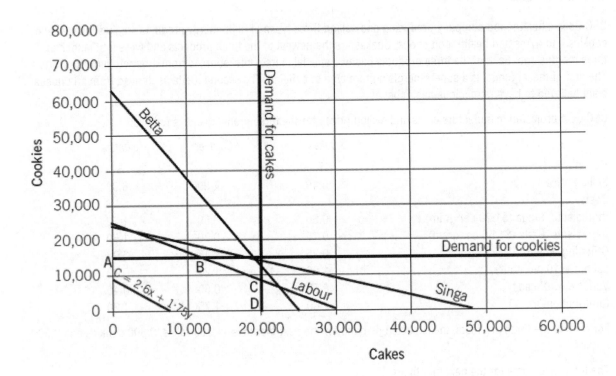

Required

(c) (i) Explain what the line labelled 'C = 2.6x + 1.75y' on the graph is, and what the area represented by the points 0ABCD means. **(4 marks)**

(ii) Explain how the optimum production plan will be found using the line labelled 'C = 2.6x + 1.75y' and identify the optimum point from the graph. **(2 marks)**

(iii) Explain what a slack value is and identify, from the graph, where slack will occur as a result of the optimum production plan. **(4 marks)**

Note. No calculations are needed for part (c).

(Total = 20 marks)

Answers

DO NOT TURN THIS PAGE UNTIL YOU HAVE
COMPLETED THE MOCK EXAM

A PLAN OF ATTACK

Managing your nerves

As you turn the pages to start this mock exam a number of thoughts are likely to cross your mind. At best, examinations cause anxiety so it is important to stay focused on your task for the next three hours! Developing an awareness of what is going on emotionally within you may help you manage your nerves. Remember, you are unlikely to banish the flow of adrenaline, but the key is to harness it to help you work steadily and quickly through your answers.

Working through this mock exam will help you develop the exam stamina you will need to keep going for three hours.

Managing your time

Planning and time management are two of the key skills which complement the technical knowledge you need to succeed. To keep yourself on time, do not be afraid to jot down your target completion times for each question, perhaps next to the title of the question on the exam. As all the questions are **compulsory**, you do not have to spend time wondering which question to answer!

Doing the exam

Actually doing the exam is a personal experience. There is not a single **right way**. As long as you submit complete answers to all questions after the three hours are up, then your approach obviously works.

Looking through the exam

Section A has 15 OTQs. This is the section of the exam where the ACCA examining team can test knowledge across the breadth of the syllabus. Make sure you read these questions carefully. The distractors are designed to present plausible, but incorrect, answers. Don't let them mislead you. If you really have no idea – guess. You may even be right.

Section B has three questions, each with a scenario and five objective test questions.

Section C has two longer questions:

- Question 31 is a traditional performance assessment question requiring a discussion on financial and non-financial performance of a business. There are plenty of easy marks available in this question. Make sure you lay out your percentage change calculations clearly and discuss possible reasons and implications for each one.

- Question 32 looks at limiting factors and linear programming. There is a lot to do on this question so make sure you don't over-run on time. You may want to start with part (c) first if linear programming is your strength.

Allocating your time

BPP's advice is to always allocate your time **according to the marks for the question**. However, **use common sense**. If you're doing a question but haven't a clue how to do part (b), you might be better off re-allocating your time and getting more marks on another question, where you can add something you didn't have time for earlier on. Make sure you leave time to recheck the MCQs and make sure you have answered them all.

Section A

Each question is worth 2 marks.

1    $27.40

OAR for fixed production overheads ($72 million/96 million hours) = $0.75 per hour

Total manufacturing costs (300,000 units × $20) = $6,000,000
Total design, depreciation and decommissioning costs = $1,320,000
Total fixed production overheads (300,000 units × 4 hours × $0.75) = $900,000
Total life-cycle costs = $8,220,000

Life-cycle cost per unit ($8,220,000/300,000 units) = $27.40

2   22,500

Two units of Y and one unit of X would give total contribution of $18.
Weighted average contribution per unit = $18/3 units = $6
Sales units to achieve target profit = ($90,000 + $45,000)/$6 = 22,500

3    $6,800

3,000 units should use 10 kg each (3,000 × 10) = 30,000 kg
3,000 units did use = 29,000 kg
Difference = 1,000 kg favourable
Valued at $6.80 per kg ($68/10 kg)
Variance = $6,800 favourable

4   Critical strategic information can be summarised

The tracking and summarising of critical strategic information is done by an Executive Information System (EIS).

The other three options are all likely to be potential benefits which would result from the introduction of an ERPS.

5   Flow cost accounting

Under a system of flow cost accounting, material flows are divided into three categories – material, system, and delivery and disposal.

6   Effectiveness

Exam success will be a given objective of a school, so it is a measure of effectiveness.

7   Variance analysis

Variance analysis is not relevant to target costing as it is a technique used for cost control at the production phase of the product life cycle. It is a feedback control tool by nature and target costing is feedforward.

Value analysis can be used to identify where small cost reductions can be applied to close a cost gap once production commences.

Functional analysis can be used at the product design stage. It ensures that a cost gap is reached or to ensure that the product design is one which includes only features which customers want.

Activity analysis identifies and describes activities in an organisation and evaluates their impact on operations to assess where improvements can be made.

8   If working from home, departmental employees must use a memory stick to transfer data, as laptop computers are not allowed to leave the department

A memory stick is much more likely to get mislaid and compromise security than a password-protected laptop. It is likely that memory sticks could get lost or that information is left on home computers.

In the context of the scenario all the other options are good practice.

9

Labour time available	YES
Machine time available	NO

If the values for R and N are substituted into the constraints:

Labour required = (3 × 500) + (2 × 400) = 2,300 hours which is less than what is available, so there is slack.

Machine time required = (0.5 × 500) + (0.4 × 400) = 410 hours which is exactly what is available, and so there is no slack.

10   19.8%

Revised annual profit = $190,000 + $10,000 profit on the sale of the asset = $200,000

Revised net assets = $1,000,000 − $40,000 NBV + $50,000 cash − $250,000 cash + $250,000 asset = $1,010,000

ROI = ($200,000/$1,010,000) × 100 = 19.8%

11   Increasing the efficiency of the maintenance routine for Process 2

Throughput is determined by the bottleneck resource. Process 2 is the bottleneck as it has insufficient time to meet demand.

The only option to improve Process 2 is to improve the efficiency of the maintenance routine. All the other three options either increase the time available on non-bottleneck resources or increase demand for an increase in supply which cannot be achieved.

12    $400 adverse

An operational variance compares revised price to actual price.

20,000 kg should cost $0.40 per kg at the revised price (20,000 kg × $0.40) = $8,000

20,000 kg did cost $0.42 per kg (20,000 kg × $0.42) = $8,400

Variance = $400 adverse

13   Material cost only

The material price when flexed is higher than budget while the external environment shows that prices are reducing. This indicates that although suppliers lowered their prices, the manager has still overspent which indicates poor performance.

When sales volumes and prices are flexed, it can be seen that the manager has performed better.

14

It is useful if significant economies of scale can be achieved	CORRECT
It is useful if demand for a product is highly elastic	CORRECT

Penetration pricing involves setting a low price when a product is first launched in order to obtain strong demand.

It is particularly useful if significant economies of scale can be achieved from a high volume of output and if demand is highly elastic and so would respond well to low prices.

15    $120

Total material budget ((1,000 units × $10) + (2,000 units × $20)) = $50,000
Fixed costs related to material handling = $100,000
OAR = $2/$ of material
Product B = $2 × $20 = $40

Total labour budget ((1,000 units × $5) + (2,000 units × $20) = $45,000

General fixed costs = $180,000
OAR = $4/$ of labour
Product B = $4 × $20 = $80

Total fixed overhead cost per unit of Product B ($40 + $80) = $120

Section B

Each question is worth 2 marks.

16   450 lunches

The maximin rule selects the maximum of the minimum outcomes for each supply level.

For Mylo the minimum outcomes are:

450 lunches – $1,170
620 lunches – $980
775 lunches – $810
960 lunches – $740

The maximum of these is at a supply level of 450 lunches.

17   960 lunches

The minimax regret rule selects the minimum of the maximum regrets.

Demand level	Supply level			
	450	620	775	960
	$	$	$	$
450	–	190	360	430
620	442	–	217	322
775	845	403	–	230
960	1,326	884	481	–
Max regret	1,326	884	481	430

The minimum of the maximum regrets is $430, so suggests a supply level of 960 lunches.

18   Expected values will ignore any variability which could occur across the range of possible outcomes. Expected values can be applied by Mylo as he is evaluating a decision which occurs many times over.

Expected values do not take into account the variability which could occur across a range of outcomes; a standard deviation would need to be calculated to assess that, so Statement 2 is correct.

Expected values are particularly useful for repeated decisions where the expected value will be the long-run average, so Statement 4 is correct.

Expected values are associated with risk-neutral decision makers. A defensive or conservative decision maker is risk averse, so Statement 1 is incorrect.

Expected values will take into account the likelihood of different outcomes occurring as this is part of the calculation, so Statement 3 is incorrect.

19    $191

This requires the calculation of the value of perfect information (VOPI).

Expected value with perfect information = (0.15 × $1,170) + (0.30 × $1,612) + (0.40 × $2,015) + (0.15 × $2,496) = $1,839.50

Expected value without perfect information would be the highest of the expected values for the supply levels = $1,648.25 (at a supply level of 775 lunches).

The value of perfect information is the difference between the expected value with perfect information and the expected value without perfect information = $1,839.50 – $1,648.25 = $191.25, therefore $191 to nearest whole $.

20

The investment is more sensitive to a change in sales volume than sales price	FALSE
If the variable costs increase by 44% the investment will make a loss	FALSE
The investment's sensitivity to incremental fixed costs is 550%	TRUE
The margin of safety is 84.6%	TRUE

The investment's sensitivity to fixed costs is 550% ((385/70) × 100), so Statement 3 is correct.

The margin of safety is 84.6%. Budgeted sales are 650 units and BEP sales are 100 units (70/0.7), therefore the margin of safety is 550 units which equates to 84.6% of the budgeted sales, so Statement 4 is therefore correct.

The investment is more sensitive to a change in sales price of 29.6%, so Statement 1 is incorrect.

If variable costs increased by 44%, it would still make a very small profit, so Statement 2 is incorrect.

21    $2,920,000

An 80% activity level is 210,000 units.

Material and labour costs are both variable. Material is $4 per unit and labour is $5.50 per unit.
Total variable costs = $9.50 × 210,000 units = $1,995,000
Fixed costs = $750,000
Supervision = $175,000 as five supervisors will be required for a production level of 210,000 units.

Total annual budgeted cost allowance = $1,995,000 + $750,000 + $175,000 = $2,920,000

22    $593,000

Variable cost per hour ($850,000 − $450,000)/(5,000 hours − 1,800 hours) = $125 per hour
Fixed cost ($850,000 − (5,000 hours × $125)) = $225,000
Number of machine hours required for production = 210 batches × 14 hours = 2,940 hours
Total cost ($225,000 + (2,940 hours × $125)) = $592,500, therefore $593,000 to the nearest $'000.

23   When the budget is flexed, the sales variance will only include the sales price variance

If the budget is flexed, then the effect on sales revenue of the difference between budgeted and actual sales volumes is removed, and the variance which is left is the sales price variance.

24   1 and 2

Flexible budgeting can be time-consuming to produce as splitting out semi-variable costs could be problematic, so Statement 1 is correct.

Estimating how costs behave over different levels of activity can be difficult to predict, so Statement 2 is correct.

A flexible budget will not encourage slack compared to a fixed budget, so Statement 3 is incorrect.

It is a zero-based budget, not a flexible budget, which assesses all activities for their value to the organisation, so Statement 4 is incorrect.

25   1 and 4

Spreadsheets can be used to change input variables and new versions of the budgets can be more quickly produced, so Statement 1 is correct.

Sensitivity analysis is also easier to do as variables are more easily changed and manipulated to assess their impact, so Statement 4 is correct.

A common problem of spreadsheets is that it is difficult to trace errors in a spreadsheet and data can be easily corrupted if a cell is changed or data is input in the wrong place, so Statement 2 is incorrect.

Spreadsheets do not show qualitative factors; they show predominantly quantitative data, so Statement 3 is incorrect.

26　Customer requirements for quality, cost and timescales are more likely to be included in decisions on product development.

The company will focus on designing out costs prior to production, rather than cost control during live production

Target costing does encourage looking at customer requirements early on so that features valued by customers are included, so Statement 2 is correct. It will also force the company to closely assess the design and is likely to be successful if costs are designed out at this stage rather than later once production has started, so Statement 4 is correct.

Statement 1 explains a benefit of flow cost accounting. Statement 3 explains the concept of throughput accounting.

27　$2.05

Target price is $45 and the profit margin is 35% which results in a target cost of $29.25. The current estimated cost is $31.30 which results in a cost gap of $2.05.

28　Using standard components wherever possible in production
Use the company's own online gaming websites for marketing

Using more standardised components and using its own websites for marketing will reduce processing and marketing costs.

Using cheaper materials and trainee designers will reduce costs but could impact the quality and customer perception of the product, which would impact the target price.

29　The target cost will remain the same and the cost gap will increase

The change in the learning rate will increase the current estimated cost, which will increase the cost gap.

The target cost will be unaffected, as this is based on the target selling price and profit margin; neither of which are changing.

30　Labour resource usage is high in services relative to material requirements.

Services do use more labour relative to materials.

The other three statements are incorrect as uniformity is not a characteristic of services, there is no transfer of ownership and although it is difficult to standardise a service due to the human influence, target costing can still be used.

Section C

31 Jungle Co

> **Text reference.** Performance analysis is covered in Chapter 16.
>
> **Top tips.** You need to perform some calculations in order to have enough to discuss. Percentage change calculations are key. In your discussion, it is important to suggest why things have changed and how this might affect other parts of the business.
>
> **Easy marks.** The easy marks are for the percentage change calculations.
>
> **Examining team comments.** Marks are awarded for percentage change calculations but not for calculations of absolute change. Points such as 'Cost of sales have decreased by 18%. This is a good performance.' were common but, apart from the calculation, scored no marks. Answers which looked at why cost of sales might have decreased, or what impact that might have had, scored many more marks.

Marking scheme

	Marks
Sales volumes (up to 2 marks per revenue stream)	8
COS and gross margins	5
Administration expenses/customer complaints	3
Distribution costs/late deliveries	2
Net profit margin	**20**

Sales volumes

Since prices have remained stable year on year, it can be assumed that changes to revenue are as a result of increases or decreases in sales volumes. Overall, revenue has increased by 15%, which is a substantial increase. In order to understand what has happened in the business, it is necessary to consider sales by looking at each of the different categories.

Household goods

Although this was the largest category of sales for Jungle Co last year, this year it has decreased by 5% and has now been overtaken by electronic goods. The company changed suppliers for many of its household goods during the year, buying them instead from a country where labour was cheap. It may be that this has affected the quality of the goods, thus leading to decreased demand.

Electronic goods

Unlike household goods, demand for electronic goods from Jungle Co has increased dramatically by 28%. This is now Jungle Co's leading revenue generator. This is partly due to the fact that the electronic goods market has grown by 20% worldwide. However, Jungle Co has even outperformed this, meaning that it has secured a larger segment of the market.

Cloud computing service

This area of Jungle Co's business is growing rapidly, with the company seeing a 90% increase in this revenue stream in the last year. Once again, the company has outperformed the market, where the average growth rate is only 50%, suggesting that the investment in the cloud technology was worthwhile.

Gold membership fees

This area of the business is relatively small but has shrunk further, with a decrease in revenue of 30%. This may be because customers are dissatisfied with the service that they are receiving. The number of late deliveries for Gold members has increased from 2% to 14% since Jungle Co began using its own logistics company. This has probably been at least partly responsible for the massive increase in the number of customer complaints.

Gross profit margins

Overall, the company's gross profit margin (GPM) has increased from 37% to 42%. While the GPM for electronic goods has only increased by 1 percentage point, the margin for household goods has increased by 10 percentage points. This is therefore largely responsible for the increase in overall GPM. This has presumably occurred because Jungle Co is now sourcing these products from new, cheaper suppliers.

Gold membership fees constitute only a small part of Jungle Co's income, so their 2 percentage point fall in GPM has had little impact on the overall increase in GPM. Cloud computing services, on the other hand, now make up over $12m of Jungle Co's sales revenue. For some reason, the GPM on these sales has fallen from 76% to 66%. This is now 14 percentage points less than the market average gross profit margin of 80%. More information is needed to establish why this has happened. It has prevented the overall increase in GPM being higher than it otherwise would have been.

Administration expenses/customer complaints

These have increased by 60% from $1.72m to $2.76m. This is a substantial increase. The costs of the customer service department are in here. Given the number of late deliveries increased from 2% to 14%, and the corresponding increase in customer complaints from 5% to 20%, it is not surprising that the administration costs have increased. As well as being concerned about the impact on profit of this increase of over $1m, Jungle Co should be extremely worried about the effect on its reputation. Bad publicity about reliable delivery could affect future business.

Distribution costs

Despite an increase in sales volumes of 15%, distribution expenses have increased by less than 2 percentage points. They have gone down from $0.16 to $0.14 per $ of revenue. Although this means that Jungle Co has been successful in terms of saving costs, as discussed above, the damage which late deliveries are doing to the business cannot be ignored. The company needs to urgently address the issue of late deliveries.

Net profit margin

This has increased from 19% to 25%. This means that, all in all, Jungle Co has had a successful year, with net profit having increased from $15.6m to $23.8m. However, the business must address its delivery issues if its success is to continue.

Gross profit margins	31 August 20X6	31 August 20X5
Household goods	40.00%	30.00%
Electronic goods	36.00%	35.00%
Cloud computing services	65.81%	75.77%
Gold membership fees	92.86%	95.00%
Overall	42.39%	37.19%
Net profit margin	25.15%	18.95%

Increase/decrease in revenue	
Household goods	−5.27%
Electronic goods	28.28%
Cloud computing services	90.18%
Gold membership fees	−30.00%
Total revenue increase	14.99%

Increase/decrease in cost of sales	
Household goods	−18.80%
Electronic goods	26.31%
Cloud computing services	168.35%
Gold membership fees	0.00%
Total cost of sales increase	5.46%

	31 August 20X6	31 August 20X5
Increase in administration expenses	60.47%	
Increase in distribution expenses	1.82%	
Increase in other operating expenses	27.27%	
Increase in costs of customer service department	120.93%	
([$1,900,000 – $860,000]/$860,000)		

	31 August 20X6	31 August 20X5
Customer complaints as % customers	19.72%	4.92%
Delivery cost per $ of revenue	$0.14	$0.16

32 CSC Co

Text references. Limiting factors and linear programming are covered in Chapter 4.

Top tips. Part (a) is not particularly difficult but does require some care. Read the requirement carefully and ensure that you use quantities (not dollar values) to calculate your optimum production plan. Part (b) says that no further calculations are required so don't waste time performing any. Part (c) requires you to have a good understanding of how linear programming works.

Easy marks. Part (a) has easy marks. There are also easy marks in part (b) for realising that breach of contract will have legal, reputational and unethical implications.

Examining team comments. Responses to part (a) were poor, with students ignoring the fact that the company had entered into a contract and also omitting to calculate the material shortage. Part (b) was also disappointing as many students focused purely on financial factors. Part (c) was answered well overall. However, although most students identified the iso-contribution line and feasible region on the graph, few could explain what they meant.

Marking scheme

				Marks
(a)		Calculating shortage of Betta		1.5
		Contribution per gram of Betta		1
		Ranking		0.5
		Optimum production plan		2
		Profit		1
				6
(b)		Each valid point		1
			Maximum	4
(c)	(i)	Identification and explanation of the iso-contribution line		2
		Identification and explanation of the feasible region		2
				4
	(ii)	Explaining how to use line for identification of optimum point		1.5
		Identification of optimum point		0.5
				2
	(iii)	Explaining what slack values are		1
		Identifying Betta as slack		1
		Identifying Singa as slack		1
		Identifying slack demand for cookies		1
				4
				20

(a) (Step 1) Calculate the shortage of Betta for the year

Total requirements in grams:

Cakes: grams used per cake	0.5
Expected demand	11,200
Total required:	5,600
Cookies: grams used per cookie	0.20
Expected demand	9,800
Total required:	1,960
Shakes: grams used per shake	1
Expected demand	7,500
Total required:	7,500
Overall total required:	15,060
Less available:	12,000
Shortage:	3,060

(Step 2) Contribution per gram of Betta and ranking

	Cakes	Cookies	Shakes	Shakes (contract)
	$	$	$	$
Contribution per unit	2.60	1.75	1.20	1.00
Grams of Betta per unit	0.5	0.2	1	1
	$	$	$	$
Contribution per gram	5.20	8.75	1.20	1.00
Rank	2	1	3	4

(Step 3) Optimum production plan

Product	Number to be produced	Grams per unit	Total grams per product	Cumulative grams	Contribution per unit	Total contribution
Shakes (contract)	5,000	1	5,000	5,000	1.00	5,000
Cookies	9,800	0.20	1,960	6,960	1.75	17,150
Cakes	10,080	0.5	5,040	12,000	2.60	26,208
Total contribution						48,358
Less: fixed costs						(3,000)
Profit						45,358

(b) **Breach of contract with Encompass Health (EH)**

It would be bad for business if CSC Co becomes known as a supplier which cannot be relied on to stick to the terms of its agreements. This could make future potential customers reluctant to deal with them.

Even more seriously, there could be legal consequences involved in breaching the contract with EH. This would be costly and also very damaging to CSC Co's reputation.

If CSC Co lets EH down and breaches the contract, EH may refuse to buy from them any more and future sales revenue would therefore be lost. Just as importantly, these sales to EH are currently helping to increase the marketability of CSC Co's shakes. This will be lost if these sales are no longer made.

Therefore, taking these factors into account, it would not be advisable to breach the contract.

(c)   (i)   This line is what is called the 'iso-contribution line' and it is plotted by finding two corresponding x and y values for the 'objective function'. At any point along this line, the mix of cakes and cookies will provide the same total contribution, 'C'.

Since each cake provides a contribution of $2.60 and each cookie provides a contribution of $1.75, the objective function has been defined as 'C = 2.6x + 1.75y'. This means that the total contribution will be however many cakes are made (represented by 'x') at $2.60 each plus however many cookies are made (represented by 'y') at $1.75 each.

The area OABCD is called the 'feasible region'. Any point within this region could be selected and would show a feasible mix of production of cakes and cookies. However, in order to maximise profit, the optimum production mix will be at a point on the edge of the feasible region, not within it.

(ii)   The further the iso-contribution line is moved away from the origin, 0, the greater the contribution generated will be. Therefore, a ruler will be laid along the line, making sure it stays at exactly the same angle as the line, and the ruler will then be moved outwards to the furthest vertex (intersection between two constraints) on the feasible region, as represented by either point A, B, C or D. In this case, the optimum point is 'C', the intersection of the 'labour' constraint and the 'demand for cakes' constraint.

(iii) A 'slack' value could arise either in relation to a resource or in relation to production of a product. It means that a resource is not being fully utilised or that there is unfulfilled demand of a product. Since the optimum point is the intersection of the labour and the demand for cakes lines, this means that there will be three slack values. First, there will be a slack value for cookies. This means that there will be unsatisfied demand for cookies, since the optimum point does not reach as far as the 'demand for cookies' line on the graph. Also, there will be slack values for Betta and Singa, which means that both of these materials are not actually the binding constraints, such that there will be more material available than is needed.

ACCA
Performance Management

Mock Exam 2 – Specimen exam CBE

Question Paper: 3 hours
ALL FIVE questions are compulsory and MUST be attempted

DO NOT OPEN THIS PAPER UNTIL YOU ARE READY TO START UNDER EXAMINATION CONDITIONS

Section A – All FIFTEEN questions are compulsory and MUST be attempted

Each question is worth 2 marks.

1   A company manufactures two products, C and D, for which the following information is available:

	Product C	Product D	Total
Budgeted production (units)	1,000	4,000	5,000
Labour hours per unit/in total	8	10	48,000
Number of production runs required	13	15	28
Number of inspections during production	5	3	8
Total production set up costs	$140,000		
Total inspection costs	$80,000		
Other overhead costs	$96,000		

Other overhead costs are absorbed on a labour hour basis.

Using activity-based costing, what is the budgeted overhead cost per unit of Product D?

  ○ $43.84
  ○ $46.25
  ○ $131.00
  ○ $140.64

2   The selling price of Product X is set at $550 for each unit and sales for the coming year are expected to be 800 units.

A return of 30% on the investment of $500,000 in Product X will be required in the coming year.

What is the target cost for each unit of Product X (to two decimal places)?

$ [   ]

3   P Co makes two products, P1 and P2. The budgeted details for each product are as follows:

	P1	P2
	$	$
Selling price	10.00	8.00
Cost per unit:		
Direct materials	3.50	4.00
Direct labour	1.50	1.00
Variable overhead	0.60	0.40
Fixed overhead	1.20	1.00
Profit per unit	3.20	1.60

Budgeted production and sales for the year ended 30 November 20X5 are:

Product P1   10,000 units
Product P2   12,500 units

The fixed overhead costs included in P1 relate to apportionment of general overhead costs only. However, P2 also included specific fixed overheads totalling $2,500.

If only product P1 were to be made, how many units would need to be sold in order to achieve a profit of $60,000 each year (to the nearest whole unit)?

[   ] units

4   Which **TWO** of the following statements regarding environmental cost accounting, are true?

☐   The majority of environmental costs are already captured within a typical organisation's accounting system. The difficulty lies in identifying them.

☐   Input/output analysis divides material flows within an organisation into three categories: material flows; system flows; and delivery and disposal flows.

☐   One of the cost categories used in environmental activity-based costing is environment-driven costs which is used for costs which can be directly traced to a cost centre.

☐   Environmental life cycle costing enables environmental costs from the design stage of the product right through to decommissioning at the end of its life to be considered.

5   To produce 19 litres of Product X, a standard input mix of 8 litres of chemical A and 12 litres of chemical B is required.

Chemical A has a standard cost of $20 per litre and chemical B has a standard cost of $25 per litre.

During September, the actual results showed that 1,850 litres of Product X were produced, using a total input of 900 litres of chemical A and 1,100 litres of chemical B.

The actual costs of chemicals A and B were at the standard cost of $20 and $25 per litre respectively.

Based on the above information, which of the following statements is true?

O   Both variances were adverse.
O   Both variances were favourable.
O   The total mix variance was adverse and the total yield variance was favourable.
O   The total mix variance was favourable and the total yield variance was adverse.

6   A budget is a quantified plan of action for a forthcoming period. Budgets can be prepared using a variety of different approaches.

Match each of the following statements to the correct budgeting process.

Statements		Budgeting approach
Builds in previous problems and inefficiences		Beyond budgeting
Recognises different cost behaviour patterns		Incremental budgeting
Focuses employees on avoiding wasteful expenditure		Activity-based budgeting
Focuses on controlling the causes of costs		Rolling budgeting
Always extends the budget one year into the future		Flexible budgeting
Uses adaptive management processes		Zero-based budgeting

7   A leisure company owns a number of large health and fitness resorts, but one is suffering from declining
     sales and is predicted to make a loss in the next year. As a result management have identified a number of
     possible actions:

     (1)   Shut down the resort and sell off the assets
     (2)   Undertake a major upgrade to facilities, costing $4.5m
     (3)   Undertake a minor upgrade to facilities, costing $2m

     The upgrades are predicted to have variable results and the probability of good results after a major upgrade
     is 0.8, whereas the probability of good results after a minor upgrade is 0.7.

     The company is risk neutral and has prepared the following decision tree.

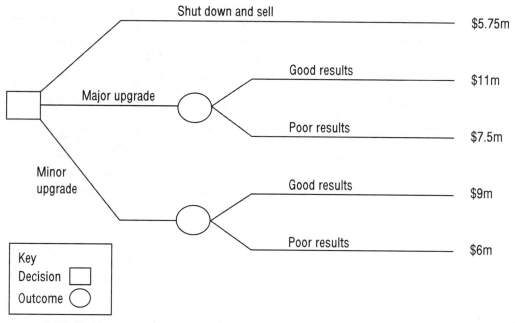

     Which decision should the company make?

     O   Shutdown and sell
     O   Undertake the major upgrade
     O   Undertake the minor upgrade
     O   Undertake the major upgrade if results are good

8   A company has the following production planned for the next four weeks. The figures reflect the full capacity
     level of operations. Planned output is equal to the maximum demand per product.

Product	A	B	C	D
	$ per unit	$ per unit	$ per unit	$ per unit
Selling price	160	214	100	140
Raw material cost	24	56	22	40
Direct labour cost	66	88	33	22
Variable overhead cost	24	18	24	18
Fixed overhead cost	16	10	8	12
Profit	30	42	13	48
Planned output	300	125	240	400
Direct labour hours per unit	6	8	3	2

     It has now been identified that labour hours available in the next four weeks will be limited to 4,000 hours.

Rank the products in the order they should be manufactured, assuming that the company wants to maximise profits in the next four weeks.

Product		Ranking	
A		1st	
B		2nd	
C		3rd	
D		4th	

9   Def Co provides accounting services to government departments. On average, each staff member works six chargeable hours per day, with the rest of their working day being spent on non-chargeable administrative work. One of the company's main objectives is to produce a high level of quality and customer satisfaction.

Def Co has set its targets for the next year.

Match the correct value for money performance category to each of the following targets for Def Co.

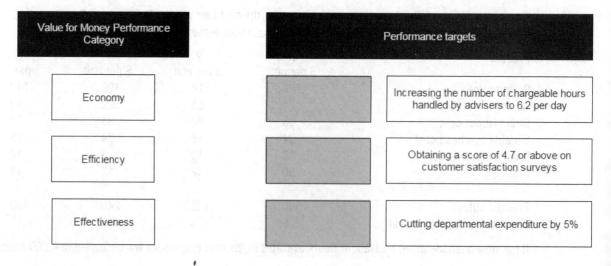

Value for Money Performance Category		Performance targets
Economy		Increasing the number of chargeable hours handled by advisers to 6.2 per day
Efficiency		Obtaining a score of 4.7 or above on customer satisfaction surveys
Effectiveness		Cutting departmental expenditure by 5%

10 Different types of information systems provide the information which organisations need for strategic planning, management and operational control.

Match the following characteristics to the relevant information systems.

Characteristic

| Summarises internal data into periodic reports |
| Can be set up with extranet links to customers and suppliers |
| Utilises dashboard facilities and interactive graphics |
| Facilitates the immediate processing of data |

Management Information System		Transaction Processing System	

Executive Information System		Enterprise Resource Planning System	

11 Which **TWO** of the following are examples of direct data capture costs?

☐ Use of bar coding and scanners
☐ Payroll department's processing of personnel costs
☐ Completion of timesheets by employees
☐ Input of data into the production system
☐ Emails sent to staff on matters that do not relate to them

12 Which **TWO** of the following statements regarding life-cycle costing are correct?

☐ It can be applied not only to products but also to an organisation's customers.
☐ It includes any opportunity costs associated with production.
☐ The maturity phase is characterised by a rapid build-up in demand.
☐ Often between 70% to 90% of costs are determined early in the product life cycle.

13 A company manufactures a product which requires four hours per unit of machine time. Machine time is a bottleneck resource as there are only ten machines which are available for 12 hours per day, five days per week. The product has a selling price of $130 per unit, direct material costs of $50 per unit, labour costs of $40 per unit and factory overhead costs of $20 per unit. These costs are based on weekly production and sales of 150 units.

What is the throughput accounting ratio?

○ 1.33
○ 2.00
○ 0.75
○ 0.31

14   Ox Co has two divisions, A and B. Division A makes a component for air conditioning units which it can only sell to Division B. It has no other outlet for sales.

Current information relating to Division A is as follows:

Marginal cost per unit	$100
Transfer price of the component	$165
Total production and sales of the component each year	2,200 units
Specific fixed costs of Division A per year	$10,000

Cold Co has offered to sell the component to Division B for $140 per unit. If Division B accepts this offer, Division A will be closed.

If Division B accepts Cold Co's offer, what will be the impact on profits per year for the group as a whole?

○   Increase of $65,000
○   Decrease of $78,000
○   Decrease of $88,000
○   Increase of $55,000

15   Identify, by clicking on the relevant box in the table below, whether each of the following statements regarding Fitzgerald and Moon's Building Blocks model is true or false.

The determinants of performance are quality, innovation, resource utilisation and competitiveness	TRUE	FALSE
Standards are targets for performance and should be fair, achievable and controllable	TRUE	FALSE
Rewards encourage staff to work towards the standards and should be clear, motivating and controllable	TRUE	FALSE
It is a performance measurement framework suitable for service organisations	TRUE	FALSE

(Total = 30 marks)

Section B – All FIFTEEN questions are compulsory and MUST be attempted

Each question is worth 2 marks.

The following scenario relates to questions 16–20.

Glam Co is a hairdressing salon which provides both 'cuts' and 'treatments' to clients. All cuts and treatments at the salon are carried out by one of the salon's three senior stylists. The salon also has two salon assistants and two junior stylists.

Every customer attending the salon is first seen by a salon assistant, who washes their hair; next, by a senior stylist, who cuts or treats the hair depending on which service the customer wants; then finally, a junior stylist who dries their hair. The average length of time spent with each member of staff is as follows:

	Cut Hours	Treatment Hours
Assistant	0.1	0.3
Senior stylist	1.0	1.5
Junior stylist	0.6	0.5

The salon is open for eight hours each day for six days per week. It is only closed for two weeks each year. Staff salaries are $40,000 each year for each senior stylist, $28,000 each year for each junior stylist and $12,000 each year for each of the assistants. The cost of cleaning products applied when washing the hair is $1.50 per client. The cost of all additional products applied during a 'treatment' is $7.40 per client. Other salon costs (excluding labour and raw materials) amount to $106,400 each year.

Glam Co charges $60 for each cut and $110 for each treatment.

The senior stylists' time has been correctly identified as the bottleneck activity.

16 What is the annual capacity of the bottleneck activity?

	Cuts	Treatments
O	2,400	1,600
O	4,800	4,800
O	7,200	4,800
O	9,600	9,600

17 The salon has calculated the cost per hour to be $42.56.

Calculate the throughput accounting ratio (TPAR) for both services (to two decimal places).

Cuts	

Treatments	

18 Which **THREE** of the following activities could the salon use to improve the TPAR?

- ☐ Increase the time spent by the bottleneck activity on each service
- ☐ Identify ways to reduce the material costs for the services
- ☐ Increase the level of inventory to prevent stock-outs
- ☐ Increase the productivity of the stage prior to the bottleneck
- ☐ Improve the control of the salon's total operating expenses
- ☐ Apply an increase to the selling price of the services

19   What would be the effect on the bottleneck if the salon employed another senior stylist?

   ○   The senior stylists' time will be a bottleneck for cuts only
   ○   The senior stylists' time will be a bottleneck for treatments only
   ○   The senior stylists' time will remain the bottleneck for both cuts and treatments
   ○   There will no longer be a bottleneck

20   Which of the following statements regarding the theory of constraints are correct?

   (1)   It focuses on identifying stages of congestion in a process when production arrives more quickly
          than the next stage can handle

   (2)   It is based on the concept that organisations manage three key factors – throughput, operating
          expenses and inventory

   (3)   It uses a sequence of focusing steps to overcome a single bottleneck, at which point the
          improvement process is complete

   (4)   It can be applied to the management of all limiting factors, both internal and external, which can
          affect an organisation

   ○   (1) and (2)
   ○   (1), (2) and (3)
   ○   (2), (3) and (4)
   ○   (1), (3) and (4)

The following scenario relates to questions 21–25.

Chair Co has several new products in development. Information relating to two of these products is as follows:

Luxury car seat

The estimated labour time for the first unit is 12 hours, but a learning curve of 75% is expected to apply for the first eight units produced. The cost of labour is $15 per hour.

The cost of materials and other variable overheads is expected to total $230 per unit. Chair Co plans on pricing the seat by adding a 50% mark up to the total variable cost per seat, with the labour cost being based on the incremental time taken to produce the 8th unit.

High chair

Another product which Chair Co has in development is a new design of high chair for feeding young children. Based on previous experience of producing similar products, Chair Co had assumed that a learning rate of 85% would apply to the manufacture of this new design but, after the first phase of production had been completed, management realised that a learning rate of 80% had been achieved.

Chair Co uses cost-plus pricing when setting prices for its products.

21   In relation to the luxury car seat, what is the labour cost of the 8th unit?

   ○ $45.65
   ○ $75.94
   ○ $4.32
   ○ $3.04

22   The first phase of production has now been completed for the new car seat. The first unit actually took 12.5 hours to make and the total time for the first eight units was 34.3 hours, at which point the learning effect came to an end. Chair Co is planning on adjusting the price to reflect the actual time it took to complete the 8th unit.

      What was the actual rate of learning which occurred (to two decimal places)?

      ┌─────────────┐ %
      └─────────────┘

23   In relation to the new design of high chair, which **THREE** of the following statements could explain why the actual rate of learning differed from the rate which was expected?

☐   Staffing levels were stable during the first manufacturing phase

☐   There were machine breakdowns during production

☐   Assembly of the chairs was manual and very repetitive

☐   There was high staff turnover during this period

☐   There were minimal stoppages in the production process

☐   The design of the chair was changed several times at this early phase

24   Identify, by clicking on the table below, whether each of the statements regarding cost-plus pricing strategies is true or false.

Marginal cost-plus pricing is easier where there is a readily identifiable variable cost	TRUE	FALSE
Full cost-plus pricing requires the budgeted level of output to be determined at the outset	TRUE	FALSE
Cost-plus pricing is a strategically focused approach as it accounts for external factors	TRUE	FALSE
Cost-plus pricing requires that the profit mark-up applied by an organisation is fixed	TRUE	FALSE

25   Chair Co has also developed a new type of office chair and management is trying to formulate a budget for this product. They have decided to match the production level to demand, however, demand for this chair is uncertain.

Management have collected the following information:

	Demand (units)	Probability
Worst possible outcome	10,000	0.3
Most likely outcome	22,000	0.5
Best possible outcome	35,000	0.2

The selling price per unit is $25. The variable cost per unit is $8 for any production level up to 25,000 units. If the production level is higher than 25,000 units, then the variable cost per unit will decrease by 10% and this reduction will apply to all the units produced at that level.

Total fixed costs are estimated to be $75,000.

Using probabilistic budgeting, what is the expected budgeted contribution of the product (to the nearest whole $)?

$ [   ]

The following scenario relates to questions 26–30.

The Hi Life Co (HL Co) makes sofas. It has recently received a request from a customer to provide a one-off order of sofas, in excess of normal budgeted production. The order would need to be completed within two weeks. The following cost estimate has already been prepared:

		$
Direct materials:		
Fabric	200 m² at $17 per m²	3,400
Wood	50 m² at $8.20 per m²	410
Direct labour:		
Skilled	200 hours at $16 per hour	3,200
Semi-skilled	300 hours at $12 per hour	3,600
Factory overheads	500 hours at $3 per hour	1,500
Total production cost		12,110
General fixed overheads as 10% of total production cost		1,211
Total cost		13,321

A quotation now needs to be prepared on a relevant cost basis so that HL Co can offer as competitive a price as possible for the order.

26　The fabric is regularly used by HL Co. There are currently 300 m² in inventory, which cost $17 per m². The current purchase price of the fabric is $17.50 per m².

The wood is regularly used by HL Co and usually costs $8.20 per m². However, the company's current supplier's earliest delivery time for the wood is in three weeks' time. An alternative supplier could deliver immediately but they would charge $8.50 per m². HL Co already has 500 m² in inventory but 480 m² of this is needed to complete other existing orders in the next two weeks. The remaining 20 m² is not going to be needed until four weeks' time.

What is the cost of the fabric and the wood which should be included in the quotation (to the nearest whole $)?

Fabric

$	

Wood

$	

27　The skilled labour force is employed under permanent contracts of employment under which they must be paid for 40 hours per week's labour, even if their time is idle due to absence of orders. Their rate of pay is $16 per hour, although any overtime is paid at time and a half. In the next two weeks, there is spare capacity of 150 labour hours.

There is no spare capacity for semi-skilled workers. They are currently paid $12 per hour or time and a half for overtime. However, a local agency can provide additional semi-skilled workers for $14 per hour.

What cost should be included in the quotation for skilled labour and semi-skilled labour (to the nearest $)?

Skilled

$	

Semi-skilled

$	

28 Of the $3 per hour factory overheads costs, $1.50 per hour reflects the electricity costs of running the cutting machine which will be used to cut the fabric and wood for the sofas. The other $1.50 per hour reflects the cost of the factory supervisor's salary. The supervisor is paid an annual salary and is also paid $15 per hour for any overtime they work.

They will need to work 20 hours overtime if this order is accepted.

What is the cost which should be included in the quotation for factory overheads (to the nearest $)?

$ [   ]

29 Which statement correctly describes the treatment of the general fixed overheads when preparing the quotation?

○ The overheads should be excluded because they are a sunk cost
○ The overheads should be excluded because they are not incremental costs
○ The overheads should be included because they relate to production costs
○ The overheads should be included because all expenses should be recovered

30 Which **FOUR** of the following statements about relevant costing are true?

☐ An opportunity cost will always be a relevant cost even if it is a past cost
☐ Fixed costs are always general in nature and are therefore never relevant
☐ Committed costs are never considered to be relevant costs
☐ An opportunity cost represents the cost of the best alternative forgone
☐ Notional costs are always relevant as they make the estimate more realistic
☐ Avoidable costs would be saved if an activity did not happen and so are relevant
☐ Common costs are only relevant if the viability of the whole process is being assessed
☐ Differential costs in a make-or-buy decision are not considered to be relevant

(Total = 30 marks)

Section C – Both questions are compulsory and MUST be attempted

31 Carad Co is an electronics company which makes two types of television – plasma screen TVs and LCD TVs. It operates within a highly competitive market and is constantly under pressure to reduce prices. Carad Co operates a standard costing system and performs a detailed variance analysis of both products on a monthly basis. Extracts from the management information for the month of November are shown below:

		Note
Total number of units made and sold	1,400	1
Material price variance	$28,000 A	2
Total labour variance	$6,050 A	3

Notes

1   The budgeted total sales volume for TVs was 1,180 units, consisting of an equal mix of plasma screen TVs and LCD screen TVs. Actual sales volume was 750 plasma TVs and 650 LCD TVs. Standard sales prices are $350 per unit for the plasma TVs and $300 per unit for the LCD TVs. The actual sales prices achieved during November were $330 per unit for plasma TVs and $290 per unit for LCD TVs. The standard contributions for plasma TVs and LCD TVs are $190 and $180 per unit respectively.

2   The sole reason for this variance was an increase in the purchase price of one of its key components, X. Each plasma TV made and each LCD TV made requires one unit of component X, for which Carad Co's standard cost is $60 per unit. Due to a shortage of components in the market place, the market price for November went up to $85 per unit for X. Carad Co actually paid $80 per unit for it.

3   Each plasma TV uses 2 standard hours of labour and each LCD TV uses 1.5 standard hours of labour. The standard cost for labour is $14 per hour and this also reflects the actual cost per labour hour for the company's permanent staff in November. However, because of the increase in sales and production volumes in November, the company also had to use additional temporary labour at the higher cost of $18 per hour. The total capacity of Carad's permanent workforce is 2,200 hours production per month, assuming full efficiency. In the month of November, the permanent workforce were wholly efficient, taking exactly 2 hours to complete each plasma TV and exactly 1.5 hours to produce each LCD TV. The total labour variance therefore relates solely to the temporary workers, who took twice as long as the permanent workers to complete their production.

Required

(a)   Calculate the following for the month of November, showing all workings clearly:

    (i)   The sales price variance and sales volume contribution variance;   **(4 marks)**

    (ii)   The material price planning variance and material price operational variance;   **(2 marks)**

    (iii)   The labour rate variance and the labour efficiency variance.   **(5 marks)**

(b)   Explain the reasons why Carad Co would be interested in the material price planning variance and the material price operational variance.   **(9 marks)**

(Total = 20 marks)

32   Thatcher International Park (TIP) is a theme park and has for many years been a successful business, which has traded profitably. About three years ago the directors decided to capitalise on their success and reduced the expenditure made on new thrill rides, reduced routine maintenance where possible (deciding instead to repair equipment when it broke down) and made a commitment to regularly increase admission prices. Once an admission price is paid customers can use any of the facilities and rides for free.

These steps increased profits considerably, enabling good dividends to be paid to the owners and bonuses to the directors. The last two years of financial results are shown below.

	20X4	20X5
	$	$
Sales	5,250,000	5,320,000
Less expenses:		
Wages	2,500,000	2,200,000
Maintenance – routine	80,000	70,000
Repairs	260,000	320,000
Directors' salaries	150,000	160,000
Directors' bonuses	15,000	18,000
Other costs (including depreciation)	1,200,000	1,180,000
Net profit	1,045,000	1,372,000
Book value of assets at start of year	13,000,000	12,000,000
Dividend paid	500,000	650,000
Number of visitors	150,000	140,000

TIP operates in a country where the average rate of inflation is around 1% per annum.

Required

(a)   Assess the financial performance of TIP using the information given above.   **(14 marks)**

During the early part of 20X4 TIP employed a newly qualified management accountant. They quickly became concerned about the potential performance of TIP; to investigate their concerns, they started to gather data to measure some non-financial measures of success. The data they have gathered is shown below:

Table 1

	20X4	20X5
Hours lost due to breakdown of rides (see note)	9,000 hours	32,000 hours
Average waiting time per ride	20 minutes	30 minutes

Note. TIP has 50 rides of different types. It is open 360 days of the year for 10 hours each day

Required

(b)   Assess the **QUALITY** of the service which TIP provides to its customers using Table 1 and any other relevant data and indicate the **RISKS** it is likely to face if it continues with its current policies.

(6 marks)

(Total = 20 marks)

Formulae Sheet

Learning curve

$Y = ax^b$

Where   Y = cumulative average time per unit to produce x units
         a = the time taken for the first unit of output
         x = the cumulative number of units produced
         b = the index of learning (log LR/log2)
         LR = the learning rate as a decimal

Demand curve

$P = a - bQ$

$B = \dfrac{\text{change in price}}{\text{change in quantity}}$

A = price when Q = 0

$MR = a - 2bQ$

End of Questions

Mock exam 2 (Specimen exam CBE): questions

Answers

**DO NOT TURN THIS PAGE UNTIL YOU HAVE
COMPLETED THE MOCK EXAM**

A PLAN OF ATTACK

Managing your nerves

As you turn the pages to start this mock exam a number of thoughts are likely to cross your mind. At best, examinations cause anxiety so it is important to stay focused on your task for the next three hours! Developing an awareness of what is going on emotionally within you may help you manage your nerves. Remember, you are unlikely to banish the flow of adrenaline, but the key is to harness it to help you work steadily and quickly through your answers.

Working through this mock exam will help you develop the exam stamina you will need to keep going for three hours.

Managing your time

Planning and time management are two of the key skills which complement the technical knowledge you need to succeed. To keep yourself on time, do not be afraid to jot down your target completion times for each question, perhaps next to the title of the question. As all the questions are **compulsory**, you do not have to spend time wondering which question to answer!

Doing the exam

Actually doing the exam is a personal experience. There is not a single **right way**. As long as you submit complete answers to all questions after the three hours are up, then your approach obviously works.

Looking through the exam

Section A has 15 MCQs. This is the section of the exam where ACCA examining team can test knowledge across the breadth of the syllabus. Make sure you read these questions carefully. The distractors are designed to present plausible, but incorrect, answers. Don't let them mislead you. If you really have no idea – guess. You may even be right.

Section B has three questions, each with a scenario and five objective test questions.

Section C has two longer questions:

- Question 31 requires you to calculate sales variances. There are plenty of easy marks in the question. If you get stuck on the details of which numbers to use where, make an attempt at something sensible and move on.

- Question 32 looks at performance measurement. This is a classic performance measurement question with a contrast between the picture painted by financial indicators and that given by non-financial indicators. Start with the ratio calculations and then make sure that you fully analyse what the numbers are telling you.

Allocating your time

BPP's advice is to always allocate your time **according to the marks for the question**. However, **use common sense**. If you're doing a question but haven't a clue how to do part (b), you might be better off re-allocating your time and getting more marks on another question, where you can add something you didn't have time for earlier on. Make sure you leave time to recheck the MCQs and make sure you have answered them all.

Section A

1   The correct answer is: $46.25

Set-up costs per production run = $140,000/28 = $5,000
Cost per inspection = $80,000/8 = $10,000
Other overhead costs per labour hour = $96,000/48,000 = $2

Overhead costs of product D:

	$
Set-up costs (15 × $5,000)	75,000
Inspection costs (3 × $10,000)	30,000
Other overheads (40,000 × $2)	80,000
	185,000

Overhead cost per unit = $185,000/4,000 units = $46.25

2   The correct answer is: $362.50

Return: $500,000 × 30% = $150,000
Total sales revenue = $550 × 800 = $440,000
Therefore total cost = $440,000 − $150,000 = $290,000
Unit cost = $290,000/800 = $362.50

3   The correct answer is: 18,636 units

The number of units required to make a target profit = (fixed costs + target profit)/contribution per unit of P1.

Fixed costs = ($1.20 × 10,000) + ($1.00 × 12,500) − $2,500 = $22,000

Contribution per unit of P = $3.20 + $1.20 = $4.40

($22,000 + $60,000)/$4.40 = 18,636 units

4   The correct answers are: 'The majority of environmental costs are already captured within a typical organisation's accounting system. The difficulty lies in identifying them' and 'Environmental life cycle costing enables environmental costs from the design stage of the product right through to decommissioning at the end of its life to be considered'

Most organisations do collect data about environmental costs but find it difficult to split them out and categorise them effectively.

Life-cycle costing does allow the organisation to collect information about a product's environmental costs throughout its life cycle.

The technique which divides material flows into three categories is material flow cost accounting, not input/output analysis.

ABC does categorise some costs as environment-driven costs, however, these are costs which are normally hidden within total overheads in a conventional costing system. It is environment-related costs which can be allocated directly to a cost centre.

5   The correct answer is: The total mix variance was favourable and the total yield variance was adverse

Mix variance:

Material	AQSM	AQAM	Difference litres	Standard cost $/litre	Variance $
A	800	900	100 A	20	2,000 A
B	1,200	1,100	100 F	25	2,500 F
	2,000	2,000			500 F

Yield variance:

Material	SQSM	AQSM	Difference litres	Standard cost $/litre	Variance $
A	779	800	21 A	20	420 A
B	1,168	1,200	32 A	25	800 A
	(W1) 1,947	2,000			1,220 A

(W1) 1,850 litres of output should use 1,947 litres of input (1,850/0.95)

6   The correct answers are:

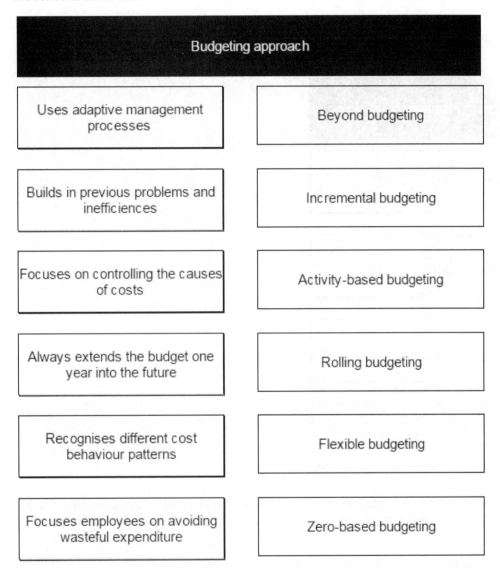

Budgeting approach	
Uses adaptive management processes	Beyond budgeting
Builds in previous problems and inefficiences	Incremental budgeting
Focuses on controlling the causes of costs	Activity-based budgeting
Always extends the budget one year into the future	Rolling budgeting
Recognises different cost behaviour patterns	Flexible budgeting
Focuses employees on avoiding wasteful expenditure	Zero-based budgeting

Beyond budgeting attempts to move away from conforming to a rigid annual budget and uses adaptive processes to encourage management to be responsive to current situations.

An incremental budget builds from the previous year's figures and so any inefficiencies will be carried forward.

Activity-based budgeting is based on the principles of activity-based costing and will attempt to identify the drivers of costs in order to formulate a budget.

Rolling budgeting are budgets which are continuously updated throughout the year by adding a new budget period once the most recent budget period has ended. This means that the budget is always extended one year into the future and so forces managers to reassess plans more regularly.

Flexible budgets are designed to show the changes in financial figures based on different activity levels and so will recognise different cost behaviour patterns.

Zero-based budgeting starts from scratch with each item justified for its inclusion in the budget and so should encourage the identification of waste and non-value adding activities.

7   The correct answer is: Undertake the minor upgrade

EV for major upgrade = (0.80 × $11m) + (0.2 × $7.5m) = $10.3m

EV for minor upgrade = (0.70 × $9m) + (0.3 × $6m) = $8.1m

Decision

Shutdown and sell	$5.75m
Major upgrade (10.3m – 4.5m)	$5.8m
Minor upgrade ($8.1m – $2m)	$6.1m

As the minor upgrade has the highest expected return that should be the option chosen.

8   The correct answer is:

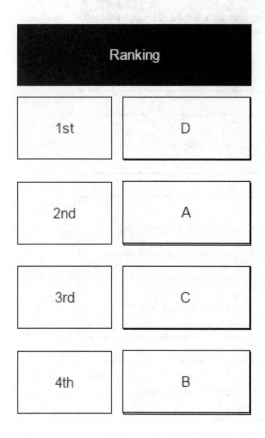

Ranking	
1st	D
2nd	A
3rd	C
4th	B

In a single limiting factor situation products should be ranked based on their contribution per unit of limiting factor, which in this case is labour hours.

Product	A	B	C	D
Contribution per unit ($)	46	52	21	60
Number of labour hours required per unit	6	8	3	2
Contribution per labour hour ($)	7.67	6.50	7.00	30.00
Ranking	2nd	4th	3rd	1st

9   The correct answer is:

Performance targets

Efficiency	Increasing the number of chargeable hours handled by advisers to 6.2 per day
Effectiveness	Obtaining a score of 4.7 or above on customer satisfaction surveys
Economy	Cutting departmental expenditure by 5%

Target 1 is measuring the rate of work handled by staff which is an efficiency measure. Target 2 is assessing output, so is a measure of effectiveness. Target 3 is a financial measure and so assesses economy factors.

10   The correct answer is:

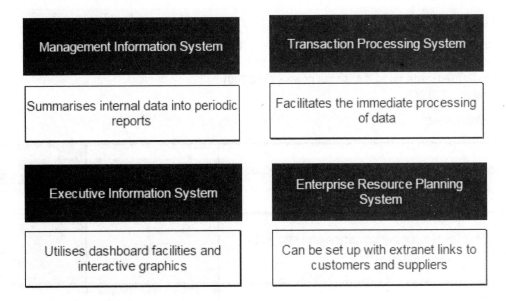

Management Information System	Transaction Processing System
Summarises internal data into periodic reports	Facilitates the immediate processing of data

Executive Information System	Enterprise Resource Planning System
Utilises dashboard facilities and interactive graphics	Can be set up with extranet links to customers and suppliers

Transaction processing systems facilitate the immediate processing of data.

Management information systems summarise data from TPS into periodic reports for management to use for decision-making.

Executive information systems draw data from the MIS and support senior managers to make strategic decisions. They usually have dashboard and interactive graphics so that the big picture can be seen.

Enterprise resource planning systems are software packages that integrate all the key processes in an organisation and so this permits data to be shared more easily between departments. It can also have extranet links set up with customers and suppliers.

11 The correct answers are: 'Use of bar coding and scanners' and 'Completion of timesheets by employees'.

Direct data capture costs is a type of data input in which there is no data entry but instead it is captured for a specific purpose.

Therefore the use of bar coding and scanners and the completion of timesheets are examples of direct data capture costs.

Time spent by the payroll department processing personnel costs and the input of data into the production system are examples of process costs.

The sending of emails to staff regarding matters that are not pertinent to them is classed as an inefficient use of information cost.

12 The correct answers are: 'It can be applied not only to products but also to an organisation's customers' and 'Often between 70% to 90% of costs are determined early in the product life cycle'

Customer life-cycle costing can be used by organisations.

It has been reported that the majority of a product's costs are determined early on, ie at the design phase.

Life-cycle costing does not include any opportunity costs associated with production.

The growth phase is characterised by a rapid increase in demand.

13 The correct answer is: 1.33

Return per factory hour = ($130 – $50)/4 hours = $20
Factory costs per hour = ($20 + $40)/4 = $15
TPAR = $20/$15 = 1.33

14 The correct answer is: Decrease of $78,000

Increase in variable costs per unit from buying in ($140 – $100) =$40
Therefore total increase in variable costs (2,200 units × $40) = $88,000
Less the specific fixed costs saved if A is shut down = ($10,000)
Decrease in profit = $78,000

15 The correct answers are:

The determinants of performance are quality, innovation, resource utilisation and competitiveness	TRUE	FALSE
Standards are targets for performance and should be fair, achievable and controllable	TRUE	FALSE
Rewards encourage staff to work towards the standards and should be clear, motivating and controllable	TRUE	FALSE
It is a performance measurement framework suitable for service organisations	TRUE	FALSE

The determinants of performance are quality, innovation, resource utilisation and flexibility. Competitiveness is a result of the determinants.

Standards should be fair, achievable and staff should have ownership of them. Controllability is a feature of the rewards block.

Rewards should be clear, motivating and controllable, so this is correct.

It is a framework designed to attempt to overcome the problems associated with performance management in service companies.

Section B

16   The correct answers are: Cuts 7,200   Treatments 4,800

Total salon hours = $8 \times 6 \times 50$ = 2,400 each year.

There are three senior stylists, therefore total hours available = 7,200.

Based on the time taken for each activity, they can perform 7,200 cuts (7,200 hours/1 hour per cut) or 4,800 treatments (7,200 hours/1.5 hours per treatment).

17   The correct answers are: Cuts 1.37   Treatments 1.58

Cuts

Return per hour = (Selling price – materials)/time taken on the bottleneck = (60 – 1.50)/1 = 58.50

TPAR = Return per hour/cost per hour = 58.50/42.56 = 1.37 (to two decimal places)

Treatments

Return per hour = (Selling price – materials)/time taken on the bottleneck = (110 – 8.90)/1.5 = 67.40

TPAR = Return per hour/cost per hour = 67.40/42.56 = 1.58 (to two decimal places)

18   The correct answers are:

Identify ways to reduce the material costs for the services

Improve the control of the salon's total operating expenses

Apply an increase to the selling price of the services

The factors which are included in the TPAR are selling price, material costs, operating expenses and bottleneck time. Increasing the selling price and reducing costs will improve the TPAR.

Increasing the time which each service takes on the bottleneck (the senior stylists' time) will only reduce the number of services they can provide, so this will not improve throughput.

Throughput accounting does not advocate the building of inventory as it is often used in a just-in-time environment and there is no point increasing the activity prior to the bottleneck as it will just create a build-up of work-in-progress. Neither of these will improve the rate of throughput through the process.

19   The correct answer is: The senior stylists' time will be a bottleneck for treatments only

The existing capacity for each activity is:

	Cut	Treatment
Assistants	48,000	16,000
Senior stylists	7,200	4,800
Junior stylists	8,000	9,600

If another senior stylist is employed, this will mean that their available hours will be $(4 \times 2,400)$ = 9,600.

This will give them capacity to now do 9,600 cuts (9,600 hours/1 hour per cut) and 6,400 treatments (9,600 hours/1.5 hours per treatment).

As a result, the senior stylists will still be the bottleneck activity for treatments but for cuts the bottleneck will now be the junior stylists as they can only do 8,000 cuts compared to the senior stylists of 9,600.

20   The correct answer is: (1) and (2)

The theory of constraints is focused on identifying restrictions in a process and how to manage that restriction (commonly termed a bottleneck).

It is based on the concept of managing throughput, operating expenses and inventory.

It does use a series of focusing steps but it is not complete once the bottleneck has been overcome. In fact it is an ongoing process of improvement, as once the bottleneck has been elevated it is probable that another bottleneck will appear and the process will continue.

It cannot be applied to all limiting factors as some, particularly those external to the organisation, may be out of the organisation's control.

21   The correct answer is: $45.65

Learning curve formula = y = ax^b

Cumulative average time per unit for 8 units: Y = 12 × 8$^{-.415}$= 5.0628948 hours.
Therefore cumulative total time for 8 units = 40.503158 hours.
Cumulative average time per unit for 7 units: Y = 12 × 7$^{-.415}$= 5.3513771 hours.
Therefore cumulative total time for 7 units = 37.45964 hours.
Therefore incremental time for 8th unit = 40.503158 hours − 37.45964 hours = 3.043518 hours.
Total labour cost for 8th unit =3.043518 × $15 = $45.65277

22   The correct answer is: 70.00%

Actual learning rate

Cumulative number of seats produced	Cumulative total hours	Cumulative average hours per unit
1	12.5	12.5
2	?	12.5 × r
4	?	12.5 × r^2
8	34.3	12.5 × r^3

Using algebra: 34.3   = 8 × (12.5 × r^3)
                  4.2875 = (12.5 × r^3)
                  0.343 = r^3
                  r   = 0.70

Therefore the learning rate was 70.00%.

23   The correct answers are:

Staffing levels were stable during the first manufacturing phase

Assembly of the chairs was manual and very repetitive

There were minimal stoppages in the production process

An 80% learning rate means that the learning was faster than expected.

Factors which are present for a learning curve to take effect are a highly manual and repetitive process (so staff can become quicker the more they perform the same series of tasks), no stoppages to production (so the learning rate will not be lost whilst staff are idle) and a stable workforce (so the learning process does not have to keep restarting).

If there is high staff turnover, stoppages in production and continual design changes, then the learning rate will not be effective and should be slower.

24   The correct answers are:

Marginal cost-plus pricing is easier where there is a readily identifiable variable cost	TRUE	FALSE
Full cost-plus pricing requires the budgeted level of output to be determined at the outset	TRUE	FALSE
Cost-plus pricing is a strategically focused approach as it accounts for external factors	TRUE	FALSE
Cost-plus pricing requires that the profit mark-up applied by an organisation is fixed	TRUE	FALSE

As marginal costing is based on variable costs, it is easier when a readily identifiable variable cost has been established.

The budgeted volume of output does need to be determined for full cost-plus pricing as it would be used to calculate the overhead absorption rate for the calculation of the full cost per unit.

Cost-plus pricing is internally focused and a drawback of the technique is that it fails to consider external influences, like competitor pricing strategies.

The mark-up percentage does not have to be fixed; it can vary and be adjusted to reflect market conditions.

25   The correct answer is: $362,600

As the variable cost per unit is changing depending on the production level, contribution for each level needs to be calculated and then the probabilities applied to the outcomes.

Demand (units)	Contribution (per unit)	Total contribution	Probability	Expected budgeted contribution
10,000	17.00	170,000	0.3	51,000
22,000	17.00	374,000	0.5	187,000
35,000	17.80	623,000	0.2	124,600
				362,600

26   The correct answer is: Fabric $3,500   Wood $419

Fabric is in regular use, so the replacement cost is the relevant cost (200 m^2 × $17.50) = $3,500.

30 m^2 of wood will have to be ordered in from the alternative supplier but the remaining 20 m^2 which is in inventory and not needed for other work can be used and then replaced by an order from the usual supplier (30 m^2 × $8.50) + (20 m^2 × $8.20) = $419.

27   The correct answer is: Skilled $1,200   Semi-skilled $4,200

Skilled labour:

There is no cost for the first 150 hours as there is spare capacity. The remaining 50 hours required will be paid at time and a half, which is $16 × 1.5 = $24.

50 hours × $24 = $1,200

Semi-skilled labour:

There is no spare capacity, so the company will either need to pay overtime or hire in additional staff. The cost of paying overtime would be $18 per hour, so it would be cheaper to hire in the additional staff for $14 per hour.

300 hours × $14 = $4,200

28   The correct answer is: $1,050

The electricity costs are incremental as the machine will be used more to produce the new order (500 hours × $1.50) = $750.

The supervisor's salary is not relevant as it is paid anyway; however, the overtime is relevant (20 hours × $15) = $300.

29   The correct answer is: The overheads should be excluded because they are not incremental costs

The general fixed overheads should be excluded as they are not incremental, ie they are not arising specifically as a result of this order. They are not sunk as they are not past costs. This is a common misconception.

30   The correct answers are:

Committed costs are never considered to be relevant costs.

An opportunity cost represents the cost of the best alternative forgone.

Avoidable costs would be saved if an activity did not happen and so are relevant.

Common costs are only relevant if the viability of the whole process is being assessed.

An opportunity cost does represent the cost of the best alternative forgone, however, if it is an historic (past) cost, it would not be relevant.

Fixed costs can be incremental to a decision and in those circumstances would be relevant.

Committed costs are costs the organisation has already agreed to and can no longer influence and so are not relevant.

Notional costs are used to make cost estimates more realistic; however, they are not real cash flows and are not considered to be relevant.

Avoidable costs are saved if an activity is not undertaken and if this occurs as a result of the decision, then they are relevant.

Common costs are relevant if the whole process is being evaluated; however, they are not relevant to a further processing decision.

Differential costs are relevant in a make or buy decision as the organisation is trying to choose between two options.

Section C

31 (a) (i) **Sales price variance and sales volume variance**

Sales price variance = (actual price – standard price) × actual volume

	Actual price $	Standard price $	Difference $	Actual volume	Sales price variance $
Plasma TVs	330	350	–20	750	15,000 A
LCD TVs	290	300	–10	650	6,500 A
					21,500 A

Sales volume contribution variance = (actual sales volume – budgeted sales volume) × standard margin

	Actual sales volume $	Budgeted Sales volume $	Difference	Standard margin $	Sales volume variance $
Plasma TVs	750	590	160	190	30,400 F
LCD TVs	650	590	60	180	10,800 F
	1,400	1,180			41,200 F

(ii) **Material price planning and purchasing operational variances**

Material planning variance
= (original target price – general market price at time of purchase) × quantity purchased

($60 – $85) × 1,400 = $35,000 A

Material price operational variance
= (general market price at time of purchase – actual price paid) × quantity purchased

($85 – $80) × 1,400 = $7,000 F

(iii) **Labour rate and labour efficiency variances**

Labour rate variance
= (standard labour rate per hour – actual labour rate per hour) × actual hours worked

Actual hours worked by temporary workers:

Total hours needed if staff were fully efficient = (750 × 2) + (650 × 1.5) = 2,475.
Permanent staff provide 2,200 hours, therefore excess = 2,475 – 2,200 = 275.
However, temporary workers take twice as long, therefore hours worked = 275 × 2 = 550.

Labour rate variance relates solely to temporary workers, therefore ignore permanent staff in the calculation.

Labour rate variance = ($14 – $18) × 550 = $2,200 A

Labour efficiency variance
= (standard labour hours for actual production – actual labour hours worked) × standard rate

(275 – 550) × $14 = $3,850 A

(b) **Explanation of planning and operational variances**

Before the material price planning and operational variances were calculated, the only information available as regards material purchasing was that there was an adverse material price variance of $28,000. The purchasing department will be assessed on the basis of this variance, yet, on its own, it is not a reliable indicator of the purchasing department's efficiency. The reason it is not a reliable indicator is because market conditions can change, leading to an increase in price, and this change in market conditions is not within the control of the purchasing department.

By analysing the materials price variance further and breaking it down into its two components – planning and operational – the variance actually becomes a more useful assessment tool. The planning variance represents the uncontrollable element and the operational variance represents the controllable element.

The planning variance is really useful for providing feedback on just how skilled management is in estimating future prices. This can be very easy in some businesses and very difficult in others. Giving this detail could help to improve planning and standard setting in the future, as management will be increasingly aware of factors which could create volatility in their forecasts.

The operational variance is more meaningful in that it measures the purchasing department's efficiency given the market conditions which prevailed at the time. As can be seen in Carad, the material price operational variance is favourable which demonstrates that the purchasing department managed to acquire the component which was in short supply at a better price than expected. Without this breakdown in the variance, the purchasing department could have been held accountable for the overall adverse variance which was not indicative of their actual performance. This is then a fairer method of assessing performance and will, in turn, stop staff from becoming demotivated.

32   (a)   TIP's financial performance can be assessed in a number of ways:

Sales growth

Sales are up about 1.3% (W1) which is a little above the rate of inflation and therefore a move in the right direction. However, with average admission prices jumping about 8.6% (W2) and numbers of visitors falling, there are clearly problems. Large increases in admission prices reduce the value proposition for the customer, it is unlikely that the rate of increase is sustainable or even justifiable. Indeed with volumes falling (down by 6.7% (W6)), it appears that some customers are being put off and price could be one of the reasons.

Maintenance and repairs

There appears to be a continuing drift away from routine maintenance with management preferring to repair equipment as required. This does not appear to be saving any money as the combined cost of maintenance and repair is higher in 20X5 than in 20X4 (possible risks are dealt with in part (b)).

Directors' pay

Absolute salary levels are up 6.7% (W3), well above the modest inflation rate. It appears that the shareholders are happy with the financial performance of the business and are prepared to reward the directors accordingly. Bonus levels are also well up. It may be that the directors have some form of profit related pay scheme and are being rewarded for the improved profit performance. The directors are likely to be very pleased with the increases to pay.

Wages

Wages are down by 12% (W5). This may partly reflect the loss of customers (down by 6.7% (W6)) if it is assumed that at least part of the wages cost is variable. It could also be that the directors are reducing staff levels beyond the fall in the level of customers to enhance short-term profit and personal bonus. Customer service and indeed safety could be compromised here.

Net profit

Net profit is up a huge 31.3% (W7) and most shareholders would be pleased with that. Net profit is a very traditional measure of performance and most would say this was a sign of good performance.

Return on assets

The profitability can be measured relative to the asset base which is being used to generate it. This is sometimes referred to as ROI or return on investment. The return on assets is up considerably to 11.4% from 8% (W8). This is partly due to the significant rise in profit and partly due to the fall in asset value. We are told that TIP has cut back on new development, so the fall in asset value is probably due to depreciation being charged with little being spent during the year on assets. In this regard it is inevitable that return on assets is up but it is more questionable whether this is a good performance. A theme park (and thrill rides in particular) must be updated to keep customers coming back. The directors of TIP are risking the future of the park.

(b)   Quality provision

Reliability of the rides

The hours lost has increased significantly. Equally the percentage of capacity lost due to breakdowns is now approaching 17.8% (W9). This would appear to be a very high number of hours lost. This would surely increase the risk that customers are disappointed being unable to ride. Given the fixed admission price system, this is bound to irritate some customers as they have effectively already paid to ride.

Average queuing time

Queuing will be seen by customers as dead time. They may see some waiting as inevitable and hence acceptable. However, TIP should be careful to maintain waiting times at a minimum. An increase of 10 minutes (or 50%) is likely to be noticeable by customers and is unlikely to enhance the quality of the TIP experience for them. The increase in waiting times is probably due to the high number of hours lost due to breakdown with customers being forced to queue for a fewer number of ride options.

Safety

The clear reduction in maintenance could easily damage the safety record of the park and is an obvious quality issue.

Risks

If TIP continues with current policies, then they will expose themselves to the following risks:

- The lack of routine maintenance could easily lead to an accident or injury to a customer. This could lead to compensation being paid or reputational damage.

- Increased competition. The continuous raising of admission prices increases the likelihood of a new competitor entering the market (although there are significant barriers to entry in this market, eg capital cost, land and so on).

- Loss of customers. The value for money which customers see when coming to TIP is clearly reducing (higher prices, less reliability of rides and longer queues). Regardless of the existence of competition, customers could simply choose not to come, substituting another leisure activity instead.

- Profit fall. In the end if customers' numbers fall, then so will profit. The shareholders, although well rewarded at the moment, could suffer a loss of dividend. Directors' job security could then be threatened.

Workings

1   Sales growth is $5,320,000/$5,250,000 = 1.01333 or 1.3%.

2   Average admission prices were:

20X4: $5,250,000/150,000 = $35 per person
20X5: $5,320,000/140,000 = $38 per person
An increase of $38/$35 = 1.0857 or 8.57%.

3   Directors' pay up by $160,000/$150,000 = 1.0667 or 6.7%.

4   Directors' bonuses levels up from $15,000/$150,000 or 10% to $18,000/$160,000 or 12.5% of turnover. This is an increase of 3/15 or 20%.

5   Wages are down by (1 − $2,200,000/$2,500,000) or 12%.

6   Loss of customers is (1 − 140,000/150,000) or 6.7%.

7   Profits up by $1,372,000/$1,045,000 = 1.3129 or 31.3%.

8   Return on assets:

20X4: $1,045,000/$13,000,000 = 1.0803 or 8.03%
20X5: $1,372,000/$12,000,000 = 1.114 or 11.4%

9   Capacity of rides in hours is 360 days × 50 rides × 10 hours per day = 180,000.

     20X4 lost capacity is 9,000/180,000 = 0.05 or 5%.
     20X5 lost capacity is 32,000/180,000 = 0.177 or 17.8%.

ACCA
Performance Management

Mock Exam 3
December 2016 Exam PBE

Question Paper: 3 hours 15 minutes
This paper is divided into three sections:
Section A – **ALL FIFTEEN questions are compulsory and MUST be attempted**   Section B – **ALL FIFTEEN questions are compulsory and MUST be attempted**   Section C – **Both questions are compulsory and MUST be attempted**

DO NOT OPEN THIS PAPER UNTIL YOU ARE READY TO START UNDER EXAMINATION CONDITIONS

Section A – ALL 15 questions are compulsory and MUST be attempted

Each question is worth 2 marks.

1   A company makes a single product with the following data:

	$	$
Selling price		25
Material	5	
Labour	7	
Variable overhead	3	
Fixed overhead	4	
		(19)
Profit per unit		6

Budgeted output is 30,000 units.

In relation to this data, which of the following statements is correct?

A   The margin of safety is 40%
B   The contribution to sales ratio is 24%
C   The volume of sales needed to make a profit of $270,000 is 45,000 units
D   If budgeted sales increase to 40,000 units, budgeted profit will increase by $100,000

2   Which of the following statements regarding zero-based budgeting are correct?

(1)   It is best applied to support expenses rather than to direct costs
(2)   It can link strategic goals to specific functional areas
(3)   It carries forward inefficiencies from previous budget periods
(4)   It is consistent with a top-down budgeting approach

A   3 and 4
B   1 and 2
C   2 and 3
D   1 and 4

3   A manufacturing company decides which of three mutually exclusive products to make in its factory on the basis of maximising the company's throughput accounting ratio.

Current data for the three products is shown in the following table:

	Product X	Product Y	Product Z
Selling price per unit	$60	$40	$20
Direct material cost per unit	$40	$10	$16
Machine hours per unit	10	20	2.5

Total factory costs (excluding direct materials) are $150,000. The company cannot make enough of any of the products to satisfy external demand entirely as machine hours are restricted.

Which of the following actions would improve the company's existing throughput accounting ratio?

A   Increase the selling price of product Z by 10%
B   Increase the selling price of product Y by 10%
C   Reduce the material cost of product Z by 5%
D   Reduce the material cost of product Y by 5%

4   Which of the following could be a closed system?

A   Target costing
B   Public relations department
C   Controlled design tests
D   Rolling budget preparation

5   Perrin Co has two divisions, A and B.

Division A has limited skilled labour and is operating at full capacity making product Y. It has been asked to supply a different product, X, to division B. Division B currently sources this product externally for $700 per unit.

The same grade of materials and labour is used in both products. The cost cards for each product are shown below:

Product	Y ($)/unit	X ($)/unit
Selling price	600	–
Direct materials ($50 per kg)	200	150
Direct labour ($20 per hour)	80	120
Apportioned fixed overheads ($15 per hour)	60	90

Using an opportunity cost approach to transfer pricing, what is the minimum transfer price?

A $270
B $750
C $590
D $840

6   Jorioz Co makes joint products X and Y. $120,000 joint processing costs are incurred.

At the split-off point, 10,000 units of X and 9,000 units of Y are produced, with selling prices of $1.20 for X and $1.50 for Y.

The units of X could be processed further to make 8,000 units of product Z. The extra costs incurred in this process would be fixed costs of $1,600 and variable costs of $0.50 per unit of input.

The selling price of Z would be $2.25.

What would be the outcome if product X is further processed?

A $600 loss
B $400 gain
C $3,900 gain
D $1,600 loss

7   A company has produced the following information for a product it is about to launch:

	20X4	20X5	20X6
Units	2,000	5,000	7,000
Variable production cost per unit	$2.30	$1.80	$1.20
Fixed production costs	$3,000	$3,500	$4,000
Variable selling cost per unit	$0.50	$0.40	$0.40
Fixed selling costs	$1,500	$1,600	$1,600
Administrative costs	$700	$700	$700

What is the life cycle cost per unit?

A $2.81
B $2.32
C $3.22
D $3.07

8   A company manufactures a specific clinical machine used in hospitals. The company holds a 2% share of the market and the total market demand has been constant at 250,000 machines for the last few years. The budgeted selling price for each machine is $10,000 and standard contribution is equivalent to 10% of the budgeted selling price.

An initial performance review of the company's actual results showed a sales volume of 5,600 machines had been achieved. The total market demand for the machines, though, had risen to 300,000 units.

What is the market share variance for the clinical machines?

A $200,000 favourable
B $400,000 adverse
C $600,000 favourable
D $1,000,000 adverse

9   VC Co is a firm of opticians. It provides a range of services to the public, such as eye tests and contact lens consultations, and has a separate dispensary selling glasses and contact lenses. Patients book appointments with an optician in advance.

A standard appointment is 30 minutes long, during which an optician will assess the patient's specific requirements and provide them with the eye care services they need. After the appointment, patients are offered the chance to buy contact lenses or glasses from the dispensary.

Which of the following describes a characteristic of the services provided by an optician at VC Co during a standard appointment?

A   Tangible
B   Homogeneous
C   Non-perishable
D   Simultaneous

10   Which of the following methods would be **LEAST** effective in ensuring the security of confidential information?

A   Monitoring emails
B   Encryption of files
C   Dial back facility
D   Universal passwords

11   A company which makes two products, Alpha and Zeta, uses activity-based costing to absorb its overheads. It has recently identified a new overhead cost pool for inspection costs and has decided that the cost driver is the number of inspections.

The following information has been provided:

Total inspection costs $250,000

	Alpha	Zeta
Production volume (units)	2,500	8,000
Machine hours per unit	1	1.5
Units per batch	500	1,000
Inspections per batch	4	1

What is the inspection cost per unit for product Alpha?

A $23.81
B $17.24
C $71.43
D $80.00

12   Which of the following statements, regarding the existence of multiple objectives in not-for-profit organisations, is/are correct?

(1) They ensure goal congruence between stakeholders
(2) Compromise between objectives can be problematic

A   1 only
B   2 only
C   Both 1 and 2
D   Neither 1 nor 2

13   Flow cost accounting is a technique which can be used to account for environmental costs. Inputs and outputs are measured through each individual process of production.

Which of the following is **NOT** a category used within flow cost accounting?

A   Material flows
B   System flows
C   Delivery and disposal flows
D   Waste flows

14   A company has used expected values to evaluate a one-off project. The expected value calculation assumed two possible profit outcomes, which were assigned probabilities of 0.4 and 0.6.

Which of the following statements about this approach are correct?

(1)   The expected value profit is the profit which has the highest probability of being achieved
(2)   The expected value gives no indication of the dispersion of the possible outcomes
(3)   Expected values are relatively insensitive to assumptions about probability
(4)   The expected value may not correspond to any of the actual possible outcomes

A   2 and 4
B   2, 3 and 4
C   1, 2 and 3
D   3 and 4

15   In an investment centre, a divisional manager has autonomy over negotiating all selling prices, has local functions set up for payables, inventory and cash management, and uses a full debt factoring service.

Which of the following should the divisional manager be held accountable for?

(1)   The generation of revenues
(2)   Transfer prices
(3)   Management of working capital
(4)   Apportioned head office costs

A   1, 2 and 3
B   2, 3 and 4
C   1 and 3
D   1, 2 and 4

(Total = 30 marks)

Section B – ALL 15 questions are compulsory and MUST be attempted

Each question is worth 2 marks.

The following scenario relates to questions 16–20.

Hare Events is a company which specialises in organising sporting events in major cities across Teeland. It has approached the local council of Edglas, a large city in the north of Teeland, to request permission to host a running festival which will include both a full marathon and a half marathon race.

Based on the prices it charges for entry to similar events in other locations, Hare Events has decided on an entry fee of $55 for the full marathon and $30 for the half marathon. It expects that the maximum entries will be 20,000 for the full marathon and 14,000 for the half marathon.

Hare Events has done a full assessment of the likely costs involved. Each runner will receive a race pack on completion of the race, which will include a medal, t-shirt, water and chocolate. Water stations will need to be available at every five-kilometre (km) point along the race route, stocked with sufficient supplies of water, sports drinks and gels. These costs are considered to be variable as they depend on the number of race entries.

Hare Events will also incur the following fixed costs. It will need to pay a fixed fee to the Edglas council for permits, road closures and support from the local police and medical services. A full risk assessment needs to be undertaken for insurance purposes. A marketing campaign is planned via advertising on running websites, in fitness magazines and at other events Hare Events is organising in Teeland, and the company which Hare Events usually employs to do the race photography has been approached.

The details of these costs are shown below:

	Full marathon	Half marathon
	$	$
Race packs	15.80	10.80
Water stations	2.40	1.20
		$
Council fees		300,000
Risk assessment and insurance		50,000
Marketing		30,000
Photography		5,000

16 If Hare Events decides to host only the full marathon race, what is the margin of safety?

    A   35.0%
    B   47.7%
    C   52.3%
    D   65.0%

17 Assuming that the race entries are sold in a constant sales mix based on the expected race entry numbers, what is the sales revenue Hare Events needs to achieve in order to break even (to the nearest $'000)?

    A $385,000
    B $575,000
    C $592,000
    D $597,000

18   Hare Events wishes to achieve a minimum total profit of $500,000 from the running festival.

What are the number of entries Hare Events will have to sell for each race in order to achieve this level of profit, assuming a constant sales mix based on the expected race entry numbers applies?

Work to the nearest whole number.

A   Full marathon: 17,915 entries and half marathon: 12,540 entries
B   Full marathon: 14,562 entries and half marathon: 18,688 entries
C   Full marathon: 20,000 entries and half marathon: 8,278 entries
D   Full marathon: 9,500 entries and half marathon: 6,650 entries

19   Hare Events is also considering including a 10 km race during the running festival. It expects the race will have an entry fee of $20 per competitor and variable costs of $8 per competitor. Fixed costs associated with this race will be $48,000.

If the selling price per competitor, the variable cost per competitor and the total fixed costs for this 10 km race all increase by 10%, which of the following statements will be true?

A   Breakeven volume will increase by 10% and breakeven revenue will increase by 10%
B   Breakeven volume will remain unchanged but breakeven revenue will increase by 10%
C   Breakeven volume will decrease by 10% but breakeven revenue will remain unchanged
D   Breakeven volume and breakeven revenue will both remain the same

20   Which of the following statements relating to cost volume profit analysis are true?

(1)   Production levels and sales levels are assumed to be the same so there is no inventory movement

(2)   The contribution to sales ratio (C/S ratio) can be used to indicate the relative profitability of different products

(3)   CVP analysis assumes that fixed costs will change if output either falls or increases significantly

(4)   Sales prices are recognised to vary at different levels of activity, especially if higher volume of sales is needed

A   1, 2 and 3
B   2, 3 and 4
C   1 and 2
D   3 and 4

The following scenario relates to questions 21–25.

Romeo Co is a business which makes and sells fresh pizza from a number of mobile food vans based at several key locations in the city centre. It offers a variety of toppings and dough bases for the pizzas and has a good reputation for providing a speedy service combined with hot, fresh and tasty food to customers.

Each van employs a chef who is responsible for making the pizzas to Romeo Co's recipes, and two sales staff who serve the customers. All purchasing is done centrally to enable Romeo Co to negotiate bulk discounts and build relationships with suppliers.

Romeo Co operates a standard costing and variances system and the standard cost card for Romeo Co's basic tomato pizza is as follows:

Ingredient	Weight (kg)	Price ($ per kg)
Dough	0.20	7.60
Tomato sauce	0.08	2.50
Cheese	0.12	20.00
Herbs	0.02	8.40
	0.42	

In Month 3, Romeo Co produced and sold 90 basic tomato pizzas and actual results were as follows:

Ingredient	Kg bought and used	Actual cost per kg
Dough	18.9	6.50
Tomato sauce	6.6	2.45
Cheese	14.5	21.00
Herbs	2.0	8.10
	42	

21   What was the total material price variance for Month 3?

A $7.22 adverse
B $7.22 favourable
C $40.50 favourable
D $40.50 adverse

22   What was the total materials mix variance for Month 3?

A $81.02 adverse
B $41.92 adverse
C $42.88 adverse
D $38.14 adverse

23   In Month 4, Romeo Co produced and sold 110 basic tomato pizzas. Actual results were as follows:

Ingredient	Kg bought and used	Actual cost per kg
Dough	21.3	6.60
Tomato sauce	7.5	2.45
Cheese	14.2	20.00
Herbs	2.0	8.50
	45	

What was the materials yield variance for Month 4?

Note. Calculate all workings to 2 decimal places.

A $12.21 favourable
B $11.63 favourable
C $21.95 adverse
D $9.75 adverse

24   In Month 5, Romeo Co reported a favourable materials mix variance for the basic tomato pizza.

Which of the following statements would explain why this variance has occurred?

A   The proportion of the relatively expensive ingredients used in production was less than the standard
B   The prices paid for the ingredients used in the mix were lower than the standard prices
C   Each pizza used less of all the ingredients in actual production than expected
D   More pizzas were produced than expected given the level of ingredients input

25   In Month 6, 100 basic tomato pizzas were made using a total of 42 kg of ingredients. A new chef at Romeo Co used the expected amount of dough and herbs but used less cheese and more tomato sauce per pizza than the standard. It was noticed that the sales of the basic tomato pizza had declined in the second half of the month.

Based on the above information, which of the following statements are correct?

(1)   The actual cost per pizza in Month 6 was lower than the standard cost per pizza
(2)   The sales staff should lose their Month 6 bonus because of the reduced sales
(3)   The value of the ingredients usage variance and the mix variance are the same
(4)   The new chef will be responsible for the material price, mix and yield variances

A   3 and 4
B   1 and 2
C   1 and 3
D   2 and 4

The following scenario relates to questions 26–30.

Sweet Treats Bakery makes three types of cake: brownies, muffins and cupcakes.

The costs, revenues and demand for each of the three cakes are as follows:

	Brownies	Muffins	Cupcakes
Batch size (units)	40	30	20
Selling price ($ per unit)	1.50	1.40	2.00
Material cost ($ per unit)	0.25	0.15	0.25
Labour cost ($ per unit)	0.40	0.45	0.50
Overheads ($ per unit)	0.15	0.20	0.30
Minimum daily demand (units)	30	20	10
Maximum daily demand (units)	140	90	100

The minimum daily demand is required for a long-term contract with a local café and must be met.

The cakes are made in batches using three sequential processes: weighing, mixing and baking. The products must be produced in their batch sizes but are sold as individual units. Each batch of cakes requires the following amount of time for each process:

	Brownies	Muffins	Cupcakes
Weighing (minutes)	15	15	20
Mixing (minutes)	20	16	12
Baking (minutes)	120	110	120

The baking stage of the process is done in three ovens which can each be used for eight hours a day, a total of 1,440 available minutes. Ovens have a capacity of one batch per bake, regardless of product type.

Sweet Treats Bakery uses throughput accounting and considers all costs, other than material, to be 'factory costs' which do not vary with production.

26 On Monday, in addition to the baking ovens, Sweet Treats Bakery has the following process resources available:

Process	Minutes available
Weighing	240
Mixing	180

Which of the three processes, if any, is a bottleneck activity?

A   Weighing
B   Mixing
C   Baking
D   There is no bottleneck

27 On Wednesday, the mixing process is identified as the bottleneck process. On this day, only 120 minutes in the mixing process are available.

Assuming that Sweet Treats Bakery wants to maximise profit, what is the optimal production plan for Wednesday?

A   80 brownies, 30 muffins and 100 cupcakes
B   0 brownies, 90 muffins and 100 cupcakes
C   120 brownies, 0 muffins and 100 cupcakes
D   40 brownies, 60 muffins and 100 cupcakes

28   Sweet Treats Bakery has done a detailed review of its products, costs and processes and has identified the following information:

(1)   The café customer wants to negotiate a loyalty discount
(2)   A bulk discount on flour and sugar is available from suppliers
(3)   There is additional demand for the cupcakes in the market
(4)   The rent of the premises has been reduced for the next year

Which of the above statements will improve the throughput accounting ratio?

A   1 and 2
B   2 and 3
C   1 and 3
D   2 and 4

29   On Friday, due to a local food festival at the weekend, Sweet Treats Bakery is considering increasing its production of cupcakes. These cupcakes can be sold at the festival at the existing selling price.

The company has unlimited capacity for weighing and mixing on Friday but its existing three ovens are already fully utilised. Therefore in order to supply cupcakes to the festival, Sweet Treats Bakery will need to hire another identical oven at a cost of $45 for the day.

How much will profit increase by, if the company hires the new oven and produces as many cupcakes as possible?

A $55.00
B $140.00
C $95.00
D $31.00

30   In a previous week, the weighing process was the bottleneck and the resulting throughput accounting ratio (TPAR) for the bakery was 1.45.

Which of the following statements about the TPAR for the previous week is/are true?

(1)   The bakery's operating costs exceeded the total throughput contribution generated from its three products

(2)   Less idle time in the mixing department would have improved the TPAR

(3)   Improved efficiency during the weighing process would have improved the TPAR

A   3 only
B   2 only
C   1 and 2
D   1 and 3

(Total = 30 marks)

Section C – Both questions are compulsory and MUST be attempted

31   Static Co is a multinational consumer goods company. Traditionally, the company has used a fixed annual budgeting process in which it sets quarterly sales revenue targets for each of its product lines. Historically, however, if a product line fails to reach its sales revenue target in any of the first three quarters, the company's sales director (SD) and finance director (FD) simply go back and reduce the sales revenue targets for the quarter just ended, to make it look like the target was reached. They then increase the target for the final quarter to include any shortfall in sales from earlier quarters.

During the last financial year ended 31 August 20X6, this practice meant that managers had to heavily discount many of their product lines in the final quarter in order to boost sales volumes and meet the increased targets. Even with the discounts, however, they still did not quite reach the targets. On the basis of the sales targets set at the beginning of that year, the company had also invested $6m in a new production line in January 20X6. However, to date, this new production line still has not been used. As a result of both these factors, Static Co saw a dramatic fall in return on investment from 16% to 8% in the year.

Consequently, the managing director (MD), the FD and the SD have all been dismissed. Two key members of the accounts department are also on sick leave due to stress and are not expected to return for some weeks. A new MD, who is inexperienced in this industry, has been appointed and is in the process of recruiting a new SD and a new FD.

They have said:

'These mistakes could have been largely avoided if the company had been using rolling budgets, instead of manipulating fixed budgets. From now on, we will be using rolling budgets, updating our budgets on a quarterly basis, with immediate effect.'

The original fixed budget for the year ended 31 August 20X7, for which the first quarter (Q1) has just ended, is shown below:

Budget Y/E 31 August 20X7	Q1	Q2	Q3	Q4	Total
	$'000	$'000	$'000	$'000	$'000
Revenue	13,425	13,694	13,967	14,247	55,333
Cost of sales	(8,055)	(8,216)	(8,380)	(8,548)	(33,199)
Gross profit	5,370	5,478	5,587	5,699	22,134
Distribution costs	(671)	(685)	(698)	(712)	(2,766)
Administration costs	(2,000)	(2,000)	(2,000)	(2,000)	(8,000)
Operating profit	2,699	2,793	2,889	2,987	11,368

The budget was based on the following assumptions:

(1)   Sales volumes would grow by a fixed compound percentage each quarter.
(2)   Gross profit margin would remain stable each quarter.
(3)   Distribution costs would remain a fixed percentage of revenue each quarter.
(4)   Administration costs would be fixed each quarter.

The actual results for the first quarter (Q1) have just been produced and are as follows:

Actual results	Q1
	$'000
Revenue	14,096
Cost of sales	(8,740)
Gross profit	5,356
Distribution costs	(705)
Administration costs	(2,020)
Operating profit	2,631

The new MD believes that the difference between the actual and the budgeted sales figures for Q1 is a result of incorrect forecasting of prices; however, they are confident that the four assumptions the fixed budget was based on were correct and that the rolling budget should still be prepared using these assumptions.

Required

(a) Prepare Static Co's rolling budget for the next four quarters. **(8 marks)**

(b) Discuss the problems which have occurred at Static Co due to the previous budgeting process and the improvements which might now be seen through the use of realistic rolling budgets. **(6 marks)**

(c) Discuss the problems which may be encountered when Static Co tries to implement the new budgeting system. **(6 marks)**

(Total = 20 marks)

32 Lens Co manufactures lenses for use by a wide range of commercial customers. The company has two divisions: the Photographic Division (P) and the Optometry Division (O). Each of the divisions is run by a divisional manager who has overall responsibility for all aspects of running their division and the divisions are currently treated as investment centres. Each manager, however, has an authorisation limit of $15,000 per item for capital expenditure and any items costing more than this must first be approved by Head Office.

During the year, Head Office made a decision to sell a large amount of the equipment in Division P and replace it with more technologically advanced equipment. It also decided to close one of Division O's factories in a country deemed to be politically unstable, with the intention of opening a new factory elsewhere in the following year.

Both divisions trade with overseas customers, choosing to provide these customers with 60 days' credit to encourage sales. Due to differences in exchange rates between the time of invoicing the customers and receiving the payment 60 days later, exchange gains and losses often occur.

The cost of capital for Lens Co is 12% per annum.

The following data relates to the year ended 30 November 20X6:

	Division P $'000	Division O $'000
Revenue	14,000	18,800
Gain on sale of equipment	400	–
	14,400	18,800
Direct labour	(2,400)	(3,500)
Direct materials	(4,800)	(6,500)
Divisional overheads*	(3,800)	(5,200)
Trading profit	3,400	3,600
Exchange gain/(loss)	(200)	460
Exceptional costs for factory closure	–	(1,800)
Allocated Head Office costs	(680)	(1,040)
Net divisional profit	2,520	1,220
* Depreciation on uncontrollable assets included in divisional overheads	320	460

	Division P $'000	Division O $'000
Non-current assets controlled by the division	15,400	20,700
Non-current assets controlled by Head Office	3,600	5,200
Inventories	1,800	3,900
Trade receivables	6,200	8,900
Overdraft	500	–
Trade payables	5,100	7,200

To date, managers have always been paid a bonus based on the return on investment (ROI) achieved by their division. However, the company is considering whether residual income would be a better method.

Required

(a) Calculate the return on investment (ROI) for each division for the year ended 30 November 20X6, ensuring that the basis of the calculation makes it a suitable measure for assessing the **DIVISIONAL MANAGERS'** performance. **(6 marks)**

(b) Explain why you have included or excluded certain items in calculating the ROIs in part (a), stating any assumptions you have made. **(8 marks)**

(c) Briefly discuss whether it is appropriate to treat each of the divisions of Lens Co as investment centres. **(2 marks)**

(d) Discuss the problems involved in using ROI to measure the managers' performance. **(4 marks)**

(Total = 20 marks)

Formulae Sheet

Learning curve

$Y = ax^b$

Where   Y = cumulative average time per unit to produce x units
             a = the time taken for the first unit of output
             x = the cumulative number of units produced
             b = the index of learning (log LR/log2)
             LR = the learning rate as a decimal

Demand curve

$P = a - bQ$

$B = \dfrac{\text{change in price}}{\text{change in quantity}}$

A   = price when Q = 0

MR = a − 2bQ

Answers

DO NOT TURN THIS PAGE UNTIL YOU HAVE
COMPLETED THE MOCK EXAM

A PLAN OF ATTACK

Managing your nerves

As you turn the pages to start this mock exam a number of thoughts are likely to cross your mind. At best, examinations cause anxiety so it is important to stay focused on your task for the next three hours! Developing an awareness of what is going on emotionally within you may help you manage your nerves. Remember, you are unlikely to banish the flow of adrenaline, but the key is to harness it to help you work steadily and quickly through your answers.

Working through this mock exam will help you develop the exam stamina you will need to keep going for three hours.

Managing your time

Planning and time management are two of the key skills which complement the technical knowledge you need to succeed. To keep yourself on time, do not be afraid to jot down your target completion times for each question, perhaps next to the title of the question. As all the questions are **compulsory**, you do not have to spend time wondering which question to answer!

Doing the exam

Actually doing the exam is a personal experience. There is not a single **right way**. As long as you submit complete answers to all questions after the three hours are up, then your approach obviously works.

Looking through the exam

Section A has 15 MCQs. This is the section of the exam where the ACCA examining team can test knowledge across the breadth of the syllabus. Make sure you read these questions carefully. The distractors are designed to present plausible, but incorrect, answers. Don't let them mislead you. If you really have no idea – guess. You may even be right.

Section B has three questions, each with a scenario and five objective test questions.

Section C has two longer questions:

- Question 31 requires you to prepare a rolling budget and discuss budgeting systems. There are plenty of easy marks in the question.

- Question 32 looks at performance measurement. This is a classic performance measurement question on return on investment. Start with the ratio calculations and then make sure that you fully explain why you have included or excluded numbers.

Allocating your time

BPP's advice is to always allocate your time **according to the marks for the question**. However, **use common sense**. If you're doing a question but haven't a clue how to do part (b), you might be better off re-allocating your time and getting more marks on another question, where you can add something you didn't have time for earlier on. Make sure you leave time to recheck the MCQs and make sure you have answered them all.

Sections A & B

1   D   If budgeted sales increase to 40,000 units then budgeted profit will increase by $100,000. This is because 10,000 more units will be sold at a contribution per unit of $10. The fixed costs would not be expected to change.

2   B   ZBB is useful for support expenses as they are discretionary and it can be used to link strategic goals to specific functional areas so Statements 1 and 2 are correct.

3   A   As all three products are mutually exclusive the company would choose to make X as it has the highest throughput return per hour of $2. Of the four possible options only increasing the selling price of product Z by 10% would give a higher throughput return per hour of $2.40.

4   C   Any controlled testing is a closed system as the aim is to limit external influences. The other three options all require interaction with the external environment.

5   B   The minimum transfer price is $750 and product X should be sourced externally to maximise the profit of the company.

         The minimum transfer price is the variable cost of product X ($270) plus the lost contribution from not making product Y ($480).

         The lost contribution is from 1.5 units of product Y (as it takes 4 hours to make product Y and 6 hours to make product X) which is (($600 – ($200 – $80) × 1.5 = $480.

6   A   Before further processing the sales value of X (10,000 units × $1.20) = $12,000.
After further processing:

         Sales value of Z (8,000 units × $2.25) = $18,000

         Further processing costs ((10,000 units of X × $0.50) + $1,600) = $6,600.

         This gives a net return of $11,400 which is $600 less than the sales value of X.

7   C   Variable production costs ($2.30 × 2,000) + ($1.80 × 5,000) + ($1.20 × 7,000) = $22,000

         Variable selling costs ($0.50 × 2,000) + ($0.40 × 5,000) + ($0.40 × 7,000) = $5,800

         Fixed production costs = $10,500

         Fixed selling costs = $4,700

         Administrative costs = $2,100

         Total costs = $45,100

         Cost per unit = $45,100/14,000 units = $3.22

8   B   Market share variance compares revised sales volume to actual sales volume.

         Revised sales volume (300,000 units × 2%) = 6,000 units

         Actual sales volume = 5,600 units

         Difference = 400 units adverse

         Valued at standard contribution of $1,000

         Variance = $400,000 adverse.

9   D   It is simultaneous as there is no delay between the service being provided by the optician and consumed by the patient.

10   D   A universal password would apply to everyone and therefore there would be no way to trace the person responsible for printing/transferring or amending the information. The other three options are common methods for securing the confidentiality of information.

11	C	Alpha batches (2,500/500) = 5; therefore inspections required for Alpha (5 × 4) = 20.

Zeta batches (8,000/1,000) = 8; therefore inspections required for Zeta (8 × 1) = 8.

OAR = $250,000/28 = $8,928.57

Alpha cost/unit = (20 × $8,928.57)/2,500 units = $71.43

12	B	Multiple objectives often conflict and therefore do not ensure goal congruence between stakeholders. Therefore Statement 1 is incorrect. This then can lead to the need for compromise between objectives which can be problematic therefore Statement 2 is correct.
13	D	Waste flows are not a category used within flow cost accounting, however the other three categories are.
14	A	The expected value does not give an indication of the dispersion of the possible outcomes; a standard deviation would need to be calculated so Statement 2 is correct.

The expected value is an amalgamation of several possible outcomes and their associated probabilities so it may not correspond to any of the actual possible outcomes so Statement 4 is correct.

15	A	The manager will be accountable for the generation of revenues, transfer prices and management of working capital as they have control over these areas. The manager will not be accountable for the apportioned head office costs as they have no control over those.
16	B	Total fixed costs = $385,000

Contribution per marathon entry ($55 – $18.20) = $36.80

BEP = 10,462

Margin of safety (20,000 – 10,462)/20,000 = 47.7%

17	C	Weighted average C/S ratio (2 × $36.80) + (1.4 × $18.00)/(2 × $55) + (1.4 × $30) = $98.80/$152 = 65%

BER = $385,000/65% = $592,308

18	A	Weighted average C/S ratio = 65%

Revenue to achieve target profit = $885,000/65% = $1,361,538

Marathon ($110/$152) × $1,361,538 = $985,324/$55 = 17,915 entries

Half marathon ($42/$152) × $1,361,538 = $376,214/$30 = 12,540 entries

19	B	Current contribution = $12

Current BEP = $48,000/$12 = 4,000 units
Current BER = $48,000/($12/$20) = $80,000

Revised contribution = (($20 × 1.1) + ($8 × 1.1)) = $13.20
Revised fixed costs = $48,000 × 1.1 = $52,800
Revised BEP = $52,800/$13.20 = 4,000 units
Revised BER = $52,800/($13.20/$22) = $88,000
The BEP hasn't changed but the BER has increased by 10%

20	C	CVP analysis assumes no movement in inventory and the C/S ratio can be used to indicate the relative profitability of different products so Statements 1 and 2 are correct.
21	B	Dough 18.9 kg × ($7.60 – $6.50) = $20.79 favourable

Tomato sauce 6.6 kg × ($2.50 – $2.45) = $0.33 favourable
Cheese 14.5 kg × ($20.00 – $21.00) = $14.50 adverse
Herbs 2 kg × ($8.40 – $8.10) = $0.60 favourable

Total material price variance = $7.22 favourable

22   D

	Actual usage/mix kg	Standard mix kg	Mix variance kg	Standard price $ per kg	Mix variance $
Dough	18.9	20.0	1.1 (F)	7.60	8.36 (F)
Sauce	6.6	8.0	1.4 (F)	2.50	3.50 (F)
Cheese	14.5	12.0	2.5 (A)	20.00	50.00 (A)
Herbs	2.0	2.0	–	8.40	–
	42.0	42.0	0		38.14 (A)

23   A

	Standard quantity standard mix kg	Actual quantity standard mix kg	Variance kg	Standard cost per kg $	Variance $
Dough	22.00	21.43	0.57 (F)	7.60	4.33 (F)
Sauce	8.80	8.57	0.23 (F)	2.50	0.58 (F)
Cheese	13.20	12.86	0.34 (F)	20.00	6.80 (F)
Herbs	2.20	2.14	0.06 (F)	8.40	0.50 (F)
	46.20	45.00			12.21 (F)

24   A   A favourable mix variance indicates that a higher proportion of cheaper ingredients were used in production compared to the standard mix.

25   C   The actual cost per pizza will be lower than the standard cost per pizza because expensive cheese has been replaced with cheaper tomato sauce.

The usage variance equals the mix and yield variance combined. The yield variance is zero as 100 pizzas used 42 kg so the mix and usage variances will be the same.

Sales staff should not automatically lose their bonus as the reduced sales could be a result of the change in mix affecting the quality of the pizza and the new chef will only be responsible for the mix and yield variances as they have no control over the purchase costs of ingredients.

26   B

Process	Available minutes	Brownies	Muffins	Cupcakes	Total minutes required
Weighing	240	60	45	100	205
Mixing	180	80	48	60	188
Baking	1,440	480	330	600	1,410

The bottleneck is the mixing process as 188 minutes are required to meet maximum demand but there are only 180 minutes available.

Note. Four batched of brownies need to be made in order to have sufficient cakes to meet maximum demand as the cakes must be made in their batch sizes.

27   A

	Brownies	Muffins	Cupcakes
Throughput contribution ($)	50	37.5	35
Mixing minutes	20	16	12
Throughput per mixing minute ($)	2.50	2.34	2.91
Ranking	2	3	1

Optimal production plan:

Fulfil customer order	Number of cakes	Mixing minutes
1 batch of cupcakes	20	12
1 batch of brownies	40	20
1 batch of muffins	30	16
General production (based on ranking)		
4 batches of cupcakes	80	48
1 batch of brownies	40	20

Therefore the bakery should produce 80 brownies, 30 muffins and 100 cupcakes.

28   D   Reduction in rent and discounts on materials will reduce costs and will improve the TPAR.

Giving a customer a loyalty discount will reduce sales revenue and as a result the TPAR. Demand for cupcakes can increase but it will not impact the TPAR as demand is not the restriction.

29   C   Each oven has a capacity of eight hours and each cupcake batch takes two hours so four extra batches can be made.

Extra throughput = four batches × $35 = $140

Less the hire costs will result in an additional profit of $95.

30   A   As the TPAR exceeds 1, the throughput contribution exceeds operating costs and so Statement 1 is false.

Less idle time on a non-bottleneck process would not improve the TPAR so Statement 2 is false.

Improving efficiency during the weighing process would improve the TPAR as any actions to improve throughput on a bottleneck will improve the TPAR so Statement 3 is true.

Section C

31 Static Co

Text reference. Budgetary systems are covered in Chapter 8.

Top tips. There are easy marks available throughout this question so ensure you allocate enough time to each requirement. Refer to the scenario throughout your answer.

Easy marks. You should be able to score well in part (a).

Examining team's comments. On the whole this was answered quite well. However, in part (a), some candidates simply calculated the GPM from the original budget and ignored the actual quarter 1 figures. This meant that their cost of sales and gross profit figures were incorrect in their rolling budget. In part (b) some candidates noted from the scenario that many product lines had to be heavily discounted in the last quarter. This was not enough and answers needed to go on to say that that was a problem because it led to reduced sales revenues and made it difficult to increase prices to their original level in later quarters. The biggest problem for part (c) was that candidates did not read the requirement carefully or simply answered the question that they wanted it to be.

Marking scheme

		Marks
(a)	Growth rate	1
	Actual distribution cost %	0.5
	Actual GPM %	0.5
	Use of Q1 actuals	1
	Rolling budget: sales	1
	COS	1
	GPM	0.5
	Distribution costs	1
	Administration costs	1
	Operating profit	0.5
		8
(b)	Problems and improvements	6
(c)	Implementation problems	6
		20

(a) Workings

From budgeted figures: need to work out what the compound growth rate is and the distribution costs as a percentage of revenue.

Compound sales growth: $13,694/13,425 or $13,967/13,694 = 2%

Distribution costs: $671/$13,425 = 5%

From actual figures: GPM = $5,356/14,096 = 38%

Distribution costs: $705/14,096 = still 5%.

Starting point for revenue now $14,096 but compound growth rate still 2%.

Rolling budget for the 12 months ending 30 November 20X7

	Q2	Q3	Q4	Q1
	$'000	$'000	$'000	$'000
Revenue	14,378	14,666	14,959	15,258
Cost of sales	(8,914)	(9,093)	(9,275)	(9,460)
Gross profit	5,464	5,573	5,684	5,798
Distribution costs	(719)	(733)	(748)	(763)
Administration costs	(2,020)	(2,020)	(2,020)	(2,020)
Operating profit	2,725	2,820	2,916	3,015

(b) **Problems and improvements**

Problems

The use of fixed budgeting has caused serious problems at Static Co. The fact it was using inaccurate sales forecast figures led it to invest in a production line which was not actually needed, even though it knew they were inaccurate. This unnecessary investment cost it $6m and caused the return on investment to halve. Had rolling budgets been used at the time, and used properly, the sales forecasts for the remaining quarters would have been adjusted to reflect a fall in demand and the investment would not have been made.

Presumably, inaccurate sales forecasts would have led the business to get its staffing levels and materials purchases wrong as well. This too will have cost the business money. It was forced to heavily discount its goods in order to try to reach its targets at the end of the year, which was simply unrealistic. It can often be difficult to put prices back up again once they have been discounted. However, the actual results from the first quarter suggest that prices have increased again, which is fortunate.

Improvements

The use of rolling budgets should mean that a downturn in demand is adjusted for in future quarters, rather than sales simply being pushed into the last quarter, which is not a realistic adjustment. Management is forced to reassess the budget regularly and produce up-to-date information. This means that accurate management decisions can then be made and mistakes like investing in a new production line which is not needed should not happen again. Planning and control will be more accurate.

(c) **Problems trying to implement new budgeting system**

The first problem may be trying to obtain the right information needed to update the budget. The FD has been sacked and two other key finance personnel are off work due to stress. This could make it very difficult to obtain information if the department is understaffed and lacking the direction given by the FD. Staff in the finance department may not have the skills to update the budget and roll it forward, having never done it before. Similarly, the sales department is without a SD and they would usually have played a key part in reviewing figures for the sales forecasts. Hence, it may be difficult to obtain reliable sales data.

Even without this staffing issue, obtaining the correct information could be difficult as actually preparing rolling budgets is new for Static Co. Staff will need training. They are only used to preparing fixed budgets, although these have often been revised in the past to move sales into later periods. Staff are not familiar with the process of updating all of their financial information again: reviewing sales demand to realistically reforecast, updating costs, etc. This process takes time and staff may feel resentful about having to do this again, so soon after the annual budgeting process which would recently have been undertaken.

The new MD is new to this industry and therefore lacks experience of how it works. Whilst they are confident that the assumptions of the original fixed budget still stand true, they are not in a good position to know that this is in fact the case. They may be wrong and, if they are, the new rolling budget will be unreliable.

32 Lens Co

Marking scheme

		Marks
(a)	Calculation of controllable profit	2
	Calculation of controllable assets	2
	ROI	2
		6
(b)	Explanation about controllability	2
	Inclusion/exclusion explanations	6
		8
(c)	Description of investment centre	1
	Application to Lens Co	1
		2
(d)	Problems with using ROI	4
		20

(a) Return on investment

Controllable profit

	Division P	Division O
	$'000	$'000
Revenue	14,000	18,800
Direct labour	(2,400)	(3,500)
Direct materials	(4,800)	(6,500)
Divisional overheads excl. uncontrollable depreciation	(3,480)	(4,740)
Exchange gain/(loss)	(200)	460
Net divisional profit	3,120	4,520

Net assets controlled by the divisions

	Division P	Division O
	$'000	$'000
Non-current assets controlled by division	15,400	20,700
Inventories	1,800	3,900
Trade receivables	6,200	8,900
Overdraft	(500)	–
Trade payables	(5,100)	(7,200)
Net controllable assets	17,800	26,300

ROI for Division P

Controllable profit/controllable assets

= $3,120/$17,800
= 17.53%.

ROI for Division 0

$4,520/$26,300 = 17.19%

(b)   The ROIs in part (a) have been calculated by applying the principle of 'controllability'. This principle states that managers should only be held accountable for areas which they can control. This means that, when calculating 'profit' for the purposes of calculating ROI, the only revenues and costs included should be controllable by the manager. Similarly, when calculating 'net assets' for the ROI calculation, only assets which the divisional managers can control should be included.

Applying the principles of controllability, treatment of certain costs is explained below:

Gain on sale of equipment

This has been excluded from the profit figure as the decision to dispose of a large amount of equipment in division P was taken by Head Office. The divisional manager had no control over this decision.

Divisional overheads

The depreciation on HO-controlled assets has been excluded when calculating profit for ROI purposes. Again, this is because divisional managers do not control some of the assets.

Exchange gains/losses

These have been left in when arriving at a profit figure for ROI purposes. This is because the scenario states that the divisions choose to give the overseas customers 60 days' credit and it is this delay, between the point of sale and the point of payment, which gives rise to the exchange gain or loss. The managers make the choice to deal with these customers so they have control here.

Exceptional cost of factory closure

The effect of this has been removed from the 'profit' calculation as this decision was made by Head Office, not the manager of division 0. It was therefore beyond their control and its effect should be excluded.

Allocated Head Office costs

These have been excluded when calculating profit, as the divisional managers have no control over these and should not be held accountable for them.

Non-current assets controlled by Head Office

These have been excluded from the 'net assets' calculation, as these assets are not under the control of the divisional managers.

(c)   **Investment centres**

An investment centre is a type of responsibility centre in which managers have responsibility for not only sales prices, volume and costs, but also for investment in working capital and non-current assets. Both divisions do have responsibility for working capital; that is clear from the scenario. However, they only have responsibility over some of the assets. In the circumstances, it could be argued that it is correct to treat them as investment centres, provided that appropriate adjustments are made when using ROI to assess their performance.

On the other hand, however, managers are only able to sign off $15,000 of capital expenditure, which is a relatively small amount, suggesting that treatment as an investment centre is not appropriate. Bringing the divisions under Head Office control may even be beneficial as exchange rate risk can then be managed more closely.

(d) **Problems of using ROI**

The main disadvantage of using ROI is that the percentage increases as assets get older. This is because the net book value of the assets decreases as a result of higher accumulated depreciation, hence capital employed falls. This, in turn, can lead managers to hold onto ageing assets rather than replace them, especially where their bonuses are linked to ROI. It may be that division P's manager would not have made the same decision which Head Office made to invest in the more advanced technology for this reason.

Another disadvantage is that ROI is based on accounting profits, which are subjective, rather than cash flows. It is therefore open to manipulation.

Additionally, it does not take into account the cost of capital. It merely looks at profits relative to capital employed without taking into account the cost of the capital which has been invested. It is therefore not consistent with maximising returns to investors.

Review Form – Performance Management (PM) (02/18)

Name: _____   **Address:** _____

_____

_____

How have you used this Kit?
(Tick one box only)

☐ Home study (book only)

☐ On a course: college _____

☐ With 'correspondence' package

☐ Other _____

Why did you decide to purchase this Kit?
(Tick one box only)

☐ Have used the complementary Study text

☐ Have used other BPP products in the past

☐ Recommendation by friend/colleague

☐ Recommendation by a lecturer at college

☐ Saw advertising

☐ Other _____

During the past six months do you recall seeing/receiving any of the following?
(Tick as many boxes as are relevant)

☐ Our advertisement in *Student Accountant*

☐ Our advertisement in *Pass*

☐ Our advertisement in *PQ*

☐ Our brochure with a letter through the post

☐ Our website www.bpp.com

Which (if any) aspects of our advertising do you find useful?
(Tick as many boxes as are relevant)

☐ Prices and publication dates of new editions

☐ Information on product content

☐ Facility to order books off-the-page

☐ None of the above

Which BPP products have you used?

Study Text	☐	*Passcards*	☐	*Other*	☐
Practice & Revision Kit	☑	*i-Pass*	☐		

Your ratings, comments and suggestions would be appreciated on the following areas.

	Very useful	Useful	Not useful
Passing PM	☐	☐	☐
Questions	☐	☐	☐
Top Tips etc in answers	☐	☐	☐
Content and structure of answers	☐	☐	☐
Mock exam answers	☐	☐	☐

Overall opinion of this Practice & Revision Kit	*Excellent*	☐	*Good*	☐	*Adequate*	☐	*Poor* ☐

Do you intend to continue using BPP products?   *Yes* ☐   *No* ☐

The BPP author of this edition can be emailed at: accaqueries@bpp.com

Review Form (continued)

TELL US WHAT YOU THINK

Please note any further comments and suggestions/errors below.